Richard Neutra and the Search
for Modern Architecture

A Biography and History

New York   *Oxford*

OXFORD UNIVERSITY PRESS

1982

Richard Neutra

and the Search

for Modern Architecture

Thomas S. Hines

Copyright © 1982 by Oxford University Press, Inc.

Library of Congress Cataloging in Publication Data

Hines, Thomas S.
   Richard Neutra and the search for modern
architecture.

   Bibliography: p.
   Includes index.
   1. Neutra, Richard Joseph, 1892–1970.
2. Architects—United States—Biography.
I. Title.
NA737.N4H5   720′.92′4 [B]   81–22530
ISBN 0–19–503028–1   AACR2
ISBN 0–19–503029–X (pbk.)

Printing: (last digit) 987654321

Printed in the United States of America

To Dorothy

Acknowledgments

The great Yankee baseball catcher Yogi Berra once addressed a testimonial dinner by thanking everyone who had "made this occasion necessary." It is a pleasure to do the same with those who made this book "necessary" and possible. My wife Dorothy and my children Taylor and Tracy stimulated and distracted me during the long years Richard Neutra competed for my attention. My greatest debts and thanks are to them.

The Introduction tells how I met Neutra and his family and how I decided to write a book about him, and the essay on sources documents interviews, but I must give special thanks here to Neutra's wife Dione, who was described once by a friend as a "pathological truth teller." That does not mean that she, or anyone, is always "correct" or has a monopoly on the truth, but in her open-minded way, she attempted, I believe, to withhold nothing and to share information and insights without reservations or conditions. At times she laid more "truth" on me than I thought I could handle. I know she will disagree with some of my judgments and will find some of my interpretations painful, but I hope she believes that ultimately I did the subject justice. I owe many of the same kinds of debts to Neutra's sons, Dion and Raymond, and to his sister, Josephine Neutra Weixilgärtner. Finally, the Swiss wisdom and hospitality of Hans and Regula Fybel helped me to not only survive but also enjoy my ordeal.

For personal and institutional support at UCLA, I thank the faculty, staff, and students of the Department of History and the School of Architecture and Urban Planning; the expert typists of the Word Processing Center; and the staffs of the various UCLA libraries, particularly the Department of Special Collections, which houses the Neutra Archive. I owe similar debts to David Gebhard and the staff of the Schindler Collection, University of California, Santa Barbara. My research assistant, Peter Wrobel, performed numerous tasks with patience and brilliance, including the preparation of the index. Boris Ceverna-Fritz, James Sauvé, Margot Michels, and Joel Singer assisted me in the difficult deciphering and translation of Neutra's early diaries. Richard Sparacino was the ideal proofreader.

Walter Jaksch was invaluable as my chief contact in Vienna, helping me track down various elusive data. Though formal credit is given elsewhere to all the photographers of Neutra's work, I must single out Julius Shulman for his special contributions to architecture and to this book. I particularly thank the clients and occupants of Neutra's buildings for allowing me to visit them.

The UCLA Academic Senate Research Fund helped pay research expenses, and a 1979–80 Fellowship from the National Endowment for the Humanities allowed me to take off a year and complete my research.

Portions of this book appeared first as articles in *Oppositions*, *Skyline*, and *The Journal of Urban History*. Portions were also read as papers at the William Andrews Clark Library, Los Angeles, 1981, and at annual meetings of the Society of Architectural Historians in 1977, 1979, 1981, and 1982.

Hans Rogger and Robert Wohl read and criticized the first two European chapters, while the entire manuscript was scrutinized by Margaret Bach, Robert Judson Clark, Arthur Drexler, Harwell Hamilton Harris, Dorothy Hines, William Jordy, Richard Longstreth, and Adolf Placzek. I absolve them of all connection with any faults the book may have, but I thank them for making it better than it was.

The same is true for the remarkable staff of the Oxford University Press, particularly Vicky Bijur and Tessa DeCarlo, who edited the manuscript with skill and care, and James Raimes, Susan Rabiner and Mary Wander, who furnished crucial background support. Joy Taylor's sympathetic book design speaks for itself.

The old "without whom" phrase applies to them all.

TSH

Los Angeles
1982

Contents

Richard Neutra and the Search
for Modern Architecture

1. *Neutra,* Strathmore Apartments, Los
Angeles, 1937

Neutra and Modernism

"The new art is a world-wide fact," wrote the Spanish philosopher Jose Ortega y Gasset in 1925. "For about twenty years now, the most alert young people of two successive generations—in Berlin, Paris, London, ew York, Rome, Madrid—have found themselves faced with the undeniable fact that they have no use for traditional art; moreover that they detest it. With these young people, one can do one of two things: shoot them or try to understand them. . . . Who knows what may come out of this budding style? The task it sets for itself is enormous; it wants to create from nought. Later," he concluded, prefiguring Mies van der Rohe's famous modernist aphorism, "I expect it will be content with less and achieve more." Though this criticism applied generally to all the "modern" arts, Ortega was speaking chiefly of painting and sculpture, as was the French critic André Malraux when he later asserted that "the distinguishing feature of modern art is that it never tells a story. . . . Modern art is rather the annexation of forms by means of an inner pattern or schema, which may or may not take the shape of objects, but of which in any case figures and objects are no more than the expression."[1]

A major display of the "new art," Roger Fry's 1910 post-impressionist show at the Grafton Galleries in London, moved the novelist Virginia Woolf to make the blunt assertion that "in or around December, 1910, human nature changed radically."[2] In 1977, the literary critic Robert Adams would return to Woolf's cryptic pronouncement as the focal line of a lecture with the significant title "What was Modernism?" He believed she was right about 1910: "Within five years either way of that date a great sequence of new and different works appeared

in Western culture, striking the tonic chords of modernism. Ten years before that fulcrum of December 1910, modernism is not yet; ten years after, it is already. Mind," he cautioned, "I'm not talking about 'the modern world' or anything like that; just about a particular stylistic period in Western art, literature, music. . . ."[3]

Focusing on literature, Adams answered the title question of his lecture by admitting that the label "modernism" was "an inaccurate and misleading term, applied to a cultural trend that's most clearly discernible between 1905 and 1925. When it is understood to refer to distinct structural features that some artistic works of this period have in common, it's got a real meaning. . . . As it departs from that specific meaning, it gets fuzzier and fuzzier. . . . Still it's been a prevalent and widely accepted stopgap term, with a loose emotive tonality."[4]

Though the life cycle of architectural modernism stretched considerably beyond Adams's and Ortega's 1905–25 parameters, it shared with the other modern arts similar problems of taxonomic imprecision. Etymologically, the term "modern" and its derivatives evolved from the late-Latin sixth-century word "modernus," roughly meaning "just now," but it was not widely adopted before the sixteenth century, when it became increasingly necessary to distinguish the period after the Renaissance from the ancient and medieval worlds. In addition to that large but relatively specific meaning, from the sixteenth into the late twentieth century it continued to convey as well a more floating association with things "characteristic of the present and recent times; new-fashioned; not antiquated or obsolete." But in the late nineteenth century, the floating term quickened into a harder specificity as it became *the*

3

term for the "new art" of the incipient new century.[5]

Unlike the literary modernism of Eliot, Pound, and Joyce, which quoted eclectically from the whole history of civilization, modernism in architecture moved from the late nineteenth century in a relatively more determined line toward "pure," "new," and "original" statements—affecting, it was hoped, a forgetting of things past. There were exceptions, of course, conscious and unconscious. Le Corbusier, particularly, was enamored of the stark, by that time white, skeletal ruins of classicism and used them as motivating models and metaphors. A stripped, abstract classicism pervaded the modern movement, and not a few of its architects acknowledged that influence. But the dominant references of the new twentieth-century architecture were the more consciously contemporary images of the Machine Age —as allied to and expressive of the "functions" of "modern life." In 1894, when the Viennese pioneer Otto Wagner entitled a lecture and treatise *Moderne Architektur,* the term was not yet in common usage. By 1932, when New York's recently established Museum of Modern Art staged its epochal "Modern Architecture" show, the appellation was unquestioned. By 1966, when the same museum published Robert Venturi's seminal critique of modernism, *Complexity and Contradiction in Architecture,* architectural modernism—the term and the movement —was beginning to experience increasingly serious identity problems.

The rise and waning of modern architecture will form the central theme of this book. The conveyor of this theme, this quest for modernism, is the architect Richard Neutra. His work, his life experience, his search for modern architecture coincided neatly with the larger movement's life frame. With his—more acclaimed—fellow seekers of modernism, he experienced the buoyant struggles of modernism's early years, the heady successes of its mid-century ascendancy, and the perplexing strains of its slow demise.

Neutra's work first came to my attention in the early 1960s, when I was a graduate student in architectural history at the University of Wisconsin, Madison. Stimulated by my faculty mentors and the pioneering publications of Los Angeles critic Esther McCoy, I came to be especially conscious of Neutra's

great California houses—from the Lovell house of 1929 through the Kaufmann and Tremaine houses of the late 1940s. My first teaching job, at UCLA, brought me to Los Angeles in the fall of 1968, and I used David Gebhard and Robert Winter's *Guide to Architecture in Southern California* to find and investigate other examples of Neutra's work. My favorite early discoveries included his Strathmore apartments (1937) in Westwood, which I passed every day on my way to UCLA. I placed my name on the waiting list for an apartment at Strathmore, and in January 1970 my wife and I moved there.

Since Neutra still owned Strathmore as a personal investment, and since we knew he liked to revisit his buildings, we hoped someday to meet him. It happened sooner than we expected. On a Sunday in February, about a month after we had moved in, his sister-in-law Regula Thorston, who managed the property, knocked at the door and introduced Neutra and his wife Dione. Laden with cameras, tripods, and other photographic equipment, they confirmed my image of the cheerfully serious Germanic family on a ritualistic Sunday afternoon trek.

At seventy-seven, Neutra was as handsome and commanding as his pictures had suggested. He strode in and greeted us cordially. But then my recently acquired copy of the new English edition of Wingler's *Bauhaus* caught his eye, and we lost him for a quarter-hour as he sat at a table taking notes. Afterwards, having learned from his sister-in-law that I taught architectural history, he began to talk with me about the Bauhaus, at which he had been a visiting critic in 1930. He wanted my opinions on the early and late work of Gropius, Mies, Le Corbusier, Wright—and Neutra. Soon the talk became more densely philosophical and of apparently sufficient portent to make him pause for a moment, tap the table, and address the women at the other end of the room. "Ladies," he said paternally, "you would do well to listen to this."

Later yet, we talked about music, and I asked him which composers he most identified with and would most like other people to think of when they experienced his buildings, and he quickly replied, "Schönberg and Bach," clearly evoking both the "classical" and "modern" qualities that his best work conveys. He toured the apartment, somewhat puzzled by our spare but committed use of Stickley Craftsman furniture instead of Neutra Modern. Though he made suggestions for rearrangements and realignments, as he usually did when visiting his own buildings, he seemed surprised to find himself admitting that the early twentieth-century furniture and several older decorative objects worked rather well within his design. In response to my complaint about a persistent leak in the living room, he promised that either the roof would be repaired or he would present me with a personally designed bucket to catch the rainwater.

He was eager, he said, to revisit, systematically, each of his buildings in Southern California, and since he no longer drove a car, he asked if I would join him as chauffeur and companion. We made tentative plans for that tour, to be undertaken the following summer when he returned from Europe. We never took the tour together, however, for he died on April 16 in Wuppertal, Germany, while visiting and photographing one of his own houses.

The experience of living at Strathmore in the four years following Neutra's death further stimulated my interest in his work. As I got to know his wife and family, and his friends and enemies, and as I probed the vast archive of drawings and papers Neutra had bequeathed to UCLA, I began to think of writing a book about him. I was just completing a study of the late nineteenth- and early twentieth-century architect and planner Daniel Burnham, and the conflicts involved in the rise of modernism in America, and I wanted to follow that project with a study of some of the related issues and ideas as they developed in the twentieth century. Neutra seemed as ideal a focus for the second book as Burnham had been for the first. Believing that history at its best is analytical narrative, where the methodological paraphernalia pervades but never engulfs the "story," I saw in Neutra's life experience a powerful story with significant implications: the search, via architecture, on the part of Neutra and his generation for the promise and meaning of the twentieth century. The "proper" new architecture, which they agreed to call "modern," would express, define, and shape the new century. Though they would continue to insist that they were following no set style, the modernists opted for what ultimately came to be a cluster of new styles—from the hot, exotic plastic-

ity of Expressionism to the elegantly cool austerity of Rationalism, *die Neue Sachlichkeit*. In his own search for modernism, Neutra drank from both wells, though ultimately, in his best, mature work, inclining toward the images and canons of Rationalism.

Neutra was on most of the crests of the important waves in the development of the modern movement. He was born in 1892 in Imperial Vienna, the son of a small artisan-industrialist whose Jewish heritage had been tempered by several generations of secular agnosticism. His sister and brothers moved in sophisticated Viennese cultural circles, and through them the young Neutra met and was influenced by Gustav Klimt, Arnold Schönberg, and Sigmund Freud. He was early impressed by the architecture of Otto Wagner, but an even more direct influence was the maverick Adolf Loos, whose crusade against "ornament" turned Neutra's mind from the traditional styles and formulas. During World War I, Neutra served as an artillery officer in the Balkans, but he returned to Vienna in 1917 to graduate *cum laude* from the Technische Hochschule.

Leaving Austria in 1919, Neutra worked briefly in Switzerland for Gustav Ammann, the noted landscape architect, before moving in 1920 to northern Germany, where he served as the city architect of Luckenwalde. In 1921 he joined the great Berlin architect Erich Mendelsohn as a draftsman-collaborator. Neutra emigrated to the United States in 1923, worked briefly in New York, and then joined the large Chicago firm of Holabird and Roche. In Chicago he met Louis Sullivan, who was dying in poverty and neglect, and at Sullivan's funeral in 1924 he met Sullivan's disciple, Frank Lloyd Wright. Wright then invited him to Taliesin to work and study through the fall and winter of 1924.

Indeed, of the many European artists and architects who came to the United States and became American citizens in the 1920s and '30s, Neutra was one of the earliest to emigrate voluntarily. Unlike Walter Gropius, László Moholy-Nagy, and Ludwig Mies van der Rohe, who came as exiles from Nazi Germany, Neutra arrived in 1923 specifically to make contact with the world of Sullivan and Wright. Like most other young European architects, he had been greatly moved by the 1910 German publication of Wright's work, and had become convinced, with the encouragement of Loos, that America was indeed the capital of "modern" architecture.

Since most of Wright's meager practice of the twenties was centered in Los Angeles, Neutra, attracted by the possibilities of the area's climate and geography, decided to migrate there. With the encouragement of Rudolph Schindler, a Viennese school friend and former Wright associate then in California, Neutra set up a practice in Los Angeles. Ultimately his architecture became as important to California as Wright's and Sullivan's had been to the Middle West, and it continued through mid-century to dominate the California scene and to have a worldwide impact. Gregory Ain, Harwell Harris, and Raphael Soriano were among the first of numerous talented architects to work in Neutra's office or to be influenced by his work before moving on to distinguished careers of their own.

Neutra's basic architectural structure was the simple, timeless post and beam, with cantilevered roof slabs extending into space. His favorite materials were steel, concrete, stucco, wood, and glass, which he valued for both its transparent and reflecting qualities. Above all, his architecture emphasized the interpenetration of inner and outer space. As a student of Wright *and* of the new architecture of Europe, Neutra was able to bridge, perhaps better than any other architect, the frequently polarized worlds of Taliesin and Bauhaus. Yet unlike the highly idiosyncratic work of Wright, there was in Neutra's best work a combination of both Neutran personality and benevolent neutrality, a neutrality that tolerated and encouraged the client's own vision and creativity. Neutra studied the needs of each individual client and adapted his own ideas to those needs. He was especially concerned that good design be available to people of modest means and that even his most expensive architecture be translatable into less costly forms. Of all twentieth-century architects, he was the one most interested in and most knowledgeable about the biological and behavioral sciences. He wrote and lectured extensively on the psychological, physiological, and ecological dimensions of architecture. His best-known book, *Survival Through Design* (1954), had an especially wide influence in its time.

Always conscious of the broader social obligations of architects and planners, Neutra served in the 1930s and '40s as a member and then as chairman of the California State Planning Board, and as a consultant to the U.S. Housing Authority. His Channel Heights housing project for California shipyard workers of the early 1940s was an admirable and influential example of community planning. In the 1950s he and his partner Robert Alexander did planning and design work for such American cities as Sacramento and for the new island government of Guam.

When I first began a serious study of the modern movement in the early 1960s, the respectful, orthodox text was still Sigfried Giedion's *Space, Time and Architecture*—the "Giedion Bible," we called it then. But as a child of the sixties I soon encountered the opposing "post-modern" critique of modernism itself, epitomized and best stated in the writings and buildings of Robert Venturi and Charles W. Moore. Moore reacted to what he believed to be the modern movement's overly stark sobriety and called for more wit and irony and color in architecture. And in 1966, with his book *Complexity and Contradiction in Architecture*, Venturi launched a brilliant attack on the "puritanically moral language of orthodox Modern architecture" with a plea for an architecture that was "hybrid rather than 'pure,' compromising rather than 'clean,' distorted rather than 'straightforward,' ambiguous rather than 'articulated' . . . inconsistent and equivocal rather than direct and clear." In his call for "messy vitality over obvious unity," Venturi challenged the modern movement in its most vulnerable areas.[6]

The ensuing post-modern critique proved a healthy and stimulating corrective to much that was dull or dead in "late modern" design. But the critique was not only a bracing purgative for architects and architecture; it was equally important for historians of modernism. No longer could historians write, as did Giedion's generation, in the "puritanically moral language of orthodox modern architecture."

We can and must look at modernism with fresher eyes and more critical detachment now. But that does not mean that all criticism should or can be negative. The arguments of those who espouse post-modernist theories may be no less one-sided than the arguments they reject of modernist true believers. Charles Moore's valid, convincing call for "architecture with a memory" must not deaden our memory of that architecture called "modern." In a frequently overlooked statement from *Learning from Las Vegas* (1972), an extension of the arguments of *Complexity and Contradiction*, Venturi and his collaborators acknowledged that "since we have criticized Modern architecture, it is proper here to state our intense admiration of its early period when its founders, sensitive to their own times, proclaimed the right revolution. Our argument lies mainly with the irrelevant and distorted prolongation of that old revolution today."[7]

Some of Neutra's later work seems vulnerable to that latter indictment, but I am equally certain that most of his work, "sensitive to its own time," indeed "proclaimed the right revolution." Simple and practical, yet full of esthetic interest and variety, it provided the two essential functions of all great building art: a protective shelter from the woes of the world and a stage for confronting and enjoying life. His own life experience will serve in this book as the thread for retracing the history of the modern movement. The title and thrust of each chapter, in fact, refers not only to Neutra's own progression, but to the larger development of modern architecture as well.

2. The Neutra family, late 1890s, Vienna

Genesis

Richard Joseph Neutra lived his first quarter-century in a time and place of remarkable cultural richness —imperial Vienna, 1892–1914. And, as long as innocence allowed, he savored that place and time— the Vienna of his youth—with unabashed fervor and delight. "We who were born in Vienna and grew up there," recalled the music critic Max Graf, "had no idea during the city's brilliant period before the first world war that this epoch was to be the end and . . . that the Habsburg monarchy . . . was destined to decline. . . . We enjoyed the splendid city which was so elegantly beautiful and never thought that the light which shone over it could ever be that of a colorful sunset." Others viewed it with a darker irony. The dramatist Arthur Schnitzler remarked of the city that "if we lived long enough, every lie related about us would probably become true." To the critic Karl Kraus, *fin de siècle* Vienna was "the research station for the end of the world."[1]

But however exquisitely decadent the "city of dreams" would appear in retrospect, it was for Neutra's generation primarily a source of generative stimulation. As the capital of the overripe, far-flung Habsburg empire, it was a center and symbol of cultural energy and achievement. In art, architecture, music, opera, theater, literature, philosophy, science, technology, and medicine, it not only nurtured institutions of an old established culture, but tolerated and fostered in all those areas generative dissent, opposition, and change. Frequently the new trends were pilloried or extolled as "modern." Of this avant-garde the writer Bertha Zuckerkandl remarked that "with few exceptions everything developed as if a simultaneous vision had modelled the style of our age. Mysterious links were forged connecting language, colours, forms, tones and attitudes to life."[2]

For a youth as sensitive and as talented as Richard Neutra, Vienna was a wonderful city in which to grow up. It touched and shaped him through infancy, childhood, adolescence, and maturity. It affected his psyche and his behavior for life. He was born April 8, 1892, at Josephinengasse 7, corner of Konradgasse, in the old second district of Vienna, the third son and fourth and youngest child of Samuel and Elizabeth Neutra.

His father, Samuel, born in 1844 in Beregzasz, Hungary, was the son of Wilhelm and Theresia Friedmann Neutra. The name Neutra was of Roman origin, taken by the family many generations earlier from a city and river in the old Roman Hungarian province of Pannonia. Richard's grandfather Wilhelm, who had studied medicine at the University of Vienna, died in the mid-1850s, after treating patients in a typhoid epidemic in Budapest. His wife contracted the disease while caring for him and died shortly thereafter, leaving their eleven-year-old son Samuel an orphan. Relatives arranged for him to be apprenticed, first to a tailor and then to a simple craftsman who made cowbells. He followed this period of apprenticeship with several years as a journeyman metal worker, which led to his life's career as a metallurgist, specializing in the casting of brass and bronze machinery parts.[3]

In the early 1860s Samuel migrated to Vienna, where he became a foreman in the great Austrian locomotive works at Wiener Neustadt. He took workers' adult classes and educated himself in the evenings. In 1873, with a former colleague, he bought a small metal foundry in Vienna, which ultimately employed nearly thirty workers. He designed all the casting models himself, his daughter Josephine later recalled, and was "beloved by his workers, like a patriarch." The young firm exhibited at the Vienna World's Fair of 1873 and won a bronze medal, though one of Samuel Neutra's fondest memories of the exposition was seeing the new German Kaiser Wilhelm. Later the firm found a steady commission in casting the brass and bronze parts for the city's gas and water meters.[4]

Richard admired his father's technical acumen, his high professional standards, and his stoic courage in the dangerous occupation of handling molten metals. "What a boon a real handicraft can be," he marveled. "My father had a wonderful occupation and understood it to the last dot of the i." In retrospect, Richard described his father as "an excellent man . . . completely unequivocal and virile. . . ." Samuel Neutra was relatively uninterested in high intellectual matters, Richard remembered, but was a man of great human warmth.[5]

Richard's mother was born Elizabeth Glazer in 1851 in Bisenz, Moravia. Her father died when she was young, but her brothers studied, worked, and prospered in Vienna and soon sent for their sister and mother. At the age of twenty-three, at a coffeehouse on the Praterstrasse near the Danube Canal, the beautiful black-haired Betty met Samuel Neutra, a bachelor of thirty. After less than a year's courtship, they were married on August 22, 1875. Though secular agnostics, they acknowledged their Jewish heritage with a ceremony in the temple on Viaductgasse, near the Glazer's home in the third district.[6]

The year after their marriage, with a minimal income from the still struggling foundry, the couple had their first child, named Wilhelm after Samuel's father. Two years later another son, Siegfried, was born, and in 1886 their first daughter, Josephine. In 1892 Richard arrived, fifteen years after the birth of his oldest brother.

With Richard's arrival, the Neutra household numbered eight people, including Regina Glazer, Elizabeth's mother, and a maid. For this large a family the apartment at Josephinengasse proved too small, and in 1894 the Neutras moved a few blocks to Taborgasse 72 at the corner of the smaller Lessinggasse. Located between the bustling Northwest Train Station and the broad Kaiser Josephstrasse, which led to the even grander Praterstrasse and the

3. Richard and Josephine Neutra, Vienna, late 1890s

Danube, the neighborhood had as its greatest asset the Augarten, originally a private royal park that the popular and democratically inclined Emperor Joseph II had opened to the people in the eighteenth century. As a small child, Richard later remembered, he loved to lean far out a window to glimpse a slice of Augarten chestnut trees.[7]

Neutra's earliest memory was of the Taborgasse neighborhood. "It was a four-story building we lived in," he recalled, "and our apartment was one widely winding, cold stairflight above the street floor. The windings and the cold draft are still with me in some dreams." "What happens to one, *in* one, and around one while ascending a stair," Neutra later marveled, "and what of it sticks with us as a strangely lasting memory—is to me a master specimen of what architectural experience means."[8]

His infantile "sensorial curiosity" taught him even more. "Tumbling while trying to walk erect over the mattress, I learned about gravity, resiliency, the significance of the horizontal plane. In the morning, I put my little fingers over the carved and profiled headboards of my parents' bed, where I had joined them because of anxiety in the middle of the night. . . ." He remembered watching a maid clean dust from such curlicues and "must have got then the idea that housework is always with us, but it is not a pleasure." Later, in his own more simplified designs, he would attempt to minimize the need for such chores. As a child, he slept on the mattress-covered bottom drawer of a large pull-out sofa in the parlor, where "the tall walls and towering furniture—huge, immovable, oppressive—were given me by fate, like pre-historic fossils towering around the crib of the human race." But the room contained other objects that he loved. The "stove of white, glazed Swedish tile stood catty-cornered, slender, and door high. It carried on its top a life-size, equally snow-white bust of Ludwig van Beethoven. . . . I studied and cherished his broad, sulking face." Neutra also remembered the room's few "superb industrial products, bentwood Thonet chairs with rattan seats and back . . . later replaced, when I had kneeled them through, by entirely worthless models of current art design."[9]

His favorite retreat, however, from the cold massive scalelessness of the rest of the room was under the grand piano, a "shelter, a quiet studio of my own . . . a homelike cave, a 'club,' the very best place of all." Pleasant memories, in fact, of that "dim and cozy" space would inform and pervade much of his later architecture, where low-lying canopies and shifting floor and ceiling levels responded to the human need for warmth and protection. Yet the opposite, and equally human, claustrophobic fear of entrapment also found expression in his childhood environment. He remembered that he was "so used to one and two narrow tall windows in each room of our Viennese brick and plaster apartment buildings that it struck me like a revelation when I saw, for the first time, somewhere, one fairly wide window in a room, framing one generous outlook into the outer landscape. . . ." And space-extending mirrors he loved "almost as much as windows. They were both a blessing in a small world, as our apartment was, to my eyes, hungry for space."[10]

From the narrow windows of the apartment at Taborgasse the dominant view was of the Lessing-gasse, "a drab, unpaved street with three-story buildings bordering it, and bigger boys playing ball, and jumping on the sidewalk when a horse-drawn wagon with metal milk cans passed. . . . We had no play-space really. I was an upstairs child."[11]

Yet three blocks away was the elegant Augarten, too elegant perhaps for exuberant children, whom the guards chided for damaging the lawn. Yet despite such restrictions, it was the closest Richard came in his early life to nature and fresh air. He walked there almost daily with his grandmother Glazer, sometimes accompanied by his mother and sister. And it was there, Josephine later recalled, that four-year-old Richard demonstrated his already vivid imagination and his stubborn determination in managing people. Acting out a story told him by his mother, he announced that he was Hercules, his grandmother the lion. In response to her protests that she did not feel like a lion, the grandson commanded that she play the role with fervor. "You must roar, roar, roar like the lion," he cried, in an early preview of his Viennese penchant for acting and role playing. In the park and on the street he was fascinated with horses, and back upstairs at home his later prowess as a rider was presaged. At three, he got a hobby horse and upon learning from the Hungarian maid the inciting cry "Lovacska," he shouted it as he raced the horse throughout the house. "Otherwise life was rather

tiresome," he later contended in solemn retrospection, "no playground or companions, no common activities, only loneliness." But that isolation ended when he started school.[12]

From 1898 to 1902 Neutra attended the second district primary school at Novarragasse and Blumauergasse. He then spent eight years in the humanistic Sophiengymnasium at Zirkusgasse 46. His favorite teacher there was a zoologist named Regen, "a young, tall, blond-bearded and blue-eyed Croatian," who, when speaking of his favorite interests, "became so fully absorbed that he forgot . . . the misery of teaching mischievous uninterested youngsters. The classroom dissolved, and he was either in the bush or in the meadow, collecting specimens, or in the laboratory, microdissecting them for their secrets of life and death." The history teachers, he remembered, "were good story tellers and offered rounded-out-shapes—as raconteurs do—where fuzzy, puzzling events, merely enumerated, might have become drowned in chaotic confusion."[13]

In July 1910 Neutra passed his final gymnasium examinations with distinction ("Reif mit Auszeichnung"), scoring "good" in Greek, Latin, and mathematics and "very good" in religious studies, geography, history, physics, and philosophy. In his oral examination in "Austrian Studies" ("Vaterlandskunde"), he spoke "with distinction" on "Austrian princes as patrons of art and science."[14]

Stimulated by parents, siblings, teachers, and fellow students, Neutra became an omnivorous reader. As a youth, his parents had read to him the classic myths, fairy tales, and German children's stories. Karl May's Germanic images of Indians and cowboys in the American West particularly intrigued him. He also remembered German translations of the American novel *Uncle Tom's Cabin* and the various tales of Jules Verne, "about underground and undersea travel. . . ." The one he liked best "was the wistful story of men letting themselves be shot to the moon, probably not to be heard of or seen again."[15]

In 1910 he began keeping a diary, and taking note of the authors and titles that impressed him most, from ancient writers Thucydides, Plutarch, and Marcus Aurelius to such modern classics as von Ranke's *The Papacy* and Burkhardt's *Culture of the Renaissance in Italy*. He admired Dante's "poetic

4. Richard Neutra, about age 10

elasticity" and delighted in Cervantes's *Don Quixote*. He read the Russians Gogol, Pushkin, Dostoevski, and Tolstoy; the Scandinavians Ibsen and Strindberg; and the French masters de Maupassant, Flaubert, and Stendhal. Balzac he found "colossal," "inspired," and he relished the *Noa-Noa* of Paul Gauguin. Shakespeare and Kipling were his English favorites, but he also enjoyed Sterne, Byron, Thackeray, Dickens, Galsworthy, Shaw, and Oscar Wilde. Still, his greatest commitments were to the monuments of German literature and philosophy.[16]

There was frequent mention in his notes of Goethe, Heine, E. T. A. Hoffmann, Franz Grillparzer, Gottfried Keller, and Rainer Maria Rilke. He admired the contemporary essays and lectures of Peter Altenberg and Karl Kraus, the early novels of Hermann Hesse and Thomas Mann, and the poetry of Georg Trakl and Stefan George. With Trakl, whom he would later know personally, he "once sat up in a cafe in the Neubaugasse until 5 A.M.!" He found Richard Wagner's autobiographical writings "very attracting, particularly in the beginning." Mozart's *Letters* revealed "a splendidly mad, odd fellow and amorous childlike person. . . ." He reveled in such different philosophers as Spinoza, Schopenhauer, Emerson, and Bergson, and especially admired Kant's *Critique of Pure Reason*.[17]

The first work of Sigmund Freud's of which he made special note was *The Psychopathology of Everyday Life,* though his diary notes were sprinkled with Freudian concepts and terminology. Freud's son Ernst became a school friend of Neutra, and Richard visited the Freud home frequently. "Not long ago at Freud's," he noted in his diary, "I was able to look at the collection and the books while the professor was at the desk. Pompeian frescoes . . . mummy fragments, many Egyptian bronzes, ceramics, antique vase paintings, sculptures . . . Greek gold ornaments and these books . . . the erotic work. Terrific. . . ." The contact and conversations with Freud and his family confirmed and stimulated Neutra's interest in psychology. He would continue throughout his life to value Freud's insights into the effects of the early environment on human development. He would later differ with Freud chiefly in the degree to which such influences continued throughout life to shape and alter human behavior and the extent to which human personality might be affected by them later.[18]

Neutra read without comment Otto Weininger's anti-Semitic *Sex and Character*. He was more obviously moved by the more scientifically based revelations of Wilhelm Wundt on the environmental interrelationships of human psychological and physiological factors. He read and reread the complete works of Friedrich Nietzsche, presented to him by his brother Siegfried. *The Birth of Tragedy,* which he ranked "almost higher than *Zarathustra* . . . filled me with enthusiasm as little else could." He felt that Nietzsche's letters were, by contrast, "narrow-minded . . . deaf and unacoustical because they are lacking in the wide and deep natural-scientific elements of thought and because they are lacking in almost everything that concerns the fine arts." But on March 18, 1913, Neutra noted that Nietzsche was "beginning to be lonely. Thus, speaking for me . . . he wins . . . affection."[19]

Richard's enthusiasm for reading dramatic literature was surpassed only by his typically Viennese delight in attending plays in the city's numerous theaters. His tastes ranged from the Greek classics to Shakespeare to George Bernard Shaw. But as in nondramatic literature, Neutra's theatrical favorites were the German classics, old and new. He admired Max Reinhardt and Gerhart Hauptmann, but he was even more moved by Arthur Schnitzler's dark Viennese dramas of love and death. *Der Reigen, Anatol,* and *Das Weite Land* stirred and intrigued but also depressed him with their pervasive tone of decay and despair.[20]

Hugo von Hofmannsthal remained his idol, and he left in his diary high praise for "an extraordinarily beautiful and penetrating" Hofmannsthal-Reinhardt version of the medieval classic *Jedermann.* "The arena and the three-dimensional freedom of the actors took me in completely," he wrote, "and made a deep and lasting impression on me." He attended a public lecture and reading by Hofmannsthal and though "his appearance and voice were a disappointment," the poems, as always, gave him "a lot to think about." "Hofmannsthal, Hofmannsthal, *und noch einmal*," he recorded in his diary. "I deify him in my thought and words."[21]

Indeed Neutra participated fully in the cultish Viennese worship of heroes—particularly those associated with the theater. Such cultists followed their heroes slavishly—on stage and off—and acquitted themselves even more orgiastically upon their idols' deaths. The love of grand funerals was a favorite Austrian indulgence. Neutra typified this pattern with his admiration for Josef Kainz, who was characterized by the writer Stefan Zweig as "the most beloved . . . of actors." "Kainz is dead," Neutra solemnly recorded on September 22, 1910. "It was a blow to me." He then recalled some fifteen plays in which he had seen Kainz perform. "I have wonderful memories of his death as Richard II," he wrote, "also of his acting in Hamlet. . . ." And with thousands of other mourners, Neutra attended Kainz's funeral and made note in his diary of "rain, journalists, photographers, people overcome by grief."[22]

The cult of heroes, the cult of death, and the observe and equally Viennese cult of gaiety were all refracted in the Viennese theater. But the theater not only reflected Viennese mores; it also shaped and confirmed the local penchant for "role-playing," a quality pervasive in Neutra's personality. For him, as for many of his Viennese compatriots, life followed art as frequently as the reverse. Being Viennese, noted historian William Johnston, "required incessant play-acting. Everyone from porter and street car conductor to count and emperor delighted in impersonation and witty repartee, turning each social transaction into a smoothly played scene. Although foreigners sometimes belittled Viennese politeness as pretense, participants understood that no scene, however well-acted, could produce lasting results. Instead of seeking changes, skill in acting relieved frustration by aestheticizing it. Amiability channeled into dramatics involved no downright lying; rather, as Hanns Sachs said, there prevailed 'a general insincerity, with comparatively little hypocrisy.' "[23]

The most important educational influences on Neutra were his brothers, his sister, and their friends and spouses. Wilhelm, who would become a physician and psychiatrist in Freud's circle, and Siegfried, who would become an engineer and patent attorney, had wide-ranging interests in the arts and music. Both played the violin in various orchestras and string quartets and "mingled with Arnold Schönberg and his pupils." Josephine was an artist and helped Richard learn how to draw and paint. But the person most significant in his cultural development was her husband, the art historian Arpad Weixlgärtner.[24]

The son of a Hungarian count, Arpad was twenty years older than Richard. Later a renowned Dürer and Grünewald authority, he was in Richard's youth the curator of arms, armor, and "decorative arts" at the Kunsthistorisches Museum. Among the treasures in his care were Benvenuto Cellini's salt cellar and the Imperial Crown of the Holy Roman Emperors, which he allowed his awe-struck young brother-in-law to hold and admire. Arpad was well connected in both established and avant-garde circles. He was personally acquainted with the Crown Prince Franz Ferdinand, whose assassination in 1914 would precipitate the Great War. He had known the composers Hugo Wolf and Gustav Mahler, both of whom died before Richard could meet them. But through Arpad, Neutra did meet his hero von Hoffmansthal.[25]

Most important, Arpad introduced Neutra to the great painting and sculpture collections of Vienna—from the old masters to the moderns, from the Kunsthistorisches Museum to the galleries of the Wiener Sezession. Neutra took special note of the German and Flemish masters: Breughel, Rubens, Dürer, and Holbein. A particular favorite was the austerely fetching, "fabulously good" Lucas Cranach. Of the moderns, he favored Courbet, Manet, Van Gogh, Cezanne, and Rodin, but he reserved his greatest enthusiasm for the contemporary Viennese painters Anton Romako, Egon Schiele, Oskar Kokoschka, and especially Gustav Klimt, whose studio he once visited with Arpad and Josephine.[26]

"It's a one-story house in an old, somewhat wild garden," Neutra recorded in his diary. "At both sides of the entrance . . . two sleeping heads sculpted out of boulders . . . Klimt's only plastic attempts, as he said afterwards. After a lot of knocking . . . still nothing moved. We walked around the house and knocked loudly. He finally opened up. In a blue kimono with a flat white ornament at the shoulders. He was also a little moody. He said 'Klimt' . . . when he shook my hand. He soon got out the pictures. Most of all the half-finished 'Bride' won me over. 'Leda and the Swan' and 'Adam and Eve.' A lot of landscapes, portraits, even of a dead woman. Noticeable, the Chinese influence. Klimt talks about a Chinese theater performance which he attended. . . . He says Schiele can't do as much as Kokoschka. . . . His person and everything around him has made a bigger-than-ever impression."[27]

5. *Gustav Klimt*, portrait of Margaret Stonborough-Wittgenstein, 1905

6. *Neutra,* Portrait of a Horse, 1915

The balanced asymmetry of Klimt's elegantly stylized portraits and landscapes moved Neutra greatly. His own early travel sketches, in fact, revealed the strong influence of Klimt and Schiele's compositions. But Neutra was even more taken with the abstractly architectonic backgrounds of Klimt's figure paintings and with his use of metallic paints —an effect that Neutra would later exploit in accenting and articulating his buildings.

In February 1918 Neutra made note of Klimt's premature death and its deep effect upon him. Among the artist's last executed works were six color drawings of Josephine, three of which she promised to Richard. Like most of the Weixlgärtners' personal treasures, all were destroyed when the Nazis burned their house after Arpad refused to make the symbolic gesture of surrendering the Imperial Crown to Hitler.[28]

Music and opera were important to Neutra's development and remained a source of pleasure throughout his life. "To go to hear *Tristan* or the *Meistersinger* thirty times in the standing room of the opera house was a normal occurrence," he recalled. "Beethoven, Mozart, Haydn, Schubert were all local forces, living on in my surroundings . . . Mahler and other conductors were heroes to me. . . ." Neutra revered the classical composers, especially Bach, but he was equally committed to Wagner and Bruckner and to such different contemporary figures as Richard Strauss and Arnold Schönberg.[29]

On March 31, 1913, he recorded a significant occasion in the history of modern music—a concert conducted by Schönberg, which included his *Kammersymphonie,* Alban Berg's composition on Peter Altenberg's poems, Anton Webern's *Six Pieces for Orchestra,* and Alexander von Zemlinsky's *Maeterlincklieder.* "Right at the beginning, a few people began to bawl and scream," Neutra noted, "there was talking and yelling and knocking about. The rabble just had the feeling that there was someone to butcher in a cheap manner, someone there for the taking. It was . . . shocking to witness. People who have about as much to do with art as I . . . with cards constantly made jokes which were thought to be splendid by those . . . neighbors listening. At times I thought I would jump out of my skin. After the Schönberg symphony, which despite everything made an impression of power and of an artwork on me, a hellish racket broke out.

In the second gallery, a few people were thrown out after hard scuffles. Berg's 'lieder' were interrupted by roaring [and] neighing. Earlier [Adolf] Loos had almost engaged in acts of violence. Schönberg screamed threats into the auditorium. The 'lieder' were completed. Then all limits broke. People challenged each other, were torn apart, screamed, laughed, howled. Arthur Schnitzler sat across from me in the second box. Someone yelled to the audience to behave in a civilized manner or leave. Someone yelled back 'rascal.' The former jumped down into the crowd, slapped the supposed man who had insulted him in the face. The whole assembly followed these acts anxiously. Then some more shouting. A uniformed commissioner screamed something . . . my whole body trembled out of rage. The musicians left the hall. The mob had succeeded in breaking up the concert. . . . The audience is a cowardly beast, unfriendly and hostile to art. . . ." Neutra would have occasion to recall this reaction to "modern" music when his and others' "modern" architecture later evoked similarly hostile reactions.[30]

Neutra's love of Vienna and its physical and cultural landscape did not stand in the way of his interest in the larger world beyond. In 1910, with a school friend, Edmund Kalischer, he took his first walking trip with backpack and sketchbook through the towns and forests of Bohemia and Franconia. In the latter he gloried in the old medieval towns of Rothenburg and Regensburg, and in Nuremberg the pair stayed at "the cheap Inn of the Little Swan, Zum Schwänlein, near the old circumvallating masonry, where no self-respecting tourist had stayed, maybe, since the days when artists from Holland had come to pay a return visit to Albrecht Dürer." Near Regensburg on the Danube they visited the Walhalla, a nineteenth-century variation on the Athenian Parthenon by the German architect Leo von Klenze, designed to house portrait busts of Germanic national heroes.[31]

In 1912 Neutra toured the coast of the eastern Adriatic with his friend Ernst Freud. Later that year he visited the Freud family while they were vacationing in Bozen in the Tyrol and then journeyed southward with Ernst to Venice, Verona, Florence, Genoa, and Milan. There he savored the classics of ancient and Renaissance Italy. At the time, he admitted, he "knew nothing of the then-current Cubists, and had only a slight inkling later of the Futurists in Milan." His delight in the architecture of Palladio and the sculpture of Michelangelo epitomized his general enthusiasm for the treasures of Italy. Of Palladio's Villa Rotonda, near Vicenza, he wrote, "Splendid building. Sumptuous layout. Silhouette against the sky. In the cupola room very beautiful late frescoes."[32]

In Florence, he exulted in Michelangelo's portrait sculptures of Giuliano and Lorenzo di Medici and wrote a sensitive evaluation of his reactions. He admired Michelangelo's *David* and concurred in the consensus that "the right hand . . . is perhaps the best part of the work." But of all the Davids, he delighted most in the sculpture by Verrocchio which had "something of a slender . . . Italian rogue about him. And one thinks right away that he only decapitated Goliath in order to show off a little. So charmingly insolently does he smile at me." Indeed, he confessed, "Florence and its surroundings is to me now the dearest place in the world. . . . Venice is much more like a theater, and looks like a curtain arrangement when the wind is still. Only when a puff of wind lets the sun-warmed lagoon air glide over one's skin and when one's nose picks up the smells of tar and tepid sea water . . . then one senses suddenly that everything is real momentarily." Those early journeys confirmed for Neutra the strong elements of wanderlust in his nature. Wherever he might live for the rest of his life and however important the connotations of "home," Neutra would remain the inveterate sojourner.[33]

Neutra's precocious intellectual and cultural development was complemented during his adolescent years by a correspondingly vigorous social and sexual awakening. In his Viennese student days, in his various foreign travels, and in his out-of-town, peace-time, pre-war military training, he enjoyed increasingly both the company of women and the narcissistic discovery of his own attractiveness to them. While on military maneuvers, for example, "during the body-bending exercises and the marching exercises, there passed by the barracks off and on young women who were not really remarkable specimens. The remarks caused by these circumstances made by the trainers of us recruits started me thinking. Just like the young maiden in the seraglio, who through complete isolation from all

7. *Neutra,* travel sketch 1913

men, through the lack of a fulfilling and diverting occupation, is really artificially trained to experience a powerful nymphomania, so . . . the man isolated in the barracks turns into a satyr. . . . The work that he has to do is in part a sublimation of his sex drive. . . ."[34]

Sublimation through work, however, gave way to direct experience during furloughs and nights off in the neighboring towns. On a September night in 1911, for example, with a colleague named Kohler and several amicable females, he enjoyed a typical evening of drinking and carousing. "In the midst of this a fight took place," he noted in his diary, "and the policeman was involved in it. It was funny in a tipsy way. Kohler, the landlady and I stood high up by a window, three fourths naked, and looked down at the noisy dispute. Then we rode to Vienna. . . . Hard drinking til 1 A.M. at the Rathaus." A few nights later, his whole unit celebrated. "The trumpeter danced, the whole unit danced . . . I had two girls, but especially one girl! By God, we had a good time that night! Because then, we didn't even dance but _____! On the next night . . . I was with her again." Modesty did not prevent him from remarking the next year that he and a colleague "went in every place, made eyes, and made the girls' mouths water . . . and then I danced like a fool and sang to the guitar, but I pleased a couple of girls really well and was so honestly jolly." In April 1914 he noted being "hypnotized for the first time. With two girls it worked extremely well. And I overexerted myself and had a bad night. They were cataleptic and one was even a somnabulist."[35]

A less ominous incident in 1913 revealed his comic, play-acting compulsions, as he played on the sympathies of two attractive nineteen-year-old Viennese girls, Hansi and Frieda, by pretending to be a guileless Italian tourist, able to speak only the most primitive German. "Because the story was very amusing, I have to write down a little," he confided to his diary. "I . . . presented myself in the most broken Tedesco as a train-traveling Italian. Thereupon we agreed to a rendezvous. And went to the Prater in the afternoon. . . . I mixed in Italian phrases very quickly to keep it real. Told of my adventures in the war in Tripoli. While I kept quiet, the two girls talked by my side about harmless matters which should actually be heard only by

female ears. Because I pretended to be little able at German, I let them explain to me the word 'corset.' Something like a show-and-tell lesson. . . . Afterwards I cleared myself plausibly through unfamiliarity with the Austrian money. . . . In any case, I caused jealousy and a sensation everywhere . . . when I went around on the arms of the two spruced-up girls. It was really touching to hear how the two reminded each other . . . not to cause me too many expenses in the inn. . . . Finally . . . we landed at the White Ox. I sat down there and, relieved, gave myself away. . . . Nothing remained of the very, very pert girls of the morning. Wow!! Hansi was just not to be reconciled, to be fooled soooo! She was totally put out by it. I bought roses, red ones, and pastry with almonds, but it was not successful with her. . . . But Frieda was soon all right again, very all right . . . long live love."[36]

Neutra's most serious and sustained youthful love affair was with "sweet, tenderly milk-and-blood-faced Threska Sturm. I would meet her after hours at Kroell's millinery shop in the Mariahilferstrasse" where she worked. The relationship resulted in Threska's becoming pregnant. Though doubting that their love was deep and mature enough to ensure a successful marriage, Neutra felt both delight and apprehension over the awesome fact of producing a child. Threska was apparently less ambivalent, however, and despite Neutra's anguished reluctance, she underwent an early abortion. The affair continued intermittently and stormily until after the war, when Threska married and Neutra left Vienna.[37]

Neutra also valued his relationships with close male companions. Besides Ernst Freud, Edmund Kalischer, and numerous school friends, he enjoyed the camaraderie of his army and university colleagues. Though he was convinced, as an already studious Freudian, of the bisexual component and potential in all people, Neutra's male friendships were intensely affectionate but apparently platonic. Upon bidding farewell to an army friend, Ali, he wrote in his diary: "I surely am a lucky fellow that I alone, of all those enlisted for one year, would find such a good friend—a person of rare ability . . . loved by all. For five months we lived together in complete harmony which seems unbelievable when one takes into account our ac-

8. *Neutra,* travel sketch, 1918

tually rather differing dispositions and habits of . . . life and sphere of acquaintances prior to our meeting. I was plenty sentimental when recalling our solitary walks here and there at the most impossible and most attractive places . . . and our openness towards each other and clinking the wine glasses together on summer nights and our mutual laughter while on horseback . . . and the happy things that happened to us or between us and the anger filled things and his cigarettes which we smoked and his razor which made me handsome and the new things which he could tell me and those new things which he could see in me which came from the fresh breeze of our friendship on which we feasted together. He was three years older than I and ahead of me in terms of all general practical know how. I can't really conceive of how we can get together again but I am happy over these five months." Neutra, in fact, was sufficiently moved by his friend's departure that he added on the same diary page several pertinent lines from Kipling's *Barrack-Room Ballads*.[38]

As intense as his male and female friendships may have seemed at the time, however, Neutra's closest and most formative adolescent relationships were with the members of his extended family. He owed his greatest cultural and intellectual debts to his brothers Wilhelm and Siegfried and his brother-in-law Arpad, but emotionally he was most attracted to his mother, his sister Josephine, and Wilhelm's wife Louise. His mother's death in 1905 and Louise's death in 1911 grieved him and marked him profoundly. He knew his mother was very ill with breast cancer but had no idea that her death was so imminent. "When I entered my parents' bedroom to say good-bye as usual on the way to school that fateful day," he later recalled, "my father indicated silence. My mother lay face down near him, her long shiny hair covering her and my father did not know she had been dead for several hours. I did not know it either and quietly left for school."[39]

After his mother's death, his older sister Josephine and his sister-in-law Louise became in part maternal substitutes. Quasi-facetiously he called Louise "Mama." Her premature death in early 1911 was another severe loss, and he left in his diary a description of her funeral and of their relationship. He recalled an earlier summer outing into the

countryside with Louise and Josephine to the old cloister at Heiligenkreuz "and how Louise with her black glasses on her friendly face would at times supply us with sandwiches at rest stops." They discussed the Romanesque and Baroque styles. "Then we looked at the cloister. The sun was shining on the yellow Baroque wall and the noble shadow was on the Romanesque pathway and on the old Gobelin in the church and I led the conversation, in my estimation, in a truly loving and sensible way. Louise and Josephine at least both listened to me. . . . We three of us understood each other well. . . . I also went hiking just with Louise. At those times we would talk . . . about the upbringing of [her daughter] Helene and about children and parents in general. She liked me very much and expected the most of me. . . . I too loved her very much and have treasured her since I was little. . . . I still remember . . . how she would pour coffee for me" and how she would "put the black glasses on her lovely beautiful face."[40]

Approximately a month after Louise's death Josephine married Arpad, and Richard felt a different kind of loss. "My childhood already belongs completely to the perfect tense," he wrote. "I no longer have a grandmother nor a mother nor a sister next to me. And the home into which I came at the age of 3 will no longer be ours in one month. And today I turned 19." With no one left at home but himself and his father, the two moved to Schelleingasse 46 in the fourth district, where they shared a house with Siegfried and his family.[41]

By the time Neutra started his diary in 1910, he was becoming increasingly introspective, and he used its pages to record not only his intellectual, cultural, and social development but his growing search for his own identity. At times he was painfully honest and tough with himself. "I am benumbed from cowardice," he wrote in early 1911, as he despaired of the "rotten, foul, petty, self-loving wretched core inside me. . . . And while I am writing all this down it all seems to me to be a weak-footed, weak-headed psychological sketch." He recognized, however, that such introspection served a therapeutic function and that the melancholy moods were an important counterpoise to the flippant side of life. They brought back before him memories of his past life at its worst and at its best.

He recalled a line from Hofmannsthal about "the aroma of wet trees," which struck him as a "colorful memory and as such it enters our innermost being and gives a gloomy happiness so very fulfilling."[42]

Yet in the same introspective passage he admitted that he was also "forced to think how many sensible things and even more how many funny things I know to say about myself." He was, in fact, "happy and satisfied over this self-knowledge and over the selflessness of my ability to observe my thoughts while I write about them. Then I am afraid again of the devouring vanity which annuls every simple subjective feeling for myself . . . but further inside of myself I cannot go and perhaps unconsciously, I do not want to expose any more of myself to myself. When one writes something about oneself, then one writes, after all, only how it could be or should be, logically speaking, in the constructed 'I,' but not how it really is inside oneself, if something like 'really' exists and something like a 'self' exists."[43]

"Everything in me," he admitted, "flows out toward a painful longing for the past and fear for the quick passing of time." Tunes of Hugo Wolf "come to my mind . . . which I sang at one time and their memory lays hold of me to the marrow of my bones. I see the sunlight of long ago reflecting on the street and the blue sky and the white clouds reflecting themselves on the polished windows and the polished brass door knobs of the street doors. I walk again through the misty, dusty summer evening air, perhaps coming from the Prater and then my steps come to a halt at the deserted and mysterious home with the windows where there are no curtains." Indeed, however "rational" and "scientific" Neutra would later see himself and his work as being, there remained in his nature strong, ineluctable traces of the nineteenth-century Viennese romantic. His honest quest for "rationalism," "empiricism," and "modernity" were, in fact, partially conscious efforts to counter and control such romantic tendencies, just as the interest in modernity and the future countered his fondness for the "remembrance of things past." Even at his most "scientific," Neutra remained the romantic rationalist —the idealistic, visionary, romantic engineer.[44]

He had admitted in 1910 that he was a "goggle-eyed question to myself. I hate dilettantism in whomever I even sense it. I . . . appear to myself as a dilettante, as an unrestrained . . . outsider and am so freedom-seeking that it is repugnant to me. . . . But I am expecting soon that something in me will shake me off this track in order to find out what, from the very beginning and from my soul is my vocation in life. . . ." He was already deciding, of course, that his destined vocation "from the very beginning and from my very soul" was the art, craft, business, and "calling" of architecture.[45]

"In many a life one is conscious of the days of emergent vocational choice only much later than they actually occur," Neutra later observed. "But when I was eight years old without thinking clearly, I must have decided to become an architect. My unspoken decision was the result of a ride in the new, much-talked-about subway, the stations of which were designed by Otto Wagner. In a very short time I was enamored of him, his buildings and his fights against strong opposition and public ridicule. He was Hercules, Achilles, Buffalo Bill, all rolled in one: he stood for all the heroes and pathfinders. . . . Here was a missionary and one who was breaking with a worn-out past."[46]

Neutra never studied with Wagner nor knew him well personally, but as his interest in architecture developed, he devoured the master's writings and eagerly studied his buildings and projects. As a living presence in the Vienna of Neutra's youth, as an already internationally recognized figure, Wagner would have more impact on Neutra than any of his actual teachers at the Technische Hochschule. Except for Adolf Loos, in whose studio and circle Neutra would take an active part, Otto Wagner was Neutra's most significant early mentor.

Born in Penzing near Vienna in 1841, Wagner studied between 1857 and 1863 at Vienna's Technische Hochschule and Academy of Fine Arts. The planning and styling of his early work followed traditional neoclassical biases—traces of which he would always retain. The work of his first decades was strong and compelling enough in both logic and esthetic effect, however, to win him the commissions in the 1890s for an extensive remodeling and expansion of the public works of Vienna. This entailed plans for new government offices, museums, schools, libraries, hospitals, and numerous street and park layouts, though his designs for the Danube Canal dams and the stations and accoutrements of the metropolitan rail network were the elements of his plans that were most completely realized. It was the series of rail stations of the late 1890s that attracted young Neutra and that marked in Wagner's *oeuvre* an important transition from his early neoclassical commitments to a later "new" architecture with minimal historical references. The forms of his relatively abstract and stripped-down later buildings would increasingly reflect and celebrate their structural anatomy and the nature of their materials as well as their programmatic intentions and functions.[47]

Appointed professor at the Vienna Academy of Art in 1894, Wagner synthesized these incipient principles in his inaugural address, subsequently published under the significant title *Moderne Architektur*. There Wagner stressed what the age still considered the relatively new idea that the important elements of style, form, and beauty were ultimately by-products of the general building program and should follow the architect's primary concern of designing for "modern life." As such, Wagner's philosophy was remarkably close in spirit, phrasing, and timing to the architectural manifestos of his Chicago contemporary Louis Sullivan. Along with the later, related statements of their colleagues and followers in Europe and America, such pronouncements—as reified in their buildings—furnished the spark, and later the dogma, of the developing modern movement.[48]

The growing move away from historicism, however, did not yet obviate the use of decoration, and the new forms, relatively free of historical references, were increasingly covered with organic botanical motifs. Frequently such references pervaded the forms themselves in a tactile, plastic, three-dimensional way. The "new art" encompassed not only architecture but painting, sculpture, and all types of decorative design, and its regional variations called up various descriptive labels. In France and the low countries it was called *l'art nouveau*, in the German-speaking countries, *Jugendstil*. In Vienna it took the name of *Sezessionstil*, after the Wiener Sezession, founded in 1897 by an avant-garde group of artists, including Klimt, and architects made up for the most part of followers of Otto Wagner.

Aside from the modular, geometric, steel-framed Stadtbahn stations of the 1890s, the building

of Wagner's that most interested and influenced Neutra was the Postal Savings Bank (1904–12), the first "modern" building to be granted a place of honor on the architecturally historicist Ringstrasse. The grand Ringstrasse had been developed in the mid-nineteenth century on the circular strip of demolished fortifications that had surrounded the inner city since the Middle Ages. The neo-Gothic Rathaus and Votivkirche, the neoclassical Parliament building, and the neo-Renaissance Burgtheater typified the types of Ringstrasse historicism against which Wagner and his followers were reacting. The Postal Savings Bank epitomized that reaction.

Though it contained certain abstract classical vestiges in its pyramidal profile, its tripartite vertical composition, and its overall symmetry, the bank moved farther than any of Wagner's buildings toward the ethic and esthetic the new century would call modern. Designed to fill a trapezoidal site, the Imperial and Royal Postal Savings Bank was built in two stages, 1904–06 and 1910–12. Wagner clad the outside walls with thin sheets of white marble. Heavier, slightly undulating slabs of granite covered the lower foundation walls. Large bolts holding these materials in place created a strong, lively pattern across the facade. The extruded central entrance block of the seven-story building contained seven window bays, to effect a vast square fronting on the Kochplatz. The large *Sezessionstil* lettering of "OST. POSTSPARKASSENAMT" ran across the cornice, flanked on either side by large winged acroterial figures sculpted by Othmar Schimkowitz. Rising high above the cornice was a decorative screen marked with six large ornamental wreaths. The stair and balcony railings inside and out, the face of the bolts holding the granite and marble, the acroteria, and the ornamental wreaths were all made of aluminum.[49]

Single rows of offices lining the outer sections of the four walls opened to an interior corridor that ran continuously around the building. Near the front entrance, flanked by large offices on three sides, rose the grand, triple-naved steel and glass banking room—the most significant and spectacular feature of the building. The stunningly "vaulted" steel-framed glass ceiling brought in light from above. The glazed block panels of the floor carried the light to the rooms below. The sophisticated furniture and fixtures, all designed by Wagner,

9. *Otto Wagner*, Karlsplatz Station, Vienna, 1894–97

10. *Otto Wagner*, Postal Savings Bank, Vienna, 1905, banking room

combined Machine-Age metaphor with an elegantly simple functional suitability. The aluminum "heat-blowing machines" suggested strange, otherworldly, futuristic space objects. As a student in 1913, Neutra made notes in his diary of the building's measurements and design patterns. He must have been impressed with the numerous suggestions of prefabrication and the overall effect—especially in the great banking room—of beautifully engineered machine-part assemblage. His diary note on the building's sublime proportions was punctuated with three emphatic exclamation marks.[50]

Wagner's professorship at the Academy of Fine Arts had included the establishment of his own design studio and the teaching of master classes in what came to be known as the Wagnerschule. Only a dozen or so new Academy students were admitted each year. Wagnerschule participation became a prestigious credential, and important design ideas emerged from its sessions. Indeed, the influence of Wagnerschule ideas reached far beyond the work of its immediate participants, though its alumni included some of the most creative designers of the early twentieth century.

The Wagnerschule graduates whose work touched Neutra most directly were Joseph Olbrich, Josef Hoffmann, and, ultimately, Rudolph Schindler. Visiting Olbrich's 1898 Vienna Sezession exhibition building, Neutra later remembered, "was one of the great experiences of my young life." As a student, he also recalled, "everyone in my surroundings was aware of . . . the comprehensive effort at Darmstadt," the state-supported "artists' colony" that Olbrich directed and built. He would not see Hoffmann's masterpiece, the 1907 Stoclet house in Brussels, until 1930, except in published illustrations, but long before he finally saw it, it became one of his favorite modern buildings. With murals by Klimt and interior detailing and furniture by the craftsmen of the Wiener Werkstätte, it epitomized the Wagnerschule—and more particularly the Sezession—penchant for the *Gesamtkunstwerk,* the perfectly integrated "total work of art."[51]

Despite Neutra's admiration for the Wagnerschule, he applied for admission in 1911 not to Wagner's Academy of Fine Arts, but to the Technische Hochschule or Imperial Institute of Technology, founded in 1815 as the Vienna Polytechnic Institute. After his eight years of liberal arts training at the Sophiengymnasium, he felt the need for a more professionally and technically directed curriculum to prepare him to become a practicing architect. Wagner's scheduled retirement in 1912 had already been announced, so he would not have been able to go through the Wagnerschule as his older friend Schindler had done. After graduating from the gymnasium in 1910, Neutra served his year of obligatory military service in 1910–11, and in 1911–12 began his first year at the Technische Hochschule. His second and third years were the 1912–13 and 1913–14 sessions. He would have finished in 1915 had the war not begun. In 1914, at the end of his third year, he was called to active duty. He was granted leave from the army to return to Vienna and complete his degree during the 1917–18 academic year.[52]

In his four years of study at the Technische Hochschule, he acquired a strong technical education that prepared him in the basics of design theory, architectural and freehand drawing, civil and mechanical engineering, and the physical sciences, leavened and supported by courses in architectural history. Of his forty-one graded courses, Neutra received the highest mark of "excellent" in fifteen, the second grade of "very good" in sixteen, and the third grade of "good" in nine. The fourth grade of "sufficient" he received in only one course: "Building mechanics: Iron and reinforced concrete." In his preliminary examination, the first of two general examinations, in December 1913, he was graded "Sehr befähigt" or "very well qualified." On his final examination in July 1918, he was given a unanimous vote of "excellent" ("mit Auszeichnung bestanden") by his examining committee of Professors Emil Artmann, Leopold Simony, Max Freiherr von Ferstel, and Franz Freiherr von Krauss.[53]

Other professors who left lasting impressions included Rudolph Saliger, "tough as nails," who gave him the low grade of "sufficient" in building mechanics—though higher grades in other, related courses. Karl Mayreder, husband of the Vienna feminist Rosa Mayreder, "required me to draw Ionian and Corinthian temples as a whole, and in minute shaded details as well as in neatly measured and moduled proportions." From Mayreder he earned the grade of "excellent." He got the same high mark from Eduard Veith in freehand drawing, "where I learned to draw nudes with great ease." In his last year of school he took architectural modeling from Othmar Schimkowitz, the sculptor of the winged figures on Wagner's Postal Savings Bank. In both third and fourth years he took ornamental drawing from the distinguished Wagner-schule graduate Max Fabiani, famous for his richly colored Sezessionstil Viennese apartment houses. As a student, Neutra frequently attended lectures at the Academy of Fine Arts and kept abreast of architectural activities in Vienna and beyond. On November 5, 1913, for example, he noted reading the *Yearbook* of the German Werkbund. Earlier, in 1912, he had written, ". . . I heard a really outstanding lecture by Dr. Friedrich Naumann. A colossal, inspired fellow on the 'Werkbund.'" Yet however generally fulfilling Neutra found the Technische Hochschule and the formal Viennese academic life, his most enriching Viennese architectural association was, undoubtedly, his connection with Adolf Loos.[54]

Born in 1870 in Brno, Moravia, Loos took courses at the State Polytechnic College, Reichenberg, Bohemia, before studying architecture from 1890 to 1893 at the Dresden College of Technology. He followed this with three years of travel and sporadic work in England and the United States. In America he was especially moved by the emerging Chicago School of skyscraper architecture. There he encountered the powerful geometry and the organic ornamentation of Louis Sullivan, who in an oblique criticism of his own style had written in 1892: "It would be greatly for our esthetic good if we should refrain entirely from the use of ornament for a period of years in order that our thought might concentrate acutely upon the production of buildings well formed and comely in the nude." Whether or not Loos knew of Sullivan's pronouncement at that time, he encountered Otto Wagner's orations on related themes when he settled in Vienna in 1896.[55]

In the next decades, Loos combated the rise of Olbrich and Hoffmann's lush *Sezessionstil* and seized on the need for the sublimation of architectural ornamentation as one of several highly polemical personal crusades. His essays, published chiefly in Viennese newspapers, were passionate and engagingly argued, if frequently contradictory, manifestos. Positive as well as negative enthusiasms

motivated Loos. He loved the best of Greek and Roman architecture and he admired the stern early nineteenth-century Berlin neoclassicist Karl Friedrich Schinkel. He was a fervent Anglophile and Americanophile. He was especially drawn to William Morris and the late nineteenth-century English Arts and Crafts movement. "The simplest rush seat made by man's hands," he remarked, referring to Morris's commitment to handicraft, "is a thousand times more valuable than the richest leather embossing produced by machine."[56]

He seemed unembarrassed by the contradiction between this view and his equally exuberant support for machine technology devised and run by noble engineers. He extolled, for example, the mass-produced bicycle: "Does not the spirit of Periclean Athens permeate its forms? If the Greeks had had to build a bicycle, it would have been exactly like ours. . . . Are there today still people who work like the Greeks? Oh yes! The English as a people, the engineers as a profession. The English and the engineers are our Hellenes." He claimed to find Austria, by contrast, backward and unprogressive, and in 1903 he started a short-lived journal significantly titled *The Other: A Journal for the Introduction into Austria of Western Civilization*. But despite his battles with "the formalism of an old culture," Neutra later observed, Loos "was built very much in the Viennese tradition" and was "the most Viennese person I can imagine."[57]

Loos's first decades in Vienna yielded a small but significant group of commissions for new or remodeled buildings, including shops, cafés, bars, flats, and detached villas. Lean, spare, and simple, in keeping with his credo, they achieved interest and elegance via crisp geometry, the subtle interlocking of interior spaces, the modulation of floor and ceiling levels, and the use of rich interior materials. Loos combined fine woods, marble, mirrors, and metals in such commercial commissions as the Kärtnerbar (1907). In such residential projects as the Steiner and Scheu villas (1910, 1912), he countered the stark, unornamented, usually concrete façades and the hard interior marble and tile with warmer woods—in the Arts and Crafts manner—for ceiling beams, cabinetry, and built-in furniture.

It was the quality of Loos's architecture, the bravado of his frequently outrageous iconoclasm, and his obvious personal charisma that drew stu-

11. *Adolf Loos*, Steiner House, Vienna 1910

12. *Loos*, Steiner House, interior

13. *Loos*, Kärtner Bar, Vienna, 1907, with portrait of Peter Altenberg

dents from the Academy and Hochschule to his lectures and to his smaller, more informally structured studio-salon. One such student was Richard Neutra, who in the fall of 1912, during his second year at the Technische Hochschule, entered Loos's studio and became a loyal follower. In October 1912 Neutra confided to his diary, "I was with Loos and I'm hearing 'Internal Construction' and 'Knowledge of Materials' with him. I'm not myself entirely clear about him." But a month later he seemed to be "clear" and believed that he had "created a pleasant and favorable impression on him." On November 10, 1912, Neutra accompanied Loos on an inspection visit to his house for the Scheu family, then nearing completion, in the Hietzing district of Vienna. He also followed him on visits to furniture craftsmen and stonemasons. He made detailed notes and sketches in his diary of the materials and dimensions of half-a-dozen Loos residences, including the Steiner house, which he would later claim, less than convincingly, "never interested me at all." He acknowledged being more moved, however, by the stark, interlocking geometry of the Scheu house.[58]

Every Thursday Neutra joined a group at the Deutsches Haus café, where Loos held forth at a specially reserved table. "I have already talked with Loos about everything possible," Neutra noted. "His standpoints are almost never invulnerable, but they are always interesting and probably honestly founded. And he has a relationship to very, very much." Neutra recalled several different occasions when he had sat up late talking with Loos and his friends in various cafes and "once in *his Kärtner-bar,* which is splendidly beautiful. . . . He knows how to talk beautifully about [Peter] Altenberg, about trips in Africa, about his architectural friends and foes. He has a collection of Kokoschka at his place that I think isn't too bad, in part. . . . He has three [full-time] intelligent pupils that look up to him like God. Almost deservedly: he reserves so much concern, so much sympathy for them. He got me a ticket to a Schönberg concert: 'Pierrot Lunaire,' a few songs, really beautiful and poignant." In the café and tavern meetings, Neutra would later recall, Loos "would speak with a very low voice and sometimes accentuate a humorous turn—and there were many humorous turns—with a very slight smile. One had to listen attentively over the noise

in the restaurant to hear him. . . . His face was wrinkled and at the same time young."[59]

Indeed, Neutra later insisted, he felt that he was "a plagiarist of Loos—as he is revealed in his words rather than his work—and that personality impacts, integrated and fused, are more important than any kind of formal borrowings and loanings." But as his own later work would demonstrate, Neutra borrowed more than he may have realized from Loos's actual buildings, particularly their mixture of richness and austerity and their subtle interaction of volumetric spaces. The thing about Loos that "stayed with me most," Neutra concluded, "was his faith in and almost cult of 'lastingness,' as compared with passing fashion. He was reaching out for some contact with history, to produce this 'lastingness' despite the fashions of the day."[60]

A more immediate legacy for Neutra was Loos's passion for the people, the culture, and the architecture of America. It was largely Loos's faith in the promise of American life that ultimately propelled Neutra to the United States. And this growing interest in American architecture, particularly Sullivan and the Chicago School, was quickened for Neutra by his discovery in 1914 of the work of Frank Lloyd Wright. He encountered Wright, as did most Europeans of his generation, via the 1910–11 publications of Wright's work in German by Wasmuth, the Berlin publishing house. A diary entry of June 23, 1914, noted C. R. Ashbee's introductory essay to Wright's work, and in a letter of June 14, 1914, to his friend Rudolph Schindler, Neutra wrote that he was "engrossed" in Wright's work and was struck with his "ability to be both serious and monumental without stressing symmetry." Wright's open, flowing floor plans especially interested Neutra, with their interlocking spaces and sophisticated circulation patterns. In his call for an "organic" architecture, designed "from the inside out," growing out of the site and the building program and the nature of the building materials, Wright confirmed and extended many of the ideas Neutra had encountered in the work of Wagner, Sullivan, and, in certain ways, Loos. Neutra made rough sketches in his diary of the plans of Wright's Oak Park "Wohnhäuser" for the Huertley, Martin, and Gale families, the house for Susan Dana in Springfield, Illinois, and the Darwin Martin house in Buffalo, New York.[61]

The Wasmuth presentation of Wright's work revealed to Neutra "the fantastic living culture of some unknown people. It was just like seeing pictures of houses for people in another world. . . ." He hardly knew how to place these so-called Prairie houses, though he imagined something "like the pampas of Argentina, but still inhabited by red Indians, with tepees as a backdrop, and in the distance a thundering herd of bison. In this untouched flat, level, and far-reaching paradise, Wright was creating low buildings with tremendous shading roofs and long ribbon windows, like those of the venturesome transcontinental trains which looked out on a free breezy landscape. . . . I made up my mind that I would have to see it with my own eyes; no one in Europe was doing anything like it. Whoever he was, Frank Lloyd Wright, the man far away, had done something momentous and rich in meaning. This miracle man instilled in me the conviction that, no matter what, I would have to go to the places where he walked and worked."[62]

Neutra's friend Rudolph Schindler, whom he had met in 1912, had been similarly inspired by Wright and by his teacher-mentor Sullivan and, along with Neutra in Loos's studio, had imbibed enough enthusiasm for the United States to prompt him to make a pilgrimage there. Schindler answered an advertisement for a position in the Chicago office of Ottenheimer, Stern and Reichert and in early 1914 left the Old World for the New. "Schindler is going to America in a few days," Neutra noted in his diary on January 5, 1914. He must have envied his older friend's adventure, and apparently planned to follow him in 1915 upon completing his degree at the Technische Hochschule.[63]

Yet before Neutra could finish his schooling and visit the country of Sullivan and Wright, Europe exploded and the Great War began—taking Neutra deep into the maelstrom and delaying for nine years his journey to America. In June 1914, following the assassination by Serbian nationalists of Archduke Franz Ferdinand, the heir to the Austro-Hungarian throne, Neutra was called to active duty and sent to the Balkan front. But even by August, when the fighting began, Neutra could hardly have known how painful and rending the war and the subsequent peace would be—to himself and to the world that had shaped his development.

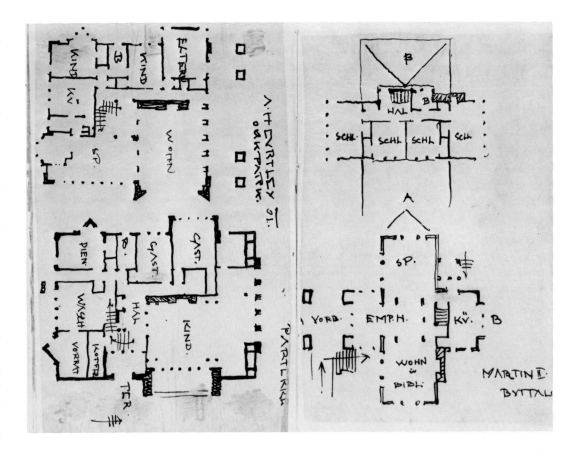

14. Pages from Neutra's diary, 1914, with drawings of floor plans of Frank Lloyd Wright houses

15. *Neutra*, Officer's Tea House, Trebinje,
ca. 1915

Trial

In contrast to the richness, security, and relative comfort of his childhood, adolescence, and early manhood in Vienna, the next decade of Richard Neutra's life was for the most part one of war, illness, and transience. It was indeed a time of trial, but also of promise, both for him and for modern architecture.

A reserve lieutenant in the Imperial army, Neutra was sent in June 1914, as war became imminent, to the village of Trebinje, a remote artillery outpost near Dubrovnik on the eastern shore of the Adriatic. After the outbreak of hostilities in August, he and his small garrison had orders to monitor the movements of enemy ships sailing up the coast and to fire only in case of coastal invasion. No such incidents occurred in his sector, however. The only armed combat Neutra saw was with Slavic partisans in Albania and Montenegro. The greater enemies were the familiar war-time scourges of disease, malnutrition, tedium, fatigue, inclemency, and alienation. Ultimately Neutra suffered them all, though in the early months of relative innocence he enjoyed certain aspects of military life.[1]

Since his initial reserve stint in 1911, he had taken delight in horseback riding, a pursuit he continued to cultivate in the Balkans. His baggage also contained his usual supply of books, and he read whenever circumstances permitted. An ever-observant traveler, he relished the sight of new people and places and frequently made sketches of the physical and cultural landscape. He was especially intrigued by the vestiges of old Islamic Turkish architecture throughout the Balkans. But his professional skills lay largely in abeyance. In Trebinje he designed only an officers' "teahouse," a modest structure that primitively anticipated his life-long penchant for simple post and beam pavilions.

One of the most painful aspects of the war for Neutra was witnessing the misery of the uprooted civilian populations. "The saddest thing one can see," he wrote in his diary in early 1916, is "small, weak children, very pregnant women, old people, sick people" who "carry the most shabby/sorry household goods under lamentations or in sorrowful resignation out into the night. . . . Today an old man collapsed completely." More directly debilitating was the presence of disease. While deployed across the border in Albania, Neutra's battery—"some three hundred and forty-five men and about six officers, including myself, accompanied by something like a hundred pack horses—contracted malaria, cholera, or typhoid; toward the end only about sixty-five men remained, with me as their last officer. . . . When I finally succumbed to my infection, I was taken away in a horse-drawn cart," and "being an officer came under a roof. . . . This was the beginning of my long journey through hospitals —something like eighteen in as many months— slowly inching my way north" to Austria. Throughout the two-year ordeal with malaria Neutra received systematic doses of quinine. "But the treatment usually ended with a new attack and chill when the bedstead and the whole floor began to vibrate with my trembling. Afterward, when my temperature had reached its peak and I started to sweat, the water actually dripped from under the mattress. This went on for a long time, and the attacks always returned again."[2]

By late 1916 his condition as a slowly recuperating patient in a hospital near Vienna led to occasional convalescent furloughs, and ultimately to the longer leave to complete his degree. One such

16. *Neutra*, Army snapshot of troops on maneuver, (1915(?))

17. *Neutra*, travel sketch, 1916

visit home in November 1916 coincided with the death of Emperor Franz Josef and the portentous end of his sixty-eight year reign. Neutra watched part of the funeral from the roof of the museum with Josephine and Arpad, who later reminded him that "from the disorder in the unfolding procession . . . you drew sad but correct conclusions as to the fate of dynasty and monarchy." It was, as Richard recorded in his diary, "a procession of ghosts. But . . . totally without any romantic eeriness. . . . No music at all, I don't know why! All of this pageantry without any bearing, without form, without direction, even without any seriousness. . . . The new Kaiser looked terrible, almost frantic, very skinny. . . . A few generals and a few Hungarian dignitaries walked pell-mell in front of the funeral coach. Behind our young Kaiser the Bulgarian Tzar ran more than walked. . . . Next to them, totally mixed up, high officers, highest civil servants in gala uniform . . . I join in. A confusion. People in groups everywhere. Military barricades, police. No sad atmosphere or mood at all. The tension which existed . . . is released. All the more stuffy, dull, heavy these empty heads seem to me, which search for all kinds of things, for the way home, for a girl, for a coffeehouse, who knows what. . . . Why must pageantry exist any longer when the bearing, the respect, even the form is dead? Since, after all, all are so 'enlightened.' . . . I am wiped out, sad, frustrated. . . ."[3]

Neutra's sense of ironic melancholy continued on a more personal level in a diary entry of the following year as he acknowledged the essential loneliness of all human existence. "I have the first quarter of a century behind me," he wrote on January 17, 1917. He lamented the years that had been and would be wasted by the war, years that could have been spent developing his life as an architect. "The circumstances made it impossible to have success. I cannot blame myself for it. However, I feel already that any success could not dissolve today's tragic mood. If I have not had any success, have I missed out on happiness? No! That's quickly enough answered. No! No! I am content and usually was so. This contentment occasionally changed to happiness. . . . with no effort at all. . . . I reject the pretext: perhaps you are chagrined that your wonderful youth is over. No. Actually something inexhaustible has been left to me. . . . *It is clear to me today that happiness is not the goal and the satisfaction of human life. . . . We race toward an understanding, a relationship to life, the better we succeed without any mishaps, the happier we are. However frequently we may succeed, however, penetrating our understanding may be, however influential we may be in it or above it, we are not the world itself. We cannot identify with it. All of us remains, I remain, solitary, locked out, even if millions of us try to ingratiate ourselves to each other.*"[4]

A serious recurrence of malaria and strong indications of incipient tuberculosis led in 1918 to further hospitalization in Trenčin, Slovakia, where on November 11 Neutra learned of the Armistice. Still too ill to return to Austria, he stayed on, convalescing in a civilian home recommended by a friend and fellow patient, Lieutenant Herzka. In late 1918 he returned to Vienna long enough to clear up personal business and get a visa to Switzerland. He arrived in February 1919 at Elsa Telekey's rest home in Stäfa, a bucolic village on the north shore of Lake Zurich. Telekey was a nurse known and recommended by Neutra's friend Herzka and his Trenčin landlord. Exhausted, emaciated, and determined to escape the defeat-drenched atmosphere of Vienna, Neutra looked for resuscitation to untainted Switzerland and to "Schwester Elsa's" medical and dietary care.[5]

Supported by small savings from his army pay and by funds advanced by his family, Neutra slowly began to recuperate and gain weight. Restless to pursue the career for which he was trained, he sought work in Zurich, but in the depressed postwar building market he was unable to secure an architectural position. He settled temporarily for an interesting job in Otto Froebel's famous old Zurich nursery and landscaping firm. There, through the summer of 1919, he worked under the tutelage of the noted Gustav Ammann and developed an interest and facility in botany, landscaping, and site planning that would serve him well the rest of his life. The kindly Ammann, furthermore, became not only an influential mentor but a sympathetic friend, allowing the poor veteran to supplement his meager salary by "grazing" in the nursery's fecund vegetable garden. In Zurich, Neutra also attended the Technische Hochschule studio of the progressively minded architect Karl Moser, and experienced a brief but significant refresher course in design. Neutra accompanied Moser's class on a sketching expedition to Neuchâtel, honing his drawing skills with intricate sketches of antique furniture and architectural interiors.[6]

And at Elsa Telekey's "Erholungsheim" boarding house he encountered the Niedermann family, who would come to have great influence in his life. The first Niedermanns he got to know were eleven-year-old Regula, a medical ward of Schwester Elsa's, and her ancient artist grandfather, Alfred, who came for Sunday dinners. Both were charmed by the dashing *Ingenieur* and arranged a dinner invitation for Neutra to the family home nearby. He arrived with the obligatory, though lusher than average, flowers, carefully selected at the nursery, and met Regula's parents, Lilly and Alfred, Jr., and her older sisters Doris, Verena, and Dione. Especially when compared with the local Swiss bumpkins, Dione and Regula recalled, Neutra fulfilled their image of Viennese elegance. He told funny and sophisticated stories, he walked splendidly erect, bowed from the waist, clicked his heels, and kissed the ladies' hands. His financial plight still forced him to wear his Austrian military uniform, shorn of insignia, which added to the overall effect of gallantry. Though still thin from his war-time illnesses, he was already regaining his health and vigor. Dione remembered that with his black hair and flashing blue eyes Richard Neutra was a handsome and impressive man. Yet though the eighteen-year-old Dione would later become his wife, Neutra admitted that in the beginning he was most attracted to her beautiful young mother. Called "Mütterli" by her family, the warm and intelligent Lilly Niedermann became through the years a sympathetic substitute for the mother and older sisters Neutra had lost in his youth. She and Dione would remain his closest friends and confidantes for life.[7]

The Niedermann daughters quickly adopted Richard as an honorary brother and arranged for him to come for weekly dinner visits. But Neutra's familial love for all the Niedermanns was coupled increasingly with a growing special interest in Dione, a fresh, innocent girl, nine years his junior, of obvious intelligence and musical talent. Through the spring and summer of 1919 their relationship developed slowly—and surreptitiously. Dione feigned illness and fatigue to convince her parents to send

18. *Neutra*, Self-portrait, 1917

19. *Neutra*, drawing in Karl Moser's class, Switzerland, 1919

20. *Neutra*, sketch of Regula Niedermann, 1919

her for several weeks to Elsa Telekey's rest home. There the romance blossomed so obviously that the Niedermanns arranged for a cooling-off period and sent Dione to Vienna to stay with friends and to study music. Though immensely fond of Richard and appreciative of his talent, they frankly deemed the twenty-seven-year-old charmer a poor prospect for their eldest daughter. His low-paying position at the Froebel nursery did not augur well for his professional future, and like most Swiss citizens of their era, the senior Niedermanns possessed an inherited anti-Semitism. Later this prejudice—milder than that of many of their countrymen—succumbed to more rational feelings; all four of their daughters ultimately married Jews. In Vienna, Richard's family received Dione warmly, and the two lovers continued their relationship via an intense correspondence.[8]

In September 1919, just as Dione was leaving Switzerland, Richard found an architectural job with the small firm of Wernli and Staeger in the village of Wädenswil, to which he commuted across the lake. His dismal working conditions, together with his loneliness and longing for Dione and his recurring memories of the depressing war years, diminished his relatively high spirits of the spring and summer and drove him to the depths of numbing despair. Such alternating periods of elation and depression would become a lifelong pattern. "I walk through the frosty air to my ugly basement room. . . . Dawn is coming and my dusty table is covered with suffocating papers. Five different tasks to work on. All empty cheerless drafting without rhyme or reason. The façades disgust me; I don't understand the sections but all has to be copied, like a treasure for posterity." He was depressed not only by a dull job, but by the bitterly cold weather as well. "I wish I could get out of Europe," he wrote, "and get to an idyllic tropical island where one does not have to fear the winter, where one does not have to slave but finds time to think, or even more important, can have a free spirit."[9]

His friend Rudolph Schindler was not on a tropical island, but he *was* in America. His position with Wright in Chicago and his prospects of moving to sunny California to supervise Wright's projects there tantalized Neutra and rekindled his desire to emigrate as soon as possible. A travel poster Neutra had seen in Zurich reading "California Calls You"

stayed in his mind. He later told Dione that he kept repeating those words "in a kind of commando tone," thinking "This is the way you will jump onto the boat that will carry you to California." He kept the three-word slogan in "my heart as a suggestive formulation. I thought to myself: 'What one wishes ardently has to be repeated in a pregnant sentence . . . over and over again.' " Once, after a period of depression, Neutra was able to gain relief simply by directing "my mind across land and water toward America from where just yesterday I received a short but refreshing letter from Rudolph Michael." He could not understand Schindler's hints of restlessness with America and suggestions that he might be planning to return to Europe. "You can hardly imagine how badly timed your idea of returning here seems to me," Neutra wrote in the fall of 1919. "To say nothing of the material ruin here, the psychological collapse is so total that it affects even the healthiest like a contagious disease. . . . I am not so much broken as deeply uprooted in my whole being. Everything in me cries for impregnation while I am surrounded by the saddest impotence." He wondered indeed "if patience is only stupidity! A young man has to act, not wait, not dry up in an out-of-the-way place."[10]

Later, in a letter to Dione, he admitted that the months in Wädenswil were among the darkest of his life. In addition to his other problems, he had experienced in Switzerland more than ever before the effects of anti-Semitism. The "prejudice against my race made me unhappy," he wrote. "I could not even make a modest start in my profession. Everything seemed set to humiliate me. While I sat at my drawing board behind my boss, I was shaken, tearless, by a terrible inward spasm of silent sobbing. . . . I suffered unspeakable loneliness. . . . I often thought of suicide. . . ." But Neutra's depression became so intense that, instead, it turned back on itself "because I clearly realized that my end had come if I did not help myself." His way out of the abyss included a relatively healthy dose of narcissism: "I prescribed for myself a certain cure to divert my mind from circling around my constant sorrow and start thinking of something else. All during the winter I washed my whole body, mornings and evenings, with cold water and did gymnastics. My young body, stripped of its military clothing, so permeated by despair . . . gave me back some self-confidence, and this body, which was I, began to interest me again. I recognized myself as a human being and was able to capture the measure of things."[11]

Since Dione had been sent to Vienna to try to forget Richard, the two were forced to correspond surreptitiously. In the spring of 1920, however, Samuel Neutra became critically ill with the influenza that was sweeping Vienna, and Richard was called home. Before he left Switzerland, he spoke to Lilly Niedermann of his love for Dione and of his intention of seeing her again. Convinced by this time of the depth of their relationship, she consented and gave her blessing to the courtship. Though Samuel Neutra died shortly after his arrival,[12] Richard decided to stay on in Vienna and attempt to find work. In the depressed Viennese economy, however, there was very little building and there were virtually no openings in architectural offices. While looking for work he boarded with Arpad and Josephine and spent as much time as possible with Dione. He enjoyed introducing her to the Vienna of his youth—the buildings of Loos and Wagner, the Schönbrunn and Belvedere palaces, and the museum and theater world. Her Viennese hosts were the Albert Scheus, close friends of her parents and clients of Adolf Loos. Neutra had admired the new Scheu house as a student before the war, and he relished his new associations with it and its owners. The Scheus were prominent in Viennese society and were active in avant-garde political and cultural circles. Through them and their friends, Dione and Richard met such figures as the composer Eric Korngold and attended private recitals of his work in progress.[13]

But such vestiges of the city's pre-war cultural life could not hide the political, economic, and social problems that pervaded post-war Austria. "The misery in Vienna is such as I anticipated," Neutra wrote to Mütterli. "Dione is hardly aware of it." Most people lived on potatoes and little else. Neutra fully appreciated the relative prosperity of Switzerland when his attentive mentor Gustav Ammann mailed him packages of hearty Swiss cheeses, sausages, and preserves. The Niedermanns sent similar provisions to Dione and the Scheus. It was, in fact, the Scheus' involvement in social relief causes that led to Neutra's finding a job with the American Friends' Relief mission as a research assistant and

21. *Neutra* in Switzerland, 1919

29

22. *Neutra*, municipal housing, Luckenwalde, Germany, 1921

German-speaking liaison between the Quakers and local government officials. "I make appearances at the various ministries, labor commissions, meet the heads of various institutes," he wrote to Mütterli. "I unearth statistical material regarding wage conditions, salaries, the setup of various organizations who could receive help from the Society. This week, for instance, I have visited all trade unions" and "am able to get an interesting bird's eye view of the income and unemployment situation. . . ." This would serve him well later when he became more interested in larger-scale social and economic planning. His dealings with the British and American Quakers, moreover, forced him to improve his English and further whetted his desire to go to America. His belief that this contact might facilitate his emigration in fact prompted him to remain in Vienna rather than return to Wernli and Staeger. He did not realize until later that his association with the pacifist Quakers—who had opposed America's entry into the war—would jeopardize rather than enhance his rapport with immigration officials.[14]

Dione returned to Switzerland in April and Neutra continued his work for the Quakers. Their serene worship services relaxed and stimulated him. His favorite member of the mission was an older American social worker named Frances Toplitz, who became a lifelong friend. For an English missionary Neutra even designed a small English country house. In the end it was not built, but as one of his earliest residential designs it gave him great pleasure and incentive to continue. He sent copies of the plans to Dione and Mütterli for comment. His accompanying letter displayed his taste for irony and the witty, spirited side of his frequently depressive nature. After such a brilliant triumph, he predicted, "someone will possibly let me build a margarine factory or the Mozart Festival Hall in Salzburg! Or I could learn like a flash the trade of hair styling in order to make myself useful to this world, so that when I finally abdicate, everybody will sigh in consternation: 'Irreplaceable!' "[15]

The wait in Vienna for fate to rescue him and transport him to America or "some idyllic tropical island" lasted longer than he expected. He worked part-time in a small architectural office and fleetingly considered a vague job offer in Java. In October 1920, however, a less exotic but more realistic opening occurred in the Berlin architectural firm of Pinner and Neumann. His old friend Ernst Freud, then practicing in Berlin, helped secure him the job, and Neutra quickly left Vienna for the German capital. Pinner and Neumann, however, had hired Neutra on the strength of a large new commission they expected to get, and when it fell through shortly after his arrival they were forced to dismiss him. Failing to find a steady job after weeks of searching, Neutra survived on part-time work as an assistant to a lamp maker and as an extra in a Berlin theater. His new round of bad fortune stunned and depressed him. In early 1921, however, he found work in the office of the architect Heinrich Staumer, and later in the spring he heard in Staumer's office of an opening for the position of city architect in the nearby town of Luckenwalde.[16]

He applied for the job before it was publicly advertised and got it on the strength of his academic credentials and his practical experience in Switzerland. Working as city architect under the director of city planning for this small city of 26,000, he designed a public housing complex in a chastened version of a *gemütlich* German folk idiom. It was built, he recalled later, for "the resettlement of industrial workers who, for dearth of dwellings after the war and during the depression after the defeat, had been living in urban basements. Now while working on semi-rural housing plans, I watched from all too close by as a town family transplanted into rustic circumstances went to pieces, with each member following a different pamphlet on how to raise potatoes, how to fertilize and water the vegetable patch and what to·feed the ducks. The human issues behind the 'hard economic facts' fascinated me to reverberate through all my life as a 'houser.' " He was, he wrote to Dione, "decidedly a person who learns a lot whenever he sees something new. . . . Here there are for instance all sorts of technical considerations with regard to economy. On the other hand I have much contact with the settlers, learn to observe how people react who start to become homeowners, the advantages and disadvantages of cooperatives for disadvantaged people, observe the behavior of men and women and have a chance for a look into various peculiar family situations." Yet whatever

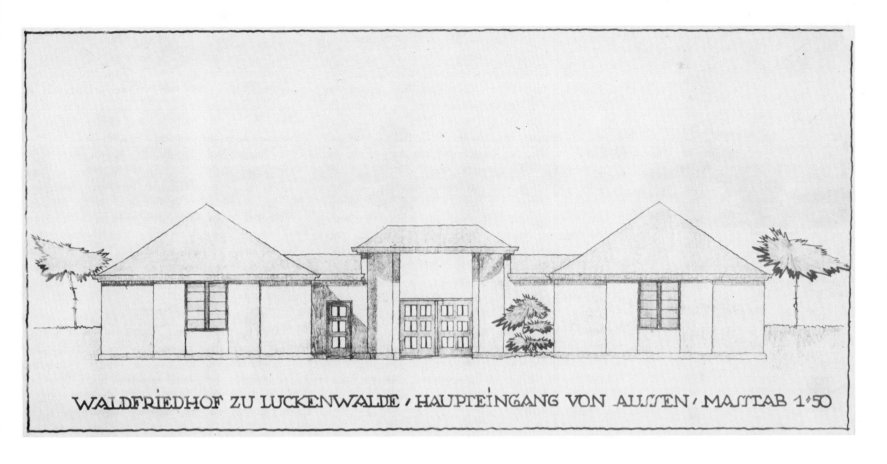

WALDFRIEDHOF ZU LUCKENWALDE · HAUPTEINGANG VON AUSSEN · MASSTAB 1:50

the problems, he was certain that living in such a development would be, for himself at least, "ten times more pleasurable than a subdivision of elegant villas."[17]

His more stylized design for the municipally sponsored forest cemetery allowed him to switch "from housing the live and quarrelsome to housing the peaceful and dead." There he combined an inflection toward the natural site and vegetation with formal, ordered areas of bordered paths and reflecting pools. The latter areas included a chapel, an entrance gate, and administrative and maintenance structures, whose low-hipped roofs and minimal ornament reflected Neutra's efforts to fuse official building standards with the work of his Viennese mentors and with various "modern" elements from Wright's Prairie School. "The forest cemetery is my child," he wrote Dione, "and for seven months, I exerted all my effort and defended it against its enemies and their stupidity." He realized that his training with Ammann had not only helped him get the job but also given him the necessary expertise to deal creatively with its horticultural and landscaping potential. As his first

major reified design, it gave him pleasure and strengthened his confidence. During this time he also designed gardens for the Berlin clients and friends of Ernst Freud and for the country estate at Gaglow Cottbus of the parents of Ernst's wife Lux. He enjoyed being part of a small, vital community and for social and professional reasons joined the Luckenwalde Men's Glee Club. "At the weekly song meetings," he recalled, "I worked hard while drinking a goodly number of steins around the long table in the inn."[18]

Though his success and relative contentment in Luckenwalde would have allowed him to stay there longer, his ambition to get on and to play for bigger stakes pulled him back to the magnet of Berlin. His immediate motivation was an advertised opening in the office of the great young avantgarde architect Erich Mendelsohn. When the interview yielded an immediate job offer he gave notice in Luckenwalde and, in October 1921, moved back to the German capital. Even before seeing any of the younger man's work, Mendelsohn was certain, he confided to his wife, that Neutra was "an artist." Erich Mendelsohn's quick rise to the front rank of

23. *Neutra,* entrance gate to Forest Cemetery, Luckenwalde, Germany, 1921

24. *Mendelsohn*, Einstein Tower,
Potsdam, 1919–21

post-war German architecture intrigued and attracted Neutra. Born in Allenstein, East Prussia, in 1887, Mendelsohn studied architecture at the technical institutes of Berlin and Munich, graduating and beginning practice in 1912. Before the outbreak of war, he survived chiefly by selling his paintings and by designing stage sets, window displays, and *Fasching* carnival costumes. In those years he became fascinated with the Expressionist movement in art and architecture, an interest he developed in numerous visionary building sketches during the war years. He served on the Russian and then the western front, and following the war he settled in Berlin, where his war-time sketches were exhibited in a remarkable exhibition at the Cassirer Gallery. The frequently tiny drawings suggested buildings of great scale and power, "skirted by one contour" as Mendelsohn described them, "bulging, protruding, and retracting—suggesting the elastic tension of the steel and concrete structure, and, to be sure, the young architect's mental tension, as well!"[19]

Indeed, Mendelsohn's vision so impressed several associates of Albert Einstein's that he was asked in 1919 to design the new astronomical observatory to be built in Potsdam, dedicated to carrying on Einstein's researches and named in his honor. Its swelling, curving, organic form brought to life the qualities of Mendelsohn's hitherto visionary drawings. The interiors and landscaping were just being completed when Neutra joined Mendelsohn's office. "Yesterday morning I was in Potsdam and visited the Einstein Tower," he wrote to Mütterli in the fall of 1921. "There are tree-covered hills on top of which stand the observatories and among the trees the houses of the professors and the stargazers. The last and newest one is our Einstein Tower. . . . From the cupola, I viewed the snowy silent landscape. The whole building is filled with smoke from the burning coal fire that is to dry out the interiors. Einstein's assistant . . . is impatiently waiting to start his work so that he can show these earthlings—what? Also, the stars are waiting. However, we meanwhile had to paint and build in furniture. Kepler, Copernicus and Galileo are happy in heaven that the work progresses." Because of his botanical and landscaping background, Neutra worked with the landscapers. He was delighted to deal with the "greatest nurseryman of Germany,

Karl Foerster," to whose work Gustav Ammann had introduced him earlier. They decided ultimately on "stately Cleopatra trees, . . . white wonder asters coycoides," and "fall heather, which keeps on blooming when the first snow falls."[20]

Neutra had already been aware of the Einstein Tower via the German press, and of Mendelsohn's more geometrically "rational" Steinberg-Herrmann hat factory commission for Luckenwalde (1921–23), a project for which Neutra did drawings and models after he joined Mendelsohn's office. Neutra had also been stimulated by an article on Mendelsohn by Herman G. Scheffauer that had appeared in the American journal *The Dial* in March and had been sent to Neutra by his American friend Frances Toplitz. "It is significant," Scheffauer had written, "that Erich Mendelsohn's basic principle of a new language and a new liberation for architecture came to him shortly before the great catastrophe which engulfed the hollow and jerry-built structure of his civilization." Scheffauer was certain that Mendelsohn's early visions and projects "prove that the artist, the master builder, is not defunct; that the true creator need only place his ear to the giant heart of the epoch and link himself to the chain of its energies in order to find those forms in which the age would express itself."[21]

Mendelsohn stressed the need to fuse the functionalist-rationalist realities with the dynamic visions of Expressionism. "[F]unction without sensibility remains mere construction," he argued in a letter to his wife in 1919. "If the rationalist's blood does not freeze and mere imagination goes a step further toward ratio, then they may unite. Otherwise both will be destroyed—the functionalist by a deadly chill in his veins, the dynamicist by the heat of his own fire. Thus, function plus dynamics is the challenge!" To Neutra's taste, Mendelsohn frequently strayed too close to the heat of dynamicism. There was in his work "too much sculpturing and molding," he wrote Mütterli. "We should not be sculptors." At the same time, he had to admit, he was glad that Mendelsohn did "not adhere to mere common sense, under whose banner some atrocities are perpetrated in the building sector." Shortly after joining the office he confessed to Dione that he was "not quite clear yet what significance I may have for this establishment, but Mendelsohn interests me very much. He belongs to the 'other [Expressionist]

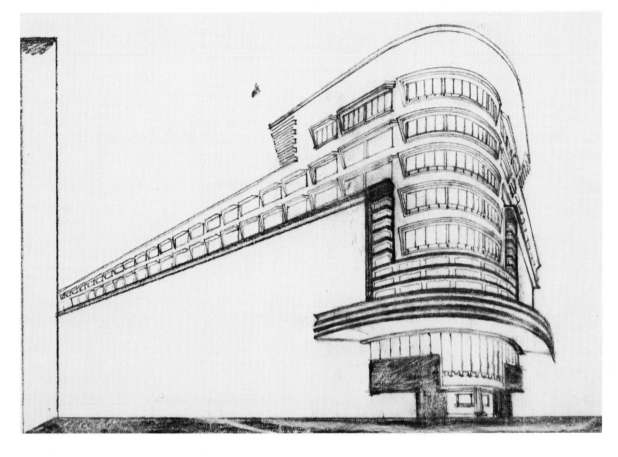

26. *Mendelsohn and Neutra*, addition to *Berliner Tageblatt* building, 1921–23

25. *Neutra*, for Mendelsohn, addition to *Berliner Tageblatt* building, Berlin, 1921–23

27. *Neutra*, for Mendelsohn, interior design for *Berliner Tageblatt* building, 1921–23

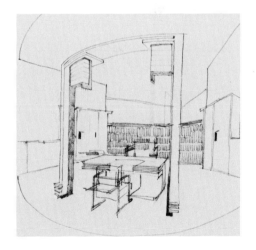

side,' but is a very diligent man with a method, a will, a goal, and a belief." Mendelsohn "asserts that he has a lot of work for me and believes I am 'his man,' " he wrote to Mütterli. "Probably he is in error. My intention in joining him was to observe the left radicals from nearby. It seemed to me that he is the only one of this group who has large commissions. Although I am very adaptable, there is a different spirit alive in me." He kept abreast of the work of the other "left radicals" via journals and exhibitions. On one winter Sunday he attended two shows of the new art and architecture, one featuring the work of Walter Gropius and his Bauhaus colleagues, the other a Russian show: "Kandinsky in both places. . . . Strange was a moving vibrating rod, held in place by some mechanical clock, called Kinetic Sculpture, which means moving sculpture, by Gabo. In principle quite good. A water jet in a Bologna piazza is just as much a moving sculpture, as is a lion cut from granite. A pendulum clock is also a sculpture in this sense. The world is vast and many ideas have validity. . . ."[22]

The first major job that Neutra handled for Mendelsohn was the remodeling and enlargement of the *Berliner Tageblatt* building for the powerful Mosse newspaper family. Neutra joined Mendelsohn's office shortly after the Mosse commission was obtained and shared credit with the sculptor R. P. Henning as Mendelsohn's collaborator. Neutra detailed Mendelsohn's initial conceptions, most likely made various original design contributions, and was placed in charge of working drawings and supervision. He did numerous sketches and design studies for Lachmann Mosse's great corner office and for furniture there and throughout the building. To the existing nineteenth-century five-story structure were added two-and-a-half floors and a new, similarly styled streamlined packaging for all eight levels of the main corner entrance. The sleek new envelope fit comfortably astride the older building, though it left no doubt that the new portion was the dominant element. "As one is building from the top downward," Neutra wrote Dione, "the effect is that of a new building. It is worthwhile for me to have such a decisive part in this monumental

33

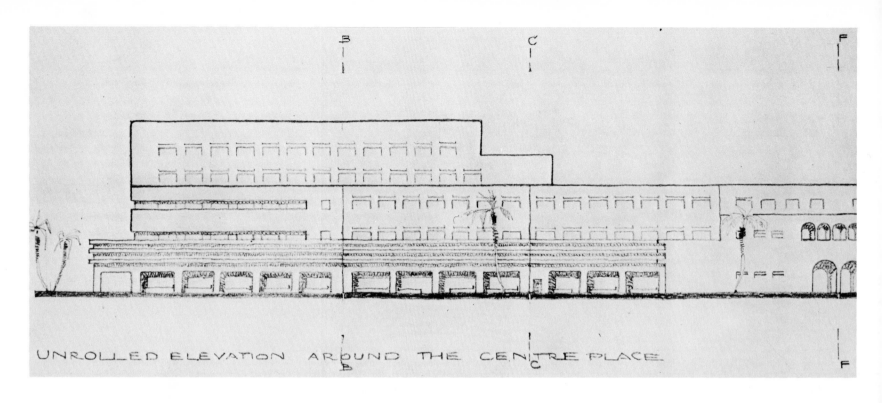

UNROLLED ELEVATION AROUND THE CENTRE PLACE.

28. *Neutra and Mendelsohn,* winning design in Haifa Competition, 1922

structure. I am very curious to know how long I shall have a chance to participate. Some very exotic constructions occur, but I could greatly benefit not only on account of the technical and artistic procedures but also by having to deal directly with the clients, the contractors, and subcontractors. I must give Mendelsohn due credit because he always introduces me as his collaborator and not only as his underling." And Mendelsohn's respect for Neutra was not just politeness. "Herr Neutra is at his peak," Mendelsohn wrote his wife. "In Neutra I have certainly the most reliable support. . . ."[23]

A letter Neutra sent to Frances Toplitz suggested that he had not only executed Mendelsohn's designs but had a part in their conceptualization. "In the closest collaboration with my boss," he wrote, "I have designed an important monumental building from its very first conception to the last detail; I have drawn the plans and supervised this difficult building. . . . Terrible battles have taken place with the old-fashioned building department officials. Most of them I had to conduct myself. The debate reached even the Lord Mayor of Berlin and only through the might of the 'Berliner Tageblatt' . . . could the matter be pushed through. There is no doubt about it that this newfangled building on which I spent so much energy will be the talk of the town for a long time to come."[24]

A contractor's error occurred during building that left a painful impression on Neutra. Heavy loads of sand were left on an upper-floor concrete slab that had not sufficiently hardened. When the slab collapsed and crashed through several floors, over a dozen newspaper workers were killed. Though he was in no way responsible for the accident, Neutra's closeness to the scene caused him intense grief and made him sensitive for the rest of his life to the danger of such calamities in any building enterprise. Fortunately, in his own later work no such incidents occurred.[25]

Neutra also worked closely with Mendelsohn on an ultimately unexecuted commercial project for Gleiwitz, Silesia, and, most notably, on an entry for a competition for a commercial center of shops, theaters, and restaurants in Haifa, Palestine. The long, plain, low-slung concrete buildings they designed for Haifa were inflected both functionally and formally to the hot desert climate and topography. Their vast wall planes of unornamented masonry were accented chiefly by long bands of ribbon windows and crisply cantilevered balcony projections. Though the Haifa design placed first in the competition it was never executed. Yet while Mendelsohn was away in Palestine in 1922, a commission came to the office for which Neutra apparently had virtually complete design responsibility—

a group of ten small detached houses for the building contractor Adolf Sommerfeld in the Zehlendorf section of Berlin. Pleasantly sited on a wooded terrain, the houses had plain white concrete facades, accented chiefly by corner ribbon windows and cantilevered corner balconies. The chief novelty of the houses, at the instigation of the builder, was a revolving floor in the central living area that allowed for a flexible extension and reorientation of the living room to the dining room, music room, or library. Berlin newspaper skeptics predicted disaster when the husband entertaining business clients inevitably pushed the wrong button and accidentally aligned the living room with his wife in the bath. Though the actual controls and room arrangements made such juxtapositions impossible, the revolving stages were later removed from the designs. Throughout his years with Mendelsohn, Neutra also designed gardens for their clients—as he continued to do for Ernst Freud and his Berlin contemporary Arthur Korn.[26]

The social and professional contact with Freud, his only old friend in Berlin, was especially important to Neutra. Ernst had followed his architectural course at the Technische Hochschule in Vienna with another year of training in Munich, where he had met his future wife Lux, a classical scholar from a wealthy, established North German Jewish family. Her ties to Berlin had persuaded them to settle there. "I had dinner yesterday with Ernst and Lux Freud," he wrote Dione in late 1921. He found Lux "extremely intelligent and not just a bluestocking; she was much more open yesterday. She comes from a very rich family, but what is even more decisive for the life of this young couple, she has social connections [which ensure] that he has plenty of work and a very good income. Although Ernst's family is not poor, they have just enough to be able to live without worries. He is blond and has an imposing personality, full of temperament and humor, and a good heart. Our relationship is a very cordial one, but not quite natural, as my own situation is so difficult. He admires me and thinks I am very gifted, but an outsider. I think his wife liked me. They accompanied me to the railway station. As she has just recovered from a difficult confinement, she took her husband's arm and, after awhile, mine also. I felt very strange. It seems so long ago that a woman hung on my arm. . . . My way is not his, who could find professional work through high society connections. He is independent and will become rich. . . . However, if one *is* somebody and has reached a certain inner balance, one can perhaps find one's way in this machine. I lent Ernst your 'Demian' and he liked it very much."[27]

35

29. *Neutra and Mendelsohn,* Zehlendorf Housing, 1923

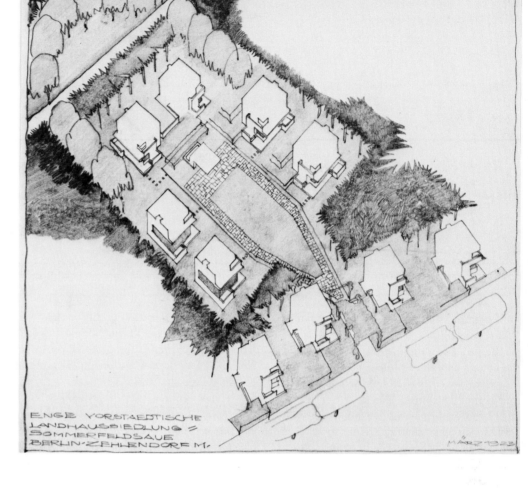

30. *Neutra and Mendelsohn,* Zehlendorf Housing, Berlin, 1923

Neutra valued many aspects of his association with Mendelsohn, both professionally and socially. There was an air of excitement and of big things going on—not only at the office but in the Mendelsohn home. Mendelsohn's wife Louise was a beautiful, talented, and intelligent woman, and Neutra appreciated her sophistication and hospitality. She played the cello, and both she and her husband moved in the highest musical and social circles. When Dione came to Berlin for a three-month visit in the winter of 1922, they helped arrange for her to study cello with their friend Hugo Becker, one of the leading cellists in Germany. Neutra greatly enjoyed the Mendelsohn's parties and musical evenings. But other aspects of the relationship were strained. Unknowingly foreshadowing the attitude his own employees would later take toward him,

Neutra felt that Mendelsohn was too hard a taskmaster—demanding too much and paying too little. Mendelsohn had instituted a sliding pay scale to help offset the mounting inflation, but Neutra argued that his real wages were always too low. In July 1922, however, Mendelsohn responded to his importunings with a proposal, Neutra wrote Dione, that "would enslave me like a Versailles treaty. To earn a few thousand marks more, I have to promise to abstain from any other work and promise, in case I leave him, to leave Berlin for three years so that he can be sure I am not taking any clients away from him. . . . Well, I am not particularly attached to Berlin, nor do I have work here. . . . Mendelsohn has made a tremendous career all by himself, has made a name for himself and has connections. He needs much technical help and he can always find it

when he pays a fee. He is and can be choosy. He is financially independent and has a well-organized office above all probability. . . . His proposals show a higher regard for me than whatever flattering words he could tell me. That he makes such ridiculously difficult conditions to prevent me becoming his competitor . . . is of course also flattering for me. So I have all reason to be in good spirits."[28]

But Mendelsohn's treatment of other employees made Neutra nervous. "As I feared, mischief has occurred," he wrote Dione in October 1922. "Without any previous warning, Mendelsohn gave notice to Bruggemann just before winter, when it is difficult to get another job. . . . That's how the world ticks if one wants to achieve success. When I observe such goings-on, I have a presentiment that my success will be a medium one, unless I can

learn to become a brilliant scoundrel. . . ." Mendelsohn, he wrote on another occasion, "is an artist who thinks only of his art and this permeates his personality. As far as form is concerned his behavior toward me could not be more correct or, given his character, hardly less open and without ulterior motives." Sometimes indeed, Mendelsohn was "thoroughly . . . inconsiderate," but "at the present time, it is hardly possible to find better conditions in Germany as an employee than those offered to me. At the moment, an association with Freud or Korn does not seem feasible." In summary, he admitted to Mütterli, "I have never stopped being amazed at how I have been able to hold on to this position, how I could achieve this balancing act and still hold on to my integrity."[29]

Neutra's relatively secure position with Men-

31. *Neutra and Mendelsohn*, Zehlendorf Housing, 1923

32. *Neutra*, snapshot of Lux and Ernst Freud, Berlin, 1921 or 1922

delsohn and his gradual salary increases convinced him that after more than three years of courtship, he and Dione could finally get married. They had tacitly known and agreed for some time that this should happen, and the date was set for late December, during the Christmas holidays of 1922. Since they had first met in early 1919, circumstances had forced them to spend much more time apart than together. For this reason, and because their marriage date had been so uncertain, Neutra had insisted that they wait until they were permanently together to consummate their sexual relationship. Sexually active since youth and believing himself knowledgeable in the mysteries of sexual psychology, Neutra reasoned that, for Dione especially, anxieties would be lessened during the long periods apart if she remained a virgin, and they practiced abstinence in their physical relationship. If Neutra strayed from this vow as a Berlin bachelor, he left no record in his letters or diaries. During Neutra's Berlin period, as before, he and Dione sustained and clarified their relationship through an increasingly intense correspondence. In his letters to her and to other friends, Neutra revealed much, not only about his relationship with Mendelsohn, but about his personal development, goals, and problems.[30]

"Dione . . . my future wife," he wrote to Frances Toplitz, "is mobile and adaptable as far as one can see now. I hope to God she will be able to bear all inconveniences and unexpected changes that will confront her with patience, as she wants to be my companion. I cannot help it that my path is not quite a bourgeois one. . . ." He trusted he could balance his artistic needs for isolation with the personal and professional needs for gregarious interaction. "Anyone who wants to build must learn to *live* with difficulties and worries," he acknowledged. "An all-around life is the school of the architect. In the final realization, the architect is probably a hermit, but he cannot always have been a hermit." He had expressed the same ambivalence to Dione with his characteristic pessimism—tempered by irony. "All architects who are successful have social connections . . . but I abhor politics and 'society' and the whole rigmarole." On the other hand, he admitted, "when I am in a dejected mood, I question my isolation. I have no relation to the socialists, nor the capitalists, nor to the Jews or the Gentiles. A real genius, unappreciated of course, a real

Beethoven. Of course I am a thousand times more cunning and clever than Beethoven, but he can surely write better violin concertos. By the way, only a single one."[31]

In a letter to Mütterli he touched on the same issues but on a more practical level. He did not instinctively "like to go around dressed like a dandy," but then again he knew he paid "much too little attention to my exterior. I would experience a much easier and readier acceptance from possible clients and could have advanced much quicker and have been spared much demeaning work if I had tried with all my might to put up an appearance. My future career *is* dependent on this external success. I have hoped that through you I shall become neater, cleaner and wear pants that are better pressed. . . . It is prudent to hide one's peculiarities from one's fellow man; otherwise one cannot enjoy them. Unfortunately, for an architect private connections are often the only preparation for his future career. No one will entrust a 200-million mark commission to a youth dressed up like an artist."[32]

As their marriage approached, Richard and Dione corresponded about their plans, needs, and devotion to each other. Only occasionally was their bliss ruffled by uncertainties. One such unsettling incident was occasioned by Dione's unpleasant encounter with a rich Jewish family in Basel and her naive equation of their "Jewishness" and "gaucheness." Having imbibed more than she may have realized of her parents' anti-Semitism, she wrote Neutra frankly that "your race strikes me as very peculiar and alien to mine. How strange, too, that I always completely forget that you belong to it. I don't know whether I hurt your feelings if I tell you that you do not belong to them, because with you, one has the impression that you stand above everything and simply are a human being. I don't quite know how to express myself." Her acquaintances in Basel "were each a different type, but all equally disagreeable."[33]

Her remarks elicited from Neutra a ringing declaration on the dangers of "classification." He admitted that he would probably have had the same reaction she did to the particular circle she encountered in Basel. "I do not have the wretched feeling of a renegade writing this, a renegade is one who denies his origin, his parentage, as do Germans in a hundred countries. . . . [A]ll the

Jewish families I grew up with have no resemblance to the circle you describe. How this is so I simply cannot tell you. Ask Arpad, who in his heart abhors Jews much deeper than your family does. . . . Where, however, can I find my social connections, as the European world is made up of Gentiles and Jews? I would love to build a house for Rabindranath Tagore. But among the Hindus, Confucians, Fire Islanders, one can also find obnoxious cliques. Jews, Jews, Jews. The cunning one, the grasping one, the dirty one, the good one, the wise one, the enlightened one, the idealistic one, the prophetic one, the talker, the visionary, the supporter of art, the usurer, the communist, the benefactor, the bourgeois, the broker, the journalist, the educated Jew, the scholarly one, the bibliophile, the operetta singer, the soldier, and the idealistically striving student. All Jews, a handful in the European world. My father, for instance, was not among those just cited. He was first a metalworker, then a master journeyman. A metal pourer, a metal lathesman, a metal fitter. Well, what does it all mean? Nothing as far as I can see."[34]

Later, when Dione's father suggested that he might avoid social and professional embarrassment if mention of Richard's religion were deleted from the wedding banns, Neutra refused to give in and insisted that he be identified as *Mosaisch*. He wrote Mütterli a long and moving letter about his parents and his relatives, describing them with unabashed pride and affection. Denying their Jewishness would be an affront to them and to him, since "the blood that courses through my veins is even more meaningful as it naturally and mysteriously came through them to me. . . ." "If you want happily to be my wife," he wrote Dione, "you must understand me and let me be my own self. How would it help you to have a husband who thinks less of himself and more about people who turn up their noses? There is anyway *no escape from that.* I was an Austrian officer and Prussian civil servant. Some people turned up their noses and after a while ceased to do so. I had a thousand occasions to feel bitterly hurt. . . . How would you feel if my relatives liked you personally but secretly feared you might bring shame and disgrace on the family?" Later on, he concluded, "if fate grants it, then your and my children will be *your* and my children and I have no idea how to educate them 'confessionally.' However it is my firm resolve to behave in such a way

33. Dione and Richard Neutra, wedding photograph, Hagen, Germany, 1922

that later on they can acknowledge, without an anxious heart, that I was their father and my parents their grandparents." Ultimately, the Niedermanns appreciated Neutra's steadfastness. Their love for him, moreover, and their pride in his achievements helped to overcome their earlier biases.[35]

Indeed, the discussion of Neutra's Jewishness was a relatively minor dark note in an otherwise exemplary in-law relationship. Neutra's overall mood became increasingly exuberant as the wedding date approached. He was, he wrote to Mütterli, "in the mood to cry hurrah! To whom? To Mütterli, who will have a new son, to Dionerl, who will get a fine specimen of a husband. Hurrah to America, Hurrah to Europe, to the occident, to the solar system!" The civil wedding ceremony took place on December 23, 1922, in the city hall of Hagen, the Rhineland city to which Alfred Niedermann's work had taken him and his family. A festive reception followed at home and then a wedding trip through central Germany. In early 1923 the couple settled into a tiny Berlin apartment, altered and enhanced by Richard's innovations. Working for Mendelsohn was as demanding as before and there was no end in sight to the galloping inflation, but newlywed euphoria carried them along. They relished the city's rich musical and cultural life. They also enjoyed the hospitality of the Mendelsohns and Freuds, though both couples moved in circles beyond the Neutras' modest income. Lux Freud's intelligence and warmth appealed strongly to Dione and confirmed the older friendship of Richard and Ernst.[36]

Though Neutra always claimed he was an unpolitical person, his environmental concerns continued to involve him in the larger, connected social and political ethos. The Niedermanns were especially interested in such matters and stimulated his political awareness both before and after his marriage to Dione. Compared with Switzerland and especially with Austria, Germany seemed to Neutra relatively viable and dynamic—even in the turbulent 1920s. Basically he supported the Weimar experiment in representative democracy and despaired of the extremists, both left and right, who opposed it. Though he had no illusions about the old, lost "unity" of the Austro-Hungarian empire, he regretted the political fragmentation of the German-

speaking peoples and supported the eventual unification of Germany and Austria. "I have a much better impression of Berlin than I expected," he wrote Alfred Niedermann soon after his arrival in late 1920. "Such huge organisms have a great deal of inertia that help them to overcome many hurdles. At the moment there is a crisis and rumors of a putsch . . . from the left. . . . The extreme Socialists are really repugnant. . . . Also the Independents seem to be discredited through their division. In Bavaria I hear talk of a breakup and here everybody abuses the government. . . . It is disgraceful that the junction between Austria and Germany is opposed in the North as well as in the South at a time when all other nations convulsively try to draw together." In the crucial matter of housing, Berlin had "had very progressive building laws which will tide them over for quite a while. Immense building areas have been opened for expansion. . . . I have criss-crossed Berlin on foot from one end to the other. . . ."[37]

He was pleased to find in his wanderings that there existed an old as well as a new Berlin. "Narrow-breasted low row houses with steep roofs mirror their oscillating fronts in a canal just like in Holland," he wrote. "This sight evokes memories of the Berlin novels of E. T. A. Hoffmann." But the new industrial areas were equally impressive, if somehow forbidding in their vastness. Siemensstadt, for example, with its factories and workers' housing, was "a gigantic development to be compared only with a North American one and then again quite different. . . . In the Middle West, according to my friend Schindler, it is the potent fertility of the endless prairie which produces the high-rise and bank buildings and commercial enterprises, while in the West are the untold riches found under the ground. But here we are in Germany, in the middle of an old, used-up continent. . . . Despite all this, such a vast expansion and development. If the war, through a 'happier' outcome at the Battle of the Marne, could have been favorably ended in the first campaign, who knows what would have happened? Here the pinnacle of a period in world history would have been expressed through a new city."[38]

He thought Oswald Spengler's *The Decline of the West* far too pessimistic about the possibilities of city planning. "His ethical attitude toward the metropolis I agree with," he observed. "His spite-fulness toward city planners, however, is unfounded and contemptible. This sort of comprehension would be a reactionary triumph of irrationality. The housing of multitudes *is* a problem to be solved by a genius. . . . The conceptions of city planners are unspeakably more diversified than Spengler assumes. The city planner as an active functionary is the noble enemy of the speculators and a splendid expression of our period. Spengler is too pessimistic. Therefore: what makes sense? A thought occurs to me: what if country living catches up with the flux of development . . . what if living in the country and communications with the centers of culture changed in our century and the *enforced* isolation was obliterated and all cultural advantages could be enjoyed. . . . Fresh air here, speakeasies and museum treasures there?" To confirm his argument, he then drew upon his images of America, garnered from Loos and from Wright's Wasmuth folio. "Have the farmers in the Middle West of the USA not wonderful libraries? Do they not speed in their Ford automobiles to concerts in Chicago. . . .?"[39]

Like most "Germans" of whatever persuasion, Neutra found the *Diktat* of the Versailles Treaty unrealistically harsh and the cause of many of the country's current problems. His correspondence revealed him to be a typical, loyal Weimarite: "I know that Germany is unhappy, but that neverthe-less all other countries believe in its future potential. I know that a vast number of German people are completely innocent in the present unhappy state of affairs, are sad about it and suffer, although inno-cent. . . . My work is not politics. For me the more I have to swallow of it, the more it stinks. In con-trast the stock exchange is at least more open and straightforward. All of this is not my cup of tea. However, when I contemplate how terribly difficult it is to govern Germany and to find acceptance abroad and at home, I lose the courage for cheap fault-finding criticism."[40]

Yet however much he was beginning to em-pathize and identify with the problems and the vulnerabilities of his adopted Germany, Neutra remained even more fascinated with the United States, the fatherland of Sullivan, Wright, and Henry Ford, Indeed, if Wright was Neutra's first American hero, Ford was certainly the second. "It

would not be far fetched," observed Harwell Harris, one of Neutra's later students, "to think that Neutra came to America because America was the home of Henry Ford. Ford was more amazing to Euro-peans than to us who saw in him our own features. . . . Europeans were prepared to worship the ma-chine." *Fordissimus* became a European phenome-non. What Neutra appreciated most about Ford was not so much the styling of his cars as the way he put them together, in prefabricated assembly-line mass production—a method, a process, an effect that Neutra would strive to translate into archi-tecture.[41]

Neutra read everything he could about America and was delighted when Frances Toplitz bought him a gift subscription to *The Nation*. "This magazine seems to be profound and progres-sive in the best sense of the word," he wrote her. "I read with the greatest interest how severely these men criticize their own country and must unabash-edly admit that we do not have any such periodical in Germany. Would you be so kind and send me a few lines outlining how this publication was cre-ated, how this 'Nation' which was founded in 1865, came about? It appears to be very modern and radical. Is there any connection between this 'Na-tion' and the Quakers? Is there any connection between the 'Nation' and the 'New Republic'? I read both of these publications quite often in Vienna." Neutra reiterated his enthusiasm for the magazine in another letter to Toplitz which she then paraphrased and forwarded to the editors with-out his knowledge. He was flabbergasted one evening while reading his *Nation* in the Berlin subway to find under the heading "Selbstkritik" his letter to the editor—his first published statement in and about America. It contradicted somewhat his earlier assertion that there was too *much* criticism of Germany within its various warring factions. Most likely, he intended to differentiate between irre-sponsible partisan criticism of the vulnerable Weimar government and a deeper self-criticism of German national goals and values. "I read your paper with the greatest interest," his letter to the editor began, "and several friends read the copy when I get through with it. But your sharp criticism of conditions in your country does not lead us to value your country any less. On the contrary we marvel that it brings forth so much self-criticism.

Our fatherland is weak in that today. . . ."[42]

Neutra's fascination with America and his determination to go there had in fact never flagged. It had been most intense during his depressed postwar years in Switzerland and Austria, but even after finding more stable and promising work in Germany, he had continued to pursue this goal. The chief obstacle in his way was the fact that the United States would conclude no peace treaty with Austria until August 1923. Until then Austrian nationals, being "enemy aliens," could not be admitted. Pending signing of the treaty, Neutra's only hope was to obtain a waiver. Such Quaker contacts as Frances Toplitz; John Fisher, the Goshen College professor; and James J. Forrestal, the prominent Chicago lawyer, gave him information and encouragement, though their pacifist reputations hurt Neutra's chances in the eyes of immigration officials more than he realized. Rudolph Schindler and his wife, Pauline Gibling, furnished cautious encouragement and support. As a native American citizen, Pauline was ultimately able to give more substantial help than was Schindler.[43]

"Dear Miss Gibling," Neutra wrote in November 1920, in his still primitive English, "I thank you very much for your kind letter and am happy that you think so friendly for myself. Even now in Berlin, one of my hearty wishes stays to come in your country and to learn at the right place. Mr. Schindler wrote me so often that just there a young architect finds the best possibility to be educated—and my custom is to believe and to estimate what he says. . . . Please excuse my weak English." By 1920, Schindler had moved to Los Angeles to supervise construction of the colossal house and cultural center Wright had designed for the socialite-socialist Aline Barnsdall. He was also strongly considering joining Wright in Japan, where the older architect hoped to follow his Imperial Hotel triumph with a number of other promising commissions. Schindler discussed with Wright the likely possibility of Neutra's joining them in Japan—which Neutra was prepared enthusiastically to do—but when Wright's Japanese prospects failed to materialize, the discussion returned to the idea of Neutra's working for Wright in the Middle West or with Schindler in California.[44]

By the end of 1920 the State Department had twice rejected Neutra's application for a visa, and in early 1921 he wrote to Dione with obvious bitterness: "Why should you be indignant that the American State [Department] does not admit an alien officer? It is a new sacrifice that I have to pay for this German escapade. You know very well that it is only one of many. Wealth, shaken health, my best years. The 'Austrian participation' soon vanished from our consciousness during the war. But no one gives a hoot about granting me or people like me any benefits."[45]

He kept discussing his American future with the Schindlers, Frances Toplitz, and an old Vienna school friend, Henry Menkes, who was then living in New York. Menkes warned Neutra that he would find aspects of American life appalling—the ethnic biases, the social and economic injustices—and he must have shocked Neutra when he debunked one of his heroes with his description of "Jewbaiting, as they call it here, with Henry Ford, the famous auto maker, organizer, philanthrop and friend of Edison as its leader!" Menkes was willing to admit, however, that Neutra could overcome all obstacles with his talent and energy and "achieve shining results. America after all is still a splendid starting point for people of your caliber. . . ."[46]

In April 1923 the Neutras learned that Dione was pregnant—a fact that forced them to make a new assessment of their needs, goals, and immediate plans. Neutra's relationship with Mendelsohn had become increasingly tense and promised to become only more so with time. With the arrival of a child, the Neutras' tiny one-and-a-half room apartment would have to be abandoned. As "foreigners" in Germany, the Neutras had little hope of getting a larger one, since German citizens had priority on the long waiting lists. There was also the likelihood that America would soon enact stricter immigration quotas. These factors made Neutra realize that if he was ever going to America he must do it soon, and he redoubled his efforts to get a visa. Talk of a peace treaty was in the air and gave him new encouragement. When the treaty was signed on August 24, 1923, the way was cleared. The affidavits of support already in his file from John Fisher, Pauline Schindler, and other American citizens led to a visa. Henry Menkes offered to help him get temporary work in New York and get on his feet before proceeding west. Because the early months in America would be so transient and uncertain, Dione would stay in Hagen with her parents and would join Neutra after the birth of their child —expected for December. Their initial plan was to go to America for several years and keep open the option of staying or returning.[47]

"Just now I have terminated one of the best, perhaps *the* most prestigious and highly paid position for an employed architect," Neutra wrote Mütterli. "I leave this office whose future looks promising to me. For a year and a half, I helped it along with all my might and perhaps excessive devotion." Mendelsohn had not yet responded to his resignation, though "all this time he has shown extraordinary cordiality toward me and one tenth of it is probably even genuine. I want to keep him in good memory. . . ." Mendelsohn soon attempted to counter Neutra's resignation "with the greatest compliments. Never had he had such a collaborator, could hardly ever find a comparable one. . . ." But with visa in hand, Neutra was determined to leave. His savings bolstered by the Haifa prize money and a recent lucky stock-market investment, he sailed from Hamburg on October 13, 1923, on the S.S. *Laconia*.[48]

As he crossed the Atlantic at the age of thirty-one, he must have reflected—at that propitious moment—on the state and the progress of his life and his art. Obsessed with the inexorable passage of time, he must have cursed again the accidents of history that had delayed and impeded his career as an architect. Still, he must also have been forced to acknowledge that his education and development —in its more intense moments—had furnished rich beginnings for a potentially successful life. He had no doubts about his debts to his parents, his siblings, Arpad, Dione, and the Niedermanns. He was probably less conscious and appreciative— then and later—of his recent debts to Mendelsohn. He had indeed apprenticed with an architectural giant, whose power and inventiveness would shape his thinking more than he knew. He had also encountered fleetingly in those intense Berlin years the exciting new work of Walter Gropius, Ludwig Mies van der Rohe, and their German contemporaries—architects with whom he would increasingly identify.

At the time, however, he was most consciously appreciative of Wagner, Loos, Wright, and his near contemporary Schindler. He was fortunate, he had written of Wagner to Mütterli earlier, "to grow up from childhood on in a city where the greatest artist in the architectural world radiated in all directions. I was too young to be [Wagner's] immediate pupil, but I imbibed a lot most recently through my friend Schindler, who studied with him without being his favored pupil, as he was much too independent. For the last ten years I have looked upon my friend as the coming man and so far have not had any counterindications. Through this friend I have received information about another genius in our art. Ever since I had a chance to study his drawings thoroughly, he has become my cherished example. . . . Perhaps it is only a hidden love for my country that keeps me from admitting that Frank Lloyd Wright is the greater artist. But the kinship between these two great spirits remains incredible in this moment in history and they never knew each other; half the earth separated them and both had entirely different antecedents. . . . It is difficult to assess Otto Wagner's importance and realize that he represented the best in our old cultural life and at the same time achieved a metamorphosis into a real future, into a new world. . . . A time will come when one will view these men as one now views Alberti or Bramante. They loom more important than the reigning princes of their period. . . ."[49]

Indeed, he wrote Dione later, "there are in our art only a handful of men who strive with a pure heart, and those one knows. There may also be a few unknowns like my friend Schindler. All else was created out of a spirit of speculation, a seeking for originality, dancing on one's head, or just imitating and changing examples of former periods. All these people have no ethical calling to be architects or teachers of human beings. I am modest and not a conceited fool; above all I know the limits of my gifts or even more those of my interest for the daily, worldly battle." The "daily, worldly battle" had tried and tested him over the last decade. Still, he admitted that "the time will probably come when I feel that this early period may be the happiest one, even if in a later one I should be successful."[50]

On October 24, 1923, with a third of a century already behind him, Neutra arrived in New York to begin a new adventure of trial and exploration.

34. *Neutra*, sketch of Brooklyn Bridge,
New York, 1923

Exploration   1923–1926

The first three years of Neutra's life in America were exciting—if uncertain—ones of exploration and search. In 1923 he exchanged his relatively secure position with Mendelsohn for a far less certain existence in a strange country with a new language, just as he had earlier left the even more secure position at Luckenwalde for the experience of working for Mendelsohn. In both cases the motive was the same—to seek new experiences, understand new things, and continue to educate himself as an architect and human being. This restless search for the possibilities of the new architecture and indeed for the essence of architectural experience would continue through the years. By 1926, after brief but generative periods in New York, Chicago, and Spring Green, Wisconsin, he had settled in Los Angeles, where he would live the rest of his life.

Neutra debarked in New York on October 24, 1923. "On account of the fog," he wrote Dione, "we could hardly see anything of the imposing entrance to New York. The Statue of Liberty was merely a shadow against the fog. When we arrived at the Cunard pier we had to pass a lengthy immigration inspection. . . . Thus one enters a new part of the world in turmoil, hardly even noticing it. Now came a thorough customs inspection. My roll of drawings evoked an unusual and lengthy inquiry. . . ." His only friends in New York were Henry Menkes and Frances Toplitz, both of whom received him warmly. En route to Menkes's apartment, where he would stay, he "took in with pleasure all these huge building shapes. Twenty-first Street at first glance appeared very shabby to me," but Gramercy Park "immediately took my fancy. It is a small green spot with a few trees . . . surrounded by small, bigger, and huge buildings with wildly protruding contour lines, silhouetted against the sky. This tiny spot represents a forgotten peace, and one hears nicely the striking of the huge Metropolitan Life Insurance Building clock tower from Madison Square where the traffic rushes by."[1]

After settling into Menkes's tiny apartment, Neutra continued to explore New York, which was filled, he wrote Dione, "with wild accidental beauty. In contrast to this, whatever was planned looks woefully inadequate. However, I surely do not know any other city that is so picturesque, not even Vienna, Hildesheim, or Prague. For decades this city has been, *is* in constant motion, changing its profile. Out of the growing mass the inner core rises always higher and floods gigantically along the riverfront into the open countryside. . . . Not so long ago this teeming Manhattan Island was a silent nature scene like the Hudson and Catskill Mountains," a landscape, he believed, "as beautiful as the Rhine Valley. . . ." The building that seemed to impress him most was the turn-of-the-century Flatiron Building at Fifth Avenue and Broadway, a wedge-shaped skyscraper by the Chicago firm of D. H. Burnham. The area he liked best was around Madison Square. "Especially on Saturdays and Sundays," he wrote, "I hear the syncopated music from a 'dance paradise palace' on Fourteenth Street. Fifth Avenue, with its twirling, colorful, illuminated advertising signs, its throng of men, with shops open until 1 A.M., is only a stone's throw from my boardinghouse entrance." New York, he concluded, was probably "the most depraved city of America, but large sections of this town are quieter and are built with more common sense than our world capitals."[2]

He enjoyed talking "with Americans whose ancestors came over as one of the first settlers," but he suspected that "the real Americans of today are not those from colonial days, but the immigrants from yesterday, the hurrying ones that transact business, that have hardly the time to play baseball." Soon after he arrived, he wrote Dione, he "took a walk through the East Side, where the Jews have settled in unbelievable masses and from where they advance into the highest strata of society. Sometimes very fast. Above all they have an unbelievable thirst for knowledge." He then visited "the metal shops of the Palestinian and Syrian Jews, saw the unbelievable masses of people that poured out of all sorts of evening seminars. . . . Finally I came to the Chinese in Chinatown. All of this is very strange. . . ." New York, he felt, with all its diversity was indeed "the city of Loos."[3]

He despaired of American wastefulness and what he perceived to be a throwaway syndrome "with many excellent new buildings and very many neglected ones." The same lack of care applied to "footwear, automobiles, street paving. . . . It is the country where one continuously buys new socks and discards the old ones. . . . Everything is in flux and whatever is dying disappears before you can say Jack Robinson." His ambivalence toward contemporary American mores was countered, however, by his perception of earlier American cultures. At the Museum of Natural History he was especially moved by the example of the Pueblo Indians, "the people who influenced the modern California building activity. Whole villages were built in one block on the top of a mountain. These cubes with hardly any windows are more than one story, have terraces in front of the setback of the upper stories. It is impossible to fathom the complexity of this agglomeration of building cubes." Later, in the 1930s, his own California architecture would continue to echo the influence of the Southwest pueblos and cliff dwellings.[4]

Of the unending American possibilities he wrote Dione, "I do not have the time, the money, and the opportunity to see 'everything.' But in my own bittersweet way, I shall battle to gain experience, of course not in the Stoic manner like the Indians, or with an Anglo-Saxon fortitude. They do not show any emotion regarding painful experiences. According to the flowing of all my inner resources I become depressed, can laugh, see the comic side of a situation, can despair about the horrible mechanical inertness or see what may be flowering in the future. With regard to 'nationalism,' I hope to be able to contemplate it with ever growing detachment. Love for country, for the peculiarities of its people I treasure much more, and it is more natural to me than the patriotism of the state. Should there be a subsequent emotion above the love for one's country, it could be love for humanity as a whole. . . ."[5]

With the help of Henry Menkes, Neutra got a job with the architect C. W. Short, commuting, against the flow, to the office in Brooklyn from his lodgings in Manhattan. After several months there he moved on, briefly, to a better-paying job in the office of Maurice Courland. The work in those offices inspired him no more than had that of Wernli and Staeger in Switzerland. "Here in New York among the architects," he wrote Dione, "I have encountered provincial stick-in-the-muds. I had thought the people here would be more innovative, more on the move." In addition to such disappointments and to the problems of learning a new architectural vocabulary, it was also disconcerting to have to change from the orderly metric system to the chaotic American system of measurements. He took such frustrations in stride, however, as he looked forward to finding more interesting work in the West and as he worked on a stimulating independent project in New York for an international Zionist committee: the building in Jerusalem of a new library of Jewish culture. Planned as the central feature of the new Hebrew University then rising on Mt. Scopus, the library was the special project of Professor Heinrich Loewe, a leading German library expert, who had come to America to raise funds. The committee included the physicist Albert Einstein, the rabbis Stephen Wise and Mordecai Kaplan, and leaders of the Jewish business community. Neutra left no indication of how he met Loewe or how he so quickly ingratiated himself with Loewe and the committee. In those early months as an unassimilated immigrant, he evidently found comfort in associating himself with international Jewish cultural activities. His collaboration with Mendelsohn on the Haifa project obviously strengthened his credentials and capacity for handling the new assignment in Palestine.[6]

35. *Neutra*, unbuilt design for a Jewish Library, Jerusalem, 1923

Indeed, Neutra's striking and sophisticated preliminary design owed much to Mendelsohn's influence and to their jointly designed Haifa commercial buildings. It was also reminiscent, on a greatly enlarged scale, of Wright's hotel for Mason City, Iowa (1909), which Neutra had seen in the Wasmuth, and of Gropius and Meyer's 1914 model factory at the Cologne Werkbund exhibition, which Wright's hotel had influenced. The low, horizontal central entrance section of the library was framed by enveloping wings of progressively increasing height. "Each succeeding terrace," the promotion brochure read, "is thrown into deep and refreshing shadow by boldly projected roof eaves which are not only ornamental, but most beneficial in the glaring Palestine sun. Bound to the structural purpose of the building are its fidelity to the architectural tradition of the country and its inherent monumental significance due to its unique situation." The low central service portion of the first floor was flanked by a two-story envelope of reading rooms and a higher three-story outer layer of offices and book stacks. The rear stack area was designed to be easily expandable. Even though Loewe and the committee praised Neutra's design and published his preliminary drawings in their brochure, they ultimately chose a more literally traditional neo-Romanesque design by Kornberg and Chaikin, which was built on Mt. Scopus in the late 1920s.[7]

Throughout his months in New York, Neutra looked forward to moving west. In anticipation of this he read "with infinite slowness" Sinclair Lewis's *Main Street*—which tempered his idyllic notions of rural and small-town American life and deepened his appreciation of the more hectic urban scene. Though his ultimate destination remained California, a stop in Chicago still seemed imperative— to meet Wright and Sullivan and see their buildings firsthand. At that time, however, Wright was experiencing enormous personal and financial problems, the solution or evasion of which led to a vexing elusiveness. But Neutra could not follow Schindler's suggestion to come directly to Los Angeles. "As far as your trip to the far west is concerned," Schindler wrote in January 1924, "I should think you should not hurry into it as long as you can make a living in New York. The 'season' there is no doubt more interesting than the one in Los Angeles would be. However, I believe that Los Angeles provides a better starting point to develop an independent future. The building activity is phenomenal and life is agreeable. I therefore give you the advice to come west in the spring when you have had your fill of New York. Wright is in Wisconsin over the holidays. He has an office here, but little to do. I hardly think he has work for you at the present time. Your architectural past is hardly of interest to him, which you would understand once you worked for him. On the whole," Schindler concluded with obvious disillusionment, "you had better get accustomed to the fact that the only thing which could give you prestige in 'Usonia' is a full bag of money. Quality is not considered. . . ."[8]

Neutra stayed in New York as long as he did only to await news from Dione that their baby had arrived safely. Being on the East Coast made the distance between them seem less formidable. A son was born on January 6 and named for Frank Lloyd Wright. The delivery had been difficult, but otherwise all seemed well. The joy of becoming a father was tempered only by the pain of separation. Neutra enjoyed thinking of his child's future life, "filled with anxieties, joy, sorrow and pride for the parents. It may not be a blessing if the child should become more prominent than the parents," he averred, "just . . . as it might be painful if he is of lesser worth. Ernst Freud, for instance, does not have his father's prominence, and still, as far as I know, he is a most beloved son and quite deservedly so." What worried Neutra most was whether he would "have time for the boy? If not, it will be my loss. If one is observant, one can learn much from one's child. No one can educate you more significantly, it seems to me, than a child."[9]

He had wanted to leave New York earlier, he wrote Dione in late January, but had waited for Loewe to return to the city so that they could further discuss the library project. "I have given up my job, to my employer's sorrow but not to mine. However, in Chicago there will again be laborious job-hunting, because I have to be prepared to wait there to meet Wright, if at all possible." He reiterated his belief that Chicago was "the important center for the new architecture. It seems I have, as

usual, to convince myself with my own eyes and have to pay my apprentice premiums. Nobody gives me presents and that is fine with me. I shall have to work for everything and I recognize even more the simple fact that I do not have a guide or a counselor but must grope around and find my way." He admitted that in some ways he was sorry that he could not "simply travel directly to Los Angeles and finally and for a long time unpack my belongings and eventually store them in our cupboards. However only for your sake. As far as I am concerned I can readily see that the time to settle down has not yet arrived and that I have to acquire more knowledge about the minutiae of our profession in order to gain a better overview. . . ."[10]

He left for Chicago in late February, traveling across New York State and lower Ontario. In Buffalo he delighted in Sullivan's Prudential Building, though he left no record of seeing Wright's Larkin Building. He saw the Prudential by twilight and found the ornament especially mesmerizing. It gave him, in fact, "a new insight into the work of Sullivan and Wright." By comparison with the Prudential terra cotta, he believed, "the Viennese ornamentation of Olbrich and Klimt appears to have a paucity of ideas. . . ." He was also pleased that "the building shows from the outside quite clearly the steel skeleton behind the exterior 'cover.' "[11]

Upon his arrival in Chicago Neutra was disappointed, he later admitted, not to step out onto the broad, open prairies where Wright's "Prairie" houses supposedly stood. Yet even the surprisingly old-fashioned and smoky Illinois Central train station could not dampen his delight in the Chicago Loop as he walked west to Hull House on Halsted Street. His Chicago patron, James Forrestal, was a friend of Jane Addams and had arranged for Neutra's temporary lodging at her famous settlement house. Addams gave him the room of a regular tenant who was out of town for several weeks and "talked to me as much as I could understand with my poor grasp of English." During his short stay on Halsted Street, Neutra especially enjoyed teaching several children's drawing classes. "This evening," he wrote Dione, "I was at the Art School of Hull House. Everything surrounding is Greek, all advertising, everything. . . . The Greek and Italian children are very gifted. Perhaps they will make it. . . ." When Neutra's stay at Hull House ended, he moved to an apartment in the North Shore suburb of Highland Park. Neutra was fascinated and appalled by Chicago. It was, he suggested, "a fat, dirty, healthy child with great potential." The crime rate shocked him, and the visual, aural, and olfactory pollution—especially that caused by the automobile—disturbed him and made him reconsider the contribution of his hero Ford. "An evil-smelling hood of gasoline fumes," he lamented, "hovers over this land."[12]

Approximately a week after arrival, however, his outlook brightened when he landed a job with Holabird and Roche, the large, old, prestigious firm that, along with Adler and Sullivan and Burnham and Root, had pioneered the development of the skyscraper in the late nineteenth century. By the 1920s Holabird and Roche had, like the Burnham firm, shifted esthetically to a more eclectic and conservative track, but structurally and organizationally it continued to work in the Chicago School tradition. It was to observe and absorb those technical achievements that Neutra joined the firm as draftsman #208. "For the time being," he wrote Frances Toplitz, "I am mostly interested in the organization of this art factory." His experiences as a draftsman and then as a multilingual liaison man on the firm's new Palmer House Hotel would form the core of his later work *Wie Baut Amerika?* ("How America Builds"). He was intrigued with the complex composition and function of the American hotel building and "in general, the composite multipurpose downtown structure." Near the Palmer House, for example, "one could live and die in the Temple Building, which had a church on top—without going out. One could have every service, from a haircut and manicure to medical assistance . . . have Mass said . . . buy theater tickets, bet on a horse, eat dinner, open a savings account, arrange for insurance, stock transactions, divorce, and even get (before remarrying) one's nose fixed by a plastic surgeon while waiting for one's pants to be pressed."[13]

Observing and participating in the building of the vast Palmer House confirmed Neutra's "admiration for the United States' precise though repetitive industrialized technology," with its rich marketing and distributing possibilities across a continent-wide area without tariff boundaries. "To a Euro-

pean it seemed that such a tremendous market would provide the opportunity and give rise to cautious research which would usher in a beneficial, growing, wholesome industry, especially in the field of building supplies, and would . . . foster modern architecture as no other could: not only did it have ingenuity and the machines to service a new auxiliary of broadly adaptable fabricates, but above all . . . it had the distribution system," including "mail-order houses and their pattern of distant control."[14]

Neutra performed well for Holabird and Roche. At the end of his stay with them the firm's chief draftsman wrote a letter recommending him "to anyone requiring the services of a first class architectural draftsman, or in any capacity requiring faithful devotion to duty." In the year he spent "assisting in the making of plans and detail of the Palmer House," he was found to be "unusually efficient in carrying out whatever was given him to do. He has had an excellent education, both general and technical, and is a man of sterling character."[15]

In Chicago, as in New York, Neutra managed to find a challenging design commission independent of his regular job. Again it was for a Jewish client —this time a new North Shore temple for the congregation of a Rabbi Sonderling. Neutra left no indication of how he met Sonderling, though the contact could have come through acquaintances in his North Shore suburb of Highland Park or through Chicago-area participants in the Jerusalem library project. He undertook the project "without any remuneration" and solely to stimulate "my heart and brain in order to keep my capability for serious design problems." The building was to be smaller and less complex than the Jerusalem library and was formally an inversion of the larger building. It consisted chiefly of a long rectangular upper room for congregational worship with a subdivided basement level for less formal activities. Double stairways from the street-level entrance led up to the main space. A major feature of the interior, decorative as well as functional, was a long narrow slit of a skylight that ran horizontally across the length of the ceiling and continued as a vertical stripe down the center of the back wall. An early rendering of the front and side indicated natural stone trim in the manner of Wright's work of the teens, but in what was presumably Neutra's final

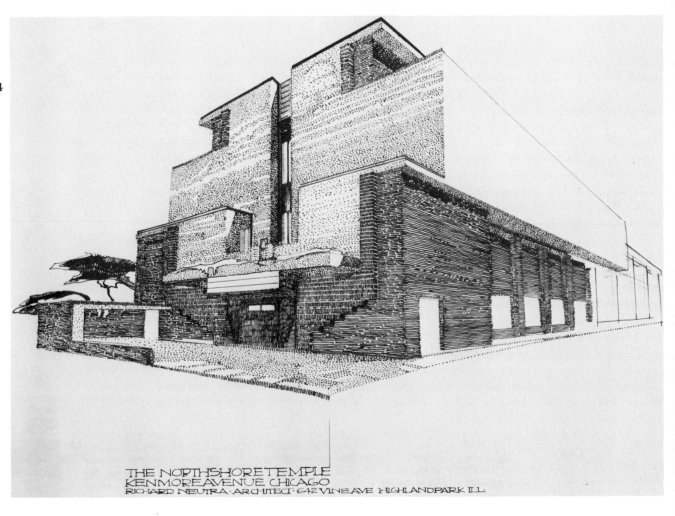

version, the rough stone gave way to smoother, plainer surfaces reminiscent of Mendelsohn and predictive of Neutra's own maturer style of the 1930s. As with the Jerusalem library, Neutra's North Shore temple was never built.[16]

Shortly after arriving in Chicago, Neutra began a systematic pilgrimage to all of Wright's buildings—from the Willitts house in Highland Park to the Robie house in Hyde Park to the Coonley house in Riverside and the numerous structures in Oak Park and River Forest. The buildings he found as wonderful as he had expected, but he was deeply disappointed by most of the residents' indifferent attitudes toward them. In his own later architecture, consequently, he carefully monitored the reaction to his work not only of the initial commissioning client but of later generations of occupants as well. His visit to Wright's Robie house epitomized the problem. In his early thoughts about the experience, he recalled, "my heart always

skipped when I imagined the moment: I would ring the doorbell and ask in very broken English, 'Is Mr. Robie in?'" But when Neutra finally arrived and rang the bell, the answer he got was "'Mr. Robie? Never heard of him.'" The owner had bought the house some years back and . . . wasn't at all enthusiastic about it. . . ." When Neutra asked why she bought the place, "she answered, cold fish, 'I got it very cheap. The man who owned it had to get out.' No, she didn't particularly like it and she had all kinds of petty criticisms." In fact, he wrote Dione, "the people who live in these houses were rather awful. I had always hoped that this new architecture would produce a different human being. I am sorry to be proved wrong. The houses have changed hands many times. Mixed furniture and frightful additional fixtures. New buildings in the neighborhood are equally terrible. The prairie surroundings have disappeared. . . . The most beautiful of all the buildings," he wrote, "the Coonley house . . . I reached only after having lost my way and when it was almost dark. I have to go back once more." Having thoroughly absorbed the plans and façades of Wright's buildings via the Wasmuth publications and now having seen them in actuality, he was in fact not sure they "could teach me anything decisive anymore." As a European modernist who had already observed the cooler, more abstract work of Loos, Mendelsohn, Mies, and Gropius, he now found some of Wright's earlier Shingle Style work of the 1890s *retardataire*. "His own studio," he observed, "looks as dated to me as a Makart or Boecklin studio."[17]

Yet for the most part the buildings were as momentous as he had expected. He despaired of the owners' apparent indifference to them and, even more, of the morbid and critical fascination that most Chicagoans seemed to have for the tragedies and complexities of Wright's personal life. In 1909 Wright had left his wife and family and run off to Europe with Mamah Cheney, one of his clients. Upon their return they had found Oak Park socially hostile to them, and Wright had built a great house, Taliesin, on the family's farm near Spring Green, Wisconsin, where he and Mamah lived and from which he commuted to his work in Chicago. In 1914 a deranged servant set the house afire and then brutally murdered Mamah and six other people, including three of her visiting children. Following this bizarre tragedy, Wright's next female companion and second wife, Miriam Noel, became emotionally unstable and by the early and middle 1920s was harassing Wright unmercifully. With few commissions coming in, Wright's financial problems also deepened. He moved elusively back and forth between the Middle West and Los Angeles, the scene of his few recent jobs, and Neutra despaired of actually ever catching him, "as he lives such an unstructured life. Everybody tells me—unasked—about his private family affairs. It's like Arrowsmith's 'Gopher Prairie.'" He found it disturbing that Chicagoans could "judge so harshly other men's faults." Anyone to whom "I start to mention the modern movement in turn starts quickly to regale me with scandal stories about him."[18]

But Neutra was determined to meet and work with Wright—if only briefly—and he continued to discuss his plans and vexations with Schindler, who wrote on April 14 that "Wright has now definitely left Los Angeles. Wednesday he will be in Chicago and promised to get in touch with you. Your impatience regarding Wright has no sense whatever. If you intend to work for him, you have to be able to give yourself completely. He is devoid of consideration and has a blind spot regarding the qualities of other people. I believe, however, that a year in his studio would be worth any sacrifice, especially in his marvelous house Taliesin. In case you want to come to California—any time is propitious. . . ."[19]

In his early weeks in Chicago, while waiting expectantly to catch up with Wright, Neutra had lost no time in seeking out his other hero, Sullivan. While attempting to locate Wright and to see his buildings, he had met the publisher Ralph Fletcher Seymour, a friend of Wright, Schindler, and Sullivan. Seymour was one of several who were contributing to Sullivan's subsistence. And it was he who apparently introduced Neutra to the aging architect. Later Neutra called on the impoverished Sullivan at the shabby Warner Hotel. He took with him the copy he had gotten through Loos and Schindler of Sullivan's *Kindergarten Chats*, for which Neutra had tried unsuccessfully to find a publisher in Berlin. In good German fashion he also took Sullivan flowers, he wrote Dione, "because I believe he has a tender heart and not many friends. L. H. Sullivan is not as significant as Otto Wagner is, but for his part of the world he was for a long time the keenest and most enterprising architect. Now he is worn out and hopeless. . . . In Chicago they all tell me that the new architecture is dying out. Where on this globe can I find a place where there are no defeatists?"[20]

Neutra sent the flowers up to Sullivan's room "and was a little afraid that he might be embarrassed because an American likes to appear well-to-do and would prefer to receive a guest in splendid surroundings. After a quarter of an hour he came down fully dressed and ready for an outing, the poor man. He invited me to have dinner with him at the Cliff Dwellers' Club. I did not accept but drove with him in the taxicab. Groaning a little, he smoked several cigarettes. His heart and God knows what other ailments seemed to torment him. If the weather improves, the doctor told him, he might make it, but the weather has become much worse. 'What is happening here? Who is working for the future? I have no hope!' he said." When Neutra assured him that his work had indeed made a difference not only in Chicago and America but in Europe as well, Sullivan replied, " 'Perhaps in Sweden and Germany but not here.' " Neutra was pleased to find that "Holabird and Roche impress him. Once they were equals with Sullivan and Adler. Now Sullivan is a poor devil and remembered only in the history of architecture." Neutra apparently saw Sullivan several times in his first months in Chicago, but as he had predicted to Dione, the weather—and Sullivan's condition—got worse. "While talking to him," Neutra confessed, "I really believed that what I told him might comfort him. However, heart pains are worse than this kind of comfort."[21]

Sullivan died on April 20, 1924, and it was at his funeral in Graceland Cemetery that Neutra finally met Frank Lloyd Wright. He "looked ill at ease in front of a lot of hometown adversaries," Neutra noted, and "compensated for it by his dandyish appearance. He was well dressed, carried a cane, and wore oxfords with fairly high heels." He "has the head of a lion resting on a somewhat well-proportioned body," Neutra wrote Dione shortly after the meeting. He "is truly a child but not a well-behaved one. God only knows. He is one in a million. . . ." Wright apologized for not having gotten in touch with Neutra sooner and, following the funeral, took him out to dinner and invited him to come to Taliesin. " 'I don't have any work you know,' " Wright stated. " 'A modern architect can't have any work to speak of in this country—especially not in Chicago.' "[22]

Neutra was delighted to accept his invitation and made plans to visit in early July. He then returned to Highland Park and to Holabird and Roche and awaited Dione's arrival. Since the national quotas were filled, she was admitted under a special professional musicians' provision. Under these circumstances, however, she was not allowed to bring her infant son. Later, with Wright's help, Frank's visa was secured, and his grandmother Niedermann brought him to Wisconsin to his parents in the fall of 1924. It happened, however, that coincident with Dione's arrival Schindler had business in New York, and Neutra had the pleasure not only of rejoining Dione after an eight-month separation but also of seeing his old friend for the first time in

ten years. Dione found Schindler the charming bohemian she had expected, with no tie and wildly flowing hair. "He laughs a lot and radiates cheerful optimism," she wrote her mother. "Perhaps all this is only a mask, one cannot guess. It is unfathomable, although at first it does not seem so. . . ." Earlier Neutra had written Schindler a letter of introduction to Frances Toplitz. "He has a commission in your world metropolis," he informed her. "He is a good and gifted man with little interest in society. He could tell you interesting things if you can induce him to speak. . . ." Later, after they had all met and been together in New York, Neutra observed to Toplitz that indeed Schindler was "the most progressive architect in the circle of my acquaintances. He is not an applied artist, not a gambler, does not make pleasant jokes. He is an engineer who is using his all-comprising knowledge logically. When we met after ten years' separation, we were not disappointed in each other. To find this out was as important for my future path as it is in the case of Wright."[23]

At their first meeting, Wright had apparently offered Neutra a job at Taliesin, since Neutra told Toplitz that he and Dione had been invited shortly after Dione's arrival "to spend a weekend in Spring Green. This would give me a chance to come to a definite decision and I would have Dione's advice based on her sound instincts." The trip was a rich experience. Upon reaching the house, Neutra felt "as though I were in a Japanese temple district, whatever I thought that might look like. Taliesin was completely removed from anything I had known before and here there did live a man who fitted it." Dione described the visit with unabashed awe in a letter to her parents. They were met at the Spring Green station by a Taliesin apprentice, Werner Moser, the son of the architect Karl Moser under whom Neutra had studied briefly in Zurich. "We passed a wonderful lake-like river, ascended a curve, and suddenly there we were without noticing the house. It is . . . quite low and winds around a hill like a snake, becoming higher only on top of the hill. It is impossible to describe the first impression. . . . Then one becomes somewhat anxious at the thought of soon being in the presence of a genius. . . ." She was not disappointed when "Wright came to greet us. He is well built, elegant, of middle height, with a significant head, which could perhaps be best compared to that of Liszt." Dione delighted in the community of apprentices, especially Werner Moser and his wife Sylva and a young Japanese couple, Kameki and Nobu Tsuchiura. "All these young people," she observed, "have a charming relationship to each other. In reality they are alone in this world because one sees no neighbors, only meadows, forests, sky, and Wright. A great admiration for him unites them all" despite the fact that "often they have to work nine hours, although there is hardly any work." The Taliesin living room she found especially "wonderful. Very low, with a beautiful fireplace corner and above all an unspeakably magnificent view. The landscape is so untouched and lonely that it opens one's heart." In the studio, "Wright fetched miraculous items from his Japanese treasure trove. Magnificently painted screens in gold and silver on which were painted either colored flowers or clouds with birds or dark green fir boughs, also magnificent embroideries, marvelously colored fabrics. . . ."[24]

The next "glorious day" also seemed "fabulously unreal." Moser showed them "parts of the house, which has been built in many periods and has innumerable corners. We came to a basement piled high with books. Imagine now that here his magnificent gigantic edition by Wasmuth rots, molds by the hundreds. . . . In the afternoon Wright drove us around the country in his car. The first thing that strikes you is the barns, which are all red. Here as well as in Highland Park there are small wooden houses, all built in good taste and without many decorations. We came through a luscious forest. . . . All very lovely and untouched. This estate is like a fairyland. Wright speaks in a winning, agreeably self-assured manner and one feels that he loves this his native country very deeply. All his ancestors lived around here on farms. . . . After the drive we three sat in his room, and, when we asked, he showed us his drawings . . . and we saw with deep devotion and great admiration how God's spirit and soul are mirrored in this man, with all the mystery of what is beyond understanding. His buildings in Los Angeles are quite marvelous," she concluded. "And this man has nothing to do . . . he sits without work on his wonderful estate and carries innumerable construction ideas with him, but they are probably too beautiful to fit into our world." To elucidate the

37. Frank Lloyd Wright and Richard Neutra, 1924

situation in which he found himself now that he had left the mainstream of Chicago architecture, Wright once told Neutra, "with sad reference to himself, the story of a monkey caught and roped by a planter on his porch. And how the monkey bit off the rope . . . during a long night and went back to the jungle. There he was torn limb from limb because he was different; he had a rope around his belly no other monkey had."[25]

Wright negotiated with Neutra during the summer of 1924 about coming to work for him, and in early November wrote that "$160.00 per month and your board is what I had in mind—altho' in excess of my practice in such matters, I believe you will be able to earn it. . . ." Delighted finally to be working for his idol, Neutra gave notice at Holabird and Roche, and the Neutras moved to Taliesin. Schindler had warned that "the winter will not be pleasant—beautiful—but too cold for

38. *Neutra,* drawing for Frank Lloyd Wright, Automobile Observatory, Sugarloaf Mountain, Maryland, 1924

39. *Neutra,* drawing for Frank Lloyd Wright, Automobile Observatory, Sugarloaf Mountain, 1924

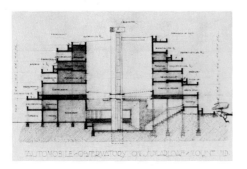

this lightly constructed house." And Dione wrote her mother that indeed "poor Richard has to work in a very cold studio . . . as we have no radiators. Despite all these shortcomings our stay here is like a dream." Neutra did drawings and design studies for several interesting projects Wright had on the boards in 1924, none of which were ever executed. They included a "reinforced concrete skyscraper" for the National Life Insurance Company; a chapter house for the Phi Gamma fraternity at the University of Wisconsin in Madison; a "big country estate of a millionaire for the California mountain desert," presumably the "Scotty's Castle" or the Doheny Ranch project, near Los Angeles; and a drive-in recreation tower for the entrepreneur Gordon Strong, planned for Sugarloaf Mountain, Maryland, between Baltimore and Washington.[26]

Apparently conceived by Wright with input from Neutra, the circular Sugarloaf Observatory contained bars, restaurants, shops, dance floors, and service areas. Enveloping the building were ascending and descending vehicular and pedestrian ramps and periodic parking slots, where motorists could leave their cars while using the various facilities or the observation platforms. Although somewhat unrealistic in its provisions for auto traffic and storage, even by 1920s standards, the building evoked through its streamlined styling the Age of the Automobile. Neutra drew renderings, floor plans, sections, and elevations while Wright was away in California during December 1924. Later, in 1925, after Neutra had left, Wright added a planetarium to the building's collection of diversions, but retained the basic concepts of the early studies. Nothing in Wright's *oeuvre* before that time predicted the observatory's streamlined circular forms—features and qualities of a decidedly Mendelsohnian stamp, which Neutra may well have imparted to the scheme. The circle and spiral would play an increasingly important role in Wright's subsequent work. Neutra would later enjoy pointing out the obvious similarities between the Sugarloaf Observatory of the mid-1920s and Wright's Guggenheim Museum of the 1950s. In addition to the architectural projects, Neutra also assisted in the assembly and translation of the graphic and verbal materials published in the special reviews of Wright's work in the Dutch journal *Wendingen* and the German *Baugilde.*[27]

While Richard worked at the drawing board, Dione practiced her singing and cello and enjoyed performing for the Taliesin "family" and for occasional visitors. It was during the Neutras' Wisconsin sojourn that Olgivanna Lazovich, later to become Wright's third wife, made her first visit to Taliesin. She danced before the fire, Dione recalled, to Dione's accompaniment of Schubert's "Der Erlkönig." In his *Autobiography,* in a chapter entitled "The Merry Wives of Taliesin," Wright later recalled how the three young couples kept his spirits up and constituted, in effect, his "immediate family. A happy one because they were all good to what was left of me at that bad time. . . . Dione was a genius, good to look at, played her cello and sang while playing, doing both with real style: her own." Indeed, Neutra wondered in a letter to Mütterli if they would "ever again be so happy."[28]

Only once during their idyllic stay at Taliesin, Neutra remembered, was the euphoric spell broken by a moment of tension. It came when Neutra mistakenly showed Wright a note and a gift from their Chicago acquaintance Ralph Fletcher Seymour, Louis Sullivan's friend, who along with Sullivan's disciple George Elmslie had gathered up the drawings and the few meager possessions that Sullivan left at his death. Among the things that had been retrieved from a pawnshop was Sullivan's topaz stickpin, sent now to Neutra because of his "enthusiasm and friendliness to the old master." Neutra later admitted that "I, who was nobody, rushed around the table and showed the pin to Mr. Wright. 'Do you recognize it?' He shook his head, and I gave him the letter. It was a mistake. He read and silently gave me back these tokens. He seemed sad." Later Neutra wrote Seymour that "your considering me a worthy heir of something that Sullivan owned has immensely encouraged me through the many dark hours of being derided and seeming to fail to reach any goal in this difficult profession. . . . Always when I had a tough time, I used to look at the pin and read your letter. . . . I wonder whether you guessed what you contributed to my effort and career when you wrote me suddenly that I, an unknown young man, was worthy to have that token and would live up to it."[29]

In addition to helping receive Olgivanna, the Neutras enjoyed meeting other visitors to Taliesin, including Wright's oldest son Lloyd. "In Los

40. The Neutras at Taliesin with Wright and apprentices, 1924

41. Dione and Richard, Taliesin, 1924

Angeles, he makes architecture in his father's style," Richard wrote Frances Toplitz, "perhaps not as forward-looking as . . . his father—but beautiful. Personally he is a nice young man who, however, seems to have business arguments with his genius father, whom he nevertheless admires. . . ." The most celebrated visitor while the Neutras were at Taliesin, however, was none other than Erich Mendelsohn, who stopped for several days during his 1924 American tour. While Wright and Mendelsohn had obvious respect for each other's work, their substantial egos and their frequently acerbic candor might have become uncomfortably abrasive had they been able to understand each other. Fortunately Wright's knowledge of German was as limited as Mendelsohn's English. Neutra, as the bemused interpreter, diplomatically tempered the sharper edges of the exchange, which if translated literally would have likely resulted in offending both men. Neutra enjoyed observing that as it turned out, both men managed to remain friendly for life. Neutra regretted that Mendelsohn, in his rather short tour, "has formed a judgment about this country which is as negative as it is superficial. I don't think it is possible," he wrote Frances Toplitz, "to get a correct idea about this district of human civilization without paying the price as I do; to know it by patiently working here."[30]

To get still another perspective on "this district of human civilization," the Neutras realized that they must end the Wisconsin idyll and move on to California—their ultimate American destination. They were flattered that Wright tried to persuade them not to leave. If and when he ever wanted to come back, Wright told Dione, Richard could always find work with him. "I don't see why he has to leave," he remarked. "Anybody can leave here, but a few only are allowed to stay. So why . . . not enjoy this place and this situation?" When Dione replied that being happy and comfortable was "not the single aim . . . in coming to this country," Wright observed significantly in that traumatic period of his own life: "Getting more mature, I have found out that being happy *is* the single aim we have to have in mind and no time is lost when spent on this purpose. Fame and money help . . . only a little."[31]

With mixed feelings of regret and expectation, they decided to leave at the end of January. Schindler continued to offer encouragement. "Do you have a clear picture of the West," he had written earlier, "or is it, as it is for so many, a nostalgic urge? In any case, here you can make a living just as well as in Chicago and, for a foreigner, with better auspices for a future and an agreeable way of life. I would be very pleased to receive you here

42. Lilly Niedermann, center, with Dione, Frank, and Richard Neutra, Taliesin, 1924

43. Mendelsohn, Wright, and Neutra, Taliesin, 1924

and help you over the initial difficulties; as far as it is in my power, we shall not starve." They crossed the country by train the first week of February 1925, stopping en route for a brief holiday at the Grand Canyon. Schindler welcomed them at the Los Angeles station and drove them to his home on King's Road in Hollywood. It was raining, Dione remembered, and the house seemed dark—but wonderful.[32]

Schindler had designed the double house in 1921, for himself, his wife Pauline, and a couple of their friends. Clyde and Marion Chase. The central and commonly shared room was the kitchen, which connected the two main apartments, with a smaller guest apartment and garages to the west. The plan was essentially an interlocking of three roughly *L*-shaped wings. Rather than the conventional designations of "living room" or "bedroom," each of the residents had his or her own "spaces" labeled with his or her initials: RMS, SPG, MDC, and CBC. The major building materials were concrete, redwood, glass, and canvas. Along the north and south prop-

erty lines and wherever else privacy was most desirable, heavy, slightly battered concrete slabs were poured in molds and tilted into place, with opaque glass slit interstices, forming beautifully textured fortress-like walls. By contrast, in other spaces, sliding glass and canvas door-walls opened to patio gardens—all flush with the building's concrete slab foundation. Subtly positioned clerestory windows provided gentle and unexpected sources of light. Two small upstairs "sleeping baskets" reached by a narrow stairway from each of the two major apartments became miniature observation towers greeting each other across the flat roof planes. The open outdoor spaces of the 100-by-200-foot lot were, in fact, as carefully conceived as the covered interior ones. Defined chiefly by gradations in level, by juxtapositions with walls, and ultimately by hedges, canebrakes, and other foliage, the patios and gardens gradually assumed the character of outside rooms. The house was, as Schindler himself suggested, cave, tent, and pavilion. Its references were not so much to Wagner's Vienna as to Wright's Prairie School, the Southwest Indian pueblos, the timeless esthetics of Japanese design, and the inside-outside possibilities of California living.[33]

The Neutras first stayed in the guest apartment and then moved to the larger north apartment originally occupied by the Chases. Their rent seemed high for the time, but the beauty of the house—and for Richard, the closeness to Schindler's studio—justified the expense. At first the two families cooked and dined communally, but when the Neutras moved to the north apartment, they set up their own kitchen in a corner of their bedroom. Still, Dione wrote her mother, "Schindler told Richard that he feels a sentimental attachment to him and considers our two families a 'unit.' Whether they can collaborate remains to be seen. . . . Unfortunately Schindler has only small commissions."[34]

Almost as unique as Schindler's remarkable house was his volatile wife Pauline, who alternately and unpredictably intrigued, attracted, vexed, and alienated the Neutras. Pauline had come from a wealthy East Coast family and had followed her four years at Smith College with a job teaching music at Jane Addams's Hull House. The way in which she and Schindler had met epitomized their fervent quest for "modernism"—in art and in life. The meeting took place at Chicago's Orchestra Hall at

the American premiere of Sergei Prokofiev's "Scythian Suite," which had been full of radical new sounds, Pauline later recalled, that had so stunned and delighted her that she could not bear to sit through the second half of the program, which featured the "ancient" music of Carl Maria von Weber. Leaving the hall at intermission, she met a friend with a gentleman escort, both of whom were equally dazzled by the new music and were also leaving the concert before von Weber could break the spell. The gentleman escort turned out to be Schindler, and his courtship of Pauline, an obvious kindred spirit, followed. They married in 1919 and moved to Los Angeles the next year.[35]

In her relationship with the Neutras, Pauline, or "Ghibbeline" as the Neutras called her, was by turns cordial and abrasive, and was particularly critical of Dione's "narrow" attitudes in such areas as education, nutrition, and child rearing. Never before in her relatively sheltered life, Dione later recalled, had she been so mercilessly scrutinized and ridiculed. This was tempered however by the Neutras' appreciation of the Schindlers' sophisticated social life and avant-garde circle of friends. In the 1920s and after, the house on King's Road was an important center for advanced social, cultural, and political activities. Leftist political groups, of particular interest to Pauline, frequently used the house as a meeting place. The modern dancer John Bovington, who occupied the guest apartment, astonished and delighted the King's Road circle with his "erotic" dances in the courtyard depicting the

"ascent of man." Dione felt, however, "very different in comparison to the women here" finding "the extravagance of [their] dresses . . . indescribable," and attracting "attention because I wear no make-up." Most astonishing, however, was the fact that "occasionally at parties I am introduced as someone who claims to be happy. This is apparently an unknown phenomenon here. In Germany I never heard so much talk of broken marriages and nervous breakdowns. . . ."[36]

Gradually the Neutras settled into King's Road and in their own way participated in its mood and style of life. Describing his first visit to the house as an awe-struck young student, Harwell Harris recalled that "Dione Neutra (I didn't know who she was) walked through the room and smiled. She was barelegged, wearing sandals and something resembling a toga (unbleached muslin, I believe) with that ribbon drawn above that completely untroubled brow. She didn't interrupt my thoughts; she merely suggested that this mountain I was on was maybe Mount Olympus."[37]

With the Schindlers the Neutras began exploring Southern California—from Los Angeles's Chinatown to the desert community of Palm Springs. In 1926 Richard and Dione bought a second-hand Franklin and took longer trips to San Francisco and Carmel, and to La Jolla to visit the honeymooning Frank and Olgivanna Wright. They enjoyed the movies, especially the early talkies, and delighted in the concerts at the Hollywood Bowl. They visited all of Wright's California buildings, but their hap-

44. *Schindler*, Schindler House, Los Angeles, 1920–21

45. Pauline Schindler, *ca.* 1918

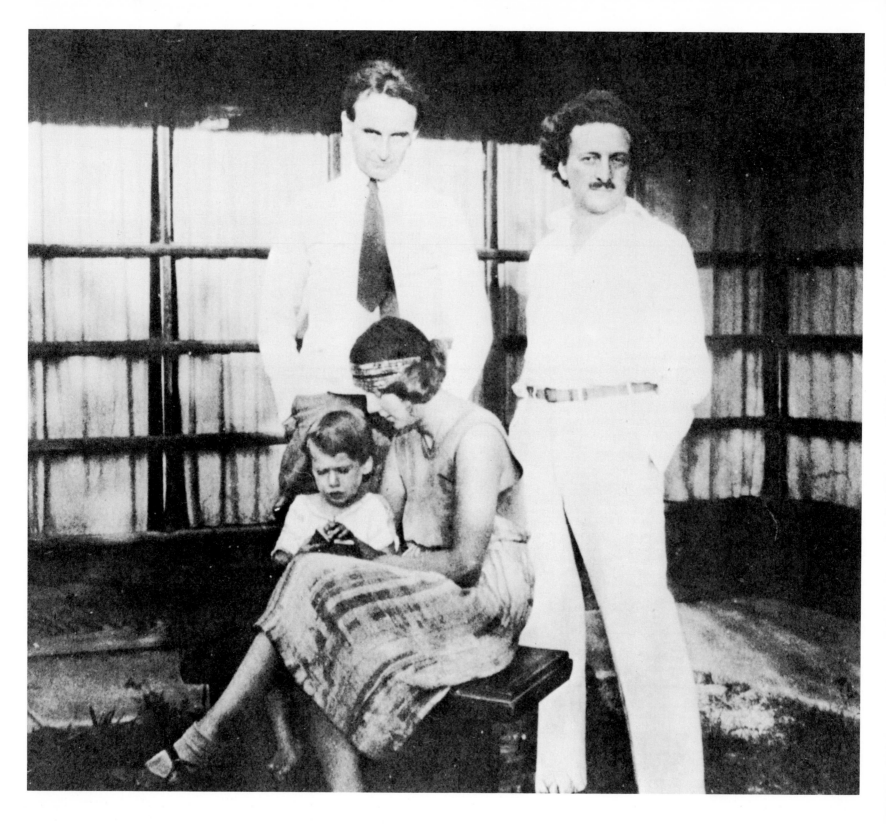

46. Neutra, Schindler, Dione, and Dion
Neutra, Los Angeles, 1928

piest new discovery was the work of Irving Gill, who had come to California in the 1890s after working alongside Wright in the Chicago office of Louis Sullivan. Gill practiced a starkly chastened version of the then-current Spanish Colonial Revival, drawing inspiration from the Spanish Mission period and from the earlier indigenous Southwest architecture of the Pueblos, an esthetic to which Neutra and Schindler were also drawn. The crisp, abstract cubistic geometry of Gill's buildings, with their flat roofs and ribbon windows, aligned him in the eyes of Neutra's generation as much with the modern movement as with the Spanish Colonial Revival. Neutra must have reflected on Gill's similarities to Loos. These qualities were exhibited a block up the street on King's Road, in Gill's handsome Dodge house (1916). Nearer downtown was his Banning house (1910) and out near the beach in Santa Monica was his Horatio West Court (1919)—all of which Neutra photographed avidly. Pervading the Neutras' first impressions of California was their delight in the exotic climate and topography— "ocean, forest, desert, snow, palm trees, South Sea fishes," Neutra noted, "all . . . in 2–3 hours driving."[38]

In 1926, their second year in California, a second son, Dion, was born to the Neutras. But their joy in his arrival and development was marred by their growing awareness that Frank, their firstborn, was mentally retarded. The "difficult delivery" of 1924 had boded more problems than anyone had suspected. In certain ways Frank had seemed a healthy and precocious infant, but his failure to talk and to communicate normally presaged the deeper problems that would soon become manifest. Caring for him properly was difficult, frustrating, and enormously time-consuming. For both Richard and Dione the pain was immense. Frank's illness would remain the great tragedy of their lives.[39]

For the first year and a half of Neutra's residence in Los Angeles the degree of his and Schindler's genuine collaboration was minimal, as Schindler allowed him minor participation on projects that were already in hand. Chiefly this involved assistance with drafting and the handling of landscaping. For example, Neutra did the landscaping for Schindler's Howe house in Los Angeles (1925) and the Lovell beach house in Newport Beach (1926). In 1925 they jointly designed a fetching

pergola and wading pool for the west front of Barnsdall's Hollyhock House. Neutra soon realized, however, that given Schindler's unaggressive penchant for residential and small-scale projects the situation would not change, and in 1926 he would propose an ambitious collaborative plan and framework for landing larger, nonresidential commissions —the Architectural Group for Industry and Commerce (AGIC). This would constitute a major turning point in Neutra's career, of course, and would affect Schindler's work as well.[40]

But until that point, to pay the rent and feed his family Neutra had to supplement his meager earnings from Schindler with outside employment in larger Los Angeles architectural offices. The first employer was the historicist architect Gordon Kaufman. "He treats me excellently," Neutra wrote Dione's parents, "and his commissions are executed in Florentine early Renaissance style. The marvelous large illustrated publications that form the source material awaken my longings for Italy, but Los Angeles is beautiful." Neutra's major work for Kaufman was on the Eisner house (1925), built on the southwest corner of Sixth and Muirfield Streets in Los Angeles. Neutra did working drawings for elevations and floor plans and may have influenced certain design concepts—especially the walls, steps, terraces, and asymmetrically fenestrated elevations of the east façade. He left Kaufman for a better-paying job with Rudolph Meier, an architect "who knows nothing, but has a first-class commission and therefore pays unusually well." On one project, presumably for a school, Neutra wrote that he was "able to conceive and execute the twenty sheets of technical drawings all by myself after the twenty preliminary drawings had been accepted by the client. Even the construction I figured out in part, and two perspective drawings of mine were published in the *Los Angeles Times*." Meir "suddenly . . . discovered that my designs have a similarity to those of Wright (I wish they had). In reality they are tame compromises." A third employer was the Fidelity Construction Company, for whom Neutra served as the chief designer of the ultimately unexecuted California Lamb's Club, in Hollywood. The mass of the proposed building rose in stepped Art Deco segments, with lower wings featuring Spanish colónnades. "Of extreme Spanish design," the promotion brochure averred, "the architect has in-

47. *Neutra*, photographs of Irving Gill, Horatio West Court, Santa Monica, California, 1919, as published in *Amerika* (1930)

48. *Neutra*, for AGIC, unbuilt (?) design for a "Spanish House," Santa Monica, California, ca. 1927

49. Los Angeles, 1850s

geniously made plans which approach the ideal in clubhouse construction, the designer's conception faithfully adhering to the club's paramount policy of refinement and comfort." During these same years Neutra also designed several Spanish Colonial houses for traditionally minded clients in West Los Angeles, though the houses were apparently never built.[41]

Neutra worked downtown all day on these jobs, usually returned to King's Road by 6:30 P.M., and frequently followed dinner with several more hours in Schindler's studio working on joint projects. He also continued work on two connected personal projects begun much earlier—a utopian city design he called "Rush City Reformed" and his book on American building, *Wie Baut Amerika?* or *How America Builds*. "I get up at 5:00 A.M. and work for two hours on my own projects," he wrote Mütterli. "At 10:00 in the evening I like to go to bed, which is noticed because Schindler's friends like to stay up until 2:00 A.M. This is really too much for me. A smoke-filled night means less to me than a clear head in the morning."[42]

"Rush City Reformed" was the name Neutra gave to the series of visionary urban designs he had started in Berlin and continued in New York, Chicago, and Wisconsin. The words "Rush City" evoked the fast pace of American life and, with irony, the legendary boom towns of the frontier. Neutra's elegant drawings emphasized traffic and transit systems of rail and motor corridors cutting with a Spartan and geometric rigidity through vast cityscapes of tautly aligned high-rise slabs. The dramatic and sometimes frightening images recalled the earlier pre-war designs of the Italian Futurist Antonio Sant'Elia and the contemporaneous urban visions of Ludwig Hillbersheimer and Le Corbusier. The schematic austerity of the general perspectives gave way, however, in detailed close-up studies to a more human and rational specificity. The detailed studies, for example, showed connecting bridges and freeway access ramps which were totally missing in the general renderings. The vermiculate character of the one- and two-story low-rise housing areas for families with children furnished a functional and esthetic counterpoise to the rigid geometry of the high-rise towers. Fetchingly small-scaled drive-in markets acknowledged the increasing significance of the automobile in modern life. School buildings with outdoor corridors and minimally adorned community centers prefigured Neutra's—and Mies's—esthetic of the 1930s and '40s. The early Rush City drawings also included a nearly mature version of

Neutra's famous Ring Plan School, with its circle of connected classrooms opening onto outside patios. For economy of space, the roof of the ring served as an athletic track and the central court as a protected playground. A fourteen-story tower design of strikingly cantilevered glass curtain walls and of convincingly balanced vertical and horizontal elements strongly prefigured the noted Pennsylvania Society for Savings Building, Philadelphia (1932), by Lescaze and Howe. For harbor and light-manufacturing districts, low conical, vault-like structures suggested factories and warehouses into which transit and industrial operations were obviously to be "plugged." A monumental "terminal" building would serve as the nexus between underground rail lines and surrounding above-ground airport facilities. While the overall gestalt of Neutra's Rush City recalled contemporary European images, the high-rise towers reflected the Chicago School. The drive-in markets and lower buildings, on the other hand, were obviously influenced by the automobile culture and horizontal sprawl of Los Angeles.

"Rush City Reformed" would continue to evolve into the 1930s as Neutra—with the help of student apprentices—would develop new aspects of this city of the future and rationalize and humanize its original thematic shell. It was typical of Neutra that instead of making random and disparate utopian sketches, he collected these visionary ideas and images into a relatively unified "system." Though Rush City was never—and was probably never intended to be—reified in toto, it would serve Neutra the rest of his life as a generative reservoir of ideas and possibilities for solving real problems of architecture and urban design. In a later exegesis and rationalization of these early schemes, Neutra would insist that "Rush City Reformed" did "not base itself on an abstract and theoretically rigid scheme," but was "rather a series of efforts a quarter century ago, to study urban problems in a scientific manner, expressing a belief in the wholesome flexibility of city planning." Whether or not Neutra's more relaxed mood of the 1950s faithfully captured his more obviously polemical and doctrinaire intentions of the 1920s, he lamented the continuing fact that an "unstable social economic order" had "not yet permitted valid methods of construction, financing and usage of land to develop in accordance with existing technological advance."[43]

Neutra used Rush City, as it had developed by 1926, to illustrate the book *Wie Baut Amerika?*, which he completed that year. He had written the greater part of it in Chicago and Wisconsin and finished it at King's Road. Roughly the first third dealt with general problems and possibilities of American architecture and urban design—traffic and transportation, stations and terminals, zoning, the New York setback law, and various other environmental regulations. The second, central portion used the new Palmer House Hotel as a case study and examined in minute detail the progress of construction and the organization of the building and the building force. This section contained dozens of the construction photographs Neutra had taken while working on the job for Holabird and Roche. The last part of the book treated new building methods and materials not exemplified in the Palmer House. It featured smaller buildings and included Rudolf Schindler's poured concrete Pueblo Ribera houses, La Jolla (1923), and Frank Lloyd Wright's inter-

50. *Neutra and Schindler*, pergola and wading pool for Aline Barnsdall, Hollyhock House, Los Angeles, 1925

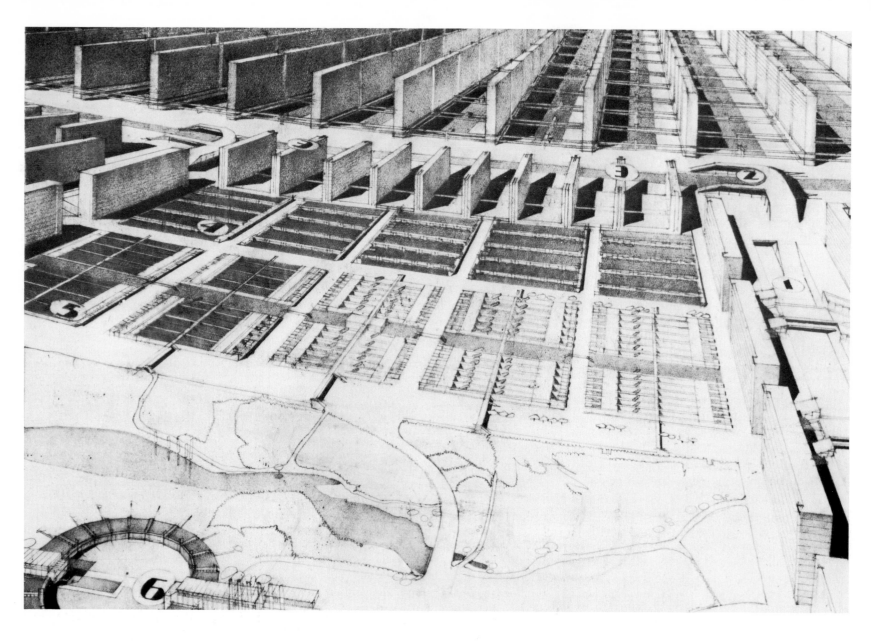

51. *Neutra*, "Rush City Reformed," late 1920s

52. *Neutra*, "Rush City Reformed,"
community center, late 1920s

53. *Neutra*, "Rush City Reformed," late 1920s

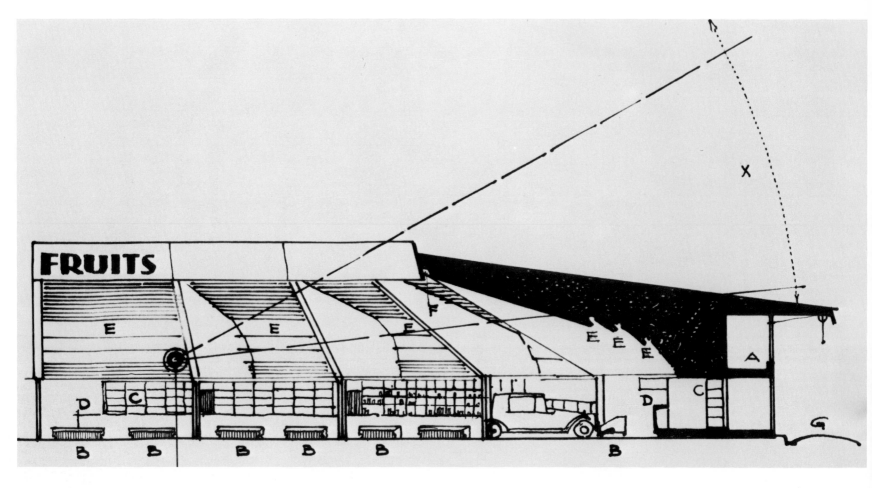

54. *Neutra*, "Rush City Reformed," drive-in market, late 1920s, detail

locking, prefabricated concrete-block Los Angeles houses of the early 1920s. Neutra reiterated the impact of Pueblo Indian forms on modern California design and cited Lloyd Wright's Oasis Hotel, Palm Springs (1922), as an example of a structure in "sensitive conformity to the landscape." The book was permeated with paeans to modernity, prefabrication, and interchangeability of parts, all symbolized for Neutra by *Sweet's Catalogue* of building materials.

Compared with the sprightliness and poetic beauty of his letters, the style of *Wie Baut Amerika?* was ponderous, convoluted, and occasionally obfuscatory. Neutra frequently made insufficient distinction between description and prescription, between what was and what ought to be. The book as a whole was more descriptive than interpretive, and its mountains of data were tediously formidable. Yet however commonplace his details of American building would seem half a century later, they were eagerly seized upon when the book was first published in January 1927 by the prestigious house of Julius Hoffmann of Stuttgart. Neutra had sent the completed manuscript to Dione's parents and had

deputized them to place it, negotiate with publishers, and handle all proofreading. The Niedermanns sent it to a number of German presses and were delighted when Hoffmann accepted it, advertised it widely, and printed 4400 copies. Its seventy-seven pages contained 102 illustrations. Neutra's original title had been "Amerikanischer Kreis—Amerikanisches Bauen" ("American Orbit—American Building"), but the publisher argued that the shorter *Wie Baut Amerika?* would have more impact. The book sold briskly to a worldwide audience 'and elicited enthusiastic reviews—both in America and in Europe.[44]

Commissar Lunacharsky of the Soviet Ministry of Education read it "with the greatest pleasure" and promised Neutra that it would be read by Soviet artists and architects. The *Architects' Journal* of London found it "an admirable short textbook on contemporary American practice" which "should prove invaluable to the student. . . ." The *Berliner Tageblatt's* reviewer believed it offered solutions to many of "our European problems" and hoped that it would be read by laymen as well as by professionals, since "an informed public is the base for a new impetus in architecture. . . ." The Swiss *Magazine for Politics and Culture* asserted that the book should "be of interest to all readers who are concerned with the social and economic conditions of the present," and noted that many of Neutra's ideas were similar to those of Le Corbusier. However, it insisted, in comparison to the highly literary and utopian quality of Le Corbusier's "aesthetic manifestoes," one saw in Neutra "a man who proceeds with utmost logic. He is a worker who says only what he can prove, who creates only projects that can be built."[45]

In the United States, historian Henry-Russell Hitchcock reviewed the book for the *Architectural Record* and compared the author with Le Corbusier, Gropius, Mies, and Oud. Neutra was, he believed, "one of the less than half a dozen architects working in this country—all but Wright, of whom he is the only worthy follower, foreign trained—who are as fully convinced as the leaders of French, German and Dutch architecture of the essential relation between modern design and the methods and materials it works with: with the architect of 'Rush City' as with the architect of Pessac, of Dessau, or of Rotterdam, architecture is the aesthetic crystallization of the engineering solution of the building problem. Creation is again, as in the time of great structural architectures of the past, a possibility, and nowhere more so than in America."[46]

One of the most favorable and significant reviews—in the obscure Los Angeles *City Club Bulletin*—was written by Pauline Schindler, who saw the book as "an interpretation of modernism and its expression in architecture . . . an affirmation and optimistic estimate of modern American civilization and architecture." Pauline extrapolated the essence of Neutra's message better perhaps than any other critic. This was no doubt due as much to their conversations at King's Road as to her reading of the book itself. She characterized succinctly much of the ideology of Neutra's wing of the developing modern movement. "Building and city planning should not be concerned solely with superficial decoration and ornamental beautification," she agreed. "Worn out symbols are discarded. Changing social and economic forces modify our manner of living. Growing industrialism and accumulating population demand housing reform for wage earners, adjustment of transportation and traffic. . . ."

55. *Neutra*, skyscraper, "Rush City Reformed," late 1920s

She found it exciting that, "in this age, decried as artistically arid, a new architectural style is slowly taking form out of these problems, impelled partly by the force that shapes cities, partly by the congress of international inventiveness, usually termed the building supply market. . . . Development of the new style is characterized by an impersonal generality. It is being created not mainly by the professional architect, but by manufacturers of building materials and specialties. . . . These factors, catering to and controlling a nation-wide de-

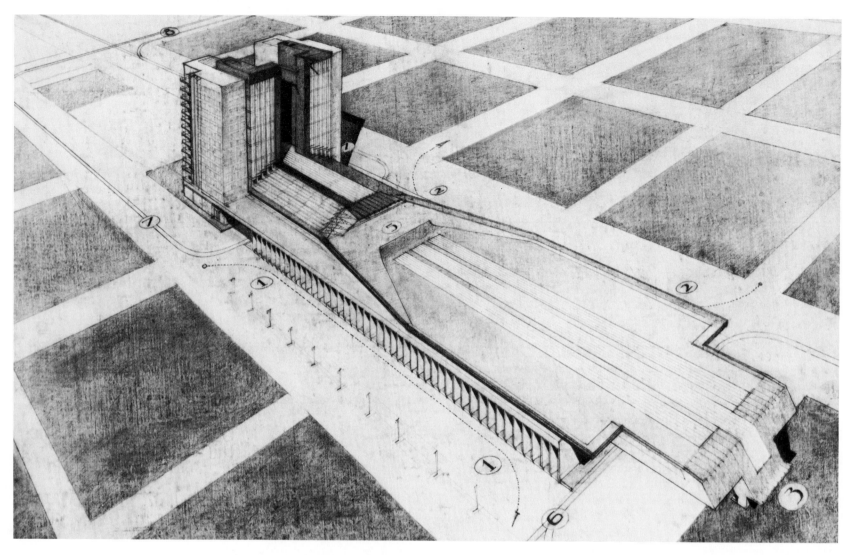

56. *Neutra*, Terminal Building, "Rush City Reformed," late 1920s

mand, necessitate mass production by extensive machinery, improving the output, raising standards, creating a new quality type of great vitality."[47]

She was certain that "aestheticists of Ruskinian order may deplore this method, but they are blind to the urgency of present conditions and the fertile necessities, which like a compelling fate, encompass the modern creative mind. . . . Formerly, quality depended on luxurious requirements of the wealthy and manual skill of individual craftsman . . . now it is developed by means of an extensive engineering apparatus, the perfection and profitable maintenance of which is based upon mass production, mass consumption and economy of cost. . . ."[48]

Pauline Schindler must have sensed already that while Neutra called convincingly for an impersonal, new architecture of prefabricated industrial parts—as the only means of meeting the new

century's building needs—there was also in his nature an urge to play the role of the Old Heroic Architect in the manner of Wagner, Mendelsohn, Sullivan, and Wright. As a nonanonymous prophet and exemplar of the new order he could, of course, do both. It was a need not uncommon among revolutionary personalities. In attaining work and publicizing it to get more, Neutra would grow through the years more and more aggressive. The noble ends increasingly seemed to justify the means. The American capitalist marketplace, he was quick to perceive, demanded and responded to vigorous self-promotion. The more famous he and his work became, the more impact his ideas would have.

By 1926, after long years of exploration, Neutra had begun to find and announce his ideals and goals. Now it remained to develop and realize them with actual buildings on actual landscapes.

57. *Neutra* and apprentices, Lehigh Airports Competition, 1931

58. *Neutra and Schindler,* final design for
League of Nations Building, 1926

Breakthrough

1926–1930

The last half of the decade of the twenties was crucial for Richard Neutra and the developing modern movement. No other period in the history of modern architecture saw the realization of so many acknowledged masterworks. At Dessau, Germany, in 1926, Gropius was completing the building of the Bauhaus. In Rotterdam, between 1927 and 1930, J. A. Brinkmann, L. C. van der Vlugt, and Mart Stam finished their epochal Van Nelle factory for C. H. Van der Leeuw. Erich Mendelsohn, during the same years, was designing his great Schocken department stores in Stuttgart, Chemnitz, and Nuremberg. At Paimio, Finland, in 1929, Alvar Aalto began that city's famed tuberculosis sanatorium. The same year saw the construction of Mies van der Rohe's short-lived but immortal pavilion for the German Werkbund at the Barcelona Exposition. In 1930 Le Corbusier completed the Villa Savoye at Poissy, near Paris. In 1927, the *chef d'oeuvre* of European housing developments was realized at Weissenhof, near Stuttgart, with prototype housing designs by Mies, Gropius, Le Corbusier, Stam, Peter Behrens, Hans Scharoun, and J. J. P. Oud. In the United States, the only contemporary works of comparable stature were George Howe and William Lescaze's Philadelphia Savings Fund Society Building (1929–32); Rudolph Schindler's Lovell beach house, Newport Beach, California (1926); and two Los Angeles buildings by Richard Neutra: the Jardinette apartments (1927) and the Lovell Health House (1927–29).

In his first year in Los Angeles working in and out of Schindler's King's Road Studio, Neutra's appreciation of his old friend's talent deepened. But a growing realization on the part of both men of seriously inhibiting temperamental differences countered the enthusiasm of Neutra's earlier assertion to Frances Toplitz that after ten years' separation they "were not disappointed in each other." During his first decade in the United States, Schindler had reacted to the American "go-getter" capitalistic mentality with increasingly cynical withdrawal. Beneath his outwardly benign disposition—for which he was widely and understandably loved and admired—there lay a capacity for a smoldering bitterness.

He suggested this to Neutra as early as February 9, 1915, in a letter that summarized his early views of America. He was drawn to the relatively primitive Southwest, he acknowledged, but "the civilized part is horrible, starting from the President down to the streetsweeper." He was certain that "the greed for money has taken on such dimensions that everybody is already born a cheat. Everything here is to be had for a price. . . . They are inhuman from start to finish." He did not deny, however, that "the stay here has been very beneficial to me personally. My view regarding life has become much clearer and simpler and allows less and less for compromises. Lately I ask myself more and more whether it is not a worthier goal in life to be a vagabond. Earning a living will always produce pettiness. . . ."[1]

Schindler's tendencies toward bohemian "vagabondage" and his growing reluctance to compromise or even to deal with the Establishment was strongly encouraged, Harwell Harris has averred, by his marriage to Pauline Gibling. By 1925–26, when the Neutras settled at King's Road, Schindler's work, however brilliant, was based for the most part on small jobs for relatively leftist, bohemian clients, most of them members of his and Pauline's

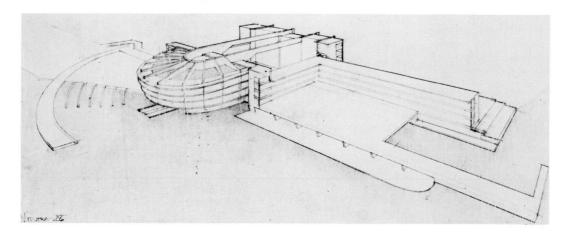

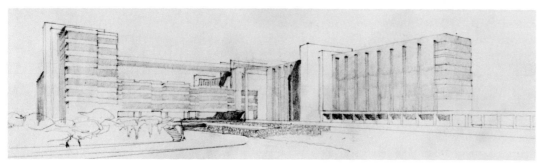

59. *Neutra and Schindler*, preliminary design for League of Nations Building, 1926

60. *Neutra and Schindler*, preliminary design for League of Nations Building, 1926

bitions, he knew that he had to be known, heard, read, and seen, and most of all that he needed to demonstrate by building.

The earliest example of Neutra's penchant for big things was his persuading of Schindler, to join him in the 1926 competition for the League of Nations headquarters in Geneva. The Niedermanns, now living near Zurich once more, were especially eager for Richard to enter, and forwarded information, entry forms, and rules for the competition. The new League complex was to be sited on the shore of Lake Leman, facing Mont Blanc, and was to contain a secretariat of 550 offices, a general assembly hall for 2600, and an area of council, committee, press, and public rooms connected to but independent of the other two major elements. There was also to be a library and a restaurant, in addition to parking and service facilities. In August, when the entry forms arrived, Neutra stopped his other jobs and through the fall and winter of 1926–27 devoted himself full time to the project. Initially he had difficulty persuading Schindler to join him. "We still do not know whether Schindler intends to participate," Dione wrote her parents, but while waiting for him "Richard works alone and has already conceived an extraordinarily interesting floor plan and . . . a marvelous elevation. Instead of having the prescribed parking place for 25 cars, he has one for 500 cars, as well as a provision to land airplanes on the water [and] arrival by motor boats. . . ." In Neutra's initial conception, the long rectilinear secretariat and administrative wings were countered by the curvilinear assembly hall, with its rounded, Mendelsohnian lakefront elevation.[3]

In late September Schindler agreed to participate. "At the moment," Dione wrote, "they have excellent contact with each other . . . harmoniously sitting together on a bench . . . their heads in shadow, deliberating." Yet because Schindler, unlike Neutra, had a practice, with other jobs and responsibilities, and enjoyed a strenuous social life besides, his involvement in the League project was less constant than Neutra's. "R. M. Schindler's participation is minimal," Dione wrote the Niedermanns on December 7. "When I have a chance to speak with Richard at 2:00 A.M. and he tells me again: 'Schindler participated only for awhile,' or 'He didn't show up at all,' I feel as if someone had

circle. Directly related, furthermore, to his alleged lack of interest in Establishment commissions was his incapacity—outside his circle—for effective self-promotion. Later, in the 1930s, when goaded by Neutra's spectacularly effective promotional efforts, he occasionally attempted similar hard-sell tactics with pathetically dismal results.[2]

Neutra, on the other hand, was by nature more aggressive. Determined to overcome his own inhibitions and his earlier aversion to marketplace politics, he nervously but stoically pushed himself to seek and finally get larger, more important work. Even more significantly, he was willing and able, via skillful publicity, to maximize and give meaning to what would otherwise have been minor commissions. Slowly, through the years, he balanced his complex personal insecurity with a forced and occasionally strained bravado. Yet, he was not only more personally ambitious than Schindler; he was also more possessed by messianic ideas of a vision, a message, a task to be accomplished, a burden to be borne, a goal to be reached, a cause to be espoused. In order to accomplish such grand am-

hit me over the head. . . . Richard fortunately can take it with humor most of the time. In reality he is delighted to have this . . . task he learns so much from."[4]

Yet though Schindler was able to devote less time than Neutra to the project, Neutra valued his design input and looked upon the final product as a collaborative effort. Ultimately, the curved cantilevered balconies of the lakeshore facade advanced through several stages to assume the more rectilinear configuration of a reverse pyramid with progressively stepped balconies cantilevered over the lake. The style and proportions of these glazed projections, with their subtle provisions for natural indirect "clerestory" lighting, were apparent Schindler trademarks, and likely constituted his major contribution. A noteworthy functional achievement in the vast auditorium, at least as much Neutra's as Schindler's, was a system of acoustical control via movable partitions that could close off sections of the room when it was less than totally filled. To the left of the assembly hall lay a ground-floor restaurant. Two plainer, multistoried, banded-window service and administrative wings connected the assembly with the secretariat. These latter areas and the general layout tended to bear Neutra's stamp. Yet rather than representing a division of labor, the design was apparently a truly cooperative effort, each man contributing to and critiquing the whole. Though they were unsigned, by regulation, to ensure anonymity, Neutra did the elegant presentation drawings and shipped them to Europe. The Niedermanns were to serve as on-the-scene liaison agents.[5]

Neutra had initially been encouraged to participate because of the number of competition jurors publicly committed to modernism, especially H. P. Berlage, of The Hague; Josef Hoffman, of Vienna; and Neutra's old professor Karl Moser, of Zurich. Chairing the jury and serving as a bridge between modernists and traditionalists was the older Belgian *l'art nouveau* architect Victor Horta. Four of the nine jurors favored Le Corbusier's design, which was remarkably similar to Schindler and Neutra's in its general layout and its dual orientation to land and to water. But a stalemate resulted, with unpleasant complications and seemingly endless indecision. Ultimately, out of 377 entries, the jurors awarded nine first, nine second, and nine

third prizes. Nenot and Flegenheimer of Paris and Geneva were declared the winners, with three other first-prize entrants, Broggi, Lefèvre, and Vago, named as collaborators for the final design. Later it was determined that Le Corbusier should also participate, though the architect apparently most significant in influencing the design of the realized building was Joseph Vago of Rome.[6]

Neutra and Schindler's design failed to win any of the twenty-seven prizes. The Niedermanns learned why from Karl Moser's son Werner, whom Mütterli and the Neutras had known at Taliesin. Alfred Niedermann, Mütterli wrote, "visited Moser today and showed him photographs of your project, whereupon Moser said: 'That must be the project which the jurors labeled "the airplane project." I gleaned this from my father's notebook. This project just missed by a hair's breadth winning a prize. As far as I know the jurors could not understand the meaning of the overhanging balconies.'" The senior Moser had furthermore "declared that the Corbusier project really was a good one. . . ."[7]

Yet though Neutra and Schindler's entry

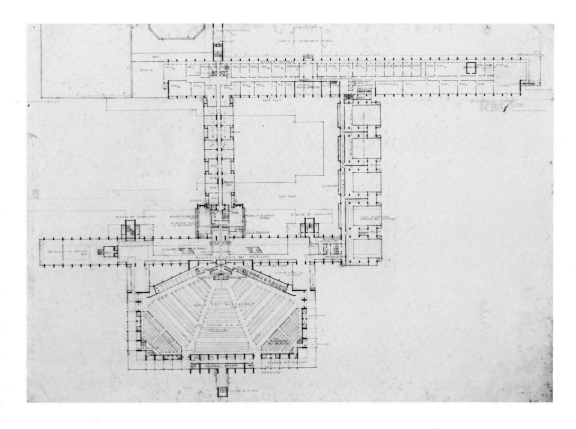

61. *Neutra and Schindler*, final design, floor plan, League of Nations Building, 1926

THEATER & STORE BUILDING — MT. VERNON AVE COLTON CAL FOR MR. H. R. COWAN LOS ANGELES — CALIFORNIA

62. *Neutra*, for AGIC, unbuilt design for Colton Theater, Colton, California, 1927

failed to win an official prize, it *was* selected in 1927, along with two other modernist entries—those of Le Corbusier and of Hannes Meyer and Hans Wittmer, of Basel—for an exhibition sponsored by the German Werkbund. The show opened in Stuttgart July 23, 1927, and then traveled to other major European centers. Since Richard was an ocean and a continent away, the Niedermanns continued to act as European coordinators and, while doing so, committed an egregious error that would gravely affect Neutra's relationship with Schindler. Strongly committed to advancing the career of their now-adored son-in-law, they inferred incorrectly from Dione's earlier letters that Richard had been chiefly responsible for the League of Nations design, and they blithely omitted Schindler's name as coauthor.[8]

When, during the frequent correspondence with his in-laws, Neutra realized that the Niedermanns were calling it the "Neutra project," he cabled them to correct the error. Dione later acknowledged that part of the fault was indeed hers, since in her letters to her parents she had, consciously and unconsciously, emphasized Neutra's role and downplayed Schindler's. But when it became apparent that the Niedermann's were insisting

on the single attribution, she wrote again to urge them to correct it. "We cannot understand that you always speak in your letters of the Neutra project despite Richard's telegrams, in which he clearly requested that it be labeled the Neutra-Schindler project. How can Richard justify this mistake in front of Schindler, who will simply not believe him, although Richard sent you two telegrams. . . ." Alfred Niedermann admitted that he was personally convinced "that you carried the lion's share in this competition and that the mention of Schindler's name is out of propriety," but promised Neutra that he would "take immediate steps to rectify this mistake. . . ." Neutra assumed the change would be made. By that time, however, with the exhibit already mounted, Niedermann was unable—or unwilling—to insist on the change, and the drawings traveled under Neutra's name alone. Though apparently initially satisfied with Neutra's apologetic explanation, Schindler would later cite this "breach of professional ethics" as a major cause of the two men's estrangement. Neutra, he apparently came to believe later, had simply not tried hard enough to counter the Niedermanns' misguided paternalism.[9]

Some of the same factors that motivated Neutra to enter the League of Nations competition also guided his efforts to broaden the scope and enhance the image of his and Schindler's cooperative efforts at home. The need for a name suggesting both larger capacities and better rapport with the American marketplace led to the acronym AGIC—Architectural Group for Industry and Commerce—a name that Neutra, not Schindler, would have tended to dream up. Intended to impress, the name sometimes merely intimidated. As a young apprentice at King's Road, Harwell Harris was instructed to use the firm's full name when answering the telephone. He recalled that this sometimes elicited a pause from the caller, an apology for having dialed an apparently wrong number, and a hang-up click, before the caller could be reassured that this was in fact Schindler and Neutra.[10]

Since Neutra had passed his licensing examination in early 1926—a hurdle that Schindler would not conquer until 1931—the promotional blurb announcing the association could state that AGIC "includes licensed architects as well as engineers and specialists in the design of storefronts, interiors and landscaping, internationally known for the progressive character of their work. . . . Interesting Architecture is the Best Advertising." As part of Neutra's efforts to promote himself and AGIC, he also sought and got, with the early help of Pauline Schindler, lecture engagements with clubs and architectural groups. His lectures on "the new architecture" became popular throughout Los Angeles and would proliferate through the years.[11]

While Schindler continued to deal separately with his independent residential commissions, work of a public, commercial, or industrial nature that found its way to the King's Road office was nominally identified with AGIC. Neutra seems to have secured a large number of these clients—speculative developers, for the most part, whose penchant for taking plunges in real estate was often stronger than their moral scruples, their credit rating, or their willingness and ability to follow through on big dreams. The rather long list of AGIC's unrealized projects ranged from hotels and apartment complexes to office buildings, shops, cafés, theaters, and drive-in markets.

More exotic prospects included an explosives factory of undesignated location and an airport-resort complex to have gone up near Bakersfield. The latter, known as the Falcon Flyers Country Club, was designed as a secluded retreat where sporting, barnstorming pilots could keep their planes and mistresses. Neutra clinched the Falcon Flyer commission through an act of picturesque heroism, as he motored up to Bakersfield on a site inspection visit with the club president, his mistress, and her two pet wolf cubs. When the wolves escaped en route, Neutra dashed into the brush and managed to recapture one. His heroic agility so impressed his clients that AGIC got the commission. Their attraction, however, to his courage—and talent—could not transcend the larger reality of the Falcon Flyers' regularly depleted treasury, and the club was never built.[12]

Though each AGIC project was, no doubt, overseen and critiqued by both Schindler and Neutra, most commissions were—despite the best intentions—the designs of one or the other associate. Each man tended to handle the jobs that he had been responsible for bringing in. Few designs bore the mark of joint authorship as clearly as those for the League of Nations competition. The Effie Dean Café and a resort hotel for Lake Elsinore,

California, were probably all Schindler's, while the "Deco" Colton Theater and the streamlined office building for the National Trading Center were apparently the work of Neutra alone. In such larger and relatively cooperative planning projects as the Richmond, California, Civic Center, AGIC utilized the talents of planner Carol Aronovici. Out of some thirty AGIC projects, only two were actually realized. The Leah-Ruth Shop, a Long Beach fashion boutique (1926), was largely Schindler's job, with minor Neutra input. The reverse was true of their other built structure, the Jardinette apartments, Hollywood (1927), the first major design of Neutra's to be built in America.[13]

The Jardinette was built for an enigmatic developer named J. H. Miller, whom Neutra met at a Hollywood party. Miller envisioned a veritable empire of luxurious Hollywood apartment houses ranging from five to thirteen stories. Similar to each other in plan, configuration, and bold reinforced concrete construction, all of the proposed buildings featured flat roof gardens, bands of steel casement windows, and projecting cantilevered balconies reminiscent of Neutra and Mendelsohn's earlier projects for Palestine. Neutra, for AGIC, prepared elegant renderings and detailed working drawings for half a dozen structures. A thirteen-story luxury building designed for the northwest corner of Franklin and Argyle avenues was to cost $1,050,000. The smaller and more modest five-story prototype Jardinette at the southeast corner of Marathon and Manhattan was projected at $110,000. It contained fifty-five apartments in 30,000 square feet. It was designed in the form of a stubby letter *U*, and the long base of the building was pushed to the back of the property, allowing the shorter wings to enclose a front courtyard. The entrance foyer in the left wing contained stairs and elevators and opened to the corridor leading to the one- and two-bedroom apartments. The building's only overt ornament was a wrought iron *J* and a series of incised lines in the concrete over the entrance porch. The balconies contained built-in planters for flowers.[14]

Had the Miller buildings been completed as planned, AGIC would have reaped handsome fees and Neutra would have accomplished an astonishing design feat. But what Neutra failed to appreciate soon enough was his capitalist patron's shaky

63. *Neutra*, for AGIC, unbuilt design for National Trading Center, Los Angeles, ca. 1927

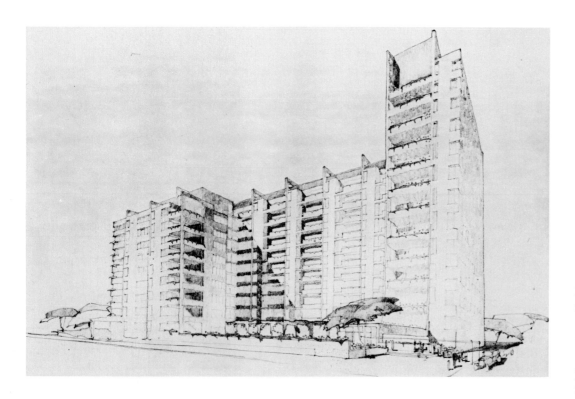

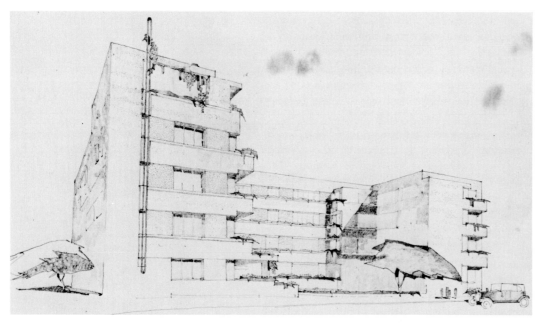

64. *(top)* Neutra, for AGIC, unbuilt apartment design, Los Angeles, 1927

65. *Neutra*, for AGIC, Jardinette Apartments, Los Angeles, 1927

financial base. For before the Jardinette—the first building—was completed, Miller acknowledged the equivalent of bankruptcy by skipping town to escape his creditors. The contractor completed and took control of the building. Miller's fly-by-night tactics left AGIC uncompensated, and the contractor-owner ultimately paid very little. Yet by adroitly managing the subsequent publicity, Neutra made the work "count" in highly significant ways.[15]

A special though unsigned report on the Jardinette in the *Christian Science Monitor*, June 12, 1928, was the first major article on Neutra to appear on the East Coast. In describing the building and its larger *raison d'être* it conveyed the essence of Neutra's modernist message: "Into the modern whirl of machinery comes the demand for better homes within the very network of this industrial mechanism." Neutra's "Jardinette," the unnamed writer believed, was a perfect example of the new trend. "This building is the expression of 1928 and could not have been built 20 years ago." In comparison to the relatively low prevailing standards for housing, "huge industrial plants arise in the latest glories of efficiency. Production attains its maximum in these well-lighted plants where the workers have the latest in modern equipment. Ventilating fans, diffused lighting, efficient arrangements in the executive offices as well as in the production departments, clean walls and floors, conveying systems, hoists and numerous other short-cuts and conveniences lighten the workers' daily tasks. But in another moment the picture may change instantly when the worker goes to his poorly lighted and ill-ventilated house. The new garden apartment house has been designed by Mr. Neutra to bridge the gap between the worker and his place of business. . . . Light and sunshine flood the apartment house and create a new harmony of family life and contentment. . . . Every room," the essay contended, ". . . is as efficiently planned for service as the most modern business office. . . . Everywhere there has been an effort to make the apartments in this building measure up to modern efficiency—and yet preserve the home atmosphere. . . ."[16]

"Imagine the possibility," the article concluded with communitarian visions of "Rush City Reformed," "of seeing an entire city block built up with these garden apartments. . . . These buildings would enclose a large community park area in the

67. *Neutra*, for AGIC, Jardinette Apartments, 1927

66. *Neutra*, for AGIC, Jardinette Apartments, 1927

center of the block for the use of children and other apartment dwellers. Hours of time and labor would be saved by maintaining community laundries, day nurseries, complete garages and equipment, janitor services, and gardeners. With such home and town planning there will be more leisure time for the city dweller. . . . Never before has the architect experienced such a flexibility of choice for expressing the modern conception of the home."[17]

The Jardinette was subsequently published in other American and European journals and elicited high praise from the critic-historian Henry-Russell Hitchcock. "The German magazines as usual have the largest group of interesting modern buildings to offer," he observed in the *Architectural Record*, but he was pleased "to note that the apartments in Los Angeles by Neutra illustrated in *Die Baugilde* are as fine and as modern as any of this German work." The Jardinette publicity also interested Walter Gropius, and when he visited Los Angeles in 1928

he expressed special delight in Neutra's apartment house.[18]

By 1928, however, Neutra was hard at work on what would become his masterpiece—the house in Los Angeles for Philip and Leah Lovell. He met them through Schindler, who had encountered them in the early 1920s. Leah was the sister of Harriet Freeman, a Los Angeles client of Frank Lloyd Wright, and it was through the Wright connection and through various mutual left-wing social and political interests that the Freemans, and then the Lovells, got to know the Schindlers. Leah, a native midwesterner, was a disciple of the liberal educator Angelo Patri and ran a kindergarten with Pauline Schindler based upon his free-association, learn-by-doing methods. A reserved, gentle person, she stood in sharp contrast to her dynamic, athletic, and extroverted husband.[19]

Philip Lovell, a native of the New York area, was a practicing naturopath, an anti-drug physician

68. Philip and Leah Lovell, late 1930s

who advocated "natural" methods of healing and preventive health care with an emphasis on exercise, massage, heat and water cures, open-air sleeping, regular nude sunbathing, and most important, reliance on a natural fresh-food vegetarian diet. Noticeably proud of his fitness and virility, an advocate of free and uninhibited sexual expression, he wrote a widely followed column in the *Los Angeles Times* called "Care of the Body." Indeed, Lovell exemplified what was already becoming—in myth if not reality—the Southern California life style. Yet his élan coexisted comfortably with a Spartan avoidance not only of drugs, but of alcohol, caffeine, and tobacco. With New-York-accented Jewish chutzpah, he expressed his opinions in rough and blustery street talk. He considered himself a "radical" in health and dietary matters and liked to associate with "radicals" in other areas—politics, economics, the arts, and architecture. He and Leah fit comfortably into the King's Road circle, which now included such sophisticated eccentrics as the German art patron Galka Scheyer. At that time, Scheyer was particularly committed to promoting the fortunes of her "Blue Four" expressionists—Kandinsky, Jawlensky, Klee, and Feininger—whose paintings she collected.[20]

In the early 1920s the Lovells lived in a pleasant though undistinguished house in the Hollywood Hills—beautifully sited with a handsome garden overlooking the city. The Schindlers and Neutras were frequent visitors. In the mid-1920s Schindler built three vacation houses for the Lovells in three widely differing Southern California environments. Two were modest—a cabin in the mountains at Wrightwood and a ranch house in the desert, at Fallbrook, near Palm Springs. The third was the epochal Newport Beachhouse. The desert house burned through no fault of Schindler's, but the improperly structured mountain cabin collapsed after a season under the weight of the winter snow. The beach house, however, was made of sterner stuff and lived to become a modernist classic.[21]

To ensure better views, as well as privacy from the public beach, Schindler lifted the main floor a story above the ground on ferro-concrete piers, allowing the beach environment to filter beneath the house. Interior balconies around the large double-story living room led to open sleeping porches, later enclosed as bedrooms. The specially equipped kitchen and bathrooms were designed to meet the Lovell's dietary and therapeutic needs. The decorative patterning of the window mullions recalled Frank Lloyd Wright. Schindler had apparently done preliminary designs for the beach house as early as 1922, but the mountain and desert houses, though designed later, had been completed first. The beach house was finished only in 1926. Neutra did the minimal landscaping.[22]

Schindler and Lovell had also discussed a larger city house, and Schindler had allegedly done preliminary sketches. But in 1927 when Lovell awarded the commission, it went to Richard Neutra. How did this happen? Over the years there emerged a Neutra version, a Schindler version, and several different Lovell versions of the story, leading to varied and sometimes contradictory interpretations. All seemed to agree, however, that by the time the beach house was finished, some degree of friction and tension had developed between Schindler and Lovell. There had indeed been cost overruns, but even more troubling to Lovell than Schindler's casual business attitude were the structural deficiencies that had caused the roof of the mountain house to collapse and the sleeping porches of the beach house to flood in the rainy season. He was vexed by Schindler's ad hoc design methods that allowed him to proceed without detailed working drawings and to alter the structure as construction progressed. For his larger, more important house in the city, which he planned to build on a difficult, sloping site, Lovell could hardly afford to take similar risks.[23]

In addition to the structural and financial problems, however, the Neutras believed there were intensely personal dimensions to Schindler's rift with Lovell. Schindler, Dione had remarked to her mother, had an "erotic makeup" which "confounds American women, who are not accustomed to this. . . . Ghibbeline is jealous and she has every right to feel thus." Despite Philip Lovell's professed liberalism in regard to sexual expression, he resented Schindler's growing infatuation with Leah Lovell, the Neutras insisted, and it was a combination of all of those factors that made him decide to turn to another architect. Sometime during this period Lovell even approached his friend, the traditionalist architect Fred Manhoff, and got from him preliminary designs in the Spanish Colonial Revival mode. But a traditional style must not have seemed right to either of the Lovells' cultivated modernist eyes, and Philip, unable to go with Schindler, turned to Neutra for a modern design.[24]

There were aspects of the two men's temperaments that should have attracted them to each other. Both were ambitious and filled with a sense of mission. "I liked him *despite* his aggressiveness," Lovell later recalled. It might have been more accurate to say he liked him *because* of it. Neutra no doubt ingratiated himself with Lovell as he did with most people who interested and impressed him. And it was likely this personality trait that Schindler remembered when he later suggested that Neutra had "taken" the commission from him. As Lovell had gotten to know Neutra, he had become increasingly impressed with the precision of his building ideas—a quality he found notably missing in Schindler. He had already commissioned Neutra to remodel his medical offices, with highly satisfying results. He would later insist that he believed, not incorrectly, that Schindler and Neutra were partners of sorts. He even apparently agreed that they might collaborate in some way on the design of the city house, but he wanted Neutra to be the architect in charge with whom he, the client, would deal. Later Lovell would deny that there had been any personal rift between him and Schindler, though he never disclaimed the professional vexations. He apparently offered Neutra the job in May 1927, and Schindler, according to Neutra, urged him to take it. Schindler, Neutra insisted, wanted no more to do with Lovell at the time and argued that if Neutra did not take the job, Lovell would give it to someone else. Neutra and Schindler's friend Galka Scheyer also urged Neutra to accept the commission. "I had a good talk with Lovell," Neutra wrote on August 24, 1927, to Dione on vacation, "and proposed quite successfully an agreement with him which he has . . . not yet signed. . . . He gave me in any case an adequate down payment. I have brought him now so far that he feels no personal grudge against R. M. Schindler and has nothing against it that he participates in the design. To be sure, he apparently wants me to be responsible for everything." But Schindler refused to participate.[25]

Neutra spent the fall and winter of 1927–28 on preliminary plans and drawings. On April 2, 1928, Dione summarized the Byzantine chain of events in a letter to her mother: "Richard refused continuously to undertake the design of the new house in deference to Schindler, whom he defended as much as he was capable of. Then Mrs. Scheyer appeared on the scene and thought that Richard's consideration was ridiculous. She worked on Schindler, on Lovell, on Richard, and finally the preliminaries were started. Richard wanted to work with Schindler, tried to involve him, with no success. This you will not be able to understand without knowing Schindler. Mrs. Lovell's sister, Harriet Freeman, has a house by Wright. She detests Lovell and tries to create as much discord in this marriage as she is capable of. She is Schindler's friend and is furious that he is not getting this commission. Yesterday, Lovell spent several hours with us to look at the plans and to discuss the situation. . . . Whatever Richard does is being criticized and ridiculed behind his back, because Schindler could have done it more beautifully. He [Schindler] remains taciturn and smiling. Lovell's advice is to pay not the least attention to what [his wife and Mrs. Freeman have] to say because it is he who makes the decisions. The more his sister-in-law speaks against it, the more he would be for it. . . . It is surely not an atmosphere for creative work. All these matters are very subtle and understandable only to the initiated. It is impossible to talk about it. It is like a tangle in a Dostoevski novel." The "tangle" was further complicated by the growing tension between Schindler and Pauline—a long-smoldering conflict that led the next year to the breakup of their marriage and to Pauline's departure from King's Road and Los Angeles.*

In 1927 Schindler had allegedly wanted nothing further to do with Lovell and had urged Neutra to take the commission. In 1928, as Neutra designed the house, he was "taciturn and smiling." It was only in later years, the Neutras would insist, after the house had become so famous, that Schindler would imply that Neutra had "taken" the commission from him.[27]

The question might be asked: What difference does it make? And the answer must remain: It

* In 1928, she moved to Carmel, where she edited a spirited local weekly newspaper, *The Carmelite*. Robinson Jeffers contributed poems. The photographer Edward Weston and Richard Neutra were listed as contributing editors.[26]

69. *Schindler*, Lovell Beach House, Newport Beach, 1926

70. *Schindler*, Samuel and Harriet Freeman, and Dione Neutra at Lovell Beach House, ca. 1928

71, 72, 73. *Neutra*, Lovell Physical Culture Center, Los Angeles, 1927

and significant house, but it is hard to believe that it could ever have been as significant in his career —or in the history of modern architecture—as the Neutra design became. The undeniable fact is that Neutra got the job and designed and built a remarkable house—both for his clients and for the cause of modern architecture. After his Jardinette apartments, it was the first mature example of the International Style in America.

The Lovell commission bore out Neutra's later contention that in "Southern California, I found what I had hoped for, a people who were more 'mentally footloose' than those elsewhere, who did not mind deviating opinions . . . where one can do most anything that comes to mind and is good fun. All this seemed to me a good climate for trying something independent of hidebound habituation. . . ." As Lovell himself said, "I was not going to build my house the same as the woman from Peoria." In both the beach and city houses, Lovell explained, the two radical young architects had "complete freedom of design. . . . They found in me a very easy mark—as long as they conformed to my [programmatic] idiosyncrasies," particularly open sleeping porches, private areas for nude sunbathing, and special provisions in the kitchen and bathing areas for dietary and therapeutic needs.[28]

Considerably more demanding and challenging for Neutra than the clients' personal "idiosyncrasies" was the difficult site, which Lovell had already chosen and acquired. Situated on a *cul de sac* at the end of Dundee Drive in the Hollywood Hills, it abutted, to the north, the beautiful, natural, city-owned Griffith Park, with views of the city to the south and glimpses of the distant ocean beyond. Just across the canyon to the west lay Frank Lloyd Wright's Ennis house (1924), and a half-mile to the south, was his Barnsdall Hollyhock House (1920), which had brought Wright—and ultimately Schindler and Neutra—to Los Angeles. Upon receiving the Lovell commission, Neutra later recalled, he "went up to the so fateful, spectacular and precarious site . . . and lonely in the midst of my worries, fell in love with it. I told myself that mankind, with a new health and population swell in store, would one day run out of level ground. It would have to build on steepness and on pre-fabricated stilts, with the living area pendant from the roof! Dr. Lovell wanted to be a patron of forward-

matters a great deal. At stake in the controversy is the issue of Neutra's ethical deportment and the tragic erosion of his and Schindler's friendship. Partially because the Lovells offered so many different and contradictory versions of the episode,* Neutra's more consistently argued and documented position emerges, in the long run, as the most logical and plausible. Whatever the motivation for Lovell's giving him the commission, the house was the turning point in Neutra's career. It is hard to imagine his life and *oeuvre* without it. If he did not "steal" the commission, perhaps he should have. Schindler would no doubt have built a beautiful

* See appendix A.

looking experiment. He would be the man who could see 'health and future' in a strange wide-open filigree steel frame, set deftly and precisely by cranes and booms into this inclined piece of rugged nature. . . ."29

Discarded preliminary sketches featured larger and simpler expanses of massing than the complex assemblage of elements in the final design. As such, the early studies predicted Neutra's basic house designs of the thirties. The final, more "industrial" design, on the other hand, was later echoed in such relatively more "institutional" structures as the Corona Avenue School and the Landfair apartment house. Neutra planned the final house on two-and-a-half floor levels. A cut in the

hillside just beneath the street furnished the base for the main middle level. Another cut, one level down, harbored the bottom half-floor of laundry, utility, recreation, and dressing rooms, opening onto the pool. The main entrance to the house was at the top, street level, which contained the family's sleeping porches and enclosed bedrooms—labeled "living rooms" on the plan. The entrance terrace off the Dundee *cul de sac* opened to a hallway leading west to the sleeping quarters and south down the stairway to the main, middle floor. Enclosed by a wall of ceiling-high casement windows looking out on the city, and gently and wittily illuminated by translucently glazed Model-T Ford headlights, the Lovell stairway became one of the grandest and

74. *Neutra*, early design for Lovell House, Los Angeles, 1927

79

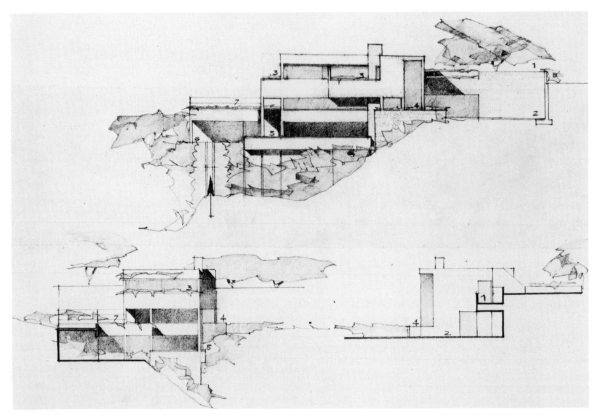

75. *Neutra*, early design for Lovell House,
1927

76. *Neutra*, final design for Lovell House,
1928

most exhilarating spaces in the modern movement repertoire. An expanded, modernist version of a fireplace inglenook offered comfortable lounging near the fire beneath the stairs. A library area, east of the stairs, nestled cave-like back into the excavated hill. The living and dining areas, west of the fireplace, soared out over the hill, completing the south half of the main, middle floor. The northern half of the middle level included guest rooms and baths on the northeast side, kitchen and service areas in the middle, and a screened eating porch on the northwest corner, later enclosed as the main dining room. Planned in consultation with the Lovells' indispensable housekeeper-cook-factotum, Mrs. Westerman, the kitchen had extra-large cutting, washing, and draining areas for the preparation of the family's vegetarian meals. At the foot of the main stairs a doorway opened to a patio and play yard, leading to the garages and to Leah's kindergarten rooms. An earlier version of the plan had placed the garage at the top floor level just off the *cul de sac*. The final location, farther down Dundee Drive, connected it more conveniently to the main middle level, making the now more spread-out composition seem not only larger but more relaxed as well.

Neutra spent most of 1928 designing and planning the house. Unable to find a contractor he believed sufficiently competent and motivated, he in effect became the general contractor himself, directing the subcontractors via detailed specifications and day-to-day supervision. The Palmer House experience had prepared him for this. Contracts were awarded in late 1928. The house was constructed during 1929. "Long before sunrise," Neutra later remembered, "I started to check every one of the thousand pre-punched bolt holes and shop-cut coverplates of my steel window-bearing I-beam columns." Above the heavy ferro-concrete foundation, which harbored the pool, rose the light steel frame that supported the building. It was the first completely steel-framed residence in America. Prefabricated, with a ⅛-inch tolerance, in portable elements transported to the site, the bolted steel frame was assembled in less than forty work hours. The myriad sections of standard, clamped-on casement windows were neatly and effortlessly slipped into place as integrally moduled parts of the surface skin. Interstitial areas of thin steel panels and concrete bands alternated with the larger, more predominating stretches of glass and heightened the effect of industrial assemblage. The bands, furthermore, moved beyond the enclosed volume into the landscape as walls and screens. This proved to

81

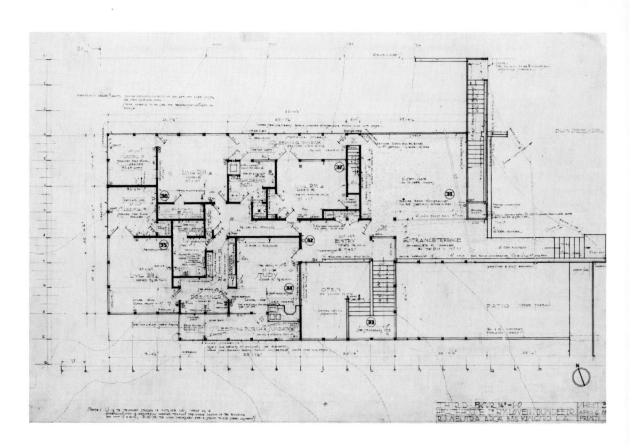

78. *Neutra*, Lovell House, 1927–29, top
floor plan

79. *Neutra*, Lovell House, 1927–29, middle
floor plan

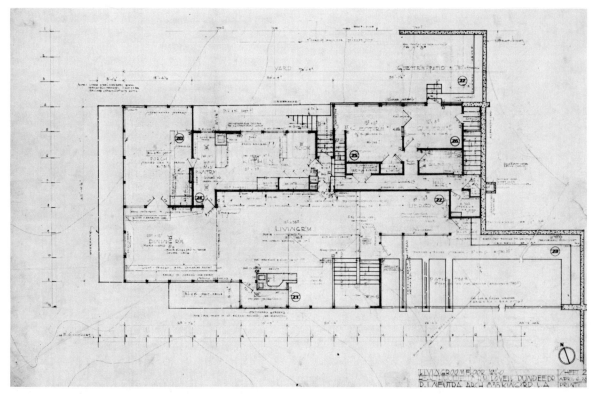

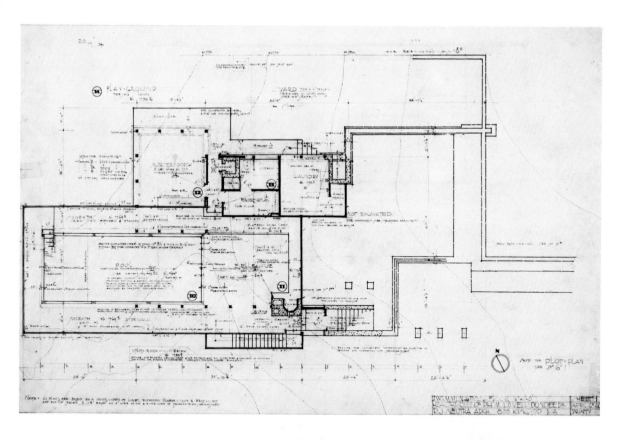

80. *Neutra*, Lovell House, under construction, 1928

81. *Neutra*, Lovell House, 1927–29, lower floor plan

82. *Neutra*, with students from Academy of Modern Art at Lovell House site: 3rd, 4th, and 5th to left of Neutra, Harwell H. Harris, Barbara Morgan, Gregory Ain, 1928

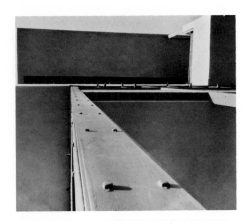

83. *Neutra, Lovell House*, 1927–29, detail

84. *Neutra*, Lovell House, under construction, 1928

be an especially effective element in the play yard area east of the living room. On the pool side they terminated in stunningly articulated upturned edges. The concrete "gunite" was "shot" onto the wire lath by long hoses extending from the mixers on the street. Open-web steel floor and ceiling joists harbored plumbing and wiring. Extended balconies and sleeping porches were suspended—not cantilevered—from the perimeter of the room frame.[30]

Indeed, filled and covered with light concrete, steel, and glass, the frame became the essence of the building. Rhetorically echoing its Chicago School origins, the frame *was* the house; the house *was* the frame. Structurally and esthetically, it gave the house its meaning. Before Neutra decided to defer to programmatic themes and call it the Demonstration Health House, he had labeled it on an early plan a "steel, glass, and shot-concrete residence in Los Angeles," Particularly on the main, image-giving southwest elevation, Neutra assembled those materials into a memorable composition. The balanced asymmetry of its rectangular geometry echoed the patterns and proportions of the abstract canvases of contemporary Dutch painters Mondrian and van Doesburg. Few modernist images attained such a cool and complex elegance.

The news of his disciple's adventurous undertaking elicited a letter from Frank Lloyd Wright: "The boys tell me you are building a building in steel for [a] residence—which is really good news. Ideas like that one are what this poor fool country needs to learn from Corbusier, Stevens, Oud, and Gropius. I am glad you're the one to 'teach' them."[31]

Neutra conceived most of the simple furniture for the house. Beds, banquettes, cabinets, and desks were generally built in, though he also designed free-standing tables and bentwood and tubular-steel chairs. The dominant interior colors were blue, gray, white, and black. Carpets and draperies were gray and beige. The metal trim was gray and most of the painted woodwork was black. The long, handsome living room lighting trough was of polished aluminum. Its light filtered downward through translucent glass panels and was reflected upward against white ceilings and walls. Throughout the interior, green plants enlivened and softened the

85. *Neutra*, Lovell House, 1927–29

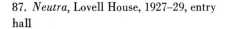
86. *Neutra*, Lovell House, 1927–29, stairway

87. *Neutra*, Lovell House, 1927–29, entry hall

sharp lines. The only jarring note in the crisply elegant geometry of the central living area was the flagstone fireplace, a misplaced legacy of Neutra's veneration for Wright. Later examples of Neutra's work would incorporate such elements more convincingly. Its intrusive presence in the 1929 house served to heighten the purity of the building's otherwise consistent industrial imagery.

The architect also supervised the landscaping. Successive layers of low concrete retaining walls followed the contours of the steeply sloping lot. Subsequently overcome by the rampant foliage, the curving walls furnished a pleasantly lyrical counterpoise to the sober orthogonal lines of the house. Green shrubs and trees were balanced with flowering plants in the blue-purple palette to complement the white-gray-blue-black hues of the façade and the interiors. Wisteria covered the "constructivist" front pergola. The carefully placed exercise and gymnastic equipment took on the character of abstract garden sculpture. Neutra's treatment of the

Lovell landscaping confirmed the effectiveness of his training with Ammann and predicted his continuing success in this area. In his knowledge of botany and his landscape design skills, he surpassed all other major twentieth-century architects.

Though Lovell would later recall it as being considerably more, the total cost of the house and its furnishings—not counting Neutra's fee or the initial cost of the land—ran, according to Neutra's final statement to Lovell, $58,672.32. His fee of 10 percent for designing the house and supervising its construction made the total—exclusive of land cost—come close to $65,000.[32]

As the house neared completion, Lovell could hardly contain his enthusiasm and devoted one of his "Care of the Body" columns to its description and celebration. "For years," he began, "I have periodically written articles telling you how to build your house so that you can derive from it the maximum degree of health and beauty. . . . Always at the end of each article was the thought, 'If I

88. *(Above, left) Neutra*, Lovell House, 1927–29, living room

89. *Neutra*, Lovell House, 1927–29, living room with Neutra furniture

90. *Neutra*, Lovell House, 1927–29, library

91. *(Above) Neutra*, Lovell House, 1927–29, detail of pergola

92. *Neutra*, Lovell House, 1927–29

93. *Neutra*, Lovell House, 1927–29, gym equipment in garden

ever build a home myself—.' " He was pleased to announce that "at last the day has arrived. We have built such a home—a home premised on the fundamental health principles and construction ideas which I have presented in my writings. . . ."[33]

He described in detail the plan, construction, and special facilities of the house. He especially relished the impact it would have on his three young sons: "This home, in a sense, is being built mainly for the little ones. It is really a social school in which they will learn their life habits. Their customs will be molded and shaped therein." The house "has many of the features which schools should have, but most of them do not." It "should be considered from a social sense . . . where friends and kin can gather—where children of the neighborhood will prolong their stay voluntarily." He hoped that Neutra's example would "introduce a modern type of architecture and establish it firmly in California, where new and individualistic architecture is necessary." Because he believed that such architecture was replicable on a more modest scale than that of his own house and because so many of its features could be "incorporated into the humblest cottage," he invited his readers to visit the

house and see for themselves. He and Neutra would be present on four successive Sunday afternoons to conduct personal tours and explain the building's multiple meanings. Officials of the Auto Club would be on hand to conduct traffic up and down the steep, narrow road.[34]

The response to his invitation was overwhelming. Some 15,000 amazed Angelenos poured through the house. For most of them, in 1929, it was simply too much to begin to comprehend. "Moon architecture," Neutra heard someone mutter in a mixture of shock, admiration, and skeptical apprehension. To counter such reservations Lovell wrote a testimonial to Neutra and posted it so prominently that all visitors saw it. "The demonstration of this building," it read, "would not be complete unless I, the owner, stated something publicly concerning Mr. Neutra and his relationship to this house. . . . The architecture he espouses is Modernistic [sic] in more senses of the word than one. That is, it is unquestionably the very best combination of the utmost in utilitarianism and beauty." Neutra "not only spent a year in the preparation of plans, but also made an intensive study of the social uses to which this house is to be put. He diligently ascer-

94. *(Above left) Neutra,* Lovell House, 1927–29

95. *Neutra,* Lovell House, 1927–29, pool, looking toward garage

96. *Neutra*, Lovell House, 1927–29, main entrance

tained the living habits of this family—our likes and dislikes—our prejudices and idiosyncrasies—and conformed his architecture accordingly. . . . Not only were plans drawn to the minutest detail—far more complete than for the average house—a necessary procedure by reason of the unique quality of this home—but he also gave it his constant supervision. . . . Such cooperation is rare, and we, as owners, desire to express this appreciation publicly to him. If we had to build a home over again or if we had to do any other type of construction, there is no architect in the city we would rather choose than Mr. Neutra."[35]

The public tours helped to make the Lovell house a major local news item. With obvious encouragement from architect and client, the Los Angeles papers promoted it intensely—presaging the acclaim it would soon begin to draw from the national and international trade and public press. Neutra himself did not hesitate to publish it in his second book on American architecture, published in 1930 as *Amerika: Die Stilbildung des neuen Bauens in den Vereinigten Staaten* ("America: The Stylistic Development of New Building in the United States"). He continued in the new book to praise and to explicate Schindler's work as he had done in *Wie Baut Amerika?*, while also presenting for the first time to his largely German audience the relatively unknown architecture of the Californian Irving Gill.[36]

He had written the book while completing the Lovell house, and in 1930, exhausted from it all, he decided to take a long working vacation—around the world to Europe via China and Japan. Dione would travel with the children directly across the Atlantic. On May 15, 1930, as he made preparations for the long journey, he sent Philip Lovell his final financial statement and thanked him for the support. "You gave me a chance to convince you—and did not expect me to be a hundred percent perfect, but simply sincere and careful, which I endeavored to be," he wrote. "I shake your hand and wish you happiness in your house and indulgence against your absent architect, who is trusting himself to the winds of the sea to bring the gospel of new architecture to the heathens of the far east."[37]

He sailed the next week for China and Japan and then through the Indian Ocean and Suez Canal to Europe. His seven years in America had been painful, exciting, and productive beyond his dreams. He needed now to ponder them and to contemplate the years ahead. Whatever the trials and triumphs of the past, the future, he was certain now, was always more demanding.

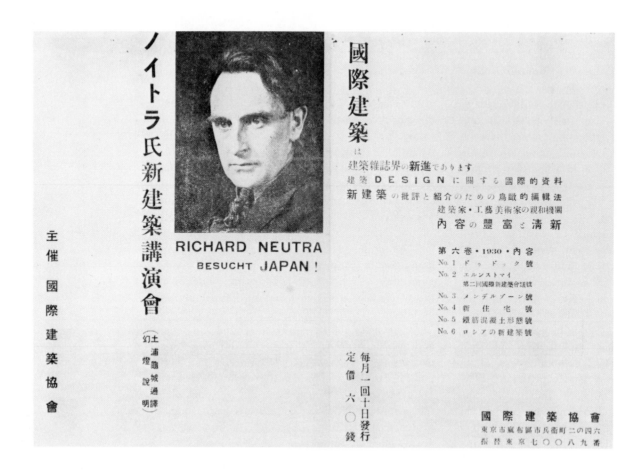

RICHARD NEUTRA
BESUCHT JAPAN!

97. Announcement of Neutra lecture in
Japan, 1930

Confirmation

The appreciative reception Neutra got in the Far East and Europe in 1930 and in the United States, especially New York, soon after confirmed the achievement of his American years and the international reputation he had begun to acquire. The high points of this new recognition included his attendance, as the American delegate, at the 1930 Brussels meeting of CIAM, the Congrès-internationaux d'Architecture moderne, his success the same year as a visiting teacher-critic at the Bauhaus, and his inclusion in the 1932 "Modern Architecture" exhibition at New York's Museum of Modern Art. These and other institutions of modernism helped Neutra to gauge his standing and confirm his relationship with his modern-architectural peers and to participate at the highest level in the international exchange of modernist ideas.

The Pacific voyage on a Japanese steamer was, for Neutra, atypically relaxed and sybaritic. He regretted that, by comparison, many of the Japanese on board exhibited a "Prussian rigidity." "You will be pleased to know," he wrote Dione, "that I am considered to be the best-looking fellow on board. I cannot imagine that I shall ever work again. All concerns having to do with architecture, or any others, except those directly physiological, appear ridiculous to me. These tropical waters may ruin my outlook forever."[1]

Neutra's hosts in Japan were Kameki and Nobu Tsuchiura, whom he had first met at Taliesin in 1924. Impressive posters and flyers announced his well-attended lectures, followed by receptions in Tokyo and Osaka. *Wie Baut Amerika?* had been widely read by Japanese architects and Neutra, to his astonishment, was received as a celebrity. One of his most vocal admirers was a young Japanese architect, Kunio Maekawa, who had studied and worked with Le Corbusier in Paris and would become one of the major links between European and Japanese modernism in the next decades. After meeting Neutra and hearing him lecture on the imperatives and techniques of an industrially prefabricated, essentially anonymous, internationally replicable architecture that would transcend regional boundaries and individual egos, Maekawa wrote an enthusiastic fan letter. "I regret so much," he began, "that I can't well express myself in your beautiful language—it's the only language with which man can sing the jazz. . . . The only thing that I've learned in Europe is that so long as the architects of today will be adhering to their rather romantic title which is 'architect' and which accompanies often so ridiculously heroic childish glory, the modern architecture in its most correct sense will never be attained." During his stay in Europe, Maekawa had found friends and colleagues from all nationalities and "we promised the eternal friendship and the glorious future collaboration. And I was so happy last night to have found one more comrade who are you."[2]

From Japan Neutra traveled to Macao, Hong Kong, Singapore, and the major cities of China. The spacious Portuguese baroque influences on the layout of Macao contrasted sharply with the more complex density of Shanghai and Canton. Neutra especially relished accompanying a Chinese acquaintance he had met aboard ship on a brief visit to his home in a remote village in the province of Kwantung. He recorded his impressions of Asian life and architecture in a series of articles for the Berlin journal *Die Form*. Despite his fascination with China and Indochina, he acknowledged with

98. *Mamaru Yamada,* Electrical Testing
Office, Tokyo, 1929

greater conviction his admiration for Japan. His *Die Form* articles on Japanese architecture stressed his love for the ancient, timeless, tea-house vernacular, as expressed and heightened in such a famous example as the seventeenth-century Katsura detached palace in Kyoto. He also championed the modernist legacies of that tradition that had come forward to clasp hands with the modern movement in the West. He especially admired the machine-like precision of such buildings as Mamoru Yamada's Electrical Testing Office of the Traffic Ministry, Tokyo. Such designs, while reflecting ancient national traditions, could almost have been signed in the late twenties or early thirties by Gropius in Germany, or Neutra in California. The Japanese designers, new and old, Neutra later reflected, worked in an atmosphere "so unbelievably different from my own background, and yet so close to my feelings of treating space and nature or giving emphasis often only by surrounding restraint." He observed with a combination of surprise and *déjà vu* "how the Japanese lightweight house fitted Japanese music and modes of living and privacy, how furnitureless small rooms corresponded to Japanese sociability, manners of eating and diet, as well as to those of dancing and watching the dance. The rich and the poor, the urban wealthy and the peasant, all had the same standard of dimensions, from tatami floor mats, sliding door panels, to tansu, built-in drawer sets. Detailing and finishing were as simple and normalized as they were superbly neat. I had been striving for all that, and I was no longer alone."[3]

From the Far East, Neutra sailed through the Indian Ocean and Suez Canal to Europe, where he met his wife and sons, who had sailed via the Panama Canal across the Atlantic. After a reunion with the Niedermanns in Switzerland, they visited the Neutras and Weixilgärtners in Vienna. There Richard especially enjoyed seeing Marlene Dietrich in Josef von Sternberg's film *The Blue Angel,* little realizing that he would later build a great house for von Sternberg in California. Neutra was particularly pleased to lecture at "the Neue Burg, the Imperial Palace, which all through my youth I had seen under construction. . . . Many people turned up whom I had known as a boy. Now they found that I was speaking with a quaint American accent." Other well-received lectures followed in

Zurich, Prague, Hamburg, Berlin, Cologne, Amsterdam, and Rotterdam. A memorable meeting occurred with Alvar Aalto, "still a young man at that time [who] came to shake hands before I spoke publicly in Frankfurt, and smilingly related how he used *Wie Baut Amerika?* to convert Finns of influence and means to overseas progressiveness." In Frankfurt, Neutra also took note of the housing projects of Ernst May and his socially progressive contemporaries. Neutra's chief regret in this increasingly demanding schedule was his failure to visit Stuttgart and see the Weissenhof *Siedlung,* which he had avidly followed in architectural periodicals.[4]

While lecturing in Basel, Neutra met the enlightened Dutch industrialist and architectural enthusiast C. H. Van der Leeuw, who invited him to visit and give lectures in Holland. Ardently devoted to the support of modern architecture and to the hygienic and psychological welfare of the workers in his Van Nelle chocolate, tea, and tobacco factories, Van der Leeuw had just completed a highly significant complex of new factory buildings in Rotterdam between 1928 and 1930. Designed by J. A. Brinkmann and L. C. van der Vlugt, with major contributions by their associate Mart Stam, the Van Nelle factories gave high priority to the human needs for light and ventilation and to industrial safety and convenience. The sophisticated packaging comprised a handsomely proportioned collage of glazed brick, steel casement windows, metal accoutrements, and other characteristic modernist trademarks. Brinkmann and van der Vlugt had also designed a deluxe modern house for Van der Leeuw where Richard and Dione stayed for a week. "It was the most modern house I had ever dreamed of," Neutra later recalled. "An assembly of technical novelties, from English sheet rubber to cover the floors and winding metal stairways to microphonic conversations at the entrance and from room to room, exhausts for cigarette smoke as soon as it left the mouth; organization down to a complicated dashboard of switches over our guest beds to activate all kinds of illumination, move the window drapes, electronically turn on hot and cold water in the bathroom."[5]

In addition to receiving them in his own house, moreover, Van der Leeuw arranged for the Neutras to spend a night in the even more famous

Schröder house in Utrecht, designed in 1924 by the Dutch *De Stijl* architect Gerrit Rietveld. Neutra was impressed by the intersecting lines and interlocking volumes of Rietveld's constructivism, but the plainer, simpler profiles of the Van der Leeuw buildings—with their explicit deference to physiological needs—appealed even more to his own tastes and convictions. He was similarly moved by the Rotterdam buildings of J. J. P. Oud and by Johannes Duiker and Bernard Bijvoet's Zonnestral sanatorium (1928), which Van der Leeuw took him to visit at Hilversum. These important early contacts with the powerful and generous Van der Leeuw would lead, in the ensuing years, to even more palpable rewards for Neutra—in particular, to the sponsoring of his own house in Los Angeles.[6]

Neutra's Berlin lecture provided the occasion for a polite but strained reunion with Mendelsohn at his sumptuous new villa, "Am Ruppenhorn." But Ludwig Mies van der Rohe—Gropius and Hannes Meyers's successor as director of the Bauhaus—was so impressed with Neutra's Berlin lecture that he immediately invited him to Dessau as a visiting teacher and design critic. Neutra found Mies taciturn but likable. On their first evening in Dessau, Neutra later recalled, "he took us to a fine restaurant downtown and we . . . came home pretty late that night. Discovering that he had misplaced the key to let us into our guest quarters in the main building, we walked around and around but couldn't drum up anyone who was awake. Finally we found an open basement window. With combined muscular force we lowered my bride into the basement in the hope that she would be able to find a way to open an entrance door from the inside. She tried her best, making her way over cellar stairs and through dark corridors, but she could not succeed. While she spent the greater part of the night in the dark basement of the building, we two were walking around outside discussing the future of world architecture."[7]

Though experiencing within its faculty and student body the reverberations of the left-right political tensions that would soon plunge all of Germany into the dark order of Nazism, the Bauhaus in the autumn of 1930 was still the world's seminal institution of modernism. Founded by Gropius in 1919 at Weimar, then forced by pressures from hostile local officials to move to Dessau in 1925, the school had flourished despite all obstacles in the few short years since Gropius had designed the epochal buildings and consolidated his brilliantly controversial faculty. In all areas of design, more than any other institution, it defended and propagated the gospel of modernism.

Though Gropius had resigned the directorship in 1928 to pursue his private practice more intensely, his spirit still hovered over both students and faculty. He had, Neutra believed, "really not forced on them uniformity, in spite of all the programmatics pronounced. . . . The people I knew, saw, and learned to appreciate in the Bauhaus were the most diversified characters one can imagine." Yet while encouraging them to express their individuality in their work and in their teaching, Gropius in his overall architectural design had emphasized "standardized and identical abodes, accommodating the most diversified people, who were certainly not convergent as artists. They were very, very personal and individual in their outlook on art and life." Neutra marveled that such individualists could live in nearly identical dwellings, in view of the opposition to such regularized habitations "for quite ordinary families of coal miners or steelworkers" in America and Europe. Here he failed to realize, as did most of his modernist contemporaries, that such architecture was appropriate for geniuses of the caliber of Paul Klee, Lyonel Feininger, Laszló Moholy-Nagy, Josef Albers, and Marcel Breuer precisely *because* they were so sophisticated and secure in the knowledge and confidence of their own individuality. "Ordinary families," on the other hand, had greater need of an individualist architecture precisely because of their inability to find and express their own personal uniqueness. But Gropius's leadership was also evident in the larger areas beyond design for faculty housing. He was, Neutra believed, "a wizard at fusing the most contrasting metals. With the steady flame and heat of his enthusiasm, he alloyed them into one pot. . . . Balanced collectivity and team spirit was his forte. This was not so pronounced in Mies, in spite of all other timeliness of his work." Though his skepticism of technological panaceas would increase in later years, Neutra was impressed in 1930 with the still prevailing "hopefulness of the Bauhaus movement, which actually believed that modern technology could give us humans all we need."[8]

99. *Brinkman and Van der Vlugt*, Van der Leeuw House, Rotterdam, Holland, with predictions of Neutra's later spiderleg outrigging, 1928

95

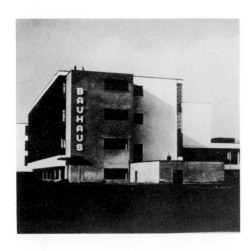

100. *Walter Gropius*, Bauhaus, Dessau, 1925

101. Neutra being met by Bauhaus students at Dessau Train Station, 1930

In their month at the Bauhaus the Neutras particularly enjoyed the company and the teaching of Klee, Albers, Feininger, and Moholy-Nagy. Dione later recalled a brilliant class of Albers's which dealt with folded paper designs. Klee, she remembered, analyzed each student's work with the careful attention an art historian might give to famous ancient masterworks.[9]

An important Bauhaus interest in the fall of 1930 was the international theater competition for Kharkov in the USSR, and Neutra used this problem as the main project for his studio. His and his students' ultimate solutions echoed aspects of his and Schindler's 1926 proposals for the League of Nations General Assembly. It would also foreshadow several of Neutra's own later theater designs, with its provisions for multidirectional covered and outdoor stages.[10]

Neutra's reputation as a teacher was confirmed by Virginia Weisshaus, the American wife of Bauhaus composer Imre Weisshaus, when she solicited opinions from several of Neutra's former students. Most, she reported, were "tremendously enthusiastic about you and said that it was marvelous," though one commented that "we never had to work so hard for anyone else."[11]

Before Neutra left Dessau, he and Mies discussed ways in which the Bauhaus system might be introduced into the United States. Neutra, it seemed to Mies, would be the ideal person to propagate the idea, and he issued a published statement, in English, to that effect. "The emancipation of the constructive arts from provincialism is highly desirable," it began. "It seems now an idea of best consequence to have this institution paralleled by a similar one on the other great continent with which the European school would work in strict cooperation and to mutual benefit. Students and professors should be exchanged for periods, methods in the construction practice of both continents, building laws and the customs in financing building activity should be critically compared, while they are demonstrated to the young men in courses of both schools. . . . Richard J. Neutra, the progressive American architect who has taught Architecture both in the European Bauhaus as in the U. S. was delegated to develop preliminary plans how to promote in America the idea of such cooperation." Yet despite Mies's endorsement and Neutra's subsequent

efforts to effect the planned union, such developments were halted by the deepening economic crisis in both America and Germany and the rapidly deteriorating German political situation. In October 1932 local Nazi opposition forced the school to move from Dessau to Berlin, and in April 1933, not long after Hitler's accession to power, the Bauhaus was permanently closed.[12]

Though the invitation to teach at the Bauhaus had come suddenly and unexpectedly in 1930, it rivaled and perhaps surpassed in significance the occasion for which Neutra had rationalized the trip to Europe—the third annual meeting of CIAM. The founders of CIAM, led by Le Corbusier and the Swiss critic-historian Sigfried Giedion, had issued a ringing declaration of principles at the 1928 organizational meeting in La Sarraz, Switzerland. These included the increasingly familiar rejection of historic styles and "antiquated formulas" and the now-standard paeans to "rationalization and standardization." Indeed, the founders asserted, "the intention that brings us together is that of attaining a harmony of existing elements—a harmony indispensable to the present—by putting architecture back on its real plane, the economic and social plane." The 1929 meeting at Frankfurt am Main took as its theme low-cost housing—the forte of its city architect, Ernst May. Neutra, already listed as CIAM's official American representative, contributed a paper in absentia.[13]

CIAM III, meeting in Brussels in 1930, focused on the related theme of the land planning and spatial organization of housing, with particular attention to the issue of low-rise "garden city" sprawl versus high-rise urban density. While both favored the latter in varying forms and degrees, Le Corbusier and Neutra reiterated in their conference papers the thrust and tone of their earlier, longer books. In his poetic affirmation of the functional beauty and power of high-rise towers in park-like green space, Le Corbusier's paper echoed many of the sentiments of his *Vers une Architecture* (1923) and his later writings on the "Radiant City." Neutra's less visionary, more pragmatic call for a combination of low- and high-rise buildings likewise recalled his arguments from *Wie Baut Amerika?* In both his book and his paper at Brussels, Neutra regaled his audience with descriptions of what was then still considered the new and amazing phenomenon of large-scale, high-rise American building construction.[14]

Though the Brussels meeting was the last CIAM conference that Neutra would attend, he continued through the years to follow its deliberations on the nature, the problems, and the future of modern architecture. His relationship with Giedion, the CIAM secretary, would also flourish as the Swiss critic became one of Neutra's ardent champions. Neutra especially valued the chance that the Brussels meeting gave him for renewing his ties with Gropius and for meeting and conversing with Le Corbusier. He particularly enjoyed visiting, with the Swiss architect, the famous 1906 Stoclet house in Brussels. Designed by the Viennese Wagnershule, *Sezessionstil* architect Josef Hoffmann and decorated by Gustav Klimt and the Wiener Werkstätte, the Stoclet house was a symbol of Neutra's national artistic heritage. Trained as a student to appreciate it through photographs, he now, upon seeing it, affirmed his loyalty to its principles.[15]

After the Brussels conference Neutra sailed for the United States. Dione stayed behind to take Frank, their mentally retarded seven-year-old son, to Vienna for psychiatric observation by Sigmund and Anna Freud. Owing to Richard's long friendship with the family, the Freuds took a special interest in the illness of the child, but they were unable to offer a cure for what was essentially a physiological problem. They did recommend, however, that the Neutras attend to Frank at home, rather than institutionalize him. This decision the Neutras later came to regret, since it had, they believed, no real effect upon Frank's condition and consumed time and energy that could have been devoted to Dion's development and to Dione's career as a musician. In the early 1940s, Frank was committed to a home for the mentally ill.[16]

"This trip has not been 100 percent successful," Neutra wrote to Schindler as he left for America in December 1930. "Above all, we have not arrived anywhere in this miserable affair with Frank." He was also less than "100 percent" sanguine about the current state of European civilization. "I have seen a lot of colleagues, many fools and a few serious men. There was a catastrophic slump all over Europe this fall. . . . Central Europe is the worst, although the external appearance of Berlin and even Munich is rather good. Much

traffic, much neon . . . and shining amusement places. . . ." Their native city of Vienna, Neutra felt, "really is impoverished. . . . At the same time I am not hopeless at all for the future of this city. But the future certainly will be different [from] the past. Another type of life and of society. The municipal dwellings are not as bad as I expected. . . . The buildings are executed in a more reliable way than the corresponding enterprises in Germany. Most of the sixty thousand dwellings are awfully small and incomplete. But life in them is much better than in the previous tenement type."[17]

Though throughout their first seven years in America the Neutras had indeed considered returning to Europe permanently, their visit in 1930 convinced them otherwise. The modernist avant-garde was larger and more successful there, but the prospects for work in Depression Germany seemed almost as bleak as in Depression America. And the Neutras sensed as well the darkening European political atmosphere. In contrast to the old, cold beauty of Germany, sunny California seemed once again to call them. It seemed, in fact, a better place to be poor. Neutra realized, however, that he must broaden his contacts beyond California, and to further this end he planned to stop for a month or so in New York.

Aboard ship in early December 1930, he pondered the immediate and the more distant future. "What is in the offing?" he wrote Dione. "The famous Modern Architect has no office, no organization, no jobs. Where can he rest his weary head? Just as I did in 1923, so I do now. I swim toward the U.S.A." New York has "a few editorial offices where one has made a note that I am supposed to be a West Coast sensation. . . . If I did not have this ridiculous prestige, it would perhaps be easier. On top of it all, there is this depression and fear of a crisis. I feel as if I were one single man against a continent. However, I have sowed so diligently, I should at least try to harvest."[18]

In New York he rented a tiny room in Henry Menkes's apartment house, as he had done seven years earlier. In an effort to "make contacts" for lecture engagements, for publication of his work, and ultimately for new commissions, he devoted most of December 1930 to the tedious process of self-advertisement. He started each day, he wrote Dione, "looking up telephone numbers in the huge

102. Neutra and students in Bauhaus Studio, 1930

103. *Neutra*, bus design, 1931

such quarters for the even more luxurious warmth of Florida vacations.[20]

The degrees and varieties of squalor appalled him: "Where, I ask myself despondently, are the rundown females? Those older ones or those who possibly have children?" Indeed, there did not seem to be any place for them. "Females, who have no place to stay, put a nickel into the subway turnstile and ride all night from Brooklyn to the Bronx and back again. . . . Here one does not think much about women, as one does in Florida, where they are beautifully dressed and promenade and flirt along the beach wall or alternately dance tango or ragtime with a tanned fortune hunter. . . . These are simply facts and 100 percent cheerless," he noted. "In any case, what a comic contrast when I take a meal for which I do not pay in one of those expensive Tuxedo Clubs, put on airs and try to make an impression. . . ."[21]

Yet by the beginning of 1931, Neutra's new quest for contacts had begun to yield results. He had met, among others, the critic Lewis Mumford, the architects Raymond Hood, Jacques Ely Kahn, Joseph Urban, Ralph Walker, and Buckminster Fuller, and the artists and designers Bruno Paul, Rockwell Kent, Paul Poiret, and Lucian Bernhard. On January 4, 1931, the latter four designers sponsored a lecture by Neutra on "The New Architecture" under the aegis of Contempora, Incorporated, their organization of "International Service of Art to Industry." On the following three successive days Neutra inaugurated Joseph Urban's recently completed auditorium at the New School for Social Research with well-received lectures on "The Relation of the New Architecture on the Housing Problem," "The American Contribution to the New Architecture," and "The Skyscraper and the New Problem of City Planning." In the latter he inveighed against the proliferation of skyscrapers in the downtown areas of cities like New York while adequate sites for lower buildings were readily available in the nearby "slums." His lectures received prominent coverage in the *New York Times* and the *New York Post*, the latter describing him as "the new type of Viennese. You will not find his like in the pages of Schnitzler or Herman Bahr. A lean, long-faced zealot, he is full of feverish energy and has very little of his countrymen's once-famous Gemütlichkeit."[22]

New York directory. . . ." Then, after making appointments, "I travel long distances to get an address, speak extensively to a vast assortment of people who usually have no time for me, do not understand what I am driving at, who tell me a lot of irrelevant matters, are *occasionally* willing to listen in a friendly way and write down my telephone number. . . . This procedure is obscure and doubtful, but the experts tell me it would be more questionable to sit somewhere unshaved and draw or develop ideas if one wants to make a career and provide a living for one's wife and children."[19]

While pursuing these frequently elusive "contacts" in the New York worlds of art, architecture, business, and journalism, Neutra could not refrain from observing the darker worlds of depression, poverty, and despair. By contrast, his own problems seemed relatively benign. Again his insightful letters to Dione revealed his knack for social observation. In the nearby Lower East Side slums, for example, he found "very little illumination, dilapidated fronts with dirty windows, rusted fire escapes. . . . I wandered toward the Bowery. Not one female in sight, only men, men, men. Some drunk, some reeling. Those that vomit into the gutter or elsewhere are increasing. . . . On every corner, someone is selling apples . . . and most people of a certain kind nowadays seem to subsist on apples." By contrast, he noted, "many shiny automobiles quickly traverse this huge proletarian quarter toward the Williamsburg Bridge." He was impressed not only by the fact that the shiny cars conveyed their passengers to comfortable and even luxurious quarters, but by the grimmer irony of the richer classes fleeing

Neutra's illustrated lectures of his and others' work also brought him to the attention of the New York Museum of Science and Industry, which commissioned a scale model of the Lovell Health House to conclude its exhibit of human habitations from cave dwellings to the present. Museum director C. R. Richards chose the house as "the most convincing and rational specimen of the new architecture . . . because of the enthusiastic recognition accorded it in Paris, Berlin, New York, and Tokyo."[23]

During his months in New York, Neutra also negotiated with Walker, Urban, and Kahn of the New York Architectural League about the inclusion, in the League's 1931 show, of several architects from Southern California, including Schindler, J. R. Davidson, Kem Weber, Lloyd Wright, and Neutra. He corresponded with Schindler at some length about such details as space allotment and the mounting of exhibits. "It is too bad the League accepted your work," Philip Johnson wrote Neutra from the Museum of Modern Art, "so that we could not take it and put it in our Show where it would have been seen better. As you know, they hid your photographs as much as they could and when I talked with Ralph Walker afterwards he told me he did not think that kind of stuff was architecture." Johnson promised Neutra he would get better treatment in the forthcoming architecture show that Johnson's museum would sponsor.[24]

The most financially remunerative and professionally gratifying connection Neutra made in New York was with Philip Johnson's father, the lawyer and financier Homer H. Johnson, of Cleveland. Johnson was a corporate attorney and large shareholder in the young but growing Aluminum Corporation of America, and he planned for Alcoa to participate with the White Motors Company in the design of a new aluminum bus. By this time Philip Johnson was well into planning, with historian Henry-Russell Hitchcock, the Museum of Modern Art's "Modern Architecture" exhibition, scheduled to open in 1932 and to include among others, the work of Neutra. And when the senior Johnson asked son Philip to suggest a designer for his new bus, Philip recommended Neutra. The flabbergasted Neutra later admitted that at the time he knew nothing about bus design, but knew he could learn. He was flattered by the offer and de-

104. *Neutra*, bus design, 1931

lighted with what, during the early Depression, was an extravagant fee. He was housed in Johnson's private club in Cleveland and was paid $150 a day. Despite his alleged impatience with high society, he enjoyed hobnobbing with the Johnsons and the Cleveland Establishment in a rented tuxedo.[25]

Homer Johnson thought it important to bring in an outside designer to confront the relatively conservative in-house designers at White Motors, who, jealous of Neutra's invasion of their territory, tried to resist him in every way possible. "I have drawn up beautiful buses," Neutra wrote his mother-in-law, against "the involved special interests of the various bureau chiefs. . . . The chassis specialist advises me to round out, make the rear more exotic; that affects only the body designer and not him, but the radiator cannot be tampered with under any circumstances. . . . I have discussions with the bumper, the aluminum seat and upholstery experts," and so on. Yet Neutra also understood that it was important that his new "Pullman of the Highway" not be so structurally or stylistically radical or so far ahead of current taste that White Motors or future customers would resist it as unsuitable or unrealistic. "Do not believe," he had written to Schindler in an early description of the project, that "great departures from the normal will be admissible." Therefore the designs were only slightly more "streamlined" and sophisticated than other buses of the period—considerably less futuristic, for example, than the slightly later unbuilt bus designs of Norman Bel Geddes. Still, Neutra's designs were advanced for their time in their relatively clean lines, their upswept rear ends, and the wavy streamline of the front cab roof. Neutra produced several different variants. The bus, however, was never manufactured. This was due in part to the foot-dragging resistance of the White Motors production chiefs, and to the steadily worsening Depression and various other factors that worked against a single, standardized, prefabricated design.[26]

In Cleveland, as elsewhere, Neutra was fascinated with the vagaries of the cultural and physical landscape and with what he perceived to be peculiarly "American" phenomena. He was intrigued, for example, by the advertisement of a large, downtown Protestant congregation brazenly offering "Spiritual Surgery" to its communicants. He was, likewise, amused and puzzled by "Sylvia's Charm School." What "in Heaven's name," he asked, "is a 'charm school'? Too bad that it is dark inside the glass door. I would like to ask the price of a cram course. . . . I speculate whether Sylvia would admit me as a student." When he was not being entertained *gratis*, Neutra slipped around the corner from Johnson's posh Union Club and saved his salary and expense allowance by eating in a diner. It was, he explained to Dione, "an imitation of a railway coach where one sits at a long counter and watches the cigarette-smoking cook while he prepares hamburgers. The principal customers are taxi drivers and occasionally an old prostitute. The already-in-Cleveland-well-known-Viennese architect is an unknown habitué in this place and saves money so that his beloved Dione . . . can join him again. . . ." Indeed, Neutra's savings from his Cleveland salary furnished his and his family's chief means of support for nearly a year.[27]

After lecture engagements in Detroit, Chicago, and San Francisco, Neutra returned to Los Angeles in April 1931. Two of his former students from the short-lived Los Angeles Academy of Modern Art, Harwell Harris and Gregory Ain, met him at the station. When the Neutras had left for Europe in the summer of 1930, they had not known exactly how long they would be gone, though they realized correctly it would be close to a year. Consequently they had given up their apartment at King's Road, which Schindler, in their absence, had naturally rented to someone else. To house his family and his work, Neutra soon located an acceptable—if

decidedly unmodern—turn-of-the-century California bungalow on North Douglas Street in the Echo Park district of Los Angeles. Here he would live until late 1932, when he would complete his own new house in the nearby Silverlake district. In the Douglas Street house he installed his studio, where he and several eager student apprentices—Harris, Ain, and Raphael Soriano—worked, without pay, on the ever-developing visionary landscapes of "Rush City Reformed." They also endeavored to translate Rush City into several actual competition projects, the most noteworthy, though unsuccessful, of which was for the Lehigh Portland Airport Competition.[28]

Harris appreciated Neutra's then-advanced perception of the extent to which "airports would become parts of the world-wide system of transportation. Of course airports would be shaped by the size and nature of planes. They would be shaped also by cities and cities' systems of transportation. What would be needed would be not airports nor air terminals but air transfers—places where one . . . leg of transportation stopped and another took over. . . . The design of the air transfer," Harris realized, was "part of the design of the city and region. So the number of factors affecting its design was now a thousand times greater than it was when we looked at the project alone and considered only what could be learned from reading, from flying and from talking to the airport manager at the infant [local] Mines Field. . . . Altho Ain and I were devoting ourselves wholly to it, it was Neutra who was directing it. The marvelous thing was that Neutra was doing his thinking, his musing, his proposing, his adopting, his rejecting with Ain and me as ringside watchers. As Neutra weighed his moves, we weighed them too. Neutra's decisions were then our decisions. In this Neutra was the perfect teacher. In watching him work, we learned in a few weeks what would have taken years had we been left to fumble our way to it."[29]

Other similarly exciting projects had followed the Lehigh Air Transfer designs in those lean years of the early thirties. In connection with Neutra's involvement as the chief American member of CIAM, he and Harris developed two documents that typified Neutra's broad, visionary thinking. To one of these Neutra gave the very Germanic designation of Minimum Existence Correlation

Chart, "with which to judge the efficiency of our designs and compare their efficiency with that of the Europeans. Bases for comparison were family size, area, cube, cost and rent." The other project was in response to a CIAM call for each national group to replan one of its cities in accordance with the most advanced thinking of the day. "Accordingly," Harris recalled, "we replanned Los Angeles as we imagined it might be in 1950 [which] was so remote and shrouded in mists one could imagine anything possible. . . ." In the central business district of this Los Angeles plan, "the twelve-story buildings were elevated to leave the ground free for vehicles. They were long, thin slabs oriented to catch the sun and spaced to insure their getting it. Shops were at second and third story levels and bordered by elevated pedestrian walks. Walks became bridges at cross streets. Streets carrying thru traffic became tunnels under other streets. Radial and circumferential boulevards, together with surface and sub-surface rails, linked together the central and outer city and the air transfers linking them with other cities. These and other projects of these early years became part of Rush City Reformed."[30]

In addition to his savings from the Johnson bus commission, Neutra's only other sources of income in 1931 were lecture fees and pittance wages from several short-run, part-time teaching jobs. Neutra taught courses for one semester at the Los Angeles College of Architecture and Engineering in architectural design, theory, and history. In the summer of 1931, Neutra and Schindler joined forces once again to teach "a course in the Fundamentals of Modern Architecture" at the older and more established Chouinard School of Art. "A seminar and two periods of practical design in the drafting room, with criticism," the brochure read. "Special consideration will be given to the dwelling and the design of its interior furnishings. The course will stress the attitude of the creative planner rather than the purely aesthetic reaction of the onlooker." The course was poorly attended and folded after one session. "Can you imagine the following situation?" Dione wrote her sister Verena. "Twice a week Richard participates with Schindler in an evening seminar. For months the school advertised all over the country. The net results are eight students. This gives you a slight indication

of the chances modern architecture has here. However, where is it better? Perhaps in Germany Richard's work would be appreciated." In 1932 the College of Architecture of the University of Southern California announced that Neutra would teach a course in architectural design, provided that a minimum of twelve students enrolled. The course failed to attract the necessary minimum and was canceled before it began. None of Neutra's teaching in the early 1930s, in fact, repeated the success of the first course he had taught in 1929 at the short-lived Academy of Modern Art. There, in addition to Harris and Ain, his students had included the future critic and photographer Willard Morgan, his wife, the photographer Barbara Morgan, and their friend, the painter Anita Delano, later an art professor at UCLA. Neutra had involved the students in the construction phase of the Lovell house—an enviable laboratory for the aspiring young modernists.[31]

In her Christmas letter of 1931, Dione wrote Frances Toplitz that "alas we have nothing enjoyable to report. This life of no work is very hard on Richard. He is very busy always, but nothing which brings in any money and this waiting, one does not know for what, gets on our nerves, sometimes. I wish there would be a reason for his going to New York or Chicago, where chances seem to be better; we realize more and more that we do not know anyone of importance here; it is such a strange town." In a letter to her sister Verena about their depressed condition, Dione warned that "your European conviction that [Richard] will be rich one day is too painful at the moment. He is not a fashionable architect. He is an experimenter, way ahead of his time. . . . Nevertheless we often are very happy together. It surely is a fact that women here work much more than they do in Europe; on the other hand we live a kind of picnic life and this I enjoy. . . ."[32]

Despite the lack of work, however, Neutra still managed to keep his name and his modernist message in full public view. "Architect Back From Long Tour" read a headline in the *Los Angeles Times* in the spring of 1931. "After touring Europe and the Orient for the past eleven months," the article announced, "where he was invited to lecture in many countries and capitals on progressive architecture, Richard J. Neutra, Los Angeles architect, has just returned to his home . . . more fully convinced than ever that it will not be long before the whole world will 'go modern' in home construction and design."[33]

The strongest confirmation of Neutra's achievement in that frustrating period of increasing fame and diminishing commissions was the Museum of Modern Art's inclusion of his work in its 1932 "Modern Architecture" exhibit. Museum director Alfred Barr's foreword to the exhibit catalogue reiterated the attributes of the "new architecture," which curators Hitchcock and Johnson had already labeled the International Style "because of its simultaneous development in several different countries and because of its world-wide distribution. . . ."[34]

"Both in appearance and structure," Barr noted, "this style is peculiar to the twentieth century and is as fundamentally original as the Greek, Byzantine or Gothic." Its esthetic principles, he asserted, "are based primarily upon the nature of modern materials and structure and upon modern requirements in planning. Slender steel posts and beams and concrete reinforced by steel have made possible structures of skeleton-like strength and lightness. The external surfacing materials are of painted stucco or tile, or in more expensive buildings of aluminum or thin slabs of marble or granite and of glass both opaque and transparent. Planning, liberated from the necessity for symmetry so frequently required by tradition is, in the new style, flexibly dependent upon convenience." The new architect "thinks in terms of *volume*—of space enclosed by planes or surfaces—as opposed to *mass* and solidity. This principle of volume leads him to make his walls seem thin flat surfaces by eliminating moldings and by making his windows and doors flush with the surface. . . . He permits the horizontal floors of his skyscraper and the rows of windows in his school to repeat themselves boldly without artificial accents or terminations. And the resulting *regularity*, which may in itself be very handsome, is given accent by a door or ventilator, electric sign, stair tower, chimney or fire escape, placed asymmetrically as utility often demands, and the principle of *flexibility* permits." Beauty in the new style "depends upon technically perfect use of materials whether metal, wood, glass or concrete; upon the fineness of proportions in units such as doors and windows and in the relationships between

these units and the whole design." Only by pondering these principles, and the models and photographs of the exhibit illustrating them, Barr concluded, could one "understand what is meant by the International Style and how it differs from the modernistic or half-modern decorative style, which with the persistence of the revived styles of the past, has added so much to the confusion of contemporary architecture."[35]

Though it included photographic examples of designs by nearly fifty architects from sixteen countries, the show focused on the work of five Americans and five Europeans. Frank Lloyd Wright was included, not as a practitioner but as a "father figure" and progenitor of the new style. Indeed, "as the embodiment of the romantic principle of individualism, his work, complex and abundant, remains a challenge to the classical austerity of the style of his best younger contemporaries." Of 'these, Le Corbusier was seen as "the greatest theorist, the most erudite and the boldest experimenter"; Gropius, "the most sociologically minded"; Mies van der Rohe, "the most luxurious and elegant"; and Oud, as possessing "the most sensitive and disciplined taste." Otto Haesler was featured as "the foremost housing architect in Germany and perhaps the world."[36]

The Americans included the Philadelphia firm of George Howe and William Lescaze, whose stunningly modern Pennsylvania Society for Savings skyscraper was just nearing completion; the Bowman brothers, of Chicago, whose "thorough study of steel construction in relation to architecture . . . may revolutionize certain phases of American architecture within the next few years"; and Raymond Hood, of New York, whose newest skyscrapers had, the curators believed, retrieved him from the depths of traditional eclecticism and brought him to the forefront of the modern movement in America. Hood's inclusion, however, seemed the most arbitrary and suspect to such doctrinaire modernists as Van der Leeuw, who refused, as a result, to become a patron of the exhibit. "They asked me to join the committee," he wrote to Neutra, "but I told them I could not possibly lend any hand if people like Hood would exhibit; only if there were *really* modern European and American architects." As a champion, furthermore, of the more *sachlich* practitioners such as Gropius, Oud, and Neutra, Van

105. *Neutra*, "Rush City Reformed," late 1920s, Ring School Plan

der Leeuw also regretted that Johnson was so "much impressed by Mies van der Rohe, whom he considers the greatest European modern architect. I do not. Well, anyway, he is helping things with his enthusiasm. . . ."[37]

All of Johnson and Hitchcock's essays on the featured architects were relatively critical. Hitchcock thought, for example, that the exterior of Neutra's Lovell house had "more complexities than are required by the plan so that the general effect is lacking in serenity." Still it was "without question, stylistically the most advanced house built in America since the War." In his Jardinette apartments Neutra had, Hitchcock believed, achieved "the first practical application in America of a consistent scheme of design based on modern methods of construction. The ribbon windows are splendidly used; but the attempt to make the bands continuous around the facade by painting the occasional intervening wall sections black is a trick of design which is hardly frank." He gave an equal amount of positive and negative criticism to Neutra's Zehlendorf housing and Ring Plan School. Alfred Barr concluded that Neutra was, partially due to his writing, "among American architects . . . second only to Wright in his international reputation" and without a doubt "the leading modern architect of the West Coast."[38]

Neutra was delighted with the show and the catalogue and acknowledged to Hitchcock that he agreed with most of his critical judgments. He also appreciated the correctness of Hitchcock's statement that "my way as a naturalized citizen and architect . . . has not been so clear and easy. Still I could not have made equally specific progress with European materials and for European purposes and in this sense, one may be permitted to consider me an American. . . ."[39]

In reviewing the show for the *New York Times,* the critic H. I. Brock spoke for most contemporary observers in finding the work generally exciting, frequently beautiful, and occasionally forbidding. He also offered what would come to be the major criticisms of the International Style through the years. He especially challenged the assertion of the sponsors that "where function is straightforwardly expressed, one type of building will not be confounded with another." Brock disagreed, and argued that in fact "it is very hard to

tell any building from any other building or guess the function of any building. A church and a factory are easy to confuse. . . . The machine-made notion of 'function' cannot obscure the fact that the historically true function of a church is to excite and keep alive religious emotion. That being the case, 'allusion to the past' may not be airily swept aside as no part of a 'straightforward' solution to the problem of church architecture."[40]

After leaving New York the exhibition traveled to Hartford, Cambridge, Worcester, Philadelphia, Buffalo, Rochester, Cleveland, Cincinnati, Toledo, Chicago, and Los Angeles. Neutra was instrumental in recruiting the California sponsors. Unable to persuade the Los Angeles County Museum of Art to host the exhibit, he arranged for a showing in the elegant and fashionable Bullock's-Wilshire department store. Designed in the late 1920s by the Los Angeles firm of Parkinson and Parkinson in the style known variously as Art Deco and zigzag moderne, the store typified, ironically, the "modernistic" or "half-modern decorative style" that the Museum of Modern Art show had castigated. Arriving in the summer of 1932, the show coincided with the Los Angeles–based Olympics, and was treated with considerable fanfare by the Los Angeles press. In connection with the exhibit, Neutra gave three lectures and numerous interviews. As a result, Dione wrote to Frances Toplitz, he had become increasingly "a figure of importance, is invited to dinners, openings and such occasions and has to wear his evening clothes quite often."[41]

As usual, Neutra handled the publicity adroitly, constantly reiterating the idea of "modernism" and challenging Los Angeles to support its development. "I am sorry," he noted in a typical interview, referring to Schindler and to other contemporaries, "that out of the fine and unique work which Los Angeles has produced through a good number of architectuarally gifted brains . . . not more has been picked out by the New York jury; but it is gratifying that our city has been given a place in this international contest." The exhibit included only his and Wright's California work. Schindler's exclusion was yet another confirmation of the widening differences between his and Neutra's work and of the growing distinction in their architectural identities.[42]

In their earlier contacts with Schindler, Hitchcock and Johnson had experienced personal as well as professional differences. Schindler had been greatly annoyed with Hitchcock's book, *Modern Architecture: Romanticism and Reintegration* (1929), which had stated bluntly that "Neutra alone is a worthy disciple of Wright. . . . His railway stations [from "Rush City Reformed"] and his houses displayed a sort of technical research infrequent in America and an integrity of aesthetic expression only found in the best work of Wright. . . ." Hitchcock was certain that "Neutra's work, although not specifically American, illustrates that the new manner can cope individually and effectively with American conditions." On the other hand Schindler, Hitchcock believed, had "paralleled with mediocre success the more extreme aesthetic researches of Le Corbusier and the men of *de Stijl*."[43]

Schindler wrote and corrected Hitchcock's incorrect citation of Neutra, rather than himself, as Wright's assistant on the Imperial Hotel. To link Neutra, Schindler went on, "with the School of Wright both in fact and especially in spirit is just as wrong as to link me with Corbusier. The reverse might be stated with some chance to find supporting arguments. Your statement concerning my work is careless as you have no real knowledge of it." Hitchcock replied that he would be happy to correct the factual errors should there be a second edition of his book. But "in matters of opinion, I am little likely to be influenced by your apparent contention that the critic is helpless entirely to mention buildings he has only seen photographs of. I hope of course to see your work in California—although frankly it would be Neutra's which would draw me there. . . . I regret that I have not pleased you and your friends, but think, pray, how little I have pleased Mr. R. A. Cram."[44]

Philip Johnson had conducted an equally tense correspondence with Schindler regarding the actual Museum of Modern Art exhibit. To Schindler's plea of early 1932 that he be included in the show, Johnson replied that the plans were "already completed and it would be impossible to include any more buildings." Schindler then asked if perhaps he could be included in the Los Angeles showing of the exhibition. Johnson replied that he was not certain but that if Schindler would send photographs of his work, "which I should be very interested in seeing, I will try to arrange for your inclusion at Bullocks Wilshire." Rather than sending the photographs, however, Schindler wrote Johnson another contentious letter: "Following your request," he wrote, "I have prepared a few photos for the architectural exhibit. However since then I have heard more about the group you are showing and hesitate to send the pictures to you. I had supposed that the exhibit was the usual chance collection of modern architecture. I know now that it is the result of a definite choice. It seems to me that instead of showing late attempts of creative architecture, it tends toward concentrating on the so-called 'International Style.' If this is the case, my work has no place in it. I am not a stylist, not a functionalist, nor any other sloganist. Each of my buildings deals with a different *architectural* problem, the existence of which has been entirely forgotten in this period of rational mechanization. The question of whether a house is really a house is more important to me than the fact that it is made of steel, glass, putty, or hot air. I would appreciate if you would let me know your opinion whether my work belongs with your exhibit." Johnson's quick reply may not have been the one that Schindler wanted or expected. "I am sorry," Johnson wrote, "that you did not receive the correct impression of our Architectural Exhibition. It is very much not a chance collection, and since only ten architects are represented, they were of course very carefully selected. From your letter and from my knowledge of your work, my real opinion is that your work would not belong in the Exhibition."[45]

Though both Hitchcock and Johnson would, several decades later, revise their opinions of Schindler and come to appreciate the special character of his work, in the 1932 catalogue they confirmed their slightly pejorative assessment, while acceding to his wishes to be classified as a "Wrightian." In America, they wrote, "there is Frank Lloyd Wright who stands alone. Those men such as Barry Byrne, Chase McArthur and Wright's son Lloyd Wright, who follow most directly in his footsteps are no more worthy exemplars of modernism than the metropolitan architects of the East. . . . R. M. Schindler in California, although trained in Europe, belongs rather with the group of Wright followers."[46]

It was curious that Schindler, while attacking

the International Style so vociferously, imbibed the style in his work of the early 1930s more fully and directly than he ever had before. This may have been partially an unconscious response to the ideas and trends so obviously in the air, but he was more likely influenced by the presence and example of Neutra himself as they talked and worked together at the King's Road studio. Such superb achievements, for instance, as the Buck house (1934), the Delahoyde and Shep projects (1935), the Fitzpatrick house (1936), and the Rodakiewicz house (1937) clearly exemplified Schindler's strong affinities for the tenets and mannerisms of the International Style.[47]

Schindler also drew from his association with Neutra a new appreciation for publicity and promotion. It was not, however, his penchant or forte. In July 1929, for example, as the Lovell Health House was nearing completion, Schindler obviously felt the need to acquire new commissions, and he solicited the attention of Josef von Sternberg. "The movie director who wants to create thorobreds," Schindler wrote, "can do nothing but wait until the public grows eyes. The architect who is limited by economic considerations, might thru some chance find a client who already has eyes. I, a pupil of Otto Wagner, of Vienna, have been trying to develop contemporary building in Los Angeles for the last eight years, without finding anyone whose imagination could follow me to the end. Miss Barnsdall who has appreciated my schemes for translucent space architecture, has so far used me to build half-breeds. You are reputed to be a contemporary artist of imagination and achievement. May I present to you a new conception of architecture, which transcends the childish freaks of the fashionable modernique decorator?" Schindler's attempt at self-promotion proved unsuccessful in the von Sternberg case. Little could he know that when the famous director, some six years later, would decide to build a modern country villa, he would commission instead the more noted Neutra and would get, in the process, one of Neutra's finest works.[48]

Despite his protestations and his cavalier stance, being excluded from the 1932 show apparently hurt Schindler deeply. It also marked yet another source of strain in his and Neutra's complex relationship. Before 1932 there had been no

"break," as frequently suggested, because of Neutra's "taking" the Lovell commission in 1927 or the Niedermann's omission of Schindler's name from the League of Nations exhibit the same year. The Neutras continued to live happily at King's Road until they left for Europe in the summer of 1930. Neutra's letters to Schindler in 1930 and '31 suggested a continuingly warm personal relationship even as professional and ideological differences increased. In 1930, Neutra wrote from Japan, Europe, and the Middle West, combining his observations of life and architecture with affectionate personal sentiments as well. "Your mother probably wrote you about our being together," he stated. "I have been ill and told her to imagine you in much better a shape than she saw me. I said you had changed to a strong, very good looking, sun-burnt man. . . ." After discussing the bleakness of Europe, Neutra asked, in his still less-than-perfect English, "And how fine is everything in LA? I wish heartily very fine. Please write me about it. . . . I shall be glad to see you again and I hope your *spirits are good*." After Neutra returned to Los Angeles in 1931, he and Schindler taught their course together at the Chouinard School of Art.[49]

After 1932 however, the relationship became increasingly cool. Again, this was due not to one particular incident, but to a slow accumulation of smoldering animosities. When they had met as students some twenty years earlier, Neutra had become, in a sense, Schindler's admiring protégé. Between 1914, when Schindler left Europe, and 1924, when they met again in America, they had maintained their friendship through an active correspondence. When Neutra had longed desperately to emigrate to America, Schindler had offered steady advice and encouragement. He had facilitated Neutra's meeting with Wright, had welcomed him and his family to his Los Angeles home and studio, and had given him bits of part-time work while Neutra got his bearings in a new environment. He had succumbed to Neutra's infectious enthusiasm for expanding their work to "commerce and industry" and had agreed to join him in the AGIC partnership. And it was there, in the late twenties, that their growing differences in personality, ideology, and modus operandi became increasingly apparent.

For whatever reasons Neutra had gotten the

Lovell commission, the house had quickly achieved the status of a masterpiece. It and Neutra's sudden fame—acknowledged now throughout the world— could hardly have failed to arouse resentment in Schindler, whose work, by comparison, had been largely ignored. And the obvious difference in their international standing was trenchantly confirmed by the 1932 show. While dismissing Schindler as a flawed and parochial "Wrightian," Hitchcock, Barr, and Johnson had trumpeted Neutra as "the leading modern architect of the West Coast." It was the 1932 show more than any other single event that brought Schindler's latent hostility to the surface. For Neutra, however, the show was a ringing confirmation of his painfully wrought achievement. Building now upon this base, Neutra produced in the 1930s a remarkable output of significant work that would substantiate his standing as a leading prophet and practitioner of modernism.

Such work would contribute another important layer to California's already rich architectural fabric. Before the arrival of Wright, Schindler, and Neutra, the dominant elements of that fabric had included the missions and related Hispanic buildings; the western variants of high Victorian modes; the Arts and Crafts bungalow; and the Spanish Colonial and other "period" revivals. In the twenties and thirties the varieties of modernism would add another significant element to those older styles and textures—even as its practitioners revolted against tradition.

The California modernists produced, moreover, a large and significant body of work *before* Mies and Gropius and their various contemporaries transferred their versions of European modernism to the East Coast and Middle West. Had history been less cruel in the Europe of the thirties, and had its modernists not been forced into exile, Neutra and Schindler and the California School would have constituted, and been recognized as, the dominant wing of American modernism.

106. *Neutra,* model house, Vienna, 1932

Modernity

The decade between the Modern Architecture show of 1932 and America's entry into World War II was the most creative period of Richard Neutra's life, the time during which he practiced most convincingly the ethic and esthetic of architectural modernity. Throughout his career, though particularly in the thirties, Neutra developed a personal vocabulary based for the most part on "impersonal" references. Though there was never such a thing as a typical Neutra building, there were patterns, formulas, themes, and motifs that distinguished his work from his modernist peers.

A typical Neutra element, for example, that could be expanded or multiplied to form a building was the long, thin, sparely supported pavilion, virtually closed on one side and very open on the other, with a cantilevered roof slab, particularly wide on the open side. The closed side, away from the view or the major activity area might have a high, narrow, frequently translucent, band of steel casement windows to let in light without compromising privacy or usable wall space. The more open side would contain large casement windows or sliding glass door-walls that dramatically integrated indoors and out. As pervasive and repetitive as such designs elements were, however, the particular character of individual buildings was ultimately determined by client, site, and program.

While pursuing his goals of replicable, prefabricated, mass-produced, low-cost, high-quality building, available and attractive to all classes, Neutra came to rely on simpler, lighter, more modular, more skeletal, more industrial means and effects than any of his contemporaries. His work, in short, more than any other architect's, reified the theories of what the International Style was *sup-posed* to be. Much of the lightness and thinness, admittedly, was nurtured by the temperate California climate, where the almost constant sun encouraged Neutra's characteristically wide roof overhangs. Protection from the sun via columned or arched verandas had long been a fact of Hispanic California buildings. The technical imperatives and imagery of modernism addressed the same problem with cantilevered slabs. Striving for "industrial" effects to suggest the possibilities of replicable mass production, Neutra frequently painted his wood surfaces silver, a "dishonest" practice according to modernist moral canons, for which he was roundly criticized. Yet because of their simple, rectangular slab construction, Neutra's buildings could vary in materials and technology without appreciable effects on the design.

Like Wright's Prairie houses, most of Neutra's buildings had a strong horizontal orientation. While the buildings of Le Corbusier usually seemed to "stand" on the land, Neutra's tended to "sit" or to "lie" there. As compared, moreover, with those of most of his modernist contemporaries, Neutra's buildings—in verdant California—reached out to embrace and intermingle with nature. His buildings were the quintessential "machines in the garden."

Throughout the thirties Neutra's office staff remained small, with seldom more than two or three assistants or, as Neutra liked to call them, architectural "collaborators." His former student apprentices, Harris and Ain, would assist him into the middle 1930s, while Peter Pfisterer, a Swiss immigrant, would remain into the early 1940s. To help get and supervise jobs in the San Francisco area Neutra employed the services of a German immigrant, Otto Winkler. In addition, moreover, to her duties as wife, mother, cook, and housekeeper, and to her frequently neglected musical career, Dione served as office secretary and stenographer. Neutra worked with numerous contractors in the thirties, though his apparent favorites were Eric Nelson and Herman Kasielke.

During those years Neutra received approximately one hundred commissions and saw the completion of over fifty of them. By this measure he built more than any of his modernist peers.* He believed his most important buildings were those that serviced the larger community—stores, factories, schools, theaters, museums, airports, and multiple-family housing developments.† Still, for all his ideological commitment to the primacy of public architecture, he realized his greatest fame and success in the design and promotion of single family houses. His house clients comprised a broad social and economic spectrum—from low-income school teachers to Hollywood moguls and millionaire aristocrats. Their only common traits were a penchant for experiment, a commitment to modernism, and, with several exceptions, a lasting fascination with their architectural mentor. The houses, themselves, fell into several simple categories, distinguishable first, by size and scale—small, medium, large, a factor usually connected to the affluence of the clients and the sizes of their families; second, by mood and image, which related most directly to the nature of materials—the "industrial" crispness of concrete, for example, versus the natural "warmth" of redwood; and third, by geographical location and setting—urban, rural, suburban, desert, mountain, or seacoast.

The first small house Neutra completed in the thirties was not in Los Angeles but in his native city of Vienna, the one and only building he would ever design there. It was one of seventy structures by thirty-two architects in the 1932 international housing exhibition built by Geshiba, a cooperative, nonprofit building society, and sponsored by the city in cooperation with the Austrian Werkbund. Other contributing architects included Adolf Loos

and Josef Hoffmann of Vienna, André Lurçat of Paris, Gerrit Rietveld of Utrecht, and Hugo Häring of Berlin. Unlike its more famous predecessor at Weissenhof (1927), which had emphasized apartment units, the Vienna exhibition focused on attached and detached single-family houses grouped in the modernist, garden-city suburb of Lainz. The Vienna correspondent to the *Christian Science Monitor* placed the exhibit within the larger context of the city's post-war housing trends. "On the one hand," he noted, "were the splendid, immense tenement blocks erected by the municipality to solve the housing problem and on the other, the large colonies of 'Schrebergärten' or allotments, with tiny huts, log cabins or bungalows, and the small weekend houses along the River Danube in the immediate vicinity of the city. The tenements handled the problem of giving thousands of families 'roofs over their heads' but they have also intensified the desire of these same people for 'homes of their own,' where independence and privacy can be enjoyed."[1]

Neutra apparently made arrangements for his project during his visit to Vienna in 1930, and designed the building upon his return to Los Angeles in 1931. A simple one-story cube with basement and roof deck, Neutra's "cottage" was the smallest in the exhibition. A rounded corner in the large living-dining room softened the wall enveloping the corner kitchen and the connected stairway to the basement. The bath and two bedrooms shared with the living room the band of ribbon windows which on the entrance side abutted the front door in what would became a characteristic Neutra *L*-shaped configuration. The stairs to the roof garden and a small, high window giving light to the bedroom balanced the larger separate casements to the left of the door. Neutra was unable to supervise construction. When he saw the house for the first time in 1955 he was dismayed by the crude detailing, the subsequent changes in his original design, and the poor level of maintenance. Nevertheless, the attempt to make "something out of nothing," to make art of a project so modest in size and budget, would remain one of his greatest life-long interests.[2]

Neutra's next significant house also had strong European connections—his own Los Angeles home and studio, inspired and sponsored by the Dutch industrialist C. H. Van der Leeuw. Since his visit to Rotterdam in 1930, Neutra had continued

---

* In this computation, multiple-unit projects that included numerous individual structures are each counted as one.

† To be discussed in Chapter Seven.

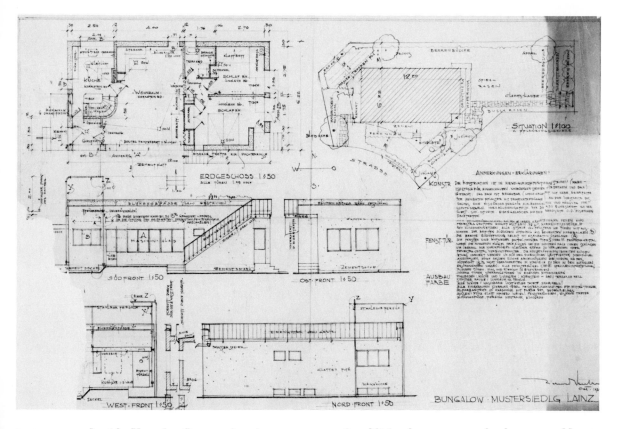

107. *Neutra*, model house, Vienna, 1932

to correspond with Van der Leeuw, but he was flabbergasted the next year to receive a call from him in New York asking if he might fly on to Los Angeles to see Neutra and his work. Van der Leeuw greatly admired the Jardinette and the Lovell house and asked Neutra to show him where he lived as well. When Neutra replied that he lived in a rented bungalow and could not afford to build a house for himself, Van der Leeuw "pulled out a checkbook and asked, 'How much do you need? . . . You pay me three percent and you build your house. How is that?' Finally I heard my voice accepting," Neutra recalled, "mentioning a ridiculously low figure. He signed the check; . . . Later I parked the car twice on the trip home. Each time the check still proved to be in my breast pocket, and I knew I was completely sober. . . ."[3]

With $3000 from Van der Leeuw and the rest borrowed from the bank, Neutra built his house on a sixty-by-seventy-foot lot fronting on the placid Silverlake Reservoir on the near northwest side of Los Angeles. Determined to make it an experimental venture, he solicited from manufacturers the most interesting new building materials, from enamel metal facing to cork floors to pressed fiber boards—to be exchanged *gratis* for the antici-

pated publicity he was sure the house would get. Learning from the old Spanish practice of building to the property lines with rear interior courtyards for gardens and privacy, Neutra designed a simple two-story wood-framed structure topped with a solarium on the flat roof deck. The deck and the second floor offered spectacular views of the nearby Silverlake and the distant snow-capped mountains. The downstairs level included a large space for the drafting room with two small adjoining apartments. The family living quarters on the second floor contained a large living-dining space equivalent to the drafting room beneath, and a kitchen, bath, and two bedrooms. From the upstairs living room, folding glass and metal doors opened to a covered, unglazed sleeping porch from which a ladder led to the roof solarium.[4]

A characteristically modernist touch along the front facade was the uninterrupted stucco band that ran beneath living room windows, continued as the sleeping porch balcony railing, and turned the corner as the two front sides of an open, uncovered, and even more abstract aedicule framing the front entrance. The soffit of the wide southwest overhang contained what would become another Neutra trademark—a lighted band that illuminated

111

108, 109. *Neutra*, VDL Research House, Los Angeles, 1932

110. *Neutra*, VDL Research House, 1932, used as background for 1936 Oldsmobile advertisement

111. *Neutra*, VDL Research House, 1932, living room overlooking Silver Lake

112. *Neutra*, VDL Research House, 1932, folding doors between living room and sleeping porch

113. *Neutra*, VDL Research House, 1932, stairway to living quarters

114. *(Above, right) Neutra*, VDL Research House, 1932, interior garden patio

the garden and, in rendering opaque the outside of the window glass, provided additional privacy at night. Neutra especially liked the idea of planning the house as a flexible cluster of smaller entities which could, whenever desirable or necessary, serve the different needs of several types of family units. It epitomized his penchant for "after the revolution" planning. He employed mirrors throughout to stretch the small spaces. "Everything had to double for something else," he recalled, "to yield increase and elasticity of use, even in the breakfast roomette, the table of which folded down over a washtub. The kitchen had access to drawers which could be heated or cooled and which opened both

ways to serve refreshments or complete meals directly into the living quarters." Later, in 1940, Neutra designed an important addition to the house in the form of a one-story guest wing, pushed to the rear property line, thus completing the enclosure of the garden patio.[5]

The original house cost approximately $3.00 a square foot, or slightly over $10,000. Because of Van der Leeuw's contribution and his own experimental use of new and varied building materials, Neutra named it the VDL Research House. Speaking to a magazine journalist, he labeled it "California moderne." The house was widely published in American and foreign journals, which prompted

a stream of interested visitors over the years. Thomas Whittemore of Boston, for example, director of the prestigious Byzantine Institute, visited the house when Neutra was away, but wrote him an appreciative and insightful evaluation. The house, Whittemore asserted, "is masterly in its integration, its aloofness, and its proximity to public life."[6]

A series of small southern California houses of both "industrial" and "natural" persuasions allowed Neutra throughout the thirties to continue demonstrating his penchant and talent for maximizing the minimum. A house for a sensitive though nonaffluent young couple, Ernest and Bertha Mosk, in the Beechwood subdivision of the Holly-

wood Hills was designed as a replicable prototype for a "steep hillsite development" (1933). The other units of this development were never built, as such, though variants were realized in Neutra's housing projects of the later thirties and forties. The Nathan Koblick house, built in 1933 near Atherton, south of San Francisco, was a rural, flat-sited variant of the Mosk hillsite idea. Designated "Rural House K" by Neutra, the Koblick house was likewise never replicated as planned and lost its intended character as suburbia encroached. Later the original house was devoured by an awkward enlargement.

The Mosks first encountered Neutra's work at

115. *Neutra*, VDL Research House, 1932, Dione Neutra on the sleeping porch

116. *Neutra*, VDL Research House, 1932, Dione and Dion Neutra on the roof deck

117. *Neutra*, Koblick House, Atherton, California, 1933

the Los Angeles installation of the "Modern Architecture" show. Bertha Mosk had sophisticated esthetic tastes. Her husband Ernest, a modest small businessman, quickly imbibed her enthusiasm for modernism. A slightly raised vertical space housed the large central living-dining room, flanked by the lower kitchen-garage wing on the north and a longer bath and bedroom wing to the south. The basement contained recreational space and additional bedrooms. A raised deck across the rear of the house was a favorite area for private sunning, entertaining, and contemplating the view. Interior partitions were of gypsum board covered with washable fabric. Above and below the rows of steel casements running continuously around the bedroom wing were wooden and stucco bands, painted to heighten the building's "machine identity" in varying hues of "silver-gray aluminum." The wooden attic band surged beyond the building's volume both as ·a pergola and sunscreen protecting the southern exposure and as an abstract gesture to nature and infinity. The importance to the building of such apparently simple statements as the silver-gray paint and the outreaching pergola were graphically demonstrated when later occupants removed the pergola and covered the silver with brown and white paint. A few months after moving in, Bertha Mosk wrote Neutra of her "feeling that now we have freedom to breathe and grow. The house is alive and so we too feel vital. . . . It was a great privilege to have been closely associated with a person who is so far ahead of his time and . . . who has given us an instrument so that we can keep up with his vision."[7]

A far different type of client was the volatile psychologist and collector Galka Scheyer, whom Neutra had first met in the King's Road days with Schindler. In 1927 she had intervened in the Schindler-Neutra-Lovell impasse and, when she sensed that the Lovell commission was not destined for Schindler, urged Neutra to take it without reservation. After the Neutras left King's Road in 1930, Scheyer occupied the north apartment. There on the apartment's concrete walls she hung her great canvases of major modernist painters, particularly those of the "Blue Four." When Scheyer began thinking of building a house in the early thirties, she apparently first considered the architect J. R. Davidson, a friend of both Neutra and Schindler. But at about that time the Davidsons moved to Chicago, where he had several jobs, and for reasons that would shortly become obvious to Neutra, Scheyer wanted to deal with an architect at closer range. She left no specific indication as to why she chose Neutra over her older friend Schindler. The Neutras surmised it was at least partially due to the breakup of the sporadic and stormy affair they had witnessed between Schindler and Scheyer after Pauline's departure. Scheyer also told her friend Lette Valeska that she wanted the "most modern" architect, and she believed that that was Neutra.[8]

Scheyer first approached Neutra in 1931 or '32. Dione remembered her visiting to discuss the project at the Douglas Street bungalow with Mme. Archipenko, the wife of the sculptor. Ain, who

118. *Neutra*, Mosk House, Los Angeles, 1933

119. *Neutra*, Scheyer House, 1934

120. *Neutra*, Scheyer House, Los Angeles, 1934

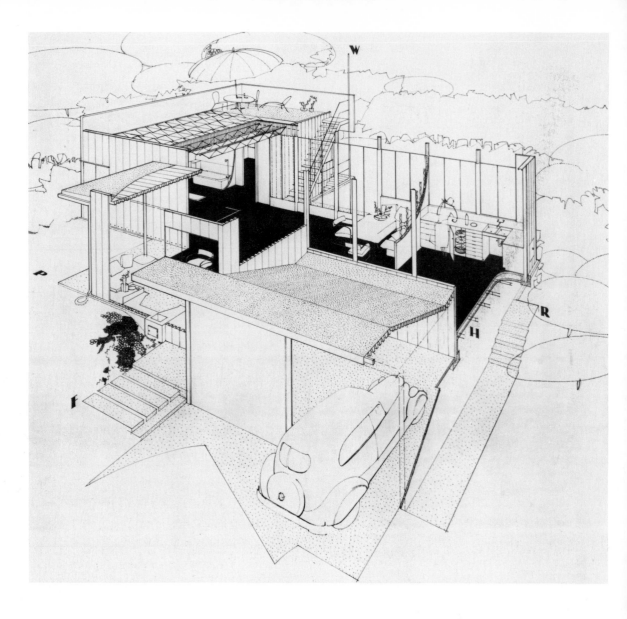

assisted Neutra on the project, recalled that in Scheyer, Neutra "met his match and vice versa." There were numerous confrontations. She would telephone, Dione recalled, at all hours of the day and night. Scheyer wanted, for example, less glass than Neutra proposed and more wall space for her paintings. Their sensible compromise was Neutra's proposal and Scheyer's acceptance of removable panels for insertion over openings, allowing for expandable exhibition space without permanently closing off the spectacular views of the city, ocean, and mountains. To reach the then-isolated site high in the Santa Monica Mountains, a primitive road was cut into the hillside, which Scheyer named Blue Heights Drive in homage to the Blue Four.

Unable or unwilling to sell many of her paintings and with only a modest income from her family's estate, Scheyer had an unusually tight budget, and Neutra brought the house in for under $3,000. The small kitchen, bath, and bedrooms allowed Neutra to give the remaining available space to the large living-exhibition room with its glazed south wall and its long adjoining porch deck protected from the sun by a wide overhang. Due to the steep slope, the rear of the top flat sunroof was level with the shaved-off mountain top. The house was completed in 1934. Because of her frequently tense and ultimately strained relationship with Neutra, however, Scheyer later turned to Gregory Ain, who had worked on the original house, when she decided in

the late thirties to add another floor at the top. Ain's competent but rather boxy third floor addition sacrificed the house's horizontal serenity for a less compelling vertical orientation.[9]

An equally small house of all-metal siding completed the same year for William and Melba Beard in Altadena, was for both Neutra and the clients a happier and more satisfying achievement. William Beard's parents, the historians Charles and Mary Beard, were friends and admirers of Neutra and had encouraged their son to commission him. William Beard was a professor of engineering at the California Institute of Technology in Pasadena and author of an important work on government and technology. His wife Melba was an active

aviator. In the Beards, therefore, Neutra encountered adventurous and sophisticated clients who were as eager as he was to build not only a comfortable and beautiful house, but one that could demonstrate experimental and replicable technological possibilities.[10]

The layout was simple. A large living-dining room with almost floor-to-ceiling casements looked northeast to the Sierra Madre Mountains. A study and bedroom lay to the northwest while the kitchen and garge faced the southeast side and front. Sliding glass door-walls connected the living spaces to the outside gardens and patios. A stairway to the flat roof deck was a prominent design feature, especially visible from the living room. More revolu-

119

123. *Neutra*, Richter House, Pasadena, California, 1936

tionary were the technological innovations of the "all-metal" house, constructed, as Neutra explained, "of cellular elements approximating a series of vertical flues side by side, with exterior air intakes, [and] automatically self-cooling exterior walls." Neutra was especially proud of the radiant floor heating, a system he would continue to utilize as it became more popular through the years. Just under 1200 square feet, the house cost less than $5000.[11]

The Beard house won the 1934 Gold Medal Award in the "small house" category of the *Better Homes in America* competition, cosponsored by *Architectural Forum* and the Columbia Broadcasting System. The awards jury, appointed by the president of the American Institute of Architects, included George Howe of Yale and was chaired by Dean Joseph Hudnut of the Harvard School of Design. It was a banner year for Neutra. In addition to the top prize for the Beard house, he received honorable mentions for the Mosk house and the Koblick house in Atherton. The jury cited the Beard house as "an admirable instance of the complete correlation of function, both internally, in the relation of parts and the circulation between them, and externally in relation to orientation and climatic requirements. Furthermore, this design is a serious study in which structure and mechanical equipment admirably express the space composition conceived as a satisfactory environment for a given set of living conditions." The Beard, Mosk, and

Koblick houses, the jury concluded, "stand out preeminently as examples of a serious and informed effort to solve the problem of American life in a given locality and under given conditions. Furthermore, a variety of materials and mechanical devices is employed with superlative skills to form compositions based on the contemporary conception of space as contained in our whole philosophy, science and way of living." The Beards were delighted with the house and with the prize.[12]

A small stucco house built in 1936 in nearby Pasadena for another Cal Tech professor, Dr. Charles Richter, was less innovative technologically than the "all-metal" Beard house, though no less appreciated by the clients. Containing 1560 square feet, it cost $4300. Richter, the seismologist who invented the Richter Scale for measuring earthquakes, worked with Neutra in rendering the house as "earthquake proof" as possible. However, it was his wife Lillian, a writer, who took the greatest interest in the design and worked most closely with Neutra in devising the simple plan and working out the details.[13]

Neutra frequently asked his clients to send him impressions of and observations about their houses. Lillian Richter's paean to minimalism, "functionalism," flat roofs, and built-in furniture would have warmed the heart of any crusading modernist—though energy conservationists might have taken a dimmer view. "We've lived for nearly nineteen months in this modern house," she wrote Neutra in January 1938. "Controlled climate, and yet close contact with nature, the combination can only be enjoyed by those among us who live amid great panes of plain glass. I like the built-in furniture which must stay where it is put. No wasting energy dragging it from corner to corner for just no reason. I like the beds built down to the floor, so there can be no dirt to sweep out. But the whole family . . . enjoys the flat roof, which we use as a solarium. Being able to use our roof gives us so much more space on this fifty foot lot than we'd have, had we built one of the old-fashioned peaked-roof monstrosities. How did the human species ever happen to think of building their homes so that the whole roof space was wasted" she asked, forgetting the timeless human enchantment with attics. "More than anything I enjoy the eager interest and the discussions that follow whenever folks know we

124. *Neutra*, Richter House, 1936

live in a modern house. Many who claim to dislike this sort of dwelling, had never seen anything but the outside of them." After living in the house over thirty-five years, the Richters were forced to abandon it in 1973 when a freeway extension demanded its demolition.[14]

Neutra's most elegant small house of the period was a desert resort cottage for Grace Lewis Miller in Palm Springs, California, 1937. It contained less than 1200 square feet, but the luxurious detailing and the added expense of building in the desert pushed the cost to $7000. Miller, a middle-aged St. Louis widow, had been interested in modern architecture for most of her adult life and had long hoped to connect it with her profession of teaching the "Mensendieck System of Functional Exercise." Attracted to the cultish California health ethos, she decided to build a studio cottage in the wealthy and fashionable resort of Palm Springs. Believing that Neutra was the best modernist in the area, she also found him a sympathetic "soul mate." It seemed natural to both of them to call the dwelling the Mensendieck House. Miller chose a site near the posh Racquet Club, whose rich and famous habitués were among her friends and clients. Miller's life and work demanded a large and stylish wardrobe and a vast array of oils and cosmetics, which called for ampler-than-usual built-in cabinets and closets. The simple plan included a large studio-living-dining room, entered from a screened porch, with kitchen,

bedroom, and baths to the west. A fetching covered reflecting pool filled the southeast corner near the porch and living room.[15]

In 1938 the Museum of Modern Art included the house in a traveling exhibition of modern domestic architecture. Miller at the museum's request described her reactions. She considered it a very "smart house," one that "lends itself easily for any kind of life . . . either close, private life, or the gay social life . . . whether there is one or more to dinner; or one or two or a crowd for tea or cocktails; or a bunch of young things, careless of their cigarette butts, for dancing. . . ."[16]

Miller especially liked the way Neutra made the pool a part of the house, tempering the heat and sunshine and casting beautiful reflections on the studio ceiling. She also appreciated his climate control devices, the wide overhangs on the east, south, and west with their screened ventilation soffits drawing a flow of fresh air between the ceiling and roof. The light cement structure with its silver-gray aluminum trim was indeed one of Neutra's minimalist masterworks, a miniature echo of Mies's Barcelona Pavilion, one of the many Neutra buildings that drew from Mies's example. Its slim, crisp detailing, its "dematerialization" of surfaces did indeed create a highly abstract effect, but never as rigid and demanding an abstraction as the Barcelona structure or so much of Mies's later work. Its abstract minimalism had a definite purpose—to

125. *Neutra*, Richter House, 1936, Richard Neutra with Lilliam Richter

126. *Neutra*, Miller House, Palm Springs, 1937

127. *Neutra*, Miller House, 1937, studio-living room-bedroom

122

128. *Neutra*, Miller House, 1937

129. *Neutra*, Miller House, 1937, studio-living room-bedroom

130. *Neutra*, Miller House, 1937, as photographed in 1979

123

131. *Neutra*, Davis House, Bakersfield, California 1937

make it defer and dissolve into the desert. Neutra's minimal landscaping was especially effective in providing an edge between desert and lawn, between nature and architecture. The rock walk formed a perfect boundary between those worlds. Typical of Neutra's design sophistication was the subtle contradiction of the straight line of the stones on the "wild" desert side of the walk and the more irregular jagged spacing as the walk met the trim lawn and approached the house.[17]

Throughout the thirties Neutra continued to build significant small houses in the International Style throughout Southern California. A two-story version of his basic stucco box for Frank and Kathryn Davis in Bakersfield, built in 1937, offered faint allusions to the older California Monterey Style with its upstairs and downstairs porches across the front. As the first modern house in a provincial California town, it evoked the usual mixed reactions. A similar arrangement of cantilevered porches in the Silverlake district of Los Angeles was built the same year for the bachelor art professor Harry Koblick, a cousin of Neutra's Atherton client. Koblick lived on the top floor of

132. *Neutra*, Ward-Berger House, North Hollywood, California, 1939

133. *Neutra*, Ward-Berger House, 1939

the duplex overlooking the lake and rented the lower unit over the street level garages. The Malcomson house, a tiny retirement cottage for an elderly Massachusetts grandmother perched on a similarly precipitous site in Rustic Canyon, Los Angeles (1937), proved that devoted modernists did not have to be young.[18]

Two small North Hollywood homes, the Barsha house of 1937 and the Ward-Berger house of 1939, were more relaxed in layout, style, and atmosphere than Neutra's earlier modernist structures of the thirties. The sliding glass wall of the Ward-Berger living room brought house and garden together with unprecedented ease. The ambience was heightened by the use of casual rattan garden furniture, inside and out, captured in a favorite photograph that was widely published and admired. The *T*-shaped stucco house for the film editor Leon Barsha and his wife Helen had an unusual afterlife. After the Barshas commissioned Neutra to design an addition to the house in the mid-1950s, they were dismayed to learn that an imminent extension of the Hollywood freeway was to consume their property. They thereupon sold the house, and the new owner moved it to Rustic

134. *Neutra*, Barsha House, North
Hollywood, California, 1937

135. *Neutra*, Beckstrand House, Palos
Verdes, California, 1940

126

Canyon, just below the Malcolmson house. Though the move itself was wholly successful, the siting on the new lot and the subsequent alterations were not.[19]

Though only slightly larger than the Ward and Barsha houses, the elegant Beckstrand house (1940) seemed bigger than it was because of its siting in the midst of an orange grove overlooking the coast of the Palos Verdes peninsula. This was also Neutra's first major encounter with zoning codes that demanded red tile, pitched roofs. Since the degree of pitch was not prescribed, Neutra utilized the minimum, so as to make the pitch virtually unnoticeable. When viewed from the ground the Beckstrand house appeared to be another flat-roofed International Style statement. Later, in the forties and after, Neutra would stop attempting to fight such codes in Palos Verdes and elsewhere and would design handsome, steeply pitched roofs.

In three small thirties houses in Southern California, Neutra eschewed, at the request of the clients, the industrial imagery of the International Style for "softer" essays in California redwood. The first of these, the modest McIntosh house of 1939, near Silverlake, was inspired by the McIntosh's young sons, eager students of modernism at the Los Angeles Art Center who convinced their more conservative parents to build a Neutra house. Proud as they were of their artistic progeny, the senior McIntoshes were willing to go only "so far" toward the brave new world of the International Style, and gladly accepted Neutra's suggestion of the more familiar and "homey" redwood as a compromise. He thereupon transferred the ribbon windows and other modernist trademarks to this medium. Schindler had already done this with success, and Wright at the same time was beginning his kindred series of "Usonian" houses. For another client, Philip Gill, a high school science teacher, Neutra designed a redwood box with a basement floor beneath the street level. (1939) But the modest Gill house took on added significance when Matilda Sweet, the owner of the property directly across the street, asked Neutra to build her "exactly the same thing." Pleased that the Gills did not object to the idea, Neutra simply reversed the layout of the Gill house and, with minor alterations on the street facade, produced a mirror image. Located on the *cul de sac* of Suncourt Terrace in the Glendale Hills, the Gill

136. *Neutra*, Beckstrand House, 1940

137. *Neutra*, Beckstrand House, 1940, living room

138. *Neutra*, McIntosh House, Los Angeles, 1939

139. *Neutra*, Gill House, Glendale, California, 1939

140. *Neutra*, modern steelcraft home,
early 1930s

and Sweet houses suggested a Neutra village. A later owner of the Sweet house largely destroyed the effect, however, by painting over the natural redwood.[20]

Neutra's interest in the small low-cost house and his penchant for both experiment and promotion led in the thirties to several significant "model house" schemes. Enthusiastic over the possibilities of building panels made of diatomaceous earth—a development that he never lived to see fully exploited—Neutra designed small housing schemes from the late 1920s into the '30s which he liked to call the "Diatom House." Never built with the diatomaceous, sea-shell aggregate as such, the design, with variations, found its way into his low-cost housing projects of the thirties and forties. Like Frank Lloyd Wright before him, Neutra delighted in designing model houses to be sponsored and marketed by popular as well as professional magazines. In 1938, for example, he contributed a design to the "Bildcost House" series of *Better Homes and Gardens*, and in 1939 to the National Small House Competition of the *Ladies' Home Journal*. Complete building plans of the latter were available for a dollar, with which buyers could then do as they wished. Neutra liked to think of the anonymous variants of his magazine houses built across the land.[21]

A close variant of the Bildcost design from Neutra's own hand was actually constructed in 1936 as a "Plywood Model Demonstration House" in the Architectural Building Material Exhibit. Sponsored by the Los Angeles Building Center, Neutra's plywood model house was the only modern offering among various "period" cottages. Operated by two ingenious and dedicated sisters, Louisa and Florence Schmidt, the Building Center solicited building materials *gratis* for all of the exhibition houses, just as Neutra himself had done for his Silverlake VDL House. For Neutra it offered—as did most of his other commissions—another chance to pay homage to *Sweet's Catalogue*, the builders' standardized

141. *Neutra*, Plywood Model House, third from left, Los Angeles, 1936, on exhibit site

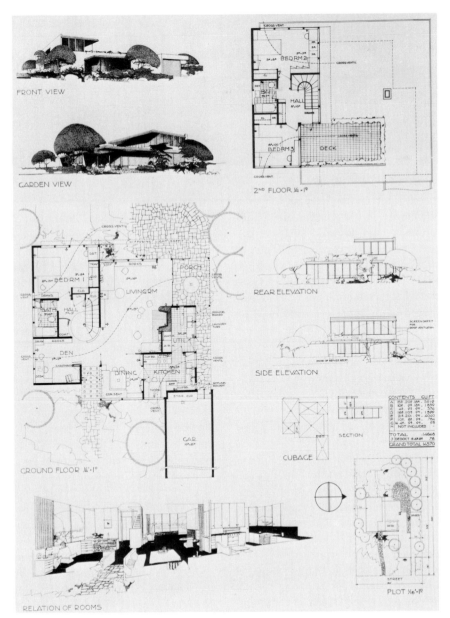

FRONT VIEW

GARDEN VIEW

2ND FLOOR ¼" = 1'

REAR ELEVATION

SIDE ELEVATION

CUBAGE

SECTION

GROUND FLOOR ¼" = 1'

RELATION OF ROOMS

PLOT ⅟₁₆" = 1'

142. *Neutra, Ladies' Home Journal* House 1939

129

143. *Neutra*, Plywood Model House, 1936,
after move to Westwood

supply catalogue. Located on the busy and fashionable Wilshire Boulevard in Los Angeles, the exhibition drew exceedingly large crowds. This was partially owing to the cunning decision of the Schmidt sisters to give all of the houses away in a raffle at the end to visitors of the exhibit. The lucky ticket holders only had to buy a lot and move their houses. The winner of the Neutra house moved it to Westwood near UCLA and soon sold it to the architect Maynard Lyndon. With its light metal frame and its plywood panels held in place by metal strips·and other industrially prefabricated parts, it was easily disassembled and reassembled. Lyndon painted the plywood in festive pastel colors. A later owner, the painter William Brice, son of the actress Fanny Brice, returned it to its original white. For Brice, Neutra later built a detached, but sympathetic, studio across the garden to the north. The plywood model house, with its terraces, patios, and articulated garden areas, seemed larger and more spacious than its 1565 square feet suggested. As such, it was something of a transition between Neutra's small houses and his grander villas.[22]

The first large house that Neutra designed after the Lovell Health House of 1929 was for the film star Anna Sten and her husband, the film director Eugene Frenke, overlooking the ocean in Santa Monica Canyon. Sten had recently arrived from Russia via Germany, imported by Samuel Goldwyn to be his studio's rival to Greta Garbo and Marlene Dietrich. Sten never became the "Russian Garbo," but she and her husband did build a great house. It was chiefly Frenke who wanted a modern building and who decided that Neutra was the best man on the scene. The elegant off-white stucco house with its glistening silver-gray trim was efficiently sited at the rear of the lot. A wall tied subtly to the entrance pergola and street-side garage assured privacy without obstructing views of the ocean and mountains. The garage unit contained showers and dressing rooms for the pool, which lay between these elements and the house. The house was essentially a large rectangle, textured by attached porches and constructivist pergolas and by a large curving bay off the front of the living room.[23]

The main door was placed asymmetrically on the east side, leading into an opaquely glazed stair hall. The two-story stairway fenestration recalled Hoffmann's Brussels Stoclet house and presaged recurring Neutra variations. The stairway railing alternated solid plaster panels with open wooden balusters, capped by a continuous chrome band. It

thus contained strong Wagnerschule memories, with related references to Charles Rennie Mackintosh. The entrance hall led south to the kitchen and pantry, north and west to the living and dining room. High French doors, west of the curving bay, opened to a terrace, which Neutra paved—surprisingly and winningly—with light blond craggy flagstone. Was this a homage to Frank Lloyd Wright? It was not a characteristic International Style juxtaposition—at least not among Neutra's European contemporaries. He had done it less convincingly in the Lovell house fireplace and would return to it later, with notably mixed results. A porch atop the curved living room bay led off the upstairs study. Bedrooms opened onto other porches with

spectacular views of the seacoast. The proportions of the Sten house were taller than most of Neutra's thirties compositions, imparting to the house a lilting verticality, as opposed to his penchant for the horizontal line. A particularly nice achievement was the downstairs fenestration, with its changes of scale and jogs of elevation. The large front living room windows continued as a transom atop the French doors leading to the terrace. The bottom of the windows of the circular bay continued the bottom line of the glazed part of the door. The top of the bay windows led from the lower line of the transom and continued around the bay to meet a thin, high band of subtly opaque glazing. This, in turn, ran along the east side of the living room to connect

144. *Neutra*, Sten House, Santa Monica, 1934

131

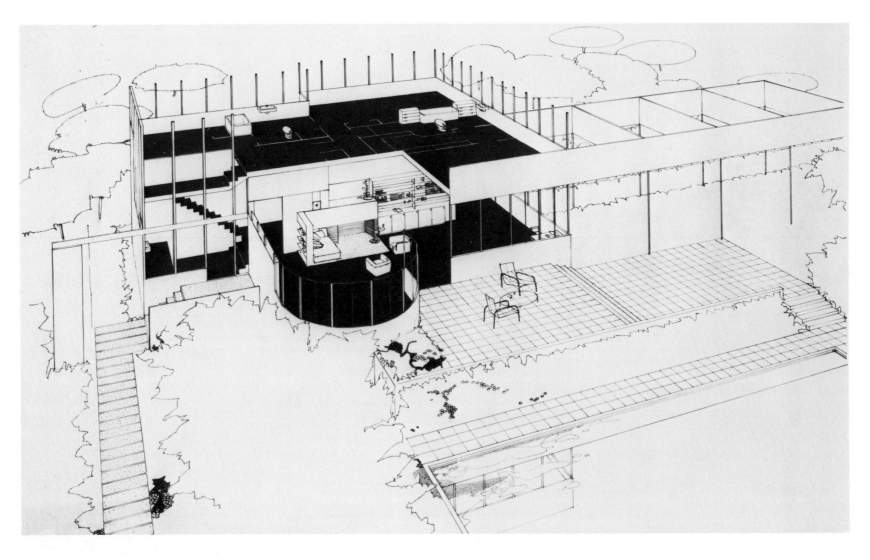

145. *Neutra*, Sten House, 1934

with the transom above the main entrance. The Sten house won first prize in the 1934 *House Beautiful* competition—the first modern house ever to win that award. It was one of Neutra's finest achievements.[24]

Most of Neutra's large Los Angeles houses of the thirties were connected with the movies and Hollywood. It was fitting that this industry, which not only survived the Depression but thrived on Americans' needs for elevation and escape, should provide major props for Neutra's fortunes of the thirties. His 1935 house in the then-rural San Fernando Valley, for the director Josef von Sternberg, would become one of his most celebrated buildings. Schindler had tried unsuccessfully in 1929 to solicit von Sternberg's patronage. Neutra left no indication whether or not he knew this, or how he and von Sternberg first made contact, but

after several years of informal conversations, the director commissioned Neutra in 1934.[25]

"I selected a distant meadow," von Sternberg recounted later, "in the midst of an empty landscape, barren and forlorn, to make a retreat for myself, my books and my collection of modern art. . . . I chose a comparatively unknown (at the time) architect to carry out my ideas of what a house should be." Designed in 1934 and completed in 1935, the house itself was a story-and-a-half rectangular structure with a double-height living room surrounded by a picture gallery balcony. Von Sternberg's exotically mirrored bath and bedroom looking out on a roof-top pool were the only other rooms on the small second floor. On the downstairs level east of the living room were a studio, kitchen, servants' rooms, and garages. The latter were divided between the garage for regular cars and the slightly larger space that would house the Rolls Royce. There was also a specially designed area for the owner's dogs. The basic shell for these exotic internal functions was a series of straightforward juxtaposed rectangles, with an aluminum cladding and a structural and service technology similar to the smaller, contemporary Beard house.[26]

To match and complement the client's personal and programmatic eccentricities, and to enliven the otherwise simple industrial facade, Neutra designed a series of remarkable special effects, which reached out into the landscape in layered vibrations. The first and most significant was the high, curving aluminum wall enclosing the front patio that led from the living room, which gave the house its "streamlined" personality. An advanced sprinkler system around the curving wall produced varied effects from a gentle mist to a battering rainstorm. Surrounding the wall, and, in broken stretches, the entire house, was a shallow moat or reflecting pool for fish and water lilies. To further exaggerate the real size of the house, a long thin wall extended from the west facade, dividing front and rear gardens. An actual ship's searchlight over the porte cochere, together with the moat and front wall, imparted a wittily "nautical" ambience to the scene. A specially designed swimming pool by the sculptor Isamu Noguchi was never constructed.

The early *bonhommie* between architect and client was by the end of 1935 becoming slightly strained. "Your lamp is very beautiful," von Sternberg wrote Neutra, "but request for a photograph of myself puzzles me. The home we built is causing me a great deal of pleasure and no little trouble with a few details." Neutra replied that von Sternberg should not be "puzzled" at his request for a photograph: "It was a significant experience indeed to be close to you." Later, however, in their respective autobiographies, the latent antagonisms of the two egoistic modernists rose to the surface. Neutra, von Sternberg mistakenly claimed, never visited the house after it was finished. He also charged that Neutra had alleged "that I kept four large cannons in this house to ward off visitors . . . cultivated black widow spiders to spin webs to conceal the outside, had a drawbridge built over a moat so no one could enter, replanted a giant rubber tree and moved it from place to place until it was at the proper angle to be viewed from a distant moun-

146. *Neutra*, Sten House, 1934, stairway

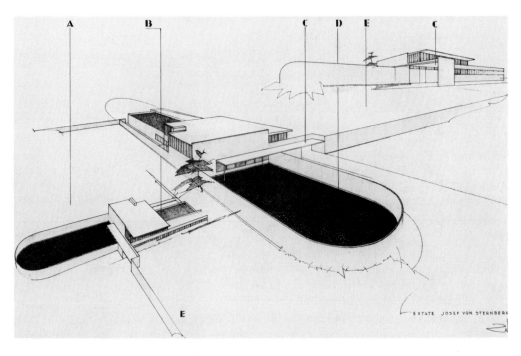

147. *Neutra*, Von Sternberg House, 1935, under construction

148. *Neutra*, Von Sternberg House, Northridge, California, 1935

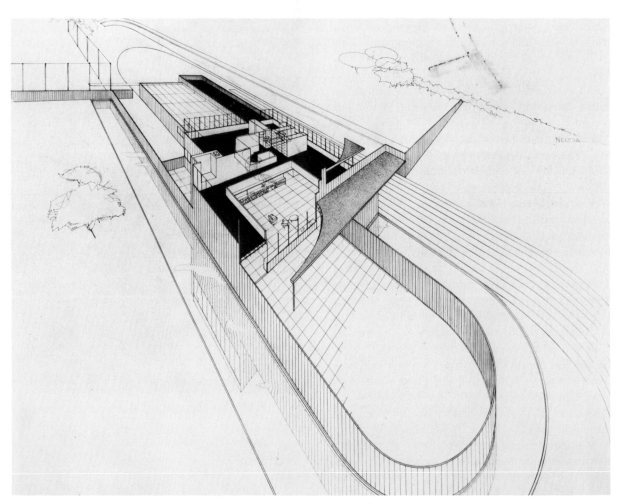

149. *Neutra*, Von Sternberg House, 1935

150. *Neutra*, Von Sternberg House, 1935

151. *Neutra*, Von Sternberg House, 1935

152. *Neutra*, Von Sternberg House, 1935

153. *Neutra*, Von Sternberg House, 1935

154. *Neutra*, Von Sternberg House, 1935

tain. . . ." Later, "meeting him when it could not be avoided, I asked him why he said things like the above, and he answered with a weird grin: 'Don't you think that helps to make you more interesting?' "27

Neutra's own autobiographical retrospections suggested that he could indeed have spun such yarns, but with an ironical intent that would not have amused the director. The house, Neutra averred, was "way out of town, and a man with a big income from a successful film . . . could be easily molested by kidnappers, who might try to cross the moat beneath the pendant optical grating during the night. It was also clear that this medieval scheme of protection was in a way primitive and outdated and would have to be supplemented by electronic devices to do away with any intruders who entered the moat as soon as they got their feet wet. Thus flipping a switch on the complex control panel over the night stand in the bedroom would

suddenly electrically charge the water of those protection basins. The idea was that while the producer . . . was sleeping late in the morning, his Persian chauffeur would, before breakfast, remove from the moat any bodies accumulated during the night so that they would not pollute the air when the sun rose in the hot climate of the wide mountain plateau. . . ." The house "had been acquired for solitude, which now had to be counterbalanced for security. . . . As an architect always must do when he serves a mobile minded human being who is the football of fate, everything had to be figured out to the last detail. However, to my embarrassment, I must admit that we ran into a big extra when we suddenly found that an electric incinerator would be necessary to dispose of the bodies fished out of the moat. The detail had completely escaped our attention."28

Finally, Neutra admitted, "there was one item which first astounded me when I brought the mag-

155. *Neutra*, Von Sternberg House, 1935

156. *Neutra*, Von Sternberg House, 1935, with Ayn Rand

nificent bathroom plans to the owner, but it is no more proper for an architect in a successful world of free enterprise—or probably anywhere—to be surprised at any time than it was for a chamberlain of the Borgias a few hundred years earlier. I had to feel with the man from dear old Hollywood when he said, 'Take out all the locks of the bathroom doors.' Worriedly he added, 'It is my experience that there is always somebody in the bathroom threatening to commit suicide and blackmailing you, unless you can get in freely.' In a moment, I adjusted myself to the natural anxiety of a wealthy producer of a world-conquering film. . . ."[29]

Despite the hyperbole of their respective retrospections, Neutra and von Sternberg were both proud of the house. "Very much later," Neutra recalled, he witnessed von Sternberg, "now white haired, revisiting his long-sold estate. He walked from one great spreading tree to the other. All he had fondly planted from five-gallon cans. Their smooth bark of once upon a time had very much changed. But he still loved them, and I did too, even more."[30]

The house was widely published in the international press and evoked virtually unanimous praise. Its minimalist elegance prompted Wright and Schindler's old client Aline Barnsdall to talk to Neutra about building for her. They had apparently been discussing the idea for some time. "I fear you are wondering," she wrote on February 15, 1939, "why you haven't heard from me regarding the house. *All* the reasons are too complicated to write but the essential one is this: I want to build just one more house, as a home, and I want time to make it contain all that I need and no more and I want to be certain that it is a place I shall want to live the rest of my life. One reason I left Olive Hill was because I always felt weary and under vitalized there. . . . I want you to see my land here at Palos Verdes. I want a house like von Sternberg's. In

137

157. *Neutra*, Von Sternberg House, 1935, bathroom

talking with Wright about it a few weeks ago, I told him that while his houses are like a St. Bernard, or perhaps the more recent ones like an eagle, von Sternberg's is like a greyhound. It taught me a lot that few minutes there, it was a new world of [minimalist] elimination and a lot of other things. . . . I don't mean I want to copy it; just get the feeling of it, the steel, aluminum and elimination, even to the vegetation. So you will hear from me again when I am ready." With the beginning of the European war that year and Barnsdall's own declining health and energy, Neutra never got to design her sleek "greyhound" house.[31]

The war also touched the von Sternberg house itself. Its ship-like ambience appealed to the Air Corps, which exploited it mercilessly as a mock bombing target. The zooming planes on the one hand and the rural isolation on the other prompted von Sternberg to sell his San Fernando castle. It passed through several hands before Ayn Rand acquired it. Though Sullivan and Wright were the apparent prototypes for *The Fountainhead*, her throbbing novel of architectural heroics, she admired Neutra greatly and was pleased to own the house. "I don't know where Miss Rand got her political ideas," Neutra enjoyed observing at cocktail parties, "but it's obvious she used me as the model for Howard Roark's sexuality." In 1971 a developer bought the property for a condominium tract and quickly demolished the castle—moat, Rolls garage, imaginary rain, and all.[32]

At about the same time he built for von Sternberg, Neutra designed another grand house for two other notable Hollywood figures—the writer Anita Loos and her husband, director John Emerson. The house, which was to have been sited directly on the Santa Monica Beach, recalled the elevations of the von Sternberg house combined

158. *Neutra*, Lewin House, 1938, view from master bedroom

159. *Neutra*, Lewin House, Santa Monica, California, 1938

with the curving bay from Anna Sten's living room. It was fated never to be built, however, as Emerson experienced at that time a severe psychological crisis. "It was a long personal story," Loos later recalled, "that had nothing to do with architecture." Much of the spirit of the Loos-Emerson design made its way, however, into a house near the Loos site of 1937 for writer-producer-director Albert Lewin.[33]

Lewin had joined MGM in 1924 and under Irving Thalberg had become head of the story department and producer of most of Thalberg's important projects, including *Mutiny on the Bounty* (1935) and *The Good Earth* (1937). Films that Lewin later wrote and directed included *The Moon and Sixpence* (1942), *The Picture of Dorian Gray* (1945), *The Private Affairs of Bel Ami* (1947), and *Pandora and the Flying Dutchman* (1951), self-consciously "arty" films that were never big box-office successes but later acquired a devoted cult

following. Lewin, observed critic Maurice Zolotow, was "one of the small number of Hollywood literati . . . who wished to raise the cultural level of pictures." He was highly attuned to the visual arts and owned a famous collection of paintings—particularly of French primitives, including Henri Rousseau. He was keenly interested in modern architecture and, knowing the Sten house, eagerly turned to Neutra.[34]

The house was built in 1938 on a long narrow slice of beachfront property. Entry was north of the street-front garages down a long walk the length of the house to the living and dining areas, which fronted the beach. The second-floor beachfront bedrooms opened onto the now-familiar balcony atop the obligatory curving bay "winter garden." Millie Lewin was listed as interior decorator. She and her husband, Dione recalled, were appreciative but difficult and contentious clients. Mary Stotherd, wife of

160. *Neutra*, Kaufman House, Los Angeles, 1937

the composer Herbert Stotherd, and owner of a noted J. R. Davidson house, remembered elegant and stimulating parties at the Lewin house where the guests included the artists Max Ernst and Man Ray, the director Jean Renoir, and the poet Charles Reznikoff. Reznikoff would further immortalize Lewin—and his house—as the prototype for the character Paul Pasha in his Hollywood novel *The Manner Music*. In the book Reznikoff, who obviously had access to Lewin's personal papers, quoted almost verbatim Lewin's letter to Neutra complaining about the photographs of the house published in a leading architectural journal. The other chief protagonist of *The Manner Music* was a writer of film scores, not unlike another real-life Neutra client, Edward Kaufman, who worked at MGM. The Kaufman house, in Westwood just off Sunset Boulevard (1937), featured the usual Neutra trademarks—

most notably the opaque two-story stairwell glazing —in a fine composition, both dramatic and serene.[35]

Neutra's largest and most significant thirties house in Los Angeles not connected with a film industry figure was the house in Laurel Canyon for the journalist Josef Kun (1936). The garage and third-floor entrance hall were flush with curving Fareholm Drive. As at the Lovell house, one entered from the top and descended two levels into the living, dining, and sleeping areas. Great balconies looked out on the city and the sea. From the street one perceived only a minimalist "gate house." Looking up from the canyon, one saw a large villa— another of Neutra's happier compositions. The Kun house was also important to Neutra and to architecture in that it signaled the debut of Julius Shulman, who on a casual visit to the house took snapshots so stunning they were passed on to Neutra.

The architect was impressed and took Shulman under his wing, helping to launch one of the century's great architectural photographers. From the late thirties on, Shulman did most of Neutra's photography as well as that of his major Los Angeles colleagues.[36]

Two Los Angeles remodeling jobs revealed different sides of Neutra's aptitudes and attitudes toward working with the existing environment. To the early twentieth-century Spanish Colonial Rajagopals house in Hollywood Neutra made in 1934 a strikingly "modern" but sympathetic addition. The silver-gray casement windows and aluminum-paneled surfaces of the new top-floor apartment quietly complemented the older Spanish motifs—neither completely overwhelming nor completely deferring to the strong personality of the building and neighborhood. In Rustic Canyon in 1937, however, Neutra did a major renovation of a shingled bungalow on the old Uplifters Ranch. The client, Albert Ruben, was an insurance executive with close business and personal ties to major figures in the film industry, particularly Albert Lewin. It was Ruben's wife Ruth who dealt with Neutra as he juxtaposed the Shingle and International Styles. He retained the original character of the open-beamed, high-ceilinged living room, painted white the shingled surfaces of the older existing structure, but gave to the building a strong modernist image with a new bedroom wing above garages and basement rooms on the street facade.[37]

The largest concentration in the 1930s of Neutra's houses outside Southern California was in the San Francisco Bay area. There he was assisted by his younger associate Otto Winkler, who helped him get some of his earliest commissions. The clapboarded Largent house of 1935 was designed to fit a long narrow corner hillside lot on Twin Peaks, and combined older memories of clapboarded, vertically attenuated Victorian San Francisco with typically Neutra fenestration and detailing. The redwood Darling house of 1937 fit just as comfortably into the Bay Area tradition of the twentieth century, with its straightforward massing of laconic, boxy, and deliberately awkward forms. It was Neutra's earliest redwood house. On the street facade, particularly, it acknowledged a kinship with the work of William Wurster, Gardner Dailey, and other contemporary purveyors of the Bay tradition,

161. *Neutra*, Kun House, Los Angeles, 1936, entrance

162. *Neutra*, Kun House, 1936, south facade

163. *Neutra*, Darling House, 1937, with Shingle Style neighbor

164. *Neutra*, Darling House, San Francisco, 1937

as well as with its older Shingle Style neighbors along steeply inclined Woodland Avenue. The rear garden elevations featured more characteristic Neutra cantilevers and ribbon windows. On all elevations, the Bay Area redwood ambience was tempered with Neutra's silver-gray trim. Mirrored interior walls expanded the living spaces. Like most of Neutra's houses of the period, the Darling house was widely published and discussed and was the recipient of awards. Near Palo Alto Neutra and Winkler also used redwood for "Three Small Houses in an Orchard," a group of cottages for three single friends who wanted clustered but separate houses sited in a communally shared orange grove. In Berkeley Neutra built a tiny redwood "cabin" for the writer Frieda Hauswith and in 1939 a larger, though equally relaxed, redwood villa for William Davey on Monterey Bay. The romantically sited seaside Davey house had an urban cedar counterpart in Neutra's contemporary De Graaf house in Portland, Oregon.[38]

In addition to the Winkler connection, Neutra had also acquired other important Bay area con-

tacts by the mid-1930s. Especially significant were the physician Sidney Joseph and his wife Emily, socially prominent San Franciscans committed to the arts and particularly to modernism. Though they never commissioned a Neutra house themselves, they introduced Neutra to several of his most important Bay Area clients—notably to the painter Mona Hofmann and her husband Arthur. The house for the Hofmanns (1937) in the fashionable suburb of Hillsborough was the first of several that Neutra did in the San Francisco area that returned completely to the high International Style and eschewed the references to the Bay Area tradition that he had used so convincingly in the woodsy Darling house. Though to its detriment it also eschewed the curving bays of Neutra's Los Angeles houses for Hollywood royalty, the Hofmann house echoed a kinship with the south. The familiar, handsome, three-story stairway glazing, the banded casement windows, the projecting terraces and balconies, the silver-gray trim, all contributed to a strong Neutra statement. Yet the Hofmann house suffered in the subtle but crucial matters of scale and proportion, particularly

on the main south elevation, where the large blank mass of the central stairway element seemed insufficiently integrated with the rest of the south facade. It appeared too bluntly, arbitrarily, and tentatively tacked on without attempting to make a statement about that condition.[39]

The well-planned interior was another matter, however, and in singing its praises, Mona Hofmann personified the modernist true believer. "The whole process of creating this four walled world of mine with Mr. Neutra and Winkler," she wrote Dione, "is second only to my psychoanalysis as a major experience." She was certain that "the most important" point was "the raised standard of living for women made possible in a modern house." This applied to the small, servantless house as well as to larger, more luxurious villas such as her own. "Built-in furniture, that need not be moved, that can be vacuumed without bending and pushing and struggling makes it possible to have a 'spring cleaning' in each room once a week. And it stays clean." But she was equally certain that "modern architecture doesn't need 'defense'. It needs re-

cruits. The longer the battle to universally establish modern architecture the more lofty the eventual pinnacle." She wrote another letter from a less lofty pinnacle. "Winning a prize," she acknowledged, "does compensate somewhat for living in a curiosity house. I'm terribly proud of the house so of course I do respond to the public interest. But you cannot imagine the deluge of people who want to see it. . . . Please, please, build four or five more modern houses in San Mateo so we can share the publicity."[40]

Neutra was happy that he could shortly oblige Mona Hofmann with other "curiosity" Bay Area houses. But if the Hofmann house represented high suburban elegance, his Ford house renovation spoke to tougher urban issues. Like Mona Hofmann, Betty Ford was an artist. A child prodigy with a sizzling IQ, she graduated from Stanford at the age of seventeen and ventured to Europe for further study and training. After a stint at the University of Munich she settled in Berlin to work with Georg Kolbe, the sculptor of the statue in the reflecting pool of Mies's Barcelona Pavilion. Forced to leave

165. *Neutra*, Davey House, Monterey, California, 1939

166. *Neutra*, Hofmann House, Hillsborough, California, 1937

167. *Neutra*, Hofmann House, 1937

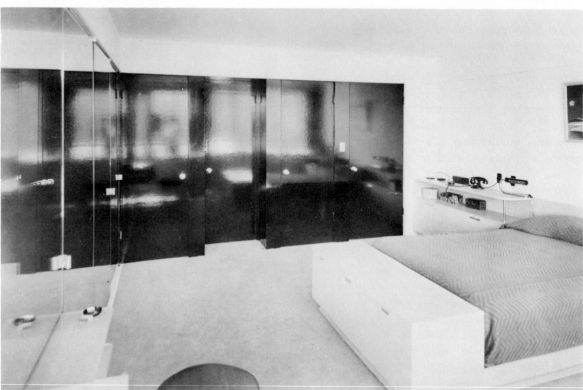

Germany with the advent of the Third Reich, she returned to San Francisco, saturated with the spirit of the Bauhaus culture that was now in eclipse as well as with Kolbe's heroic older values. By contrast, her Victorian Russian Hill row house seemed dated and dowdy, and she wondered if somehow she could not "do better." Building a new house in the midst of the Depression seemed as unrealistic as importing Mies or Gropius, but her mother reminded her of a kindred spirit in Los Angeles who might be willing to modernize the house. She contacted Neutra, and he responded eagerly with interior remodeling, particularly of her studio, and important face-liftings on front and rear additions (1937). The new bands of steel casement windows abutted the existing Victorian elements. All surfaces new and old were painted silver-gray. Delighted with the house's identity with Weimar Germany via Southern California, Ford became another loyal Neutra "soul mate" and over the years a strong champion of his work.[41]

Neutra's encounter with the row house via the Ford renovation prepared him to design a new San Francisco row house for William and Ilse Schiff, recent refugees from Nazi Germany. Despite the problems besetting Weimar Germany, the Schiffs had delighted in post-war Berlin. The *Wohnungskultur,* Ilse Schiff remembered, was "at its highest, and even the middle class was most interested in art and architecture of the new trend, the 'Bauhaus' style." She and her husband William, a physician, commissioned furniture for their Berlin apartment by Harry Rosenthal, a recent Bauhaus graduate. In 1935 they fled to San Francisco, leaving everything behind, including their furniture, but a friend was able to ship it to California. By 1938 the Schiffs were able to contemplate building a house on Jefferson Avenue near the Golden Gate Bridge. For reasons of economy they decided on a pair of stacked flats, flush with the row and close to the street. Like Betty Ford, they wanted something modern in the spirit of Weimar, and when they happened to meet Mona Hofmann and to visit her Hillsborough house, they realized happily that Neutra was their man.[42]

With an aluminum-clad band demarcating the two units, the front wall of the house was virtually all glass, recalling in miniature the famous glass wall of Willis Polk's 1917 Halidie Building a few

168. *Neutra,* Schiff House, San Francisco, 1938

169. *Neutra,* Schiff House, 1938

145

170. *Neutra*, Schiff House, 1938, roof deck

miles to the southeast. The casements extended the width of the house, even covering a segment of opaque glass block over the stairway. A designer less concerned with a unified image might have stopped the casements at the stair and let the blocks take over. The casements rendered the blocks less necessary. Yet the blocks formed a texture that appealed to Neutra, softening the interior of the stair well. A fetching garden lay nestled in the back. The alternating glass and stucco bands of the garden facade recalled Le Corbusier's Villa Stein at Garches. Over the street-level garages and a small rear guest suite was a rental apartment on the second floor of the building. The owners' two-level penthouse apartment opened to front and rear roof decks. An early photograph recorded Neutra and the Schiffs enjoying the good life there. A characteristic band of Neutra outrigging carried the wall symbolically into space and framed, in the distance, Bernard Maybeck's Palace of Fine Arts.[43]

Neutra's most famous San Francisco house was for the financier Sidney Kahn, perched over the east cliff of Telegraph Hill. It was three stories high with a basement beneath the street. All four levels had generous balconies looking south to the skyscrapers of the financial district and east across the Bay Bridge to Berkeley. An elevator at the entrance rose to the living room and bar on the top floor and the bedrooms on the middle level. The elegantly curving nearby stairway turned past glazed block windows. The stair railing alternated sleek chrome capping with glazed recessed lighting bands. The Kahns also delighted—as some clients did not —in the specially commissioned Neutra furniture. This included the noted "camel" dining table, whose legs folded in like a camel's so that when desired it could become a coffee table half as high. Because of the spectacular hillside siting, the cantilevered balconies, and certain other features of the overall gestalt, the Kahn house was labeled "the San

171. *Neutra*, Kahn House, San Francisco, 1940

172. *Neutra*, Kahn House, 1940

173. *Neutra*, Kahn House, 1940

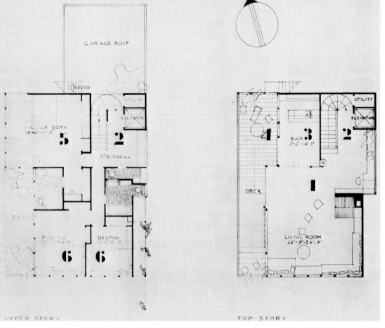

174. *Neutra*, Sciobereti House, Berkeley, California, 1939

Francisco Lovell house." Completed in 1940, the house was a source of pride and delight to Kahn.[44]

Two smaller houses in the International Style, both built in 1939 for college professors, provided a worthy finale to Neutra's Bay area building of the thirties. The story-and-a-half Sciobereti house for a University of California astronomer high in the Berkeley Hills was built of cemesto celetex panels capped with galvanized aluminum bands. In materials, plan, and overall gestalt, it recalled Neutra's 1935 all-plywood house. The crisply minimalist Sciobereti House was also noteworthy for its clients' eclectically sophisticated juxtaposition of casual rattan furniture with family heirloom European antiques. To the south in Los Altos, Neutra built a simple low-slung masterpiece for Alvin Eurich, a Stanford professor of education. Eurich had first commissioned Neutra to build a house for him while still a professor at the University of Minnesota. He had originally considered Frank Lloyd Wright, whose 1933 Willey house stood near Eurich's Minneapolis property, high on a bluff overlooking the

Mississippi, but he disliked what he perceived to be the overinsistence of Wright's work and turned instead to the more serene style of Neutra. He had formerly encountered Neutra only through publications. But shortly after Neutra presented preliminary sketches for a handsome two-story structure for the Minnesota site, Eurich accepted a job at Stanford. The move to California confirmed his decision to stay with Neutra, but his acquisition of a site in the low rolling hills of Los Altos turned him and Neutra to a one-story plan. Set slightly below the road in a splendid grove of ancient live oaks, the simple *L*-shaped house contained a bedroom wing running toward the front of the property from the central area of living and dining rooms. Despite its rather cramped entry and fireplace spaces, the house achieved brilliance in its casually elegant proportions, its comfortable, relaxed siting, and Neutra's facility with small extra touches. Here this meant chiefly a facility with walls, surging gracefully from the volume of the house to become low garden dividers and articulating screens. The front curving

175. *Neutra*, Eurich House, 1939, rear garden

176. *Neutra*, Eurich House, Los Altos, California, 1939

177. *Neutra*, Eurich House, 1939

178. *Neutra*, Kraigher House, Brownsville, Texas, 1937

wall between kitchen and garage served as a piece of abstract sculpture as well as a shield to a potentially messy service entrance. Indeed, the middle-sized Eurich house summarized much of the best of Neutra's work in the thirties, while lyrically predicting his more casual, relaxed style of the forties and fifties.[45]

Neutra's most significant houses outside California in the 1930s were for a Slavic immigrant, George Kraigher, in Brownsville, Texas, and for an eighth-generation New England patrician, John Nicholas Brown. Born in 1890 in Postojna, Serbia, Kraigher served as a mechanical engineer in World War I. In the 1930s his flying skills brought him to the attention of the newly formed Pan American Airlines, with whom he became a pilot and then a high-level executive. For logistical and diplomatic reasons, Pan Am decided to locate its hemispheric headquarters on the U.S.-Mexican border in Brownsville, and Kraigher, a worldly, sophisticated, bachelor found himself in a hot, humid, and rather bleak outpost. But as an intelligent and resourceful man, he knew that one way to cope with the less than optimal larger environment was to create for himself an optimal smaller environment, which in this case meant building an interesting house. He was not yet sure exactly what he wanted, but he thought it should be modern, and in 1936, while on a business trip to Douglas Aircraft in Los Angeles, he saw a modern house that captured his attention. He inquired, and learned that it was designed by Neutra, whom he quickly contacted and subsequently commissioned.[46]

Originally Neutra designed a simple one-story, one-bedroom house, but Kraighter then decided to have him add a guest room on top, making for a more interesting profile against the flat Texas pasture where Kraighter kept fine horses. The cantilevered overhangs furnished crucial protection from the hot Texas sun. The tubular railing around the roof deck, the high window band on the entrance side, the flat, blank stucco planes alternating with glazed ones, and the built-in furniture throughout the house comprised the usual Neutra Modern trademarks. They were not usual for Brownsville, however, except as they touched older, less abstract Hispanic chords—and the "curiosity" house became a local social mecca, where airline, army, and government executives mixed agreeably with south Texas gentry. Indeed, in what he thought would be a hardship tour Kraigher, with the help of Neutra, relished his role as a determined pioneer on the modernist frontier.[47]

In contrast to the small Texas house for Kraigher, Neutra's other most significant building outside California in the 1930s was the large vacation house for John Nicholas Brown and his family. Brown was the scion of one of the country's oldest and most distinguished families, his earliest American ancestor having settled in Rhode Island in 1638. Amassing great wealth in the eighteenth and nineteenth centuries in manufacturing, shipping, and ship building, the Browns devoted much of their fortune and their energies to philanthropy, particularly in education, medicine, and the arts. Brown University, in Providence, was established by and named for them. The death of his father and uncle three months after John Nicholas's birth in 1900 prompted the press to christen him "the world's richest baby." After graduating *magna cum laude* from Harvard in 1922 and then returning there for a master's in fine arts in 1928, Brown devoted his life to the family business interests, philanthropy, and the arts. He was a leading supporter of such cultural institutions as the Tanglewood Music Festival in Massachusetts, the Byzantine Institute in Istanbul, the American School for Classical Studies in Athens, and the Museum of Modern Art in New York. An astute yachtsman and a collector of painting and sculpture, he had a particularly keen interest in modern and historic architecture. Through the centuries the Browns had owned and enjoyed great houses, Georgian to Victorian, an interest that continued into the twentieth century. After his father's death, Brown told Neutra, "we moved to Newport, where my mother, as my guardian, built a large house for me on the Harbour" designed by Ralph Adams Cram. Later, in the 1920s, "I designed a modern bedroom in my mother's house in Boston, which, I believe, was the first modern room in New England. In 1924, I started in close collaboration with Mr. Cram to build a Gothic chapel for St. George's School in Newport and made several trips to Europe to study Gothic architecture. The chapel took four years to build and I enjoyed every detail of the building immensely."[48]

Brown's wife Anne, a journalist, was also from an established family and shared his philanthropic and artistic interests. Since earliest childhood she had vacationed with her family on Fishers Island, New York, off the Connecticut coast between Rhode Island and Long Island, an attachment which led the Browns to decide to build a summer house there in the mid-1930s. Well acquainted with the work of the major modernist architects and able to commission anyone they desired, the Browns picked Neutra, before experiencing any of his buildings, on the basis of photographs they had seen in publications and had studied more closely in the 1932 show. "Richard Neutra was certainly a genius," Anne Brown later recalled, "and, above all, which he would not care to admit, a romantic. In our opinion he topped all the graduates of the German school by combining great imagination and aesthetic ability with what we hoped was a more pragmatic approach to architecture than, let us say, Le Corbusier, many of whose buildings . . . seemed to have disintegrated rather rapidly." A visit to California to inspect "his work in and around Los Angeles . . . confirmed our judgment that he had something no other available modern architect seemed to combine, namely taste, imagination, and an element of practicality."[49]

When he received the initial, portentous phone call, Neutra had never heard of Brown, and while delighted with the enthusiasm of the prospective client, he demurred in confirming such a far-distant commitment until he had checked Brown's credit rating. Dun and Bradstreet assured the impecunious Neutra that Brown was a safe credit risk, and negotiations proceeded. In October 1936 Neutra flew to Fishers Island to inspect the site and returned to Los Angeles to contemplate the design. "We are still tingling with the thrilling excitement of your visit," Brown wrote. "I only wish it could have been longer so that we could have talked even more in detail about the many problems involved." For the next year and a half Neutra and Brown discussed the "many problems" and the details of a complex building program via personal visits, phone calls, and the most intense correspondence Neutra ever conducted with a house client. Neutra relished this contact with a family at the heart of the old American culture. Still consciously the immigrant, the amazed European fascinated with America and its diverse population, Neutra enjoyed being summoned

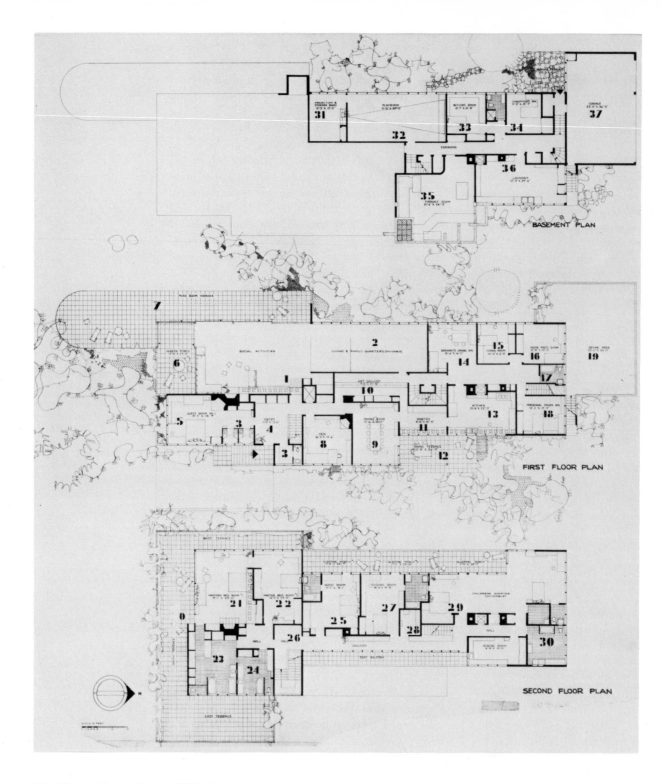

179. *Neutra*, Brown House, ("Windshield"), Fishers Island, New York, 1938

by such bona fide aristocrats. This complemented, fittingly, his equally great pleasure in designing for less wealthy clients and for such recent immigrants as the Schiffs and George Kraigher. "In spite of having had almost unlimited means," Neutra observed, his objective was to give the house "a simple dignity . . . expressing the spirit of our time and the puritanic character of New England."[50]

Throughout his career Neutra insisted that clients, particularly on residential commissions, complete involved questionnaires on their personal histories, needs, habits, likes, and dislikes. Brown later admitted that this rigorous self-analysis took him nearly a week. His detailed memorandum to Neutra reflected the life of an orderly, fastidious New England Brahmin who, despite larger humanistic and humanitarian commitments, enjoyed indulging his own needs and interests. The family, he wrote, "consists of my wife, myself, two small boys —4 and 2—my wife's maid and my valet-chauffeur . . . [and] children's nurse. . . . In addition we have in the summer, a butler, cook and housemaid. In planning the house, keep in mind possibility of additional children and governess or tutor. . . . My wife and I sleep in a double bed. I like to see my boat and an open fire from bed and do not like early morning sun. Mrs. B. likes cross draft in bedroom and large bed table on the left hand side with room for water carafe, cigarettes, ash tray, telephone books, medicines, clock, pencils, paper and bell connection to pantry and maid's room. She smokes, reads, and frequently works in bed and likes to empty cigarette and trash out of sight without getting up from bed. A built-in trash bin with chute to incinerator would be ideal."[51]

Seven pages of equally explicit direction followed for all furniture, facilities, and accoutrements for himself, his wife, his children, and the half-dozen servants, as well as details of the family's daily schedule. Sailing, he emphasized, was the family's chief interest in summer. "I like a barometer in my bedroom which can be seen from bed, and an anemometer [which] must not squeak, showing wind directions and velocity on roof with dial alongside of the barometer. A few ship models can be fitted into the wall of den where all books should be kept in built-in shelves with sliding aluminum doors. Shelves should accommodate Lloyd's yacht registers and club books. . . . I would like the signal

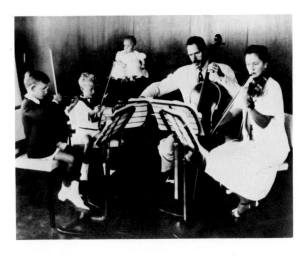

180. The Brown family at Windshield, Fishers Island, New York, ca. 1940

pole on the sun deck with convenient storage place for individual code flags under shelter in bad weather for signaling orders to the yacht. . . . I am fond of deck tennis and would like access to roof deck for this purpose. Cupboard containing rings and net should be convenient to sport deck. We would like a sports cupboard on first floor conveniently located for binoculars, cameras, sun glasses, croquet set, golf clubs and tennis nets with bins to hold one dozen each golf balls and tennis balls." With his great affinity for functional planning, modern gadgetry, and detail all housed in the most minimally and efficiently elegant packaging, Brown was in many ways the ideal modernist client and evangel.[52]

Though for Brown every detail was important, the music room was indeed "the heart of the house." In fact the building was, Anne Brown later noted, often described as "a music room, with bathrooms." This should "be the chief downstairs room of the house," Brown asserted, "and should be fairly large, dry, cool, and *soundproof* and far from the front door and neighbor's houses. It should have a fireplace, space for medium grand piano, quartet, comfortable lounging furniture, light movable straight chairs for players, large Capehart combination phonograph and radio, built-in writing desk with large surface and shelf for music paper and locker for storing phonograph records in albums, music in filing boxes and instrument cupboard with shelves for a cello, viola and several fiddles in cases, and compartments for a spare rosin, strings, mutes, etc. . . ." In response to Brown's concern that the

153

181. *Neutra*, music room, Brown House, 1938

floor not be damaged by cello pegs, Neutra typified his own concern for detail by insetting metal sockets into the floor for the peg tips. He also made proper provision for the hanging, lighting, and storing of the paintings Brown planned to use, including Lyonel Feininger's "Breakwater" in the music room. "Above all," Brown concluded, "we want the house to be unpretentious and livable, economical to build and to operate and a contrast to the Colonial family house in Providence."[53]

By late 1936 Brown could write that he and his family were "thrilled by the appearance of the house as shown in your perspectives. I realize of course that in making these perspectives you have brought the vanishing point far closer and conse-quently given the impression of a structure much larger than I imagine the house will be." He then made numerous suggestions, large and small, for changes in the plan. The boys' dining room, for example, was "much too small and not a good shape. We do not approve of the nook as shown. With a family of unknown size and the possibility of other children coming to take supper on occasion, it seems unwise to have as inelastic an eating space as shown. More fundamental than anything is the thought that the Boys' Dining Room should be dis-tinctly separate from the back part of the house except for the service entry to the pantry . . . we do not like the children being forced to use the back stairs in quite the way that you have planned."

182. *Neutra*, Brown House, 1938

183. *Neutra*, Brown House, 1938

184. *Neutra*, Brown House, 1938

Brown took care to assure Neutra that his suggestions and criticisms should "not convey to you in any way that we are not happy with the prospects . . . I realize that some of the desiderata are mutually inconsistent. On the other hand we naturally hope for as many of those things we desire as we can get!" He assured Neutra that "there is already a tremendous interest in the house here in the East. I was dining with the Department of Fine Arts at Harvard last week. Those connected with the Architectural School seemed most excited over the event of a Neutra house here in the East. I feel the house will cause a tremendous stir." This sense was heightened by the added inclusion of such innovative features as Buckminster Fuller's prefabricated bathroom units, no doubt partially championed by both Brown and Neutra for shock-effect contrast with the house's more standard, deluxe elements.[54]

Neutra, as always, wrote detailed specifications that implemented architecturally Brown's own precise intentions. Such detail frequently frustrated contractors, but Harry Polhemus, who supervised the job, wrote to Neutra upon completion, thanking him for his "patience and many kindnesses in what has been the most interesting job I have ever done. It's been a grand experience. I only hope it may be duplicated soon." Anne Brown later remembered, however, that when construction started, Neutra and the general contractor, Elliott C. Brown, "whose problems were enormous in assembling a work force up to Neutra's standards, were continuously at war . . . and in fact the poor contractor . . . who came from Long Island with an impeccable record of building palaces there, died within a year of a massive stroke. I always felt that a little epitaph should be put on his tombstone that his death may have been caused by building the Neutra house."[55]

The Browns decided to name the house "Windshield" and had stationery specially designed for it. "This is my first letter on Windshield paper, and I want you to have it," Brown wrote Neutra on August 18, 1938. "I can never tell you how much I admire the design and how much I appreciate all you have done. It is a great creation." Though the house was later published widely in architectural journals as well as in such publications as *Town and Country*, Brown adamantly refused a publication request from *Life* magazine. "Above all things," he wrote Neutra, "I do not want to have *Life* illus-

185. *Neutra*, Brown House, 1938

trate this house. I hate the vulgarity of this publication and will not subscribe to it myself."[56]

Despite the tension between Neutra and the contractors and the Browns' impatience with less-than-perfect detailing, the completed house seemed successful beyond expectations. It was, Anne Brown remembered, "aesthetically a masterpiece. Though it horrified neighbors who had built enlarged replicas of the House of Seven Gables in Salem, etc., I think it created great excitement and admiration." She recalled the remark of their four-year-old son Carter when he first saw the house from the ferry landing. "But Daddy," he said, "it doesn't look like

157

a house, it looks like a twain!" In general, she acknowledged, the house worked well functionally, though it was "noisy due to Neutra's insistence that the floors be covered with either linoleum or rubber. It ended up being almost completely carpeted." Her retrospective critique touched several of modern architecture's most vulnerable areas. The casement windows, for example, "were much too large, and hence complicated to open and close if there was any wind, and because of the immense amount of light, the view windows had to be fitted with sun-proofed glass. The servants found it harder to clean than any traditional house since every speck of dust showed glaringly—several of them quit the first summer."[57]

The Brown's greatest complaint was that Neutra failed to heed sufficiently their warnings about the area's vulnerability to storms. Sited on the second highest point of a completely exposed island, the house suffered heavy damage in the autumn hurricane of 1938. The historically unprecedented 125-mile-an-hour winds ripped away the flat roof and blew out many windows. "One of my children," Anne Brown remembered many years later "missed death very narrowly when a window, plus its aluminum frame, blew in onto his bed from the lee side of the house" minutes after he had left the room. "The near victim," she added, "was J. Carter Brown, ironically now director of the National Gallery of Art, who still loves modern architecture." Neutra was dismayed by the damage to the house, and Brown, to prevent a recurrence of the catastrophe, retained structural engineers from MIT to advise on the rebuilding. Less stoic in her reaction to the damage than her husband, Anne Brown suggested that the name of the house be changed to "Won't Shield." She recalled, however, that her husband, "who has a more equitable temperament than I, worked diligently with [Neutra] to rebuild the house . . . and the house stood nobly through five more hurricanes." In July 1939, Brown wrote Neutra that they had moved in again and "have been enjoying the house to the fullest extent. The repairs have all been completed and the house looks even better than it did last summer. We both want you to know how beautiful we think the house is and send you our congratulations. Many of our friends have visited us already and all appreciate in their varying capacities your achievement."[58]

Of all the family members, it was young

Carter Brown who apparently most loved and appreciated the house. He was, he remembered, the chief "taker-througher," relishing his role as official house tour guide. He especially loved the way the silver-gray aluminum paint reflected the changing sunlight. Indeed, he recalled, when the western façade caught the late afternoon sun the house turned red. Once this prompted a concerned neighbor to call and ask quite seriously if the house was on fire. Some thirty years later, on New Year's Eve, 1975, the house did catch fire and burned to the ground.[59]

Neutra's reputation was made and confirmed in the 1930s primarily through his houses—from the experimental cottages for the Mosks and the Beards to the grander villas for von Sternberg and the Browns. Seeing each commission as both unique *and* replicable, Neutra enjoyed this aspect of his work. Yet he placed even greater value on his public and commercial buildings and his private and public apartment housing. He called it building for "humans in groups," or taking "modernity" to the larger community.

187. *Neutra*, Laemmle Office Building, 1933

Community   1932–1942

While private single-family residences brought Neutra his greatest success and recognition in the 1930s, he believed his work for the larger community was even more significant. Commercial buildings, schools, apartments, and government housing projects were the most notable of these and were the types that most frequently saw completion. Such commissions forced Neutra to extend his attention beyond the interesting and abstractly important issue of the American single-family dwelling to the worlds of business, labor, and education and to all levels of government: municipal, state, and national. And these larger contacts forced him in turn to confront the related social and political issues of the national and international scene.

Of Neutra's commercial commissions in the 1930s, the earliest was an office building for Universal-International Pictures at the prestigious corner of Hollywood and Vine (1931–32). Neutra had met Universal's president, Carl Laemmle, through a mutual European acquaintance who had been so impressed with Neutra's lecture in Hamburg in 1930 that he recommended him to the German-American film mogul. Gregory Ain recalled that Laemmle was especially pleased with the bustle of the traffic and the human activity that Neutra had put into the presentation drawings and had remarked with pleasure, "You've got all Hollywood coming to my building." High atop the structure on either side of the sleek corner clock tower were integrally attached billboards advertising Universal's current releases. The rear service yard was an elegant essay in minimalist geometry, achieved by the repetition of *L*-shaped door and window bands in a mirror-image effect as those spare, simple elements moved outward from the corner. By making the

vents above the second-floor windows exactly the width of the first floor doors below, Neutra used a functional element to effect a striking decorative pattern. In addition to the upstairs office for the Laemmle dynasty, Neutra designed a multi-use building with a handsome café and chic, income-producing stores on the busy street floors. These shops, as well as the Coco Tree Restaurant, were trimmed and highlighted with reflecting metal and mirrored surfaces. Laemmle liked the results.[1]

Neutra employed similar effects in the Comet Orange Shop (1934) and the Leighton cocktail bar (1937) in downtown Los Angeles. In the Leighton as in the Coco Tree café for Laemmle, the leather upholstery and mirrored surfaces recalled the ambience of Loos's Viennese Kärtner bar, which Neutra had admired and frequented as a youth. Yet these designs were even more austere than Loos's, and reflected what Lewis Mumford called "that chastity, that emotional reserve, which is not so much love of ice for its coldness as a love of the crystalline forms that ice assumes." For the chewing-gum mogul Philip Wrigley, Neutra devised a stylish ticket office (1937) for Wrigley's Catalina Island resort off the Southern California coast. The permanent window display contained a model of the island. A balcony of private offices overlooked the two-story lobby. The slight opening of the balcony with tubular railing echoed the chrome of the fixtures and furniture below. Wrigley expressed his pleasure with the result by entertaining the Neutras at his Catalina estate.[2]

Neutra's design for the Scholts advertising agency (1937) near downtown Los Angeles featured a stunning corner entrance, whose protective overhang continued through the glass front into the

161

188. *Neutra*, Laemmle Office Building,
Los Angeles, California, 1933

189. *Neutra*, Laemmle Office Building,
1933, rear service yard

lobby as a lowered aluminum-faced lighting soffit. Between the long studio and layout rooms to the west and the semicircular conference room to the north lay a palm-shaded patio for the use of the employees. The handsome building contained 2300 square feet and cost $11,750. The Evans Plywood office building, Lebanon, Oregon (1940), housed plant executives and office staff on the first floor, with an apartment on the second floor for overnight visitors to compensate for the lack of hotel facilities in the rural forest area. Constructed and finished almost completely in the company's own plywood, the building illustrated the versatility of that product as a material for inside finish, exterior surfacing, and flooring. For the first-floor offices, translucent glass blocks and large transparent panes contrasted effectively with thin, high window bands of fixed and movable glass. The free-form curve of the second-floor balcony rail furnished strong counterpoint to an otherwise orthogonal structure. Also in contrast to the all-white building was the high-gloss golden-yellow porch ceiling, imparting to that element an almost metallic effect. The uncovered portion of the porch served as a sun deck.[3]

For all these enterprises, which sought to project a "modern to the minute" spirit, Neutra's sleek stores and offices provided the ideal packaging of functional requirements. They addressed themselves not only to the desired corporate image but to the comfort and delight of customers and employees as well.

Of all the public genres, school architecture interested Neutra most. His Ring Plan School design for Rush City had eschewed traditional multistoried plans in favor of a one-story ring of classrooms, which opened on one side to sheltered corridors and on the other side to patio gardens. The curving ring plan minimized the sprawl caused by the departure from the stacked multilevel plan. The model of the Ring Plan School had stirred much comment in the 1932 show as it traveled about the country, particularly in Los Angeles, where the open-air scheme seemed especially appropriate for the California climate. Conservative opposition to such new-fangled ideas was mitigated, moreover, by the effects upon both educators and the public of the devastating earthquake that struck Southern California in 1933. As older buildings were condemned or declared un-

190. *Neutra*, Catalina Ticket Office, Los Angeles, 1937

163

191. *Neutra*, Catalina Ticket Office, 1937

ing the 1932 Museum of Modern Art show, several Los Angeles educators, particularly the school principal Nora Sterry, saw in Neutra's plan the ideal setting for Dewey's "learning by doing." Sterry enlisted in her promotion campaign the additional backing of the League of Women Voters, and in 1934 the Los Angeles School Board called on Neutra to build his experimental school. The commission was for an addition to the existing Corona Avenue School in the remote district of Bell in southeast Los Angeles. Here Neutra produced the Ring Plan School without the ring. The new *L*-shaped wing finished in 1935 consisted of two kindergarten and five elementary classrooms. Bilateral ventilation and lighting came from high clerestory windows on the east above the open-porch, outdoor hallway and from the sliding glass walls on the west that opened onto the garden patios. Hedges divided each outdoor class space from its neighbors. Shade trees, adjustable awnings, and a six-foot roof-slab overhang protected the classrooms from the sun and the elements. Movable chairs and desks, easily portable between indoors and out, replaced the screwed-down school furniture of yore. Housing 250 children, the new wing cost $38,500, or approximately $3.50 per square foot.[4]

It was commonly referred to as the "test-tube school," and residents of the neighborhood likened it to "a drive-in market, an airplane hanger, and a penthouse on Mars." The *Los Angeles Times* noted, however, that it was not some futuristic dream possible only in the distant 1970s, but very much a fact of the mid-1930s. Even so, the newspaper admitted, it "differs from the customary school building like a 1936 model automobile from the original horseless carriage." The school was widely publicized in the international press. It was also filmed for Hearst's Metronome News and the noted newsreel *The March of Time*. Doyt Early, the chief state architect in the Division of Schoolhouse Planning, gave a typically enthusiastic modernist testimonial just after the school's completion. "I think that the absence of historic romancing in design is both pleasing and honest," he wrote Neutra. "There is better light in the classrooms than in any I've ever seen. The out-of-door possibilities lend freedom, variety and interest to the program, not to mention their health factors. There are some delightful color effects. I feel that you have made some fresh

safe, the need for new schools opened the door to Neutra's ideas.

Neutra was aware of the progress of similarly modern school designs elsewhere. Howe and Lescaze's Hessian Hills School, Croton-on-Hudson, New York (1931), was the most noted early example of modernist school design in America, though .its indoor-outdoor relationships were not developed as thoroughly as they would be in Neutra's schools. Johannes Duiker's modern Freiluft Volkschule (1928–30), which Neutra had seen when he visited Amsterdam, was a stack of classrooms four stories high, but with large open-air porches adjoining the classrooms at each level. Schools from the mid-1920s in the garden-city suburb of Welwyn, England, by Louis De Soissons featured classrooms which did indeed open to the outside, but via large, space-consuming variations on French doors. The essence of Neutra's contribution to the problem was not a door to the garden, but a sliding glass wall which, when opened, truly brought the outside in.

As Neutra's ideas became better known follow-

and inspiring contributions to the art, or shall I say science, of school planning. I will use it as a wedge, if I may, to encourage other districts to venture a little from the traditional."[5]

Half-way through the first school year, principal Georgina Ritchie asserted in her official report to the Board of Education that "a school has at last been built which is a distinct improvement from the standpoint of health, safety, and educational opportunity, on the antiquated type of buildings, to which we have so stubbornly adhered in face of a steadily changing philosophy of education." Fourteen years later, in 1950, Ritchie confirmed her initial evaluation. "I have yet to find in Los Angeles or anywhere else," she wrote, "a building which can measure up to the primary grade buildings at Corona. . . . Ask the teachers, the pupils, the parents and the representative people in this town what that primary building has meant to them. They are proud of it and needless to say, so am I. May many more such schoolrooms be built in the years that lie ahead." And, indeed, however experimental the "test-tube school" seemed in 1935, it became over the years an important model for school building in California and beyond.[6]

Open-air, sliding-door classrooms of the Corona type alternated with more traditionally enclosed laboratories and dormitory rooms for the California Military Academy (1935), a private Los Angeles preparatory school. Aluminum panels provided exterior cladding in the manner of the Beard and von Sternberg houses. An especially handsome element of the building was the main front entryway, where a cantilevered entrance canopy cut across the tall front windows, forming a transom and side lights. For asymmetrical effect, Neutra placed the railing wall along only one side of the entrance porch.[7]

Neutra's other large school project of the 1930s was the Emerson Junior High School (1937) on Selby Avenue in the Westwood district of Los Angeles. It was an outgrowth in certain respects of the Corona Avenue School and the California Military Academy, but the area's high student density called for a two-story structure considerably larger than the earlier buildings. Rigorously engineered to withstand earthquake shocks, the two-story structure naturally allowed for the movable-wall-patio scheme to be implemented only on the main ground

192. *Neutra*, Scholts Advertising Agency, Los Angeles, 1937

193. *Neutra*, Scholts Advertising Agency, 1937

165

194. *Neutra*, Scholts Advertising Agency, 1937

Junior High School was completed in stages. The streamlined auditorium, finished in 1939, was, Neutra believed, its finest component. In his classic historical survey, *Art and Life in America,* art historian Oliver Larkin chose Wright's Falling Water, Gropius's house at Lincoln, Massachusetts, and Neutra's Emerson Junior High School as leading examples of 1930s modernism.[8]

As with his numerous unrealized residential and commercial projects, Neutra designed public buildings which were likewise never built. In 1938 and '39, for example, he entered but failed to win competitions for buildings at Goucher College, Baltimore; Wheaton College, Norton, Massachusetts; and William and Mary College, Williamsburg, Virginia; and for the new Smithsonian Galleries in Washington, D.C. In the latter two competitions, however, Neutra's designs received honorable mentions. In 1936 he produced an ambitious and much-admired design for a Los Angeles Museum of Contemporary Art on a site in Westwood, near UCLA, but the museum was never built. Earlier in the 1930s he had hoped to build the proposed Griffith Park Observatory, and went so far as to design an elegant model, but the older and more established architect John Austin got the commission.[9]

Since his student days in Vienna, his Berlin years with Mendelsohn, and his briefer stays in New York and Chicago, Neutra had been intrigued with the problems and possibilities of the multiple-unit urban apartment house. Recalling those densely packed and populated cities, he was both charmed and perplexed by the relative lack of density of Los Angeles, a city whose sprawl and openness encouraged and fostered the detached single-family dwelling. Yet in the relatively denser sections of Central Los Angeles and in newer developing districts such as Hollywood, the need for more compact, multiple-unit dwellings was becoming increasingly apparent, even by the 1920s. The Jardinette apartments of 1927 had addressed these imperatives. Yet while stunningly "modern" in exterior packaging, the Jardinette was based on a rather old-fashioned plan that might have been appropriate to cities almost anywhere. But in the 1930s in the then-sparsely settled district of Westwood near the recently opened new west-side campus of UCLA, Neutra designed several significant apart-

floor. Whenever possible, upstairs rooms led to open roof-top terraces.

Neutra's patron on the Emerson commission was Board of Education member Margaret Clark, whom he had met as a fellow member of the prestigious Severance Club, a dining and discussion group of Los Angeles intellectuals. The initial steel-framed structure cost $5.00 a square foot. Continuing budgetary and building code constraints tried Neutra's patience. Forced to undergo surgery for concurrent appendicitis and tonsillitis shortly before the first presentation of drawings, Neutra finished the work from his hospital bed, aided by Dione and his faithful apprentice Pfisterer. At the building's dedication in the fall of 1937, a "television play" called the "Building of Emerson" was presented, with students in the roles of staff, board, and faculty members. The lead role in the play, significantly, was that of "Mr. Neutra." Emerson

ment complexes that not only acknowledged older regional traditions, but looked with prescience to the area's future density and urbanity.

Commissioned as a family investment by Joseph Rabinovitch, his mother, and other relatives, the Landfair apartments (1935–37) ultimately caused Neutra a great amount of pain. Caught between difficult, malcontent clients and a contractor who did in fact build parts of the structure badly, Neutra ultimately sided with John L. Hudson, the contractor, in a suit and countersuit between him and the Rabinovitches, a long legal entanglement that resulted in Hudson making corrections and the clients being forced to finally pay him his fee. Neutra's typically detailed specifications and supervisory memoranda made it clear, under court examination, that he was not to blame for the problems. Yet because his testimony was instrumental in forcing the clients to pay their bills to him and the builder, the Rabinovitches attempted, ultimately without success, to have the American Institute of Architects suspend Neutra's license. Despite such harassment, however, the building, as completed, was a masterwork.[10]

Composed of two one-story, five-room flats on the east side and six more compact two-story apartments to the west, the Landfair was in essence a block of densely packed row houses, with staggered set-backs, unit by unit, augmenting the effect of separate juxtaposed entities. A stairway led from the living, dining, and kitchen areas on the first floor of each of the smaller units to baths and bedrooms on the second floor, with related stairs leading from each apartment to the roof-garden sun decks. All occupants shared the common back garden. In its handsome profiles and exterior configurations, the Landfair recalled certain aspects of the apartment buildings at the Weissenhof *Siedlung* near Stuttgart (1927) by Mart Stam and J. J. P. Oud. Later the Landfair was badly disfigured in a careless conversion to student cooperative housing.

While in the Landfair Neutra composed an urbane essay on the reciprocal imperatives of density and privacy, in the Strathmore apartments (1937), two blocks to the south, he acknowledged older regional architectural traditions as well. Long impressed with the elegantly stacked megastructures of the Southwest Pueblo Indians and with the more recent bungalow courts of Southern California,

195. *Neutra*, Evans Plywood Building, Lebanan, Oregon, 1940

196. *Neutra*, Evans Plywood Building, 1940

167

197. *Neutra*, Evans Plywood Building, 1940

198. *Neutra*, Corona Avenue School, Los Angeles, California, 1935

199. *Neutra* Corona Avenue School, 1935

200. *Neutra*, California Military Academy, Los Angeles, 1935

201. *Netura*, California Military Academy, 1935

202. *Neutra*, Emerson Junior High School, Los Angeles, 1937

Neutra designed Strathmore as a modernist version of the two vernaculars. Commissioned by a client who already owned the land, Neutra decided to buy half-interest in the project. One of his earliest personal investments, it testified to his growing solvency after years of protracted financial strain.

Strathmore contained six two-bedroom, two-bath apartments and two smaller one-bedroom flats. Stacked and staggered atop each other back into the hillsides in pueblo fashion, the apartments each had a separate entrance fronting onto a central garden in the manner of the traditional California bungalow court. The six larger flats were all the same size and, with minor variations, had similar floor plans. Due to sharply breaking terrain, however, 11005 Strathmore, the street apartment on the north side, with garages underneath, featured the most interesting array of split floor and ceiling levels. From the broad central concrete stairway, smaller steps led to a front porch protected by a wide cantilevered overhang. The front door at the extreme left corner of the building was the only solid element in a wide expanse of glass that wrapped around the corner. The "weightlessness" of the door and surrounding glass planes and the general sense of a "dematerialization" of space was fostered by the slim proportions of the vertical supporting members. Fixed and movable windows were alternated in a lyrically asymmetrical Mondrianesque composition, the 3-foot, 3½-inch module of the entire building being determined by the width of the standard steel casements. Inside the

203. *Neutra*, Landfair Apartments, Los Angeles, 1937, north facade

204. *Neutra*, Landfair Apartments, 1937, east facade

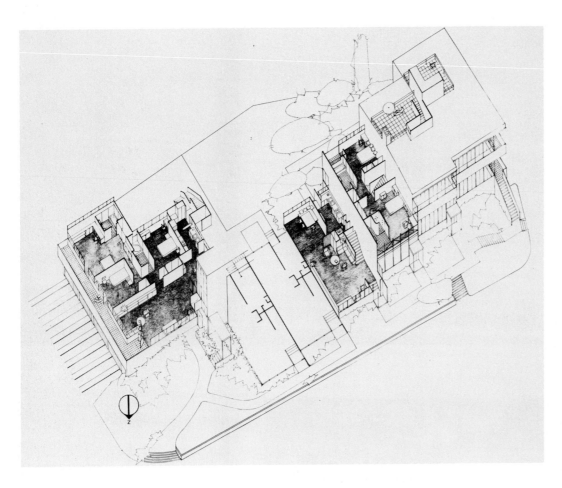

205. *Neutra*, Landfair Apartments, 1937

front elevation, with a separate side entry from the northeast studio bedroom.[11]

The first tenants at Strathmore were Dione's sister Regula Thorston and her parents, Alfred and Lilly Niedermann, who had emigrated from Switzerland to retire in Los Angeles. Regula remembered, however, that for some months they were the only inhabitants. Other early prospective tenants found the buildings too "cold," "austere," and "industrial" for their tastes. "Moon architecture . . . hospital architecture," she remembered hearing them mutter. But slowly the apartments attracted a number of interesting people, including the film stars Dolores Del Rio, Orson Welles, and Luise Rainer and Rainer's husband, the playwright Clifford Odets. Lilly Latte, companion of director Fritz Lang, kept a Strathmore apartment as her private retreat from the social whirl of Hollywood and her demanding life with Lang. Designers Charles and Ray Eames produced the first of their famous chairs in their Strathmore apartment. Later John Entenza, editor of *Arts and Architecture*, was a Strathmore dweller, as was the photographer Eliot Elisofon.[12]

In 1938 Luise Rainer confessed to Neutra "that a few years ago I, myself, was one of those who intensely hesitated to live in one of those modern houses, believing that one could never feel warm and at home inside of them. Bit by bit I went closer to such modern places, just like one comes to examine a wild animal, with jitters and a certain curiosity. In the process the revelation came over me that I was all wrong and I felt attracted more and more. . . . The clearness, the long lines of windows which allow the light to come in and the eye to rove out far, far, all of this gives you a strange feeling of happiness and freedom."[13]

Around the corner from Strathmore, on nearby Kelton Avenue in Westwood (1942), Neutra designed a modest but fetching apartment triplex as another rental investment for himself and his extended family. Lily and Alfred Niederman would move from Strathmore and spend the rest of their lives there. Two small juxtaposed ground-floor flats formed the base of the larger and more lyrical second-story "tree-house" apartment, with inviting balcony roof decks stretching into the trees at front and back. Less tautly dramatic than Strathmore and Landfair, the Kelton apartments looked ahead to Neutra's more relaxed and lyrical work of the 1940s

front door a low hardwood stairway led into the connected living and dining room area. Low railings to the side of those stairs linked up with their counterparts just beyond the glass to provide a strong example of Neutra's interpenetration of inside and outside space. As one negotiated the split-level entry into the living and dining room area, the eye was carried upward to experience a corresponding shift in ceiling heights. A hall led northwest to the kitchen and utility rooms and turned east down another stairway into the bed- and bathroom areas. The drop of the floor level was again strikingly echoed in the break of ceiling levels as the eye moved up and outward from relatively lower spaces toward the great bank of casements on the bedrooms' east walls. As with the southeast corner of the living room, the glass in the northeast bedroom studio wrapped around the corner to greet sheltering eucalyptus trees. The long, divided balcony porch ran the length of the

206. *Neutra*, Strathmore Apartments, Los Angeles, 1937, Landfair Apartments in background

207. *Neutra*, Strathmore Apartments, 1937

173

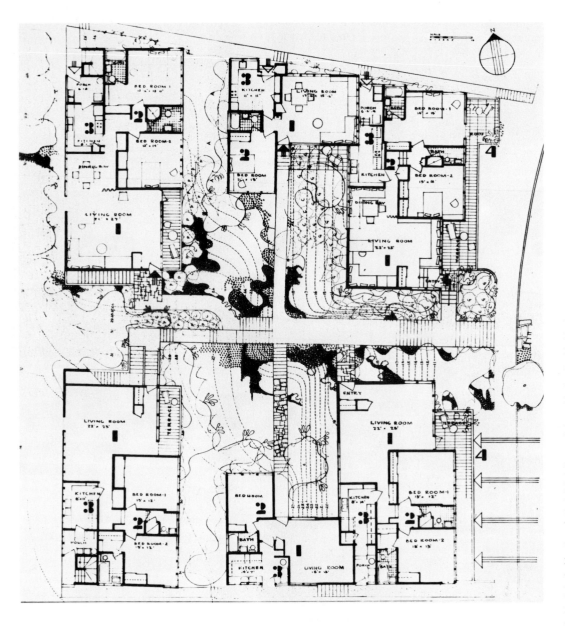

208. *Neutra*, Strathmore Apartments, 1937

versial EPIC (End Poverty in California) platform. Neutra's dreams and schemes—and his actual finished drawings of subsistence homesteads for cooperatives of unemployed workers and for migrant farm workers—came to naught in the early and middle 1930s. Later in the decade, however, his persistence paid off in contracts from such federal agencies as the National Youth Administration and the Works Progress Administration.[15]

Neutra's chief Washington patron in the late 1930s and early '40s was Colonel Laurence Westbrook, an attorney and former army officer who continued to use his military title. A native Texan, Westbrook was the first director of the Texas Relief Commission in 1931 and served with such distinction that Roosevelt called him to Washington in early 1934 to direct the nation's rural rehabilitation and drought relief program. In 1935 'he became assistant administrator of the Works Progress Administration under Harry L. Hopkins, and after resigning that post in 1936 continued to serve as chairman of the WPA advisory board while working as a private developer and consultant for large-scale federally subsidized housing projects.[16]

Hearing of Neutra through an associate, Karl Karsten, who had heard Neutra lecture in Washington, Westbrook engaged Neutra in 1938 to design the ambitious but ultimately aborted "Park Living" housing project for Jacksonville, Florida. In his own enthusiasm for Neutra's commitments to prefabricated modernist design and building, Westbrook failed to gauge correctly the conservative biases in the Jacksonville area against such modernist trademarks as flat roofs, steel casement window bands, and concrete slab foundations. Problems of financing forced Westbrook's withdrawal from the project, and local architectural jealousies ultimately decreed that more traditionally oriented Florida architects assume the work. Westbrook realized, however, that Neutra's modest remuneration hardly compensated for the time and energy he and Pfisterer had expended on the detailed Jacksonville plans, and he proceeded to use his substantial Washington connections to help Neutra get other federal commissions.[17]

One such contact was Westbrook's fellow Texan David Williams, chief architect of the National Youth Administration, with whom Neutra

and '50s. Kelton was featured on the cover of a special 1946 Neutra issue of the French journal *L'Architecture d'aujourd'hui*.[14]

As successful as he was with these private apartment developments, however, Neutra continued to dream of designing large-scale quality housing for low-income workers. He had already corresponded with the socialist Upton Sinclair, soliciting suggestions, and had supported Sinclair in his 1934 bid for the California governorship on his contro-

174

developed a close personal and professional friendship. The NYA provided young Americans with temporary jobs and with training for more permanent ones. Neutra designed several California training and activities centers, of which the units at Sacramento and San Luis Obispo were the largest and most typical. These combined offices, workrooms, classrooms with connected dormitory spaces, reminiscent, despite their board and batten construction, of the more permanent structures Neutra had designed for the California Military Academy and Emerson Junior High School. The placement and proportioning of such modernist elements as the high bands of windows gave a distinctly Neutra stamp to the buildings at San Luis Obispo. Neutra also exploited the slightly rolling terrain to particularly good effect with dramatic jogs in ceiling and window levels. The roofed but open connecting outdoor corridors also provided interesting constructivist effects as they joined and intersected the larger structural elements. Besides these major buildings, Neutra also enjoyed designing such relatively minor projects as the 1940 NYA Rose Bowl Parade float at Pasadena, which won a prize. The main feature of the float was a rose-covered model of the nation's Capitol dome.[18]

In addition to his own designs, moreover, Neutra served during 1939 and '40 as an architectural consultant to the whole western region of the NYA. In one report, he urged that the relatively "non-permanent or emergency character" of NYA structures not be used as an excuse for rearing "architectural potboilers. While such work, like any practical execution, might be considered as contributing to concrete experience, the aim to accomplish *exemplary* planning and executions, at least in the limited field of training and recreational youth centers, should never be lost sight of. The national idealism of youth should be kept stimulated." As a modernist missionary, he also insisted that "such work could in planning, detailing and design be more progressive and less hampered by prejudice and obsolescent tradition than many projects handled in a purely commercial manner. *The training in historical design and detail, the following of Victorian patterns in furniture or building style cannot play a fruitful role in the schooling of young people for today or tomorrow. Beauty should*

remain an important consideration in all work taught to and executed by youth. But it will have to be that beauty of a flush surface door, spotless paint jobs and sensitive color harmonization rather than that of renaissance mouldings and the wrought iron ornamentation of days never again to return in the lives of present youth." Pfisterer worked closely with Neutra on the NYA as well as other work of the period, and when a position opened in a higher echelon of the agency that paid more than Neutra could, Neutra recommended Pfisterer for the job. The ironic consequence of this move, however, was that Pfisterer, as Neutra's disciple, was so suited and attuned to the work that the NYA ultimately decided it no longer needed Neutra's services as a consultant.[19]

The visibility and experience Neutra gained at the NYA, however, made him a logical candidate for the California State Planning Board, whose members were charged with coordinating local planning efforts and initiating, renewing, and critiquing state-sponsored and state-related planning and construction projects. Reimbursed only for travel expenses, Neutra volunteered his time and services for the monthly Sacramento board meetings. He served as a board member and ultimately as chairman from 1939 through 1941.[20]

Between 1940 and '42 the Westbrook-Williams connection also brought Neutra important housing commissions in Texas and California, as the older need for low-cost housing was augmented by the even more pressing imperatives of defense production. By this time Westbrook was special assistant to Federal Works Administrator John Carmody, and was able to bring his ideas and influence to bear in the planning and design of housing for defense workers near the North American Aviation plant in Grand Prairie, Texas, north of Dallas. For this Avion Village, as it came to be called, Westbrook was also able to bring together several of his favorite modernist architects. David Williams was named supervising architect; another Texan, Roscoe Dewitt, served as resident architect; and Neutra was brought in as chief planner and designer. The "finger-park" layout with its emphasis on *cul de sac* residential streets owed much to the aborted Jacksonville "Park Living" plans, with which Westbrook, Williams, and Neutra had all been asso-

209. *Neutra*, Strathmore Apartments, 1937, entrance

210. *Neutra*, Strathmore, Apartments, 1937,
window pattern in study

211. *Neutra* and Luise Rainer at Strathmore
Apartments, 1937

212. *Neutra*, Kelton Apartments, Los Angeles, 1942

213. *Neutra*, Kelton Apartments, 1942

177

214. *Neutra*, Kelton Apartments, 1942

ciated. All were committed to the ethic and esthetic of modern building prefabrication, and Williams also contributed his own strong predilection for using, as suggestive models, the indigenous regional architecture of Texas.[21]

The two-story units at Avion Village indirectly imbibed this local tradition, with their gallery porches upstairs and down, and probably reflected major design input from Williams and Dewitt. The more sprawling and horizontal one-story duplexes bore Neutra's stamp more strongly, as did the central administration and community buildings, including school and recreational facilities. Everyone was delighted with the ease and speed of the prefabricated construction. An initial demonstration, Williams wrote Neutra on May 21, 1941, "was in honor of a flying visit by Col. Westbrook last Friday. We finally wound up there with '16 experimental houses . . . to get the bugs out of the method. . . . Pre-fab plumbing, integral wiring in panels. . . . Shop painted complete except for the finished roof. The contest was to prove how quickly a house could be completed. I think 57 minutes is a world record by several hours."[22]

Newspaper interviews with Neutra and Williams focused on the relatively novel issues of the prefabricated structures, the "Park Living" ambience, and the extent to which the thrust of the Avion Village was influenced by the design experiments of the air and motor age. "It is fitting," the *Dallas Morning News* quoted Neutra as saying, "that workers who are engaged in the most advanced branch of modern technological products should be housed in modern homes."[23]

In the *Los Angeles Times* Neutra emphasized the connections of this ethic with the process of prefabrication, suggesting that "the prefabricated era is just beginning after many false starts." He then pointed out a significant contradiction. "When you buy a car, you have pride in owning that make. It's been advertised and given prestige until you are proud to own that car. Prefabricated housing has been promoted in just the opposite way. It has been given no prestige by advertising. The builder tries to make the homes look deceptively as though they were individually planned." Neutra believed however that "the war boom will accustom people to prefabricated homes and that judicious advertising will do the rest." The *Times* also noted that "to keep cost down and for simplicity and convenience, Mr. Neutra thinks the house of tomorrow will be much smaller than today's. The bedrooms in his Texas community measure only 85 to 110 square feet. 'Our furniture of today is much too large for such small space,' he said. 'Another type of furniture must be used, not doll pieces, but designed for economy of space. You can get the best idea [of] what it will be like by examining the chairs in a skyliner or sleeper bus. The frames will be made of relatively indestructible hard wood or metal and there will be a minimum of upholstery. . . . An airplane chair today which can be used for sleeping makes a Morris chair look clumsy.' "[24]

Some eight years after its completion, reflecting on the afterlife of Avion Village, Westbrook proudly informed Neutra that in June 1948 "the project which you designed for me in 1940 was sold to its occupants under the Mutual Ownership Plan for a price approximating $750,000. . . ." Even on the basis of the total cost of $922,000, the recovery by the federal government after seven years was more than 81 percent of the original outlay, "compared to an average recovery for such projects as 49 percent. This comparison constitutes a highly deserved tribute to you as an architect. . . ."[25]

Between 1940 and 1942 Neutra conveyed the essence of the Jacksonville and Avion plans to four housing projects in Southern California. Two of these, Hacienda Village and Pueblo del Rio, sponsored by the Los Angeles Housing Authority in south central Los Angeles, housed largely black and Mexican-American populations. Both were team efforts in which Neutra collaborated with such other California firms as Paul Williams, Gordon Kaufman, and Wurdeman and Becket. Despite the multiple authorship, however, Neutra's hand was obvious in aspects of the site plans and in various design elements throughout the developments.

Two other projects, Amity Compton and Channel Heights, were designed entirely by Neutra's own office. Amity Compton was, again, initiated by Westbrook and sponsored by the Federal Works Agency. Due to inter-agency jurisdictional problems and various other complicating factors, Amity Compton, like Jacksonville, was never realized as planned. Neutra transferred much of its spirit, however, to the Channel Heights housing for shipyard workers near the Los Angeles harbor at San Pedro,

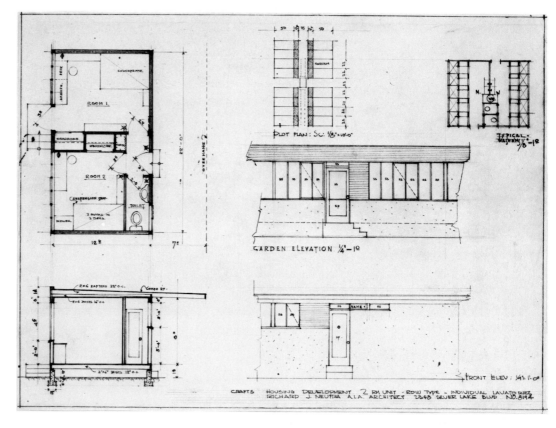

a project whose importance to the national defense effort increased as war became more imminent.[26]

Channel Heights was funded by the Federal Works Agency and, like Hacienda Village and Pueblo del Rio, was coordinated by the Los Angeles Housing Authority. It was the last permanent housing project completed after the beginning of the war, construction having begun just prior to the decree of the Federal Housing Authority that, due to the scarcity of raw materials, permitted only temporary housing for the duration of the war. The nature of the sloping 150-acre site, cut by steep ravines, on the south slope of the Palos Verdes Hills, prompted Neutra to cluster the buildings into three large super-blocks. The 222 residential structures provided housing for 600 families. Most buildings faced their streets at oblique forty-five-degree angles and offered their occupants views of the harbor and the ocean beyond. The finger-park, *cul de sac* planning, as in the Jacksonville, Avion, and Compton designs, provided both privacy and a sense of community. One-story duplexes alternated with two-story, four-family units. All were built of

215. *Neutra*, unexecuted design for migrant workers housing, early 1930s

179

216. *Neutra*, NYA Center, 1939, San Luis Obispo

217. *Neutra*, et al., Avion Village, Grand Prairie, Texas, 1941

stucco and redwood, with interiors painted in soft blues, greens, and yellows. "Sturdy simplicity and cheerful color," one critic noted, "is the keynote of the interiors." The two-story buildings featured upstairs balconies. All units contained a living and dining room, kitchen, bath, and utility and storage areas, with bedrooms ranging from one to three. Built by the Baruch Construction Company, the project had an average cost per living unit of approximately $2600.[27]

In addition to the residential flats, Channel Heights offered a store and market building, a crafts center, and a combined nursery school and community center. All were well utilized and were deemed highly successful. In contrast to the slight single pitch of the roofs of the houses, the community center featured a contrasting array of more steeply pitched shed roofs. In typically modernist fashion, there and elsewhere throughout the development, Neutra utilized glass to its maximum possibilities and emphasized the interaction between inner and outer space.

The positive reviews of the Channel Heights project that had been widely published in the Los Angeles area press persuaded Myrtle Dessery, a typical Channel Heights resident, that her family should move there when her husband Gordon became a naval shipbuilder in nearby San Pedro. She remembered her one-story duplex as being light and cheerful. She had especially liked the modern kitchen, the natural beamed ceiling, and the fact that the whole place was easy to care for. Never before or after the war, she recalled, had she lived in a more pleasant environment. Her daughter Evelyn retained childhood memories of a building that seemed "modern" but "still felt like a house." Her most lasting images more than three decades later were the shed roof, the beamed ceilings, the handsome, commodious built-in furniture and cabinets, and the spacious park-like environs.[28]

Westbrook appreciated Neutra's "care and thoroughness" and Williams declared it "one of the most thorough and competent overall developments . . . yet received in this office." Unlike the relatively successful Mutual Home Ownership transition of such projects as Avion Village in Texas, however, Channel Heights fell prey in the post-war years to larger-scale developers and absentee landlords who allowed it to fade and to deteriorate. Yet as late as 1980, when most of the units had long been demolished, visitors still sensed that somehow they "were somewhere." Amid the squalid ruins of the once modern village, a special sense of place and urbanity remained.[29]

In all aspects of his work of the 1930s, from private residences to buildings for the larger community, Neutra apparently made every effort to acknowledge the contributions of his associates and collaborators. Neutra's "system," as it evolved, borrowed from both the older European atelier idea and the corporate hierarchical organization of the large, turn-of-the-century American architectural empires. His own small office was a miniature of both systems, but theoretically and ideally it included several progressive categories through which aspirants could move: student apprentices who would work for nothing or occasionally pay fees for the privilege of learning through working; assistants who would receive 15 percent from the net income of the jobs on which they worked; and collaborators who would receive 30 percent of the net income on the jobs for which they took primary responsibility. The pay was not high, even for the top category. Neutra must have known that his most talented and ambitious disciples would ultimately move on to more lucrative and independent positions. While they were there, however, Neutra tried to supplement their pay and boost their morale by giving them credit in print whenever they worked on jobs that were published. He was commended for his not altogether customary practice by several journal editors, but was rebuked by the California State Board of Architectural Examiners. For example, in 1939 a board official, Ben G. Silver, cautioned Neutra that by attaching Pfisterer's name to his own he was aiding and abetting the practicing of architecture by someone not licensed by the board, and ordered Neutra to "refrain from using the name of . . . Pfisterer or any other unlicensed person in advertising or in connection with your work." Unless Neutra promised to adhere to such rules, Silver threatened to "refer the matter to the Southern District Board for action." Neutra replied that he would "study again the law with which I certainly wish to comply . . . although I feel very sorry that I should not be permitted to give credit after some work is successfully done to anyone who has devotedly assisted me." He had received similar

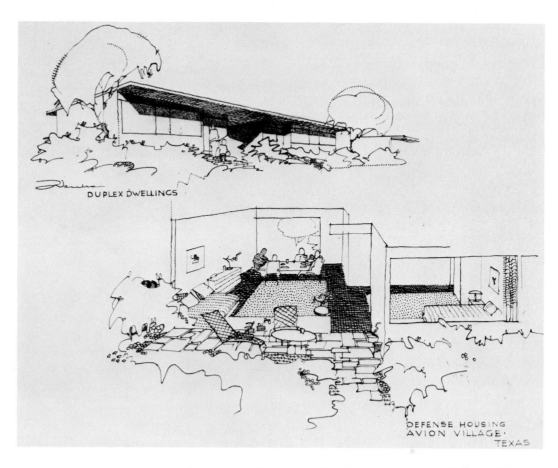

218. *Neutra*, et al., Avion Village, 1941

questions earlier in regard to Winkler and Ain but had tried to ignore them.[30]

Ain failed to appreciate Neutra's apparently real conviction that recognition was indeed more important than money and observed acerbically that being listed as a collaborator usually meant that one was not getting paid. Ain was the most critical of all of Neutra's associates of the thirties and tended, not always inappropriately, to remember the master in the darkest possible light. Neutra, Ain insisted, had a "Prussian" mentality. He could be either an officer or a private and could either command or obey, nothing in between. Ain saw Neutra, quite correctly, as a man who was probably shy and sensitive in his youth and then "gritted his teeth and went out and conquered the world." Neutra, to Ain, seemed always the immigrant who was determined to "make it" in the most "American" way but who still somehow retained a European presence. Neutra observed, for example, an almost courtly formality with both men and women. Ain

181

219. *Neutra*, Channel Heights, San Pedro, California, 1942

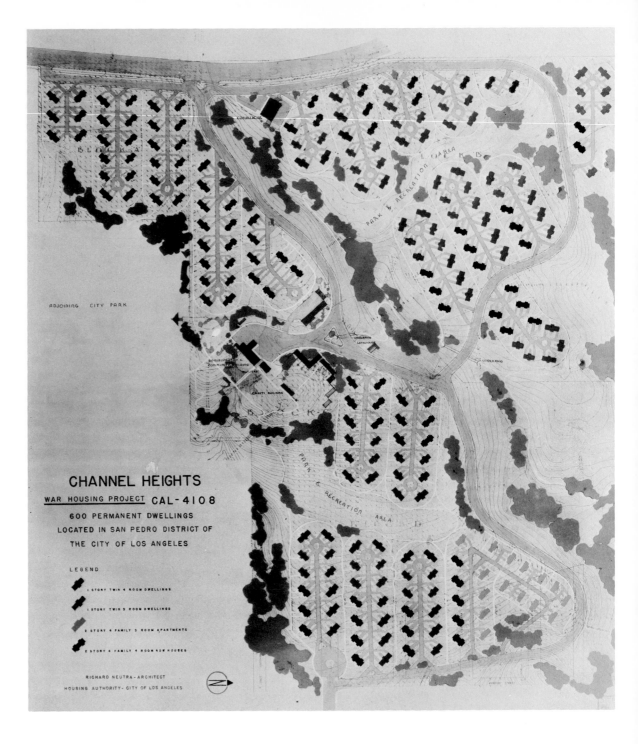

CHANNEL HEIGHTS

WAR HOUSING PROJECT CAL-4108

600 PERMANENT DWELLINGS
LOCATED IN SAN PEDRO DISTRICT OF
THE CITY OF LOS ANGELES

LEGEND

RICHARD NEUTRA-ARCHITECT
HOUSING AUTHORITY-CITY OF LOS ANGELES

objected to the fact that Neutra tended to justify and rationalize whatever contributed to the larger social and architectural mission, and that he sought so relentlessly to publicize this mission. By making this commitment to publicity, promotion, and "public relations," Ain believed, Neutra "sold his soul to the devil." He worked very hard but was too serious about everything professional and personal. Ain was particularly appalled at the "grotesque German children's stories" Neutra would tell to his son Dion. Dione saw it differently, however. "Richard is a fabulous father," she wrote in 1937. "He tells Dion the most wonderful children's stories and tries to be a moral counterbalance to the materialistic outlook on life which surrounds children here."[31]

Yet despite their obvious differences, Ain acknowledged Neutra's importance in "doing more than anyone else in the thirties to make modern architecture respectable." He *was* a great artist and educator, Ain admitted. He *was* trying to accustom the public to the idea of industrialized, prefabricated modernism, which explained his sometimes dubious penchant "for painting everything silver." This less than candid treatment of materials prompted a private joke between Ain and Harris, with the mock-serious question: "Mr. Neutra, what is the best material to build a steel house out of?" Ain felt that, for the most part, Neutra was too rigidly uncompromising, but admitted that Neutra would occasionally give in. On the Rajagopals house remodeling, for example, Neutra remonstrated when the clients insisted on too many bright interior yellows, but finally deferred to the Rajagopals' wishes—demonstrating, Ain felt, a welcomed flexibility. Ultimately, Ain admitted, much of his animosity against Neutra was based on "trivial, personal things."[32]

In March 1935, when Ain became especially critical of Neutra's design and professional policies and, at the same time, demanded a more partner-like share of the income, Neutra responded with a revealing communication. "I was very sad reading your letter," he began, "which you wrote me in this busy hour and which criticizes my work and my behavior. . . . I thank you for your frank expression of what you and your friends think of me and of what I produce. My own grievances against you I have with few exceptions always uttered with less discouraging accent than [that with which] you respond; in fact my hope was that [my criticism] may sound stimulating as the advice of a sincere friend, twenty years more experienced. I have even without using a discourteous word as older men may do in such office conversations, apologized if I thought that you might be hurt personally, an effect which indeed is contrary to my true feeling."[33]

Ain recalled that when a few months later he decided to leave the office and set out on his own, his wife Agnes vented her smoldering antagonism toward Neutra. By the time they left, she shared all of her husband's hostility toward his employer. She told Neutra that when they had first met she had

220. *Neutra*, Channel Heights, 1942

liked things about him and had thought they could be friends, but, she said, that time was over, and she was glad to be leaving the house where they had worked and lived three years. At this, to everyone's surprise, Neutra seemed visibly shaken and began to cry.[34]

As tense as the relationship was, however, both sides ultimately profited from it. Ain had given significant support to some of Neutra's most important projects of the early and middle 1930s, and Neutra knew it. As late as 1937, in a special issue of the magazine *Pencil Points* devoted to his work, Neutra continued to acknowledge Ain as one of several collaborators who had "faithfully assisted" him. The Neutra influence also had a palpable effect on Ain's later Southern California *oeuvre*. Though Ain never worked for Schindler in the regular, sustained way he had for Neutra, he liked and admired Schindler more than he did Neutra, and there were, throughout Ain's work, obvious Schind-

221. *Neutra*, Channel Heights, 1942

California. Neutra, he recalled, was the first major architect to engage and impress him as a truly serious designer. Hearing in quick succession Los Angeles lectures by Neutra and by Frank Lloyd Wright, he was more impressed by Neutra and immediately approached him about the possibilities of work. Neutra told him he could pay him nothing, but to come and bring his own India ink. For several months in 1931–32 he worked in Neutra's Douglas Street studio on the vast, ongoing Rush City project, which had also engaged Ain and Harris. When Schindler, however, saw Soriano's senior thesis at USC, he offered him part-time work for a dollar a day, which Soriano accepted—to Neutra's chagrin. But Soriano was unable to appreciate Schindler and his "chaotic" architectural ideas, and after several months returned to Neutra, whose work by contrast seemed more "sensible" and "rational." Soriano, in fact, "related" to Neutra as he was never able to do with Schindler. He worked for Neutra only briefly and sporadically before attempting in 1933 to launch his own career. Both he and Neutra were ambivalently aware of the strong Neutra mark on his later designs, from the early Lipetz house (1934), Kimpson-Nixon house (1936), and Polito house (1939) to such post-war structures as the house for photographer Julius Shulman (1950). Neutra brought "sanity" to housing in the United States, Soriano believed. Among all the moderns, he was in certain ways the first great American "rationalist."[35]

Yet Soriano's attachment to Neutra was based upon personal and social as well as professional sympathies. Both were intrigued with the poetic and mathematical relationships of music and architecture, and while strongly denying the appropriateness of the label, both were highly "romantic" rationalists. Soriano found Neutra a "warm, humane, and charming human being." When Soriano was critically injured and nearly killed by a runaway car in 1937, Neutra was probably his most attentive friend. For a year Soriano lay in a body cast in the hospital, and it was Neutra, he recalled, who came to see him more often than any other person. Soriano, in fact, marveled that as busy and as famous as Neutra was by that time, he took the time to visit him regularly. "I adored Neutra," Soriano averred, "and was resentful of those who criticized him."[36]

ler legacies. Yet in Ain's early Edwards house (1936) and Beckman house (1939) and his Dunsmuir apartments (1937), in his Avenal (1948) and Mar Vista (1948) housing and in such post-war residences as the Hurschler (1950) and Wilfong (1951) houses, the strong Neutra influence appeared again and again in details as well as in overall conception.

If Ain's attitude to Neutra was predominantly negative, the reverse was true of Raphael Soriano, another disciple of the mid-1930s who admired Neutra both as an architect and human being. Like Neutra, Soriano was a recent immigrant, a factor that may have intensified the bond. Settling in Los Angeles in his late teens after growing up on the Greek island of Rhodes, Soriano first heard of Neutra around 1930 while he was an architecture student at the University of Southern

Somewhere between Ain's palpable hostility and Soriano's affectionate admiration was Harwell Harris's characteristically measured assessment. Though his own later work owed more obvious stylistic debts to Schindler, to the earlier work of Charles and Henry Greene, and to the redwood tradition of the San Francisco Bay area, Harris acknowledged Neutra's special contributions to his education in the deeper and less tangible areas of the conceptualization and solving of architectural problems. From his early apprenticeship at the King's Road studio, where he had assisted Neutra on the Lovell house working drawings, through the period at Douglas Street following Neutra's return from Europe, when they had continued to work on the Rush City plans, Harris keenly appreciated the largeness of Neutra's vision. "Of all the things I learned from Neutra," he recalled, "integration is the most important. . . . How one thing calls for another, how one thing excludes another. . . . The marvelous thing was that Neutra was doing his thinking, his musing, his proposing, his adopting with Ain and me as ringside watchers. As Neutra weighed his moves, we weighed them too. Neutra's decisions were then our decisions. In this Neutra was the perfect teacher. In watching him work, we learned in a few weeks what would have taken years had we been left to fumble our way to it." Neutra also introduced him to major trends, ideas, and practitioners in architecture, Harris recalled, which might otherwise have taken him years to discover. Neutra subscribed, for example, to such leading European architectural magazines as *Werk, Die Form,* and *Das Neue Frankfurt,* covering the most recent European developments. He also introduced Harris to such important California contributors to modernism as Irving Gill.[37]

What bothered Harris most about Neutra was that his frequently rigid and difficult temperament shrouded his own remarkable achievements and got in the way of the important ideas and goals he was trying to promulgate. Sensitive and perceptive in so many ways, Neutra was insufficiently perceptive about his dealings with others. "Playing things by ear" was not Neutra's forte, Harris observed. There had to be a "key" to everything. There was always a planned strategy, which "was followed undeviatingly to its frequently catastrophic end." When Neutra sensed he was failing to convince a client,

222. *Neutra,* Channel Heights, 1942, market

185

223. *Neutra*, Channel Heights, 1942, school

224. *Neutra*, Channel Heights, 1942

186

for example, he assumed it was because he had not made his points clearly enough and would then proceed to pour it on even more insistently. Had Neutra better appreciated the occasional importance of the "strategic retreat," Harris believed, he might have won more battles—and commissions.[38]

Greta and J. R. Davidson confirmed this observation by recalling how Neutra sought, and lost, the commission to design a Los Angeles house for the great German expatriate writer Thomas Mann. Neutra presumed that, as the leading West Coast architectural modernist, he was the logical person to design a home for Mann, particularly in view of their Germanic connections and their artistic affinities. At a party given by the writer Vicki Baum, Neutra launched his campaign to win Mann's favor. But the novelist was so annoyed by Neutra's overinsistent manner that he muttered to someone, "Get that Neutra off my back." Later, Mann awarded the coveted commission to Davidson.[39]

But if the Mann connection was an unhappy reflection of Neutra at his worst, his relationships in the thirties with other prominent figures showed him capable of pleasantly successful human interaction. One of the associations the Neutras valued most was with the physicist Albert Einstein, whom they first met in Pasadena in 1932 while Einstein was a visiting professor at the California Institute of Technology. Neutra particularly appreciated his discussions with Einstein about the mysteries and realities of cognition and perception, carried on in intense conversations and later in correspondence. Neutra also greatly admired H. G. Wells, and when the British writer visited Los Angeles, Dione recalled that Richard enjoyed a "long conversation" with him. Neutra valued as well the widely differing personalities and intellectual achievements of the historian Emil Ludwig, the Los Angeles book dealer Jake Zeitlin, and the California journalist Carey McWilliams. The Neutras strongly identified with McWilliams's crusading liberalism, particularly on behalf of migrant workers and other California minorities. McWilliams likewise found Neutra a stimulating and engaging friend with a contagious enthusiasm for new and progressive ideas. The German-American historian and biographer Emil Ludwig was part of the large European emigré community in Southern California, whose numbers grew significantly in the 1930s with the rise of

Nazism. The composer Arnold Schönberg, a friend
of Dione's sister Regula, came frequently to Strathmore to play chamber music with their father,
Alfred Niedermann. Other emigré friends in avant-
garde music and literary circles included Ernst and
Lilly Toch and Lion and Marta Feuchtwanger.
Dione sang in the chorus of the Los Angeles Phil-
harmonic, and through that connection she and
Richard enjoyed getting to know the orchestra's
conductor, Otto Klemperer. They also delighted in
their friendship with Luise Rainer and her husband
Clifford Odets. They relished the quiet social gather-
ings at Rainer's Strathmore penthouse apartment
as well as the visits to her Hollywood studio, where
they observed with fascination the filming of her
movies.[40]

Of all the Neutras' friendships, one of the
closest was with Charles and Mary Beard, whom
they met in the early thirties when the historians
were visiting at Cal Tech. Throughout the thirties,
in Pasadena or Los Angeles or at the Beards' home
in New Milford, Connecticut, visiting, talking, and
corresponding with the Beards constituted both for
Richard and Dione an intense intellectual and emotional experience. "The evenings spent with them
belong to the highlights of our lives," Dione recalled. "Charles Beard had such a stimulating influence on Richard. Every evening Richard improvised really brilliant expositions about all possible
phases of human life based on the past as well as
projections into the future. This was applauded
and encouraged by old Beard."[41]

The affection was reciprocal. Mary Beard
acknowledged that Neutra had influenced their
thinking about architecture and life and that as
much as possible they had incorporated these ideas
into the later editions of their various histories of
the United States. "Charles," she wrote in 1939, "is
sweating in real distress over a speech he is booked
to deliver in August at a 'World Congress of Education' in NYC. He agreed to discuss democracy
and is now hard put to find out what democracy is.
We wish Neutra were here to help on this 'project.'
He would have substance illuminated by brilliant
flashes and make the thing warm and sparkling."[42]

As close as Neutra was, however, to such
luminaries in the literary and performing arts, he
was more strongly drawn to his fellow architects and
artists. Throughout the 1930s and later, he corre-

225. *Neutra*, Channel Heights, 1942

sponded with Walter Gropius, an acquaintance of
long standing, about life and architecture in Germany and America. Letters and visits were also exchanged with the architects and artists he had met
in 1930, particularly at the Bauhaus, including
Ludwig Mies van der Rohe, Lázló Moholy-Nagy,
Lyonel Feininger, and Josef Albers. There were also
light social notes to and from Le Corbusier,
Amédée Ozenfant, J. J. P. Oud, and Ernst May, and
more serious exchanges with José Luis Sert and
Sigfried Giedion about CIAM matters. Alvar Aalto,
whom Neutra had met in 1930, visited Los Angeles
in 1939 and responded enthusiastically to Neutra's
buildings and ideas. Neutra believed he helped persuade Dean Joseph Hudnut to invite Gropius to
come to Harvard in the late 1930s as a refugee from
Nazi Germany and that he was also instrumental in
facilitating Mies's similar move to the Armour Institute in Chicago. He met Mies upon his arrival in
New York in 1937 and took him to a performance
of *Golden Boy* by his friend Clifford Odets. Since
Mies understood very little English, Neutra whispered a translation to him "until all the people

187

around viciously 'shushed' me." Throughout the thirties, there also continued to arrive short, folksy, matter-of-fact communications from Neutra's mentor, Frank Lloyd Wright.[43]

Closer to home, Neutra particularly enjoyed the friendship of the great photographer Edward Weston, whom he had met in the late twenties through the Schindlers and Lovells, both of whom owned fine Weston prints. Neutra used several Weston photographs in his 1930 book on American architecture and took pleasure in the fact that Weston reciprocated the personal and professional admiration. For example, an entry in the photographer's faithfully kept "day book" early in the relationship read: "To Richard Neutra's for supper. Other guests were Mr. and Mrs. J. R. Davidson. . . . I like Richard Neutra so much and found . . . the others stimulating so the evening was a rare gathering I do not regret. Even the showing of my work was not the usual boresome task. I felt such a genuine attitude. Neutra is always keenly responsive and knows whereof he speaks."[44]

Despite this affectionate praise of himself and his achievements from friends and colleagues of such impressive stature, Neutra continued to experience throughout the 1930s the same severe rounds of psychological depression that had plagued him since youth, "that numbing loneliness, that isolation and disorganization of experience," as psychoanalyst Erik Erikson put it, "which we call neurotic anxiety." The typical patient of mid-twentieth-century psychoanalysis, Erikson observed, "suffers most under the problem of what he should—or indeed, might—be or become; while the patient of early psychoanalysis suffered most under inhibitions which prevented him from being what he thought he knew he was." As a product of both eras, Neutra, not surprisingly, combined the two types of problems.[45]

The chief cause of Neutra's depression had always been the not uncommon human tension and frustration engendered by three conflicting devils. First, there had been the compelling ambition to succeed on the grandest scale by spreading his message and documenting it with built designs. Second was his continuing fear that he was somehow not doing that quickly enough, that his life was ebbing away with that mission unaccomplished— chiefly because of insufficient amounts of work.

Third was the ironically conflicting and contradictory frustration caused by the alternation of periods of fallow inaction with periods of overwork, overload, and overcommitment, when he felt inadequate to handle the demands, confront the imperatives, and realize the possibilities thrust upon him. The most disturbing example of these conflicts lay in the problems of organizing, training, and maintaining an office staff, of taking personal responsibility versus delegating responsibility, of expanding and contracting his own resources and that of the variously prepared work force as the work itself grew or diminished.

When Neutra began to undergo psychoanalysis in 1938, he identified completely with the lament from the autobiography of H. G. Wells: "I need freedom of mind. I want peace for work. My thoughts and work are encumbered by, claims and vexations and I cannot see any hope of release from them, any hope of a period of serene and beneficent activity, before I am overtaken altogether by infirmity and death. I am in a phase of fatigue and of that discouragement which is a concomitant of fatigue, the petty things of tomorrow skirmish in my wakeful brain and I find it difficult to assemble my forces to confront this problem which paralyzes the proper use of myself."[46]

Despite his long-time belief in the wisdom and efficacy of Freudian psychology, Neutra found his psychoanalysis less than satisfying and ultimately resorted to greater reliance on self-analysis. In late 1938, moreover, he and Dione both seemed to gain sustenance from their decision to have another child. The result was the arrival of another son, Raymond Richard Neutra, in March 1939. Mary Beard predicted correctly that, temporarily at least, "the defeatism will all have passed from Silverlake Boulevard. . . . It is hard not to feel downcast at times of crisis but a person like RN cannot be kept down, you must know." By Christmas of 1939 a variety of factors, including young Raymond's arrival, had indeed made a difference, and Dione could write that "Richard's emotional frame of mind is much better, thank God. . . . We are very happy together."[47]

A generally successful antidote to Neutra's periods of depression, not only in the thirties but throughout his life, was the pleasure of travel. Once aboard the train, plane, or car, away from the pressure of running his practice, Dione observed, he became a different person—relaxed, gentle, and witty. One particularly refreshing trip took him to Mexico City in late 1937, where he visited the Mexican painter Diego Rivera and the painter's architect, Juan O'Gorman, both of whom he had long admired. Dione frequently accompanied him on such jaunts, but this time, traveling alone, he wrote her his impressions: ". . . on the sunny street, I meet the immense, the colossus Rivera and soon afterwards his diminutive, black-haired doll, his wife. Later I meet O'Gorman. . . ." The Riveras "drive me in their car through the endless metropolitan region. . . . I see the Piazza del Duomo, old palazzi. Finally we drive to Guadeloupe where thousands of Indians are on a pilgrimage from December 12th to observe the yearly Fiesta of the Holy Virgin. . . . On the way I see an excellent housing project as well as Aztec villages unchanged from a thousand years ago. Finally we reach the . . . fantastic pyramid encircled by granite stone snakes. Night falls as we carefully climb higher and higher, not wanting to break our necks on this steep incline. Then a long drive back in the darkness. We have a good time together. . . . The diminutive Mrs. Rivera lays her manicured hand on my knee or her elbow on my shoulder."[48]

When he compared it to the authentic patina of Mexico, and the various textures of his own modernist tradition, Neutra had mixed feelings about the restored town of Williamsburg, which he felt prettified the early American ambience with less than convincing success. Charleston and Savannah and the older cities of the South were different matters, however. En route to Florida on the 1938 Jacksonville project, Dione recorded their mutual delight. Charleston was "buried in lush vegetation, magnificent gardens, shaded streets. The houses are convincing and well kept, with beautifully done wrought iron, old doors, balconies. We were much impressed." Savannah "astonished us with its progressive city plan consisting of ten parks around which the houses are grouped and the streets laid out. It is quite a different America, a cozy, thoughtful, contemplative one."[49]

Two years later they felt equally drawn to the very different ambience and texture of New Mexico. The architecture of the pueblos had long impressed them. Now, enlivened by the pueblos' human in-

226. *Neutra*, travel sketch, *Twenty-Nine Palms*, California, Christmas, 1938

habitants and the drama of the corn dance, the scene moved them enormously. "Now the drums sounded and the dancers appeared," Dione marveled. "Perhaps a hundred young Indians of both sexes entered, half-naked, painted white. Accompaniment was provided by drummers who beat incessantly with rhythmic virtuosity. . . . Monotonous steps and figures, according to rigid laws, were hypnotically fascinating in their endless, endless repetition. Otherwise, mute silence, burning sun. . . ."[50]

Less dramatic journeys were also inspirational. On a lecture and NYA advisory tour through Texas in 1940, they attended, at Texas A. & M., a conference on housing, the most moving feature of which was a passionate testimonial by a Texas farm woman. While riding across the state, Dione recalled, "we noticed how dilapidated and neglected the little wooden houses looked, standing so lonesome and far apart on the plains. Although the speaker, mother of many children, consulted a copy-book somewhat nervously, one had the feeling that she had a long-desired need to speak out. She had risen at 4:00 A.M. to put her thoughts into order and following are the things she wanted: a floor without crevices so that vermin would not develop; walls without fissures so that the wind couldn't blow through; any kind of cupboard so that things wouldn't have to be stored in boxes under the bed; running water in the kitchen; an indoor privy because of the cold winters. These are things we take for granted, we who are not obliged to work one-tenth as hard as this woman does. This family is one of hundreds of thousands, or even millions, earning no more than $1,000 a year. The purpose of this conference was to find some way in which to help these millions to decent dwellings. . . ." Dione then echoed the priorities she and Richard shared with Charles and Mary Beard. "It seemed to us by the end of the conference," she concluded, "that prefabrication and state subsidies are the answer. But as long as we spend so much money for armaments, this idea remains utopian, just as it has up until now, and these poor people will have to continue existing in their miserable hovels."[51]

They then toured the state with a protégé of David Williams, "a young, charming architect, O'Neill Ford," who had already visited them in Los Angeles and was greatly excited by Neutra's work. Dione remembered that "in each town, a group of architects assembled around Richard, who seems to be a light in the darkness. All try to build 'modern.' This cannot be done without compromise. It was only in Texas that I came to realize the great influence Richard had had on the architectural profession in this country."[52]

Describing the Texas journey, Dione recounted, "I especially remember the endless hours spent on the highway because it was just during this time that Hitler conquered France. As we drove we listened to the radio, to the news of these incredible events." Those "incredible events" left their mark on the Neutras as indeed they did on most of the world, as they—and the Beards—began slowly to realize the sad necessity of armed intervention in the imminent world war. Though both Neutras had supported the socialist Upton Sinclair in his 1934 bid for the governorship of California

and were enthusiastic champions of Roosevelt's New Deal domestic policies, Richard was always less "political" than Dione and occasionally took positions to emphasize his contention that certain aspects of life were above and beyond "politics." Though appalled and frightened by Hitler's anti-Semitic policies, Neutra felt, for example, contrary to many—that the United States should *not* boycott the 1936 Olympic Games scheduled to be held in Berlin.[53]

In that time of petitions both for and against a boycott, Neutra, an Austro-American Jew, signed a petition that favored American athletic participation. The publication of this document incensed his old friend Pauline Schindler. "My dearest richard," she wrote Neutra in her stylized lower-cased prose, "are you so strangely asleep then? i do not know the individuals on this committee. for all i know they may belong to the most fashionable clubs. but are you then not at all aware that forty-two college and university presidents have within the last two weeks signed a document of boycott against the olympic games in germany? do you know that the american federation of labor is passing, through many of its unions, resolutions of boycott . . . ? that students invited are refusing right and left? and whether many or few refused, would you or i accept? to be a collaborator in anyway in the promotion of the olympic games in germany this year is simply to be a collaborator in the immense white-washing they are going to stage, to say to the world that all is well in germany, all is joyous, free, healthy, laughing. the screams of the tortured, the silence of the afraid, the suicides, the brutality, the sadisms, will be white washed, hidden, unheard in the sound of that wonderful choral singing which will sound throughout the olympic games. do you know of the british surgeon, a jew, who some months ago received in london a visitor—goering, who asked him to perform a throat operation on hitler? he was a jew. he refused. i am not a jew. but i am a human being. if you lend your name to the olympic committee in any sort of collaborative way, i shall certainly suspect that you are neither. write and withdraw your name, richard. you made a ghastly mistake in accepting. ghibbeline."[54]

Neutra apparently did *not* withdraw his name. In the same connection, Philip Johnson recalled a statement of Neutra's which, if literally interpreted, could have seemed damagingly compromising, if not perverse. "Oh, if only I could work for Hitler," Neutra allegedly told Johnson in the lean Depression years. "But Mr. Neutra, you are Jewish," Johnson responded. "Yes," Neutra replied ironically, "but he builds buildings."[55]

Yet in ways that neither "Ghibbeline" nor Johnson could know, Richard and Dione empathized and agonized with Hitler's countless victims and sensed the greater holocaust to come. While traveling in the east in 1938, for example, Dione recorded their dismay when "one comes from Washington over the bridge to Virginia" and "the bus driver rises and says: 'All Negroes to the back of the bus.' In Virginia, there are separate washrooms for Negroes and whites, which shocked me very much especially after what is happening in greater Germany." After the *Anschluss*, the Neutras worked feverishly to help his brothers and other relatives and friends—as well as desperate strangers—escape to America from Nazi-dominated Austria. Because of her marriage to the powerful Gentile museum director Arpad Weixlgärtner, Neutra's sister Josephine was not deported, but their home and personal treasures were burned by Nazi thugs when Arpad refused to relinquish the keys to the vaults and present the crown of the Holy Roman Empire to Hitler. In her Christmas letter of 1939, Dione described the ordeal of the emigrés and compared her own family's relative happiness and security to the nightmare of Europe. "Here we live really in paradise . . . ," she mused. And despite all the pain that the thirties had brought them, Richard would ultimately have been forced to agree.[56]

In the July 1937 special issue of *Pencil Points* devoted to Neutra, the first of many such magazine specials on his work, critic Henry Robert Harrison summed up current thinking on Neutra's contemporary achievements by calling him "a center of architectural stimulation." He works always at top speed," Harrison observed, "emanating an amazing energy and drive as he threads his way through the tremendous amount of work incident to a practice whose novelty demands the most careful detailing. A stream of conferences, a closed afternoon for his own drawing, and the after-dinner business

routine with his secretary, keep him busy from early morning to late night. Yet somewhere he must find time for music, painting and literature, for he talks with familiar ease the jargon of the many masters of the other arts who frequently 'drop in on their way through town.' "[57]

His home, Harrison observed, "just a flight of stairs above the busy office—is a quiet refuge with deep inviting couch-seats, long shelves of books, and windows opening on all sides to the beautiful lake and park they overlook. Here in a house of his own design he can withdraw, with his wife and two sons, to an unbelievably restful atmosphere; or entertain anyone from a movie star in regal glamour to an impromptu bull session of the entire office staff, or a committee of unemployed. The photographs convey some idea of the material elements of his architecture; but they can only hint at the spirit, the liberating feeling, which is the 'forte' of all modern design in space. . . . It has been said," Harrison concluded, "that all of his designs are deeper than just buildings. His houses, more than domiciles, point the way to a new and fuller life; his schools, more than good classrooms, are the expression of a newer and finer thought in education; his town planning, more than a clever solution of traffic, zoning, and parks, crystallizes the best thought in the economics of today's civilization. Behind the simplicity of the plans lies years of deep research; behind the architect a philosopher; BEHIND THE ARCHITECT A PHILOSOPHER—not a bad pocket definition of any creative architecture."[58]

Despite a slow start in the early days of the Depression, Neutra had indeed thrived in the thirties in California and beyond by proclaiming and documenting the idea of modernity. With single-family houses as his prime stylistic models, he had also carried that message via stores, schools, apartments, and multiple-family housing to the larger community of "humans in groups." He also knew, as the thirties ended, that for individuals and communities the future of architecture in the post-war world would be greatly affected by the moral and physical destruction now upon them and the resulting imperatives for rebuilding anew.

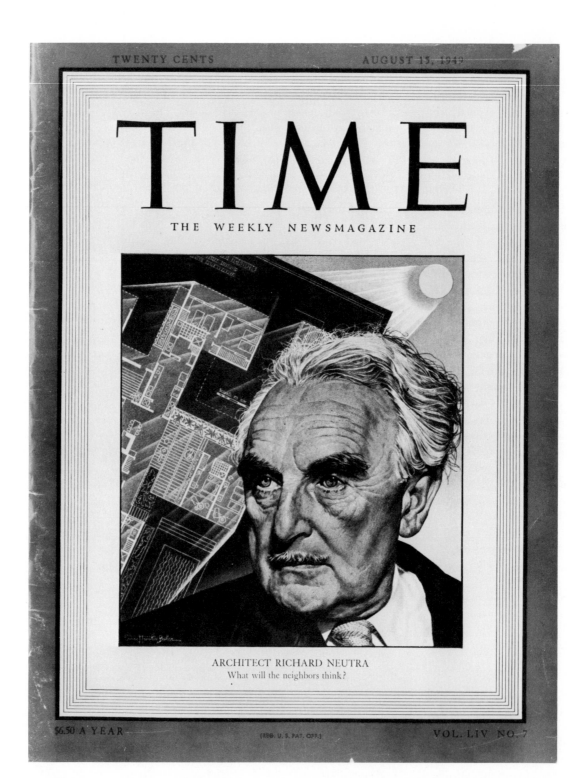

227. *Time* cover, August 15, 1949

Transition

For Neutra as for most people, the forties were trenchantly divided between the war years, which ended in 1945, and the period of post-war recovery. Both parts of the decade saw important shifts in public and professional attitudes toward the development of modern architecture. The transition in Neutra's work, which began in the early forties with such pivotal buildings as the Maxwell and Nesbitt houses, would link up in the post-war period with such masterworks as the Kaufmann and Tremaine houses. In the forties Neutra completed two major books, *The Architecture of Social Concern* and *Survival Through Design*, his most important treatise. The end of the decade marked not only the century's midpoint but a transition in Neutra's life and work as well. In 1949 his first major heart attack announced the presence of the disease that would affect him physically and psychologically the rest of his life and would eventually kill him. On the brighter side, in 1949 Neutra enjoyed appearing on the cover of *Time* magazine. In the same year, he teamed up with the architect-planner Robert Alexander on the vast Elysian Park Heights project, an effort that led to a partnership with Alexander and to the vast expansion of his practice in the 1950s.

Despite the pressures of life and work, Neutra had been an avid correspondent throughout the twenties and thirties, especially with fellow architects in America and Europe, and in 1940 the English architect Maxwell Fry reciprocated with a revealing letter about the strictures of war upon architecture and life. "You have written to me from time to time in a very friendly way and I have had messages and greetings from you," Fry began, "all of which impel me, as I sit here wondering how long the spirit can sustain a complete divorce from architecture to comfort myself by some communication with the still active world. I felt quite certain on the outbreak of war that architecture in England would be entirely eclipsed and despite some slight resuscitation of interest in the idea of research, events have fulfilled my gloomiest prognostication. It is as difficult to develop the idea of architecture without building as it would be to develop music without instruments and the loss is severe. . . ."[1]

Fry then reported on the war-time activities of the students at the Architectural Association and the members of the MARS (Modern Architectural Research) group, the English wing of CIAM. "The almost religious zeal with which the student denies himself the enjoyment of architecture until his programme is defined causes me some discomfort. . . . I was most struck by the morality of this point of view that it is somehow wicked to enjoy architecture, as I like to do, when the world is so topsy-turvy and there are so few people who will listen to reason. . . . Few people will agree to wait at all, but must be about creating a brave new world by the time they are ready to practice. . . . It is inherent of course in Le Corbusier, who issued blueprints for entirely new worlds, many of which despite the humanism of the creator, could be lived in only by a race of robots. I seem even to remember," he observed, pointing to Neutra's similar vulnerabilities, "a certain Rush City, which I can't imagine you now believe in with great fervor." Neutra was indeed beginning to question the Rush City esthetic, as his work of the forties, and later, would demonstrate.[2]

Fry's frustrations about the war and its privations applied less to Neutra than to most American architects, as he was kept busy through 1942 with his government consulting and his work on such projects as Avion Village and Channel Heights. After the completion of Channel Heights and the Nesbitt House* in 1942, however, Neutra, like Fry and most architects everywhere, found himself with little work. He was especially delighted therefore in 1943 to accept the offer of a visiting professorship in design at Bennington, the progressive women's college in Vermont. Though he enjoyed having the leisure to work on the manuscript of *Survival* and relished the contact with his sophisticated undergraduates, the Bennington experience convinced him that temperamentally he was better suited to short lecture and discussion engagements than to sustained classroom teaching. Coincident, moreover, with the Bennington year was a call from Washington late in 1943 to lead a massive design project for the post-war construction of schools, hospitals, and health facilities in Puerto Rico.

Neutra shared the liberal belief of the American-appointed governor, Rexford G. Tugwell that the horrors of poverty, illiteracy, malnutrition, overpopulation, and maldistribution of wealth had to be combated if the concurrent aims of Puerto Rican self-sufficiency and human enrichment and development were to be realized. "This small tropical island," the *Architectural Forum* observed, "strategically located between the two hemispheres, is regarded as the Latin American guinea pig in the hands of the North American experimenter. What happens in Puerto Rico may answer the question of all Latin American countries surrounding the Caribbean as well as the British and Dutch colonies in the hemisphere. Their attitude is: What shall we look forward to if the gringos or 'Yankis' have their way?"[3]

To help achieve his planning goals, Tugwell had appointed a Committee on Design of Public Works, charged with producing plans for over $50 million worth of buildings, and this committee chose Neutra as chief architect and consultant. His selection was connected to his visibly successful earlier work at Channel Heights and Avion Village and to his long-expressed interest in designing for the

tropics. Neutra made his first visit to Puerto Rico during Bennington's winter recess of 1943–44 and once again requited his *Sehnsucht nach dem Süden,* the ancient Germanic yearning for the south.[4]

Between late 1943 and early '45 Neutra established and directed an office of Puerto Rican architects and engineers who would carry on the work in the spirit of his preliminary designs. He was also the chief architect of open-air schools for more than 150 locations, of approximately the same number of rural health centers for the prevention of disease, of five large district hospitals with connected staff housing, and of such other miscellaneous structures as a home for delinquent girls. The minimalist buildings, equipped with screens and louvers, were sited so as to take advantage of prevailing breezes and were constructed of hurricane-resistant reinforced concrete in standardized, replicable, expandable sections allowing different arrangements for different sites. "Our purpose," Neutra explained, "was to avoid any institutional character, making these buildings genuinely belong to the people. . . . In front of the wide opening of the milk dispensaries," for example, "we placed a spacious porch with a concrete bench running around it, as a place for meetings, lectures, entertainments, and broadcasts. . . . Here they can play their dominoes, strum their guitars, and dance— and incidentally learn something about child care, diet, and more practical housekeeping. Usually school and health center are grouped together and placed beside the village fountain and sanitary cistern."[5]

The *Architectural Forum* commended Neutra's design approach and his sensitivity to the problems and possibilities of the tropical climate. "The outdoors," it noted, "was used as a space auxiliary with no additional building cube and no extra cost. Building types developed in the temperate zones were carefully restudied in their relationship to the function of heat economy."[6]

Neutra's Puerto Rican schools were minimalist tropical versions of the model established in the Ring Plan and Corona Avenue schools of the early 1930s. One native teacher, Olegaria de Rivera, echoed the sentiments of Los Angeles teachers a decade earlier when Corona was first opened. "The first time I came in, I was really disappointed," she admitted. "The school was closed

---

* To be discussed in connection with Neutra's post-war residential work later in this chapter.

and it looked so plain that I thought it was not a school at all. But when I opened the back door and pulled [up] the front doors, I found myself in a three-walled room with plenty of air and light. The pupils are delighted now. We feel so free and comfortable. We are not shut inside four walls. There is enough space to carry out indoor activities as well as outdoor games." She especially appreciated the "elimination of divisory lines between room and playground. . . ." As Neutra completed his work in 1945, Governor Luis Munos Marin assured him that "the task . . . we are trying to carry out in Puerto Rico has greatly benefited by your work and by the inspiration of your personality."[7]

Indeed, despite the internal rivalries within his Puerto Rican office, the occasional native resentment of his "outsider" status, and the inevitable changes in his designs as they were built in succeeding years, Neutra had reason to feel good about his Puerto Rican achievements. Throughout the forties he kept in touch with old associates about the island's development. In February 1946, for example, Herbert Johnson wrote that "Construction is going full speed ahead. In fact each day there seems to be another picture of another rural school in the making." He promised to send photographs to indicate "the changes and inoventions [sic] the 'young geniuses' of this island have added to Mr. Neutra's original plans. . . ."[8]

In addition to formulating the relatively specific Puerto Rico designs, Neutra was involved throughout the war years in larger discussions of post-war planning and reconstruction. Early in the war he was reminded of this obligation by an older architectural colleague, William Gray Purcell, then living in retirement in Pasadena. "I have long watched your work," Purcell wrote. "You correctly forecast the key to the past 15 years. It is now important to foresee the temper of this next 'post-war,' which we can be sure will be very different. . . . The reactionary old boys will never learn. When they finally seize the torch, it is a brand. . . . we have to be careful not to become 'old boys' ourselves—without realizing it. The living idea is never satisfied in the old sheath."[9]

By 1944, when CIAM activities were by necessity centered in the United States, Neutra, as the group's new president, used his office to stimulate thinking about post-war rebuilding. He represented

228. *Neutra*, District Hospital, Guyama, Puerto Rico, mid-1940s

229. *Neutra*, prototype buildings, Puerto Rico, mid-1940s

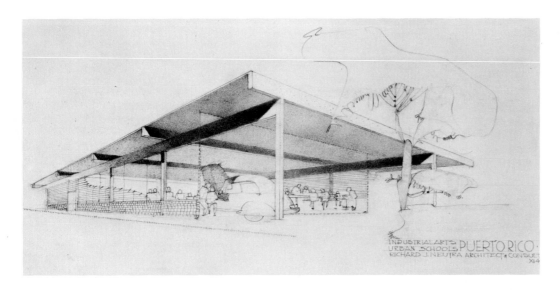

230. *Neutra*, prototype buildings, Puerto Rico, mid-1940s

CIAM at various international planning conferences, most particularly the San Francisco meeting in the spring of 1945 that gave birth to the United Nations. There and elsewhere he reiterated the views he had already expressed in *Arts and Architecture* in an article entitled "Planetary Reconstruction." Neutra argued that the tragedy of war could have paradoxically beneficent consequences as well. "By a strange inconsistency," he observed, "modern wars are significantly different from those of the past in that the victors cannot and do not really plan to eradicate, rape, or even merely abandon the losers! For better or worse, the war attitudes of a Genghis Khan can no longer fit our general situation. The dense meshwork of planetary economy does not permit it. Now the victors must somehow consider the relief and the rehabilitation of all the far spread victims of an up-to-date war, which in its wake leaves . . . enormous areas in rubble, or at least in a threatening and doubtful condition. There is even considerable doubt about what price salvage? In terms of constructive action it is well to note that many so-called physical 'improvements' turned sour long before the war ploughed them under. And they certainly ought not to be resurrected in their old form, not even for the punishment of the enemy! Once Tokyo's grimy old central railway station is down, no complaints about it should be taken too seriously. Surely everybody will be relieved."[10]

Neutra lamented the destruction of rich historical monuments and textures, but recognized that

"the chance to start from scratch is—or at least could be—a real blessing after all the misery." Many of the bombed-out sections, he argued, were not examples of great architecture or city planning. Like comparable areas in many American cities, they were merely outdated. Such areas, he noted, "make your heart sink—from elevated and surface cars in New York, Chicago, Philadelphia, San Francisco, Los Angeles, Detroit, Cleveland, and in many smaller towns emulating the larger ones. Victorian and Wilhelmian Europe is not much better. A huge percentage of structures, as well as the so-called 'city plan' on which they stand, never, at any time, could lay claim to be creatively designed, or even rationally considered as a whole. And from their haphazard first materialization—times, conditions, requirements, and locations have surely changed. . . . The modern bomb is much more advanced technically than the houses they have destroyed. Therefore, we must abolish the bombs but maintain the precision and quality level of their manufacture and convert it all to peaceful, planned pursuits." Significantly, Neutra illustrated the article with taut cityscapes from "Rush City Reformed" as well as the more relaxed designs from his recent Puerto Rico project.[11]

Neutra's obvious feelings of ambivalence toward the war's destruction were noted in the *Weekly Bulletin* of the Michigan Society of Architects. Neutra, it observed, "who disapproves of the colossal and tragic destructiveness of war as much as the next man, nevertheless can't keep his voice free of enthusiasm when he discusses the planning and architectural possibilities created by bombs and shells."[12]

Neutra emphasized, moreover, the role America should play in the rebuilding and the lessons it should learn about improving its own cities. "Unless Canada and the United States take the lead in the development of contemporary architecture, with particular emphasis on housing for low income groups, they will be outpaced by the war-torn nations of Europe," he told an audience in Vancouver. "The vast rebuilding program which is being implemented from Singapore to Le Havre will make all our cities look cheap, unless we, too, move to make our cities more contemporary." Indeed, he argued, in *Arts and Architecture*, Americans should "not exaggerate good samaritanism by spic and span reconstructions of historical Cologne and Rome, while leaving our own neighborhoods and towns in post-Victorian confusion."[13]

For at least two decades, as Neutra hoped and predicted, war's destruction would have marked effects on the rapid development and acceptance of modern architecture—as cities around the world, particularly in Europe and Asia, emerged from the rubble in starkly modern dress. And for both good and ill, America was affected by the same compulsion. As if still caught unconsciously in the bombing mentality of the war years, American planners and architects, in the name of removing "blight," seemed bent on duplicating the bombed-out open spaces of Dresden, Coventry, and Hiroshima. The density that had made cities urban and the sensibilities that had made them urbane lost out in many cases to a landscape of pock-marked "temporary" open spaces. And, indeed, as the "saturation bombing" and open spaces of the 1940s gave way in the '50s to a landscape "saturated" with modernist architecture, a reaction set in, which by the late 1960s and early '70s would supplant the ideal of modernist purity with a seemingly more timely one of post-modern eclecticism. A new generation raised on too much modern architecture began to long nostalgically in the 1960s for the textured patina that modernism had replaced and to champion the felt need for the persistence of tradition. Toward the end of his life, Neutra began vexedly to perceive this shift, though he failed to realize how much the war and the post-war rebuilding had contributed to it.

He had never, on the other hand, been entirely oblivious to the critique that would blossom in the sixties—that modern architecture was too pure, abstract, cold, sober, and colorless. While continuing to defend the ethic and esthetic, the substance and the image of prefabricated, mass-produced, industrialized architecture, Neutra argued convincingly against the anti-modernist complaint that modernism was necessarily a single monolithic entity. Rather, he demonstrated—in the forties and after—that Neutra Modern could mean several things. His succession of houses, both before and after the war, would fluctuate between the hard, cool, flat-roofed, white-and-silver International Style and a more relaxed and textured architecture of brick and wood and slanting roofs.. This repre-

231. Governor Rexford Tugwell, dedicating first rural school designed by *Neutra* in Puerto Rico, ca. 1943

sented no radical shift or disavowal of principles on his part, but a gradual embrace of pluralistic alternatives. Still, Neutra's buildings, whether wood or concrete, whether flat-roofed or pitched, continued to exude a modernist sensibility.

One of the first challenges Neutra had to confront, even in the late thirties, was that of architectural zoning boards dedicated to opposing the spread of modernism. For them the chief symbol of the movement was the pervasive flat roof, and they frequently legislated against its existence. With the 1940 Beckstrand house on the Palos Verdes peninsula, Neutra had taken advantage of the code's failure to specify the degree of pitch and had slanted the red-tiled roof at so minute an angle that from the ground it actually appeared to be flat. But after 1940, as codes became more specific, Neutra realized the futility of attempting to fight or evade them and started designing beautiful pitch-roofed houses.

The first of these was completed in 1941 in the Brentwood section of Los Angeles for the musicians Charles and Sybil Maxwell. Charles, born in

232. *Neutra*, Maxwell House, Los Angeles, 1941

233. *Neutra*, Maxwell House, 1941

Germany, had been a student of Max Reger's and had come to Hollywood in the 1920s as a composer and orchestral arranger at MGM. Sybil, a violinist, was both a teacher and performer. They met the Neutras in the late 1930s and through them got to know Dione's father Alfred Niedermann, with whom they played chamber music. The Maxwells appreciated the flow and the clean, simple lines of the Niedermann's Strathmore apartment, and when they decided to build a small house of their own they acceded to their own instincts and to Alfred Niedermann's urgings and asked Neutra to be the architect. One thing the Maxwells did not like about modern architecture was its generally low ceilings, and this in conjunction with their area's code restrictions led Neutra to open the living room ceiling to reflect the pitched roof. By glazing a portion of the gable beneath the eaves, he also predicted what became a ubiquitous trademark of American suburban architecture in the 1950s and '60s. This then-spectacular feature gave to the north elevation, opening to a garden and large flagstone terrace, a drama that was missing from the modest "American tract" houses of the time. The small redwood house cost approximately $6,750.[14]

Neutra's Van Cleef house, Westwood (1942), and Geza Rethy house, Sierra Madre (1942), included many features that the Maxwell house had introduced. In the similar Bonnet house in the Hollywood Hills (1942), Neutra paralleled the precipitous slope of the lot with one long expanse of steeply pitched shed roof. Here he alternated stucco with redwood, as he did with the shed-roofed Bald house (1941) on a level site in Ojai.

Neutra's masterwork of the early forties was a small brick and timber house in Brentwood (1942) for the NBC radio producer John B. Nesbitt. Begun just before increasing war-time scarcities prohibited private building altogether, the house's nonindustrial materials reflected client tastes as well. A gently pitched shed roof was folded over the rear glass wall with a down-turning overhang. The floors and fireplace walls were brick. Board and batten redwood covered the exterior. A lily pool outside the front entrance extended beneath the glass into the interior hallway. A broadly cantilevered overhang on the front protected the western exposure and connected the main house with the detached guest house and garage at the front.

234. *Neutra*, Maxwell House, 1941

Winner of a post-war first-place award from the American Institute of Architects, the house elicited extravagant praise from the awards jury. "Imagination abounds everywhere," the AIA jury reported. "Urban sophistication and cultural refinement have been expressed in terms of almost rustic simplicity—a juxtaposition of contrasting moods that is, in part, the key to the tantalizing delightfulness of the house."[15]

The coming of war temporarily halted private commissions, but heightened the need for war workers' housing. Neutra was given the job of designing a whole block of so-called Progressive Builders Homes erected in 1942 as part of a larger project for defense workers at the nearby Lockheed Aircraft factory in Burbank. Modest versions of the crisp, pitched-roof Maxwell and Van Cleef format, the fourteen completed FHA-sponsored detached dwellings featured bedrooms across the front with the living rooms running from front to rear and opening integrally onto fetching garden patios.[16]

Following the war, Neutra built numerous variations on both the gabled-roof Maxwell house and the shed-roof Nesbitt house. The best examples

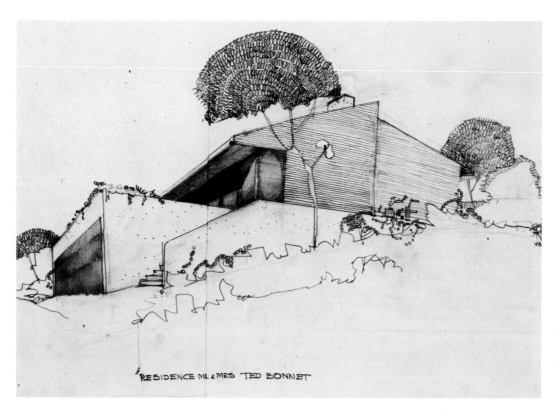

RESIDENCE Mr & MRS TED BONNET

235. *Neutra*, Bonnet House, Los Angeles, 1942

of the former type were two elegant residences of 1949, the Chase house on the old Hope Ranch in Santa Barbara and the spectacularly sited Hines house, Palos Verdes, an unabashedly pitched-roof version of the nearby Beckstrand house. Low shed roofs covered the stucco and redwood Greenberg house, Westwood (1949), and the Atwell house (1948), El Cerrito, near Berkeley. The older flat-roof esthetic reappeared as well in the starkly handsome Schmidt house, Pasadena (1945), and two fine houses near Neutra's in the Silverlake district, the Treweek house (1949) and the Earl Street Reunion house (1949). The latter especially, with its spiderleg outrigging, predicted—together with such structures as the Rourke house, Beverly Hills (1949)—Neutra's more aggressively constructivist designs of the fifties. The fetching board and batten, flat-roofed Goodson house (1948) overlooked the city from its Laurel Canyon mountaintop and seemed typical enough of Neutra's small house *oeuvre* to appear with his picture in the middle 1950s on the cover of the *Saturday Review*.[17]

Yet the finest and most celebrated of Neutra's post-war forties houses were indubitably the Kauf-

mann house, Palm Springs (1946), and the Tremaine house, Montecito, near Santa Barbara (1948). The first of these clients, Edgar Kaufmann, a wealthy Pittsburgh merchant and philanthropist, was already famous in architectural circles for commissioning Frank Lloyd Wright in 1936 to design his epochal Falling Water vacation house near Pittsburgh. Kaufmann's son Edgar, Jr., an architect, historian, and fond disciple of Wright's, wanted his father to engage Wright again to design the new Palm Springs winter house, but the senior Kaufmann, while a warm admirer of Wright, wanted for the desert house a greater feeling of lightness and openness than Wright had imparted either to Falling Water or to his own "desert house" at Taliesin West. For this new commission he found Neutra the most interesting prospect. It was not unlike Philip Lovell's decision some twenty years earlier to move from Rudolph Schindler, the designer of his beach house, to Neutra as the architect of his house in the city. Whatever the motivations in each of the two cases for moving to Neutra as the second architect, the results were salutary. In both cases the clients not only bought great houses for their personal enjoyment, but also contributed richly to architecture as well.[18]

The architect Thaddeus Longstreth, one of Neutra's chief assistants of this period, recalled how close the Kaufmann house came to never being built. Though things had loosened up considerably after the war-time moratorium, the still-tight building market and relative scarcity of materials had led to new restrictions on the building of residences costing over $40,000 unless building foundations were already in the ground by a prescribed date in 1946. Since the Kaufmann house would run considerably over $300,000, Neutra arranged for footings to be sunk the day after Kaufmann approved the preliminaries, and got the house started just before the deadline. The foundation calculations should have come later, Longstreth acknowledged, but his and Neutra's instincts and calculated guesses proved adequate everywhere except in the guest room wing, where certain minor adjustments later had to be made. The pool was laid and completed first, and Neutra enjoyed critiquing the rest of the construction while splashing and floating in the water. Kaufmann, Longstreth remembered, was quite impressed with Neutra and enjoyed coming regularly to the construction site. In his cap and overalls, he was several times mistaken for one of the workmen. Neutra likened the desert setting with its rocks and mountains to the landscape of the moon and conceived of the house as a gem-like pavilion in a small, lush oasis in the midst of a grand but relatively barren place. The house subsequently became the *chef d'oeuvre* in a suburban townscape, but it was born in the middle forties in relative isolation.[19]

Sited on a 200-by-300-foot lot, with spectacular views of the mountains and desert, the 3800-square-foot house was in the shape of a rough cross formed by two intersecting axes. From the main south entrance, a covered walk moved past garages to the entry hall, leading east to living and dining rooms and a master bedroom overlooking the pool, west to kitchen and servants' quarters, and north to an open, covered, later enclosed, patio with guest rooms beyond. To provide a raised deck for viewing the desert, Neutra baffled local authorities and skirted city ordinances against two-story dwellings by devising an open yet covered roof-top "gloriette" reached by outside stairs. Its sturdy fireplace, built-in banquettes, and adjustable louvered screen wall gave it the feeling of both an open porch and a snug, enclosed shelter. It also contributed significantly to the handsome profile of the overall structure. The relative massiveness of the house's rock and concrete walls was lightened by the equally large expanses of glass and by the "floating" quality of the silver-gray metal trim. With its overhangs, adjustable louvers, and radiant floor heating and cooling systems, the house was a model of sophisticated climate control.

Rather than building a house that appeared to have grown "organically" out of the desert, as Wright had attempted to do in Arizona at Taliesin West, Neutra designed the Kaufmann house as an obviously man-made pavilion for encountering, inhabiting, and observing the desert. The house, Neutra acknowledged, "is frankly an artifact, a construction transported in many shop-fabricated parts over long distance. Its lawns and shrubs are imports, just as are its aluminium and plate glass; but plate glass and aluminium, the water of the pool, all reflect the dynamic changes [in] the moods of the landscape. While not grown there or rooted there, the building nevertheless fuses with its set-

236. *Neutra*, Bonnet House, 1942

ting, partakes in its events, emphasises its character." The Southern California AIA awards jury, composed of architects John Dinwiddie and Eliel Saarinen and *Progressive Architecture* editor Thomas Creighton, chose the Kaufmann house for its 1947 Distinguished Award.[20]

Neutra gave Julius Shulman explicit suggestions for photographing the house. "Dusk and evening shots from the exterior into the illuminated interior of the living room, master suite and guest rooms are desirable and appropriate, like a night shot, with fire in the fireplace in the 'gloriette' roof porch, and from the roof onto the illuminated pool and garden areas." The house, he reminded Shulman, was "never static. . . . Do not take all pictures showing pool at the same hour, as the ripple or quiet reflection of water changes, clouds vary, and especially shadows and reflections on metal fascias do. The latter must be watched and no picture taken where the workmanship deficiencies are played up by side light and when they appear buckly. These pictures are not to be taken to prove the fault of the Contractor. . . . Neatness and clarity were our design intentions." Aided no doubt by both Neutra's

237. *Neutra,* Nesbitt House, Los Angeles, 1942

238. *Neutra*, Nesbitt House, 1942

239. *Neutra*, Nesbitt House, 1942

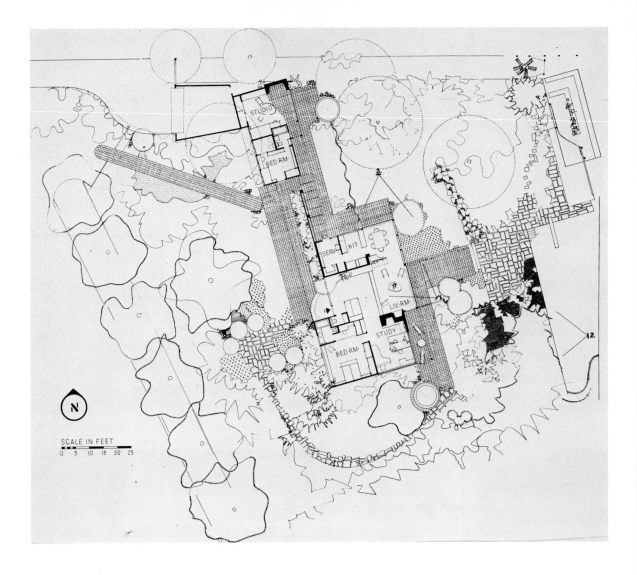

240. *Neutra*, Nesbitt House, 1942

SCALE IN FEET
0 5 10 15 20 25

and Kaufmann's insights and suggestions, Shulman's own perceptions of the building and its setting resulted in some of his most remarkable pictures. The picture taken from the east of the house and pool at twilight would become, in particular, one of modern architecture's most brilliant and famous photographs. Shulman's interpretations were widely published, and the house was internationally acclaimed.[21]

Neutra's letter to Kaufmann upon completion of the house conveyed much of the spirit that his similar letter to Philip Lovell had suggested nearly twenty years before. "In this particular world we live in," he wrote, "I have doubly appreciated you as my client, whose judgment has hardly ever been wrong in choices and modifications, and always

deeply interesting to me; and may I say how grateful I feel to you both who have greatly soft padded wherever I, or my staff, have given you a little dissatisfaction or irritation on those five thousand occasions which occur during a year and more of a wildly confused building market. . . ."[22]

Whereas the taut, pristine coolness of the Kaufmann house reflected the spirit of Neutra's work of the thirties and once again recalled Mies's Barcelona Pavilion, the more relaxed lyricism of his 1948 Tremaine house predicted his increasingly more informal esthestic of the 1950s. Warren Tremaine, a wealthy businessman, shared with his wife Katherine an interest in architecture and the arts. Even more than the Kaufmanns in Palm Springs, they became enthusiastic Neutra-ites, yet though

Neutra worked on both houses at about the same time and in fact, started the Tremaine design before he began the Kaufmann, the two structures emerged with entirely different personalities. Much of this derived from their vastly different settings and profiles on the landscape. The pristine Kaufmann pavilion obviously *sat upon* the desert; the Tremaine house, significantly, seemed to *lie within* its rolling and lushly planted garden of live oaks and succulents. Though integrally sculptural from all sides, the Kaufmann house presented a particularly dramatic front facade looking southeast across the pool. The entrance front of the Tremaine house, on the other hand, with its open garages and relatively dull expanses of flagstone diaper walls, constituted the building's least impressive facade. The Tremaine garden elevations to the north and east, however, were considerably more engaging as cantilevered concrete slab roofs seemed to float above the long glass walls that separated and integrated garden and interior spaces. The large natural boulders that covered the sites of both houses seemed to meld more successfully with the occasional and crisply trimmed flagstone walls of the Kaufmann house than with Neutra's more insistently textured use of the same material at the Tremaine house. Brilliant as always in his handling of walls that projected from the structure and penetrated the landscape, Neutra made these elements at the Kaufmann house read as dramatically visible screens. At the Tremaine house they achieved their impact in their subtle, almost furtive, extensions and disappearances into the hills and foliage. Particularly impressive in the latter case was the long, narrow terrace that bridged a small canyon connecting the main house with the pool and its accoutrements.

The Tremaine plan comprised a cross-pinwheel arrangement with an entrance hall leading northwest to a guest suite and living room, southeast to the dining room, kitchen, servants' rooms and garages, and northeast to children's and parent's bedrooms. Early discussions of a two-story plan ultimately gave way to the lower, more contextually compatible one-story profile. The largely built-in furniture was accented in each room with equally simple free-standing pieces by Neutra and other modernist designers. Soft pastels in rugs, draperies, and furniture fabrics complemented the light colors

241. *Neutra*, Nesbitt House, 1942

and textures of natural and fabricated wall and floor surfaces.

The virtually unqualified praise for the Tremaine house in the late 1940s and 1950s indicated that Neutra had struck an important nerve in regard to the needs and perceptions of the architectural public. The *Architectural Forum* particularly appreciated the way in which "the strong plastic character of the concrete frame lifts it out of the cardboard modern manner, warms it without recourse to redwood texture or soft effects." The review in *Interiors* also contrasted the warmth of the Tremaine house with the coolness of the Kaufmann. "Because he has refused to turn his back on either the naturalistic vocabulary of Wright or the international school," it argued, "Neutra's style has become an ever developing personal eclecticism, always consistent, yet full of surprises and nuances. He has demonstrated how it can beget—out of one germ of an idea—two dissimilar architectural expressions with only the vague family resemblance of fraternal twins. The Tremaine house is as well integrated with its setting as Neutra's desert house

242. *Neutra*, Nesbitt House, 1942

243. *Neutra*, Nesbitt House, 1942

PROGRESSIVE BUILDERS' HOME
RICHARD NEUTRA ARCHITECT

244. *Neutra*, Progressive Builders Homes,
Burbank, California, 1942

245. *Neutra*, Progressive Builders Homes,
1942

246. *Neutra*, Earl Street Reunion House,
Los Angeles, 1949

. . . without the cool shimmer of the glass oasis which reflects its landscape like a technological mirage. The Tremaines' California hillside home is perhaps the more warm and sensuous sibling, with its own brand of nature drama, subtle contrasts, and almost confessional structural honesty. . . ."[23]

In the mid-1940s, Neutra's penchant for experimentation found a sympathetic sponsor in the post-war Case Study House program of John Entenza's *Arts and Architecture* magazine. Acquiring the publication in 1938, Entenza turned its focus from California eclecticism toward a vigorous support of modern architecture. Until its demise in the 1960s it published practically every major building Neutra designed. Neutra keenly appreciated Entenza's commitment to modernism and his interest in the theory and history of the movement. "We just had another get together with Mrs. Theo van Doesburg and talked of olden times," he confided to Entenza in a typical communication. "I thought you would be interested that he, van Doesburg, was

inspired to some of his first abstract patterns by modern floor plans and simultaneously with his efforts and without knowing them I made in 1923 . . . the floor plans for my Diatom House. Much later on, I found Mies van der Rohe and van Doesburg developed a similar feeling for voids and solids and a horizontal plane projection. It's very interesting how a certain moment in time matures a crop of related ideas." Neutra was especially pleased that Entenza included him in the magazine's epochal Case Study programs along with such colleagues as Davidson, Soriano, and Eames. Critic Esther McCoy, a member of *Arts and Architecture*'s editorial board, recalled that by 1944 Entenza "was giving serious thought to the course that architecture should take at the end of the war. The time was ripe for experimentation; potential clients had never been more numerous, due to the halt in building during the depression years. . . ." Entenza feared that uncreative builders would flood a house-hungry country with conventional, unprogressive

247. *Neutra*, Goodson House, Los Angeles, 1948

248. *Neutra*, Kaufmann House, Palm Springs, California, 1946

plans and that too few clients would be willing to wait until the better architects got unconventional plans approved by building commissions and loan agencies. "As a result, many of the creative ideas on the drawing boards and in the minds of architects would be lost." So in 1945 Entenza announced that the magazine would become a sponsor of replicable designs for modern houses by selected architects. Though initially Entenza hoped that *Arts and Architecture* could serve as the client—commissioning and supervising the building of the houses and opening them to the public for inspection and sale—the logistical and economic realities dictated otherwise. Ultimately the clients paid for the houses after selecting the architects from Entenza's approved list. The chief advantages for clients of a Case Study designation were the discounts on building and furnishing materials provided by manufacturers in exchange for publicity credits when the houses were exhibited and published. There was also the excitement of participating in an avant-garde building program.[24]

The only Case Study design of Neutra's to be built was for a young dentist, Stuart Bailey, and his family, who bought a lot on the five-acre tract overlooking the ocean in Santa Monica Canyon that Entenza had acquired as the site for the first houses. The Bailey house was completed in 1947 as CSH #20. Its neighbors on Entenza's original site would include Rodney Walker's CSH #18 (1948), Charles Eames's famous CSH #8 for himself and his wife Ray (1949), and Eames and Eero Saarinen's CSH #9 (1949) for Entenza himself. Neutra's earlier CSH #19, designed for Warner Brothers executive Milton Scott and located next to CSH #18, was so modified by Scott and by subsequent owners that Neutra and Entenza decided to disassociate it both from Neutra's authorship and the Case Study designation.[25]

The original Bailey house was a modest flat-roofed two-bedroom, one-bath redwood structure, with the kitchen, garage, and master bedroom to the front. The large living-dining area and child's room to the rear opened via walls of floor-to-ceiling glass to a flagstone terrace and a lushly wooded garden. "Now it's tribute time," Bailey wrote

Neutra in 1958, as he commissioned him to design a new addition to the rear. "Not that I believe you will work better on my plans because I let you smell roses; surely you've had enough praise. . . ." Yet Bailey must have known that Neutra could never have "enough praise," for he went on to celebrate the fact that the house "does not just sit here passively. I feel that it acts on me in a most beneficial manner. It draws me to it. . . . After ten years, students still come from all over the world and stand here in postures of reverence, clicking their cameras and adjusting their gazes. Is it simply that they want to join a cult of which you are the high priest? Or is it that the building acts on them too—tells them some archetypal truth which sets them free?"[26]

In 1948, the year of the completion of the Bailey House, another small residence by Neutra, the Branch house, elicited from its owners less euphoric observations, which subtly foreshadowed

250. *Neutra*, Kaufmann House, 1946

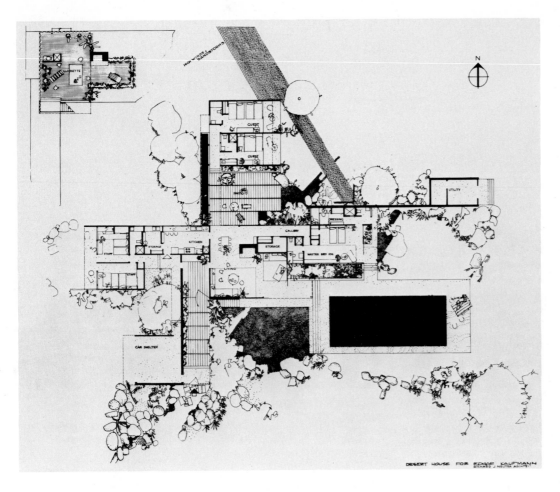

251. *Neutra*, Kaufmann House, 1946

beauty," the building was "everything we hoped our home would be."[27]

Yet by 1948 the Branches, having sold their house and moved to Santa Cruz, were surprised to find it included in a story on Neutra in *Architectural Forum*. This prompted Branch to write to a friend on the *Forum's* staff that "from all reports, the Frankels are delighted with their glass cage, and we can understand their relatively youthful enthusiasm since we once felt the same way. As for us, we're living in a 30-year-old farm house with the general proportions of a Pennsylvania barn and frankly (but don't tell Mr. Neutra) we like it a lot better. Maybe it's because we're just the sort of people who should live in a barn. But we *are* people, and we're a lot more comfortable in this old shoe of a house than we ever were as victims of the so-called functional. We have kids. We have a collie and grandmother's hand-me-downs and a wife who never could and never will keep a house according to Neutra. . . . So . . . Mr. Neutra's house is in another magazine! That's exactly where it belongs, and that's the way we felt about it even after living in it for seven years. Here we can have our dirty diapers and our peace of mind. Who, I ask you, ever saw a diaper, even a clean one, illustrated in the *Forum*? Even though there is nothing more functional. No, I'm not bitter nor even regretful. I'd just like to tell your readers why two Smart Young Things moved to Pennsylvania Dutch from Neutra Modern, and why our house of tomorrow will have to wait until tomorrow when our kids are grown and gone."[28]

Neutra was puzzled by Branch's letter, as was Stanley Frankel, the new owner, who wrote to the *Forum* in strong opposition "to the views apparently now held by Mr. Russell Branch about the 'Neutra Modern' masterpiece he sold us a year ago. From the standpoint of the young family it seems to me to present advantages unobtainable in traditional homes. Aside from its high utility to cost ratio this house appears to me, after a year of residence, to have several unusual virtues: First its flexibility— any point of the house can be reached by at least two routes. That is because the house is built around a central storage core with little waste wall and hall space. Second my wife rejoices in being able to look at the outside world instead of just at a wall in whatever room she chooses for a current job—

the critique of modernism that would blossom in the sixties. The simple two-bedroom wood and stucco structure Neutra designed for the Branches in 1942 in the Hollywood Hills resembled other houses of the early forties—though with a shed roof so slightly pitched that it read from the front and rear elevations as a conventional Neutra flat-roofed modernist building. Though they would change their minds by 1948, the clients' early reactions were ecstatic. "We want to assure you again that we are absolutely delighted with the whole house," Betty Branch wrote Neutra in 1942. "We are constantly thrilled to discover how it meets our every need and like. . . . We've been astounded that, after only one or two conferences with you, you were able to design a house that kept within our small budget but nevertheless suited us so completely." In sending Neutra the balance of his fee, Russell Branch wrote that "in liveability and

252. *Neutra*, Tremaine House, Montecito, California, 1948

253. *Neutra*, Tremaine House, 1948

254. *Neutra,* Tremaine House, 1948

255. *Neutra,* Tremaine House, 1948

256. *Neutra*, Tremaine House, 1948

257. *Neutra*, Tremaine House, 1948

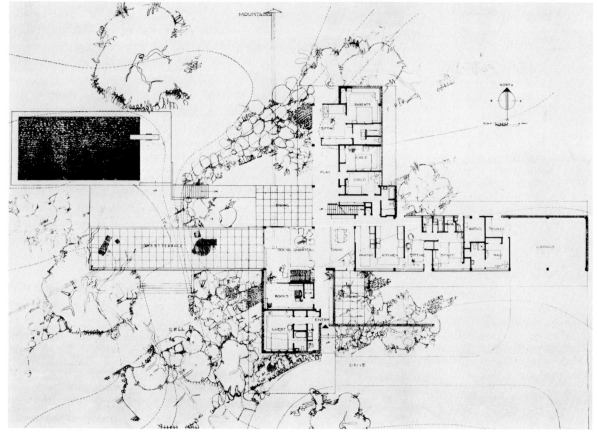

258. *Neutra*, Case Stury House for Stuart
Bailey, Los Angeles, 1946

259. *Neutra*, Case Study House for Stuart
Bailey, 1946

and in the Santa Monica mountains that is indeed pleasant. . . . Beyond this, it is our firm conviction that the former Branch House is purely and simply a thing of beauty and we rejoice in our possession of it."[29]

Despite the expressed desire in his letter to "tell your readers why," Branch later insisted that the letter was a personal statement to a friend on the staff and was never intended for publication. He apologized to Neutra and sent him a copy of his reply to the *Forum*, which tempered but did not retract his earlier statements. "Both my wife and I still feel that the house which Richard J. Neutra designed for us was a splendid realization of the ideas we took to him in 1941," he explained. "He gave us exactly what we wanted then; in fact, he gave us more than we could have hoped for, considering our small budget and construction difficulties at the time. If our ideas have changed since then, it has been in spite of our regard for Mr. Neutra and not because of him. His dwellings—as I think he'd be the first to admit—illustrate a philosophy and propound a certain way of life. It is that way of life, rather than Mr. Neutra's unassailable ability as an architect, which I question now after finding another type of house and, essentially, another mode of living. Let me put it this way. If a friend of mine came to me and said he wanted modern, I'd tell him: Go to Neutra, you can't do better. But first I'd ask that friend: Are you *sure* you want modern? Do you really want stark lines and slick surfaces and a way of life planned to the last efficient inch? Do you realize that an old-fashioned house can also be functional; that it may, in fact, function even better for families such as mine . . . and yours?" Such critiques as this would affect Neutra's work of the late forties and fifties as he worked to soften the "stark lines and slick surfaces" of the modern "way of life planned to the last efficient inch."[30]

Between the Channel Heights development of 1942 and the vast Elysian Park Heights project of 1949–52, Neutra completed relatively few important public or commercial commissions. His Elkay apartments, Westwood (1948), bore a strong resemblance, appropriately, to the neighboring Kelton apartments he had designed before the war. The strong motif of spiderleg outrigging at the Holiday House Motel in Malibu (1948) predicted the theme

260. *Neutra*, Branch House, Los Angeles, 1942

261. *Neutra*, Branch House, 1942

262. *Neutra*, Holiday House, Malibu, California, 1948

of many of his residential designs of the fifties. As one of the first motel designs by a major modernist architect, it also influenced the more anonymous and more generally adopted images of "motel modern" architecture of the fifties and later. The sturdy, respectable, but less-than-exciting designs for the Margolis Stores, Palm Springs (1945), Kaiser-Fraser showrooms, North Hollywood (1946), and Aloe Health Equipment Building, Los Angeles (1948), forecast their increasingly tired and bland commercial counterparts of later decades.

The Norwalk Service Station, Bakersfield (1947), however, took on a significance beyond its respectably "good old modern" design when its publication both in architectural and oil company journals enshrined its image in gas station typology. The client, Frank Davis, for whom Neutra had designed a house in 1938, was the area distributor for Norwalk gasoline and decided to build the station for lease as an investment. He got from Neutra a crisp emphatic design with two overlapping, slightly pitched roof slabs surging and "floating" above the glass and open spaces. It was one of the first gas stations designed by a modern master actually to be completed and was a rare example for the time of a station built in the high International Style, as opposed to the numerous contemporary Deco and Streamline Moderne stations. When Norwalk Gas was later consumed by one of the larger conglomerates with a differently named

product, the large Norwalk sign, carefully designed by Neutra, unfortunately had to be removed. It had been important to the scale and the whole design of the building, as signs frequently were to modernist structures. The Norwalk later became a bowdlerized "body shop."[31]

Neutra continued through the forties to participate in AIA, CIAM, and other professional activities. Typical of this was Princeton's 1947 Bi-Centennial Conference on the Environment, at which Neutra, Gropius, Sert, Aalto, Wright, Giedion, and several dozen more of the world's leading architects discussed the problems and possibilities of planning the physical environment. Though described as "an unprecedented assembly for an unprecedented purpose," the gathering of luminaries, while no doubt stimulated by the heady conversation, came to no ringing declaration or conclusions that promised to turn architecture in any startlingly new directions. Of greater importance to Neutra's personal and professional development was a lecture tour in 1946 to Latin America, where he observed with relish the ancient and modern monuments and conversed with students and colleagues on the needs and imperatives of Latin American architecture. His enthusiastic reception there led to his next important publication in English and Portuguese, *The Architecture of Social Concern*, which emphasized his interest in subtropical architecture as exemplified chiefly in his Puerto Rican designs. In 1948

Neutra returned to Europe for the first time since 1930 and combined the usual lecture engagements with reunions with the Weixlgärtners and other relatives and friends. In Paris, Dione recalled, they had a most impressive reception. Various student groups "received Richard with a torch parade. They put us in a twenty-year-old open Ford, flanked by two bicyclists, dressed in white robes and flowing Grecian helmets, followed by two taxicabs with a music band on the roof. Thus we were paraded down Les Champs Elysées, much to the surprise and amusement of the onlookers."[32]

Throughout the forties Neutra continued to correspond with friends and colleagues around the world. With Walter Gropius and Konrad Wachsman he discussed the possibilities of their prefabricated panel system and even produced a panel house design, though it was ultimately never built. He rejoiced furthermore in post-war reunions not only with European friends but also with such Japanese colleagues as his old Taliesin associate Kameki Tsuchiura. "I am so happy to learn that you and your affairs are in good shape," he wrote, "and that Japan which I loved, through you and from my visit, is on its way to recovery." In 1947 he mourned the death of his friend László Moholy-Nagy, and received a telling tribute from Moholy's widow Sybil. "Last week Moholy's last book *Vision in Motion* was finally published," she wrote. "It is a very beautiful and—I feel—a very important book and I want you to accept from me the copy I have mailed to you today. . . ." It was, she insisted, "through indebtedness to people like Richard that Moholy came to write this book. Moholy had great respect for Richard's creativity and he felt very much akin to the grace and life enjoyment expressed in his work."[33]

In 1949, Neutra's increasing fame and stature were confirmed by his appearance on the cover of *Time*. A *Time* feature story in 1947 had called him second in American architecture "only to the lordly Frank Lloyd Wright." Though by 1949 Neutra had been the subject of numerous feature stories and special issues of architecture journals, the *Time* cover story both reflected and increased his fame and recognition among laymen. The article, however, was more than a biographical portrait; it also surveyed the contemporary architectural scene in a related two-page spread on "Modern Houses

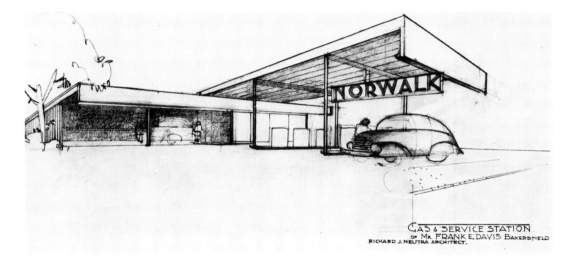

263. *Neutra*, Norwalk Service Station, Bakersfield, California, 1947

264. *Neutra*, Norwalk Service Station, 1947

265. Princeton Architects' and Planners'
Conference, 1947

across the U.S." This featured buildings by Wright, Gropius, Soriano, Breuer, Edward Stone, William Wurster, and Pietro Belluschi, but it focused on Neutra as "one of the world's best and most influential moderns." It dealt with the critique of the International Style of the thirties as too "hard and cold" for popular acceptance, but noted with approval Neutra's recent transition to softer and warmer forms and materials. "If what is now called 'modern' eventually becomes traditional in the U.S., it concluded, "it will be not merely because more and more people have learned to like it. Modern architects will have been learning too, merging clean lines, common-sense convenience and liberating openness of style with the warm overtones of home."[34]

In the late 1940s, Neutra completed the manuscript of *Survival Through Design,* a collection of forty-seven short essays that he described in the preface as "a loose yet linked cycle of writings collected over almost a lifetime." Though the book would not appear until 1954, it reflected his thought of "almost a lifetime" on sensory stimuli and human responses and the crucial relationships between the built environment and human psychological and physiological development. He was concerned, in a negative sense, with how "bad" design tends to "get on our nerves," with how design could be "the problem" as well "the solution." On the positive side, he reminded his readers, in one of the book's typical passages, that a building could "be designed to satisfy 'by the month' with the regularity of a

provider. Here it satisfies through habituation. Or it may do so in a very different way, 'by the moment,' the fraction of a second, with the thrill of a lover. The experience of a lifetime is often summed up in a few memories, and these are more likely to be of the latter type, clinging to a thrilling occurrence, rather than to the former concerned with humdrum steadiness." Here," he pointed out, "is the value of a wide sliding door opening pleasantly onto a garden. It cannot be measured by counting how often and how steadily the door is used, or how many hours it stays open. The decisive thing may be a first deep breath of liberation when one is in the almost ritual act of opening it before breakfast or on the first warm and scented spring day. The memories of one's youth and of the landscape in which it was spent seem composed, to a considerable degree, of this sort of vital recollection. There are in each life certain scattered quanta of experience that may have been of small number or dimension statistically but were so intense as to provide impacts, forever essential."[35]

In analyzing the relationship of architecture and the haptic sense, of the ways in which design "fit" or failed to meet human physiological and psychological needs, Neutra displayed his remarkable erudition but also his somewhat pretentious tendency to be the "expert" on everything from the natural and behavioral sciences to the humanities and social sciences. Frequently rich in their multilayered density, the essays tended at times toward a fragmented, episodic, and elliptical obliqueness.

And they suffered from the redundancy that had characterized his earlier writing. Like much of his architecture of the fifties and sixties, *Survival Through Design* would come to seem less and less radical as the world caught up with it and consigned it to the category of the respectably *déjà vu*. Still, most critics of the early 1950s received it as one of the era's most remarkable testaments by an architect concerned with the larger environment as well as with its myriad microcosmic components.

Maxwell Fry asserted in *Arts and Architecture* that "the appearance of a book by Richard Neutra has an interest beyond the architectural matters with which it must be concerned because among the half dozen masters of modern architecture Neutra is distinguished by his directness of approach to human problems." Robert M. Hutchins predicted in *The Nation* that "every architect and planner will read this book" and suggested that indeed "every citizen should." Lewis Mumford, on the other hand, writing in the *New Yorker,* averred that it was "not an easy book for the lay reader, or even the architect, to find his way about in, but for anyone who likes to chew over the basic problems of our lives, as related to design, it should be a useful cud, for Neutra is a thoughtful man who has gone past the phase of having pat and easy answers to the problems of architecture or life."[36]

Reviewing the book for the *Saturday Review,* Douglas Haskell saw it as heralding a shift on the part of Neutra, and perhaps of his generation, in the whole "functionalist approach, from early naive mechanistic functionalism to psychological, from concern with how architecture goes together to concern with what it is for, how it affects the user." He found the book a remarkable synthesis of the evolving thought of "one of that small group of great pioneers who transformed the art during our century."[37]

The late forties were in many ways the apogee of Neutra's career and of the larger modern movement in architecture as well. In the fifties and sixties that ascendancy would be challenged as Neutra and modernism indeed struggled for survival.

266. Richard Neutra and Robert Alexander
at Glendale Boulevard Office, ca. 1951

Crisis   1950–1960

Between the Lovell house of 1929 and the Tremaine house of 1948, between *Wie Baut Amerika?* of the late twenties and *Survival Through Design* of the late forties, Neutra had, despite his frequent despair, lived a rich and fulfilling life. The countless honors and awards, the special issues of architectural journals, and such popular recognition as the *Time* cover story had brought him to international public attention as a major designer and philosopher of modernism. Despite his gnawing personal insecurity, his desperate feelings of "time running out," of achievements lagging far behind goals, he must also have known that he had accomplished a great deal. The fame and recognition were alternately sustaining and frustrating—on the one hand, massaging his uncertain ego; on the other, creating new pressures to excel, to measure up to past praise and to the future praise he continued to crave.

How to test himself against the ambitious dreams that seemed constantly to outrun even his sturdiest accomplishments? How to do more in a quantitative way while refining and enhancing the quality of his work? How to make up for past inefficiency and wasted effort in the years remaining in his life? How to enjoy and exploit his growing celebrity without losing touch with the work that had made it possible? The last problem, which he may never have consciously confronted, would in his later years vastly affect the quality of his architectural design, the *raison d'être* of his other pursuits, because he allowed those other pursuits—lecturing, writing, philosophizing, "being famous"—to compete with design for his time and energy. His pursuit of celebrity and worldwide "importance" detracted from the time, the care, and the patient detail he had been forced to lavish on the

frequently brilliant work he accomplished *before* he was famous. Neutra was impressed with the words and example of Daniel H. Burnham, the Chicago planner, whose Nietzschean command to "make no little plans" must have appealed to his own *Übermensch* fantasies. But Neutra, unlike Burnham, was unable to delegate with any degree of comfort, or even to cooperate with others on a team. His recognition of this disturbed his self-image, especially in view of his certain belief that both were important keys to success. But whatever his problems with the division of labor and the delegation of responsibility, with departures, in essence, from the atelier mentality he had been unable to shake, he determined to expand his various horizons by overcoming his solitary, prima donna inclinations and somehow expanding the scope of his operations by finding a partner upon whom he could lean and with whom he could share the pains and pleasures of the architectural life. For different, chiefly personal reasons he had been unable to consider such a course with the assertive, acerbic Ain or the loyal, benign Pfisterer. In retrospect, he realized that a partnership with Harris or Longstreth might have come the closest to being workable.

But in the late 1940s he encountered the young architect Robert Alexander in a series of relationships which merged into partnership. For almost all of the fifties, "Neutra and Alexander" won commissions of a scale that Neutra alone had somehow never been able to acquire, though the quality of their output frequently fell behind the quantity. The agreed-upon scope of the Neutra & Alexander work was confined to the "big" areas of planning and of public and commercial architecture, conducted in an office on Glendale Boulevard, a block away from Neutra's Silverlake house. Neutra worked on his acknowledged forte, residential design, with a few loyal "collaborators" in the Silverlake studio, with no interference by Alexander.

Neutra admired in Alexander the personal "go-getter" qualities he believed so essential to success in the American marketplace, traits he had always believed he lacked and in the misguided pursuit of which he frequently seemed so awkwardly aggressive. Handsome and appealing in an all-American way, from an old, East coast family, a fraternity man and Cornell football player with an instinctive grasp of the levers of power. Alexander seemed to Neutra a potentially ideal partner. The complementary qualities of Neutra's fame and reputation likewise appealed to the young Alexander. Though each partner would ultimately disappoint the other, the partnership began with the highest expectations.[1]

Following his graduation from the Cornell School of Architecture, Alexander had migrated to California in the early 1930s, and by 1936 he had become a partner in the Pasadena office of Wilson, Merrill, and Alexander. His and his firm's most notable achievement in the late 1930s was Baldwin Hills Village, or Thousand Gardens as it was known originally, done in collaboration with the established Los Angeles architect Reginald Johnson and with the noted East Coast planner Clarence Stein, whom Johnson engaged as a planning consultant. Designed in 1937 and built in 1942 as a residential community for a private developer on a sixty-four-acre tract·of land in south central Los Angeles, the most distinctive trait of Baldwin Hills Village was its planning and design for the automobile, an acknowledgment not only of the times but of the place—the auto-possessed metropolis of Los Angeles. According to a later citation from the American Institute of Architects, Baldwin Hills provided "convenient vehicular access and parking for all its 627 dwelling units, yet is not penetrated by a single through street. The integrated pedestrian street thus created is skillfully laid out to offer its residents a remarkable variety of open spaces, ranging in scale from private patios and balconies through garden courts serving groups of apartments to the central village green, which gives unity and identity to the entire development. The buildings themselves are straight-

forward, unpretentious, serviceable. This, combined with a masterful site plan, gives the project a clarity, a serenity, a harmonious unity rarely found in 20th century urban development."[2]

In recognition of his contributions to the design of Baldwin Hills and his other planning achievements in California and elsewhere, Alexander was appointed in 1945 to the Los Angeles City Planning Commission, and in 1948 he became its president. As such, he was in close and frequent contact with the powerful Howard Holtzendorf, director of the Los Angeles City Housing Authority, the local arm of the federal government's Public Housing Authority, responsible for choosing sites and architects for the vast Los Angeles housing program made possible by the 1949 Federal Housing Act. Initially Alexander had hoped to get one of the smaller housing projects, which he could handle completely by himself. But Holtzendorf convinced him that his own favorite, the large project for Chavez Ravine, was the plum of the lot. However, to land this, the largest and most prestigious commission, Alexander would have to collaborate with a more established architect, Holtzendorf insisted, a national figure with a name and reputation he could "sell" to the board. And going through the list of other applicants for appointments, Holtzendorf favored Neutra, with whom he had worked successfully on Channel Heights. Neutra and Alexander had known each other slightly in the late thirties and early forties, and Neutra, impressed with Alexander's work on Baldwin Hills, had invited him in the mid-1940s to collaborate on a planning project for Sacramento. In 1949 Alexander returned the compliment by soliciting Neutra's participation on the new plan for Chavez Ravine, already renamed Elysian Park Heights.[3]

Chavez Ravine, at the century's midpoint, was one of those curious by-products of the rapid, sprawling, low-density, crazy-quilt growth of Los Angeles. Settled chiefly by Mexican-Americans, it merged rather vaguely into the wooded hills of Elysian Park on the north and west, but was bordered on the east and south by the oldest freeways of Southern California—the Arroyo Seco or Pasadena Freeway on the east and what came to be known as the Hollywood Freeway on the south. Following the Housing Act of 1949, it was logically targeted as the biggest and most prominent of eleven

Southern California sites to be filled with public housing under the terms of the act. With the strong backing of Los Angeles mayor Fletcher Bowron, the city council voted unanimously to approve the program and in October 1950 signed a contract between the city and the housing authority for eleven projects of 10,000 dwelling units to cost $110 million.

The Chavez Ravine project reflected many of the problems facing architecture and urban design as the nation entered the second half of the century. It also revealed dark undercurrents in other aspects of American life in the troubled 1950s. The first of several paradoxes in the Chavez Ravine story was the planners' ambivalence about changing the character of the area at all. Almost everyone among the redevelopers—including Neutra and Alexander— had to admit that the Ravine was "charming," that its people seemed happy and well-adjusted and had a rather intense feeling of pride in, and identity with, their community. As a "Mexican village" it was strongly Roman Catholic, and the church and the public elementary school were vital centers of a rich ethnic fabric. Festivals and holidays were celebrated with great esprit. Most observers commented on the lively street life, the exquisite plantings in yards and window boxes, and the *mañana* ambience of rather harmless abandon. As if to heighten the antique quality of the scene, high above the shacks, on one of the highest peaks, was a Spanish Revival villa surveying it all, the home of the noted Mexican actor Crispin Martin, the beloved "Cisco Kid. Observers remembered him walking the streets of Chavez Ravine and referring proudly to "my people." And though everyone agreed that it was indeed a slum, they felt somehow uneasy about clearing the alleged blight. Many of the buildings were by definition substandard, especially in regard to such matters as plumbing and insulation, but in the relatively benign climate of Los Angeles the cracks and crevices were less of a problem than they would have been elsewhere.[4]

Chavez Ravine posed precisely the kind of paradox that was later explicated and criticized so trenchantly in the early 1960s by Jane Jacobs in her *Death and Life of Great American Cities*, where she presented case after case in which planners, architects, and reforming politicians looked a bit closer at "blighted slums" and found there much of

267. Chavez Ravine, Los Angeles, late 1940s

268. Chavez Ravine, late 1940s

225

the vitality and neighborhood identity that good planning was ideally supposed to accomplish. Yet these planners, Jacobs asserted, lacked the wit or the courge to overcome the biases they had formed in graduate school about the nature, definition, and deserved fate of "slums."

Neutra expressed this constraining ambivalence in his early unpublished assessments of the area. It appealed quite obviously to the nineteenth-century European pastoral romanticism that pervaded so much of his modernist world view. But in his descriptions he obviously felt compelled to keep repeating the word "slum" to counter his otherwise strong approval. He referred to the inhabitants not as Mexican-Americans but as "Aztecs." He was especially fond of neighboring, admittedly neglected Elysian Park, which had been planted with eucalyptus trees as a community project in the late nineteenth century. "There is a certain human warmth and pleasantness," he remarked "a certain contact with nature in this slum which cannot be found in Harlem, New York, or along South Halsted Street, Chicago. The trees of the lovely mountain park have grown high around the strangest 'blightlocked' area that can be found in any city of America. . . ."[5]

"For fifty years," Neutra concluded ambivalently, suggesting the rationale for his and Alexander's planned improvements, the area had "resisted any development, largely due to the configuration of the grounds, which entails quite an expense in road building, utility construction and the creation of a community of urban density." "Urban density" was, in fact, the chief rationale for redeveloping Chavez Ravine. Why should such an area, the argument ran, so close to the center of a city that, like most cities, needed more housing, not be available to *more* people? Why not utilize the provisions of the Housing Act to "develop" Chavez Ravine, without—it was bravely hoped—destroying its rich assets? Neutra took this firm if somewhat naive tack, although he actually had his own personally confessed doubts. In any case, he was able to convince church, school, community, and civic leaders that the richness could and would return and would be reintegrated within the new plan.[6]

"In order to bring this rejuvenated community the benefits of transportation, shopping, and cultural facilities which it has never been able to support, numbers will count," Neutra asserted. "It is essential that the site should be fully developed with housing for over three thousand families. . . . In fitting a new community of 17,000 souls into the greater community, housing is only a part of the task, although it will settle 3360 families. Apart from this, the planners must relate intricate new and old streets and utility networks, turn traffic onto the two major freeways at the very boundary of the area, create sites through design, not independent of it for a series of . . . projects: three schools, kindergartens and day nurseries, three churches, a Community Hall with kitchen, activity rooms, indoor and outdoor auditoriums for 1500, a commercial section or trading center and managerial buildings." As much as possible, major roads would skirt rather than bisect the area, interior streets would be *cul de sacs*, and housing would face inward toward garden plots or finger parks.[7]

Economically and logistically, increased density seemed imperative, certainly to the national and local housing authorities and maybe even to Neutra, who was at least able to rationalize it. To house the estimated 3360 families, as opposed to the 1100 there at the time, there would have to be 24 thirteen-story towers and 163 two-story structures furnishing a total of 3364 units—over a third of the units projected for all of Los Angeles. Of these, 481 would contain one bedroom; 1922, 2 bedrooms; 742, three bedrooms; 202, four bedrooms; and 18 units, five bedrooms, for the more procreatively inclined.[8]

Critics in Los Angeles and elsewhere argued that the density was unreasonably high, especially for Los Angeles, where it challenged too radically the city's historic fabric and established demographic patterns—however it might compare with older Eastern cities. Among others, Clarence Stein, William Wurster, and Catharine Bauer, old friends and colleagues of both Alexander and Neutra, suggested that the planners were guilty of malfeasance in not fighting the requirements and urging lower density. The towers, they argued, would become disastrous for housing poor people in California who—semirural, or urban-suburban—had not been prepared for such a shift in living style. Later, the local chapter of the AIA would oppose it on the same grounds. Dione recalled that privately Neutra shared much of this pessimism. He wrote to Wurster to tell him how much he respected "the sincere

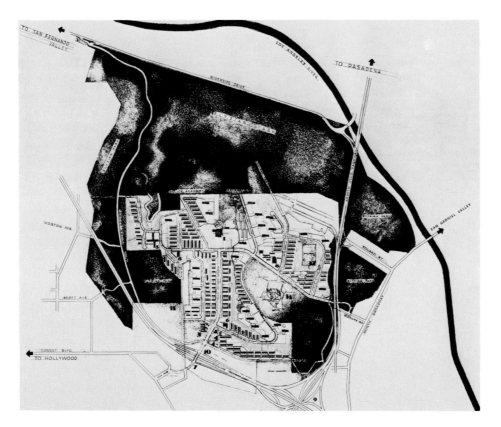

269. *Neutra and Alexander*, Elysian Park Heights, Los Angeles, early 1950s, plan

270. *Neutra and Alexander*, Elysian Park Heights, early 1950s

271. *Neutra and Alexander*, Elysian Park
Heights, early 1950s

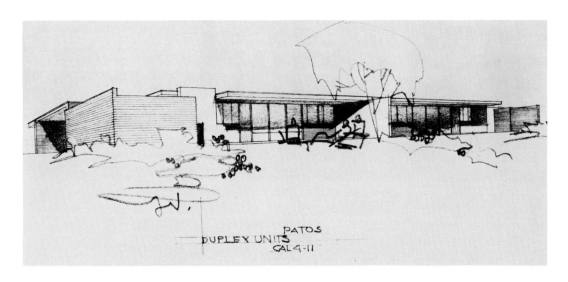

272. *Neutra and Alexander*, Elysian Park
Heights, early 1950s, low-rise apartments

stand which you have taken and expressed. We are, in this territory, still counseling with each other [as] to what possibly, apart from controversial patience, can be done to improve the situation. As I told Catharine [Bauer] too, I have had plenty of occasions to search my conscience and try to make the best human and professional decisions. . . ." Still, in public he replied obliquely, and to a certain extent accurately, to the effect that the needs and imperatives of Los Angeles in the fifties were not identical with Stein's Radburn of the twenties, and that the densities were "givens" within which they must work. Their job was to balance them with saving amenities.[9]

Neutra believed, for example, that the potentially vulnerable towers, if properly and imaginatively designed and sited, could become beautiful elements in the new Elysian landscape. Simon Eisner, the site planner of the team, recalled how Neutra spent long Sunday mornings at the site, sitting and walking, drawing in his sketchpad, imagining and placing and rearranging the towers on the hills. "However romantic it may be to dream of retaining the present charm of rural backwardness," Neutra argued in the tougher tones of the modernist reformer, "the area cannot be redeveloped with suburban bungalows. A realistic use of the site by any developer will require an urban housing solution to suit the location and must be designed to take advantage of the beautiful but very hilly terrain. In order to provide ample space between two-story buildings, with private gardens for large families, it will prove necessary to house the smaller families in need of one- and two-bedroom apartments in multi-storied buildings. An exhaustive study of the site reveals that this is a soundly conceived solution, and one which will produce the best living conditions for this particular situation." He wanted to avoid the routinely crowded siting of tall buildings in other American cities, which should be "in no way a precedent for the present project. The tall buildings here will be spaced great distances apart and in spacious groups, separated by several valleys." Identical apartments would be arranged one above the other with common plumbing stacks. In this way, Neutra argued, "a relatively small hilltop can be made to accommodate sufficient dwellings to justify the grading and road building necessary to make it available. This will automatically elevate the smaller apartments of the community to positions of unusual beauty overlooking the surrounding far-flung hills or verdure, with the ridges of the Sierra Madre rising to the north and the interesting urban scene receding to the Pacific toward the south. Every apartment will have view windows with the quality of a private balcony and access to an open recreation area on each floor. It is not hard," he concluded optimistically, "to imagine that under such conditions these apartments will be easily the most popular in the entire program."[10]

Elysian Park, alas, was beginning to resemble not Channel Heights or Baldwin Hills Village, but a green, hilly update of "Rush City Reformed." Its buildings, high and low, for good and for ill, were resolutely modernist in scale and detail. As such, they promised to exhibit the frequent elegance and crispness of Neutra's minimalist esthetic, which consciously appealed to the trained eye of the day, while touching, it was hoped, even if less consciously, the more esthetically innocent as well. This was particularly true of the project's smaller compositions, reminiscent of Neutra's earlier successes with small, modular, low-slung, abstractly asymmetrical buildings. The tower designs, on the other hand, presaged in their relative blandness the problems he would have with tall buildings later. In all cases, however, it was typical of Neutra and his generation that except occasionally in the most minimal abstractions, their attempts to recapture the area's traditional Hispanic richness included no allusions to Spanish Colonial architecture in any explicitly communicable form—as opposed to the way this was done by Neutra's fellow transplanted Californians, Irving Gill at the beginning of the century and Charles Moore toward the end.

Accommodating the towers on the more solid higher ground meant considerable grading and filling, and this in turn demanded that virtually the entire population of the ravine be "temporarily" relocated and that most of their structures and the fabric of their village be demolished. The "substandard" housing was condemned and purchased for what was allegedly the "fair price," but residents who had owned their own homes of course faced the difficulty of matching the "fair price" of their old property with the purchase price of a new home. The church, whose property was less easily condemned, held out longer and for considerably more money, and some of its parishioners managed to transfer their property to the church in order to get the same higher prices. For both owners and renters, the Housing Authority provided relocation assistance.[11]

The social and architectural merits and demerits of Neutra and Alexander's Elysian Park project would remain a fascinating and instructive subject of discussion, but of speculative discussion only, since it was ultimately never built. For as the ravine's original tenants were being relocated and their village demolished, and just before the recently approved redevelopment plans were to be opened to bid, there exploded on the scene another long-smoldering force not connected directly to questions either of architecture or of ethnic identity—that ominous specter of the early 1950s later known as McCarthyism.

A cluster of groups, institutions, and individuals, including the powerful California real estate lobby, the Home Builders' Association, the Chamber of Commerce, and, most critically, the *Los Angeles Times*, began to attack the housing program as "creeping socialism"—if not rampant communism —that was subverting from within the American values that were supposedly being defended on the hills of Korea. Though they had endorsed the program unanimously in 1949, the politically vulnerable members of the city council began to soften and to change their positions. Mayor Bowron continued to defend the program, however, and was supported by the Los Angeles unions of the AFL and the CIO, the NAACP, the League of Women Voters, and various other church, veterans', and ad hoc citizens' groups. But these organizations were simply outbought and outshouted in the press and on the air by the anti-housing forces, who pumped large sums of money into their advertising and "educational" campaign. Frederick Dockweiler, chairman of Citizens Against Socialist Housing (CASH), argued, for example, that there was "one basic issue in this campaign. That issue is, is this program Socialistic, or is it not?" Mayor Bowron's arguments for the program "had [not] removed the stamp of Socialism from the public housing program," Dockweiler charged, "but on the contrary has emphasized its collectivist pattern." And one of the councilmen, F. H. Henry, now agreed that "if we need any evidence that now is the time to stop the march on the road to collectivism, we have it in our present experience with the so-called City Housing Authority."[12]

The high—or low—point of the local McCarthyite red-baiting was reached in 1952, when an ongoing investigation by the California Senate Committee on Un-American Activities turned its attention to the Los Angeles City Housing Authority. Three highly placed members of the CHA took the Fifth Amendment when asked the fateful question, "Are you now or have you ever been a member of the Communist party?" All three were promptly fired by CHA Director Holtzendorf. One of these was CHA Director of Information Frank Wilkinson, the idealistic son of a prominent Los Angeles Methodist layman and physician. Wilkinson was a close political ally of Pauline Schindler's and a friend and client of Neutra's. Both remained loyal to him as he refused, on principle, to answer the committee's questions. Wilkinson's Fifth Amendment plea, however, convinced city councilman John Holland, "that public housing follows the Communist pattern. These are the people who are trying to wreck America. Those who have been warning us that liberty is in grave danger in this country are right." A resolution of the city council accused Director Holtzendorf of "dereliction of duty . . . in permitting Frank Wilkinson to operate for 10 years in his obvious plot to infiltrate Communists into the Housing Authority."[13]

The anti-socialist, anti-communist crusade, the focus and symbol and ideological umbrella of a highly complex cluster of anti-housing sentiments, was without doubt the crucial factor in the rapid shift from the balmy pro-housing atmosphere of August 1949, when the city council had voted unanimously to approve the program, to its 8–7 vote on December 26, 1951, to cancel the contract with the Housing Authority. In 1953, after two years of court suits and continued red-baiting, the four-term champion of public housing, Mayor Bowron, was defeated by Norris Poulson, the anti-housing candidate. Poulson then negotiated a series of complex compromises wherein the program was cut virtually in half, and Elysian Park Heights, the largest and most visible of the original eleven projects, was canceled altogether.[14]

Cleared now of most of its population, Chavez Ravine lay idle, awaiting its destiny. And later in the decade, when the Brooklyn Dodgers decided to move west and needed a home in central Los Angeles, Chavez Ravine seemed the ideal location. In 1957 the city exchanged the 315-acre ravine for the 9-acre stadium site of the old minor-league Los Angeles Angels, which Dodger owner Walter O'Malley had earlier acquired in a deal with Philip Wrigley. The contract also provided that the city would spend $2 million on "site improvement," an ironic contrast to the earlier anti-housing outcry against the city's commitments to provide sewage for the housing project. Indeed, to Los Angeles in the McCarthyite fifties, public housing seemed un-American, but baseball did not. And on September 27, 1959, ten years after it all began, O'Malley broke ground for his new Dodger Stadium. Neutra and Alexander were paid a planning fee, but no sum could compensate for their lost time and energy and their disappointment in seeing their big plans ignored. The ten-year "Battle of Chavez Ravine"— from the early debate over changing it at all, to the Neutra and Alexander designs for redevelopment, to its tragic embroilment in cold war politics, to its final, American, apple-pie resolution—framed an era in American history in which public housing was only one of the casualties.[15]

Before the demise of Elysian Park Heights, however, other planning and architectural projects cemented the Neutra and Alexander partnership. Their continuing work on the redevelopment of Sacramento led the planners to recommend the recovery of a subterranean network of basements and related areas, abandoned over the years as the river had flooded and the city had built upward. To reclaim the depressed and crime-ridden district between the riverfront and the California state capitol, Neutra and Alexander recommended an intense development of commercial blocks built around courtyards, with the drained subterranean spaces converted to storage, parking, and loading areas. The nearby riverfront would be enriched with related commercial facilities and apartment towers.[16]

The plan was "one of the most admired of the submissions" in the *Progressive Architecture* Design Awards competition of 1955, but "because of its scope and unique characteristics," it could not be classified under any of the prevailing building type categories and was given a Special Design Award in the city planning classification. While this "splendid project . . . deals with a specific site," the jury observed, "many of its features could be applied to any city suffering from 'motoritis.'" Like most such studies, the Neutra & Alexander Sacramento plans was ultimately only partially realized. "The broad brush treatment which you so nicely prepared" redevelopment director Joseph Bill observed in 1959, "still forms the structure on which, though changed in some details, a successful city rebuilding operation is now going on." Critic Allan Temko agreed that the preliminary plan was "as bold as it was sweeping, and it remains the basic concept of Sacramento today," though he regreted that city would "not achieve in this first phase of redevelopment anything like the resplendent vision offered by Neutra and Alexander ten years ago."[17]

Of even greater scope, however, was the planning and architectural commission Neutra & Alexander secured in the early 1950s for the redevelopment of the war-ravaged island of Guam. Guam had been discovered by Magellan in 1521 and controlled by Spain until 1898, when, following the Spanish-American War, it, like the Philippines, had become an American protectorate. Heavily damaged in World War II by Japanese invasion and American reoccupation, the 225-square-mile island had become a particularly important element in America's post-war Pacific defense system. Isolated from its nearest major neighbors by 1500 miles of ocean, Guam was seen as a crucial transition point between Hawaii, the Philippines, Japan, and the Asian mainland. In addition, moreover, to the physical destruction of the forties, the lush "tropical paradise" had also suffered the American-inflicted blight of automania. The American military personnel stationed there and the 25,000 Micronesian Guamanians who had bought American cars with their war-damage reparations money had between them turned the tiny island into a veritable sea of automobiles by the early 1950s. In fact, it seemed to Neutra that "almost every Guamanian has a car and many of them have three—a jeep, a truck and an automobile. On fiesta days, the area around the festival looks like the outside of an American ballpark during a game."[18]

Attempting to balance its defense priorities with the needs of the native Guamanians, the United States in 1950 established the island as a self-governing territory with an elected legislature. Carleton Skinner, the enlightened American civilian

governor, was, Alexander remembered, "an energetic young idealist with powerful dreams of reconstructing not only the physical ruins of civilian Guam, but also the social and economic condition of the Guamanians." To this end he charged Neutra and Alexander with preparing not only a physical master plan to include government buildings, schools, housing, and transportation, but an ambitious economic plan that would ultimately relieve the native population of its then-total dependence on the American Establishment. "We had dreams of a freeport," Alexander recalled, "canning home grown pineapples and locally caught tuna, as well as tourism and other activities. The Governor was familiar with Neutra's fame in designing homes and could hardly believe his good fortune in having us design a replacement for the Governor's House . . . which had been destroyed in the re-invasion." In an effort to recapture vestiges of native Guamanian culture, Neutra and Alexander conferred with sociologists and anthropologists in the early planning stages, and when visiting Guam itself "talked with everyone available, 'from the Bishop to the Boy Scouts,' as Neutra would say. . . . Twice when we were on the island," Alexander recalled, "Japanese soldiers surrendered to bus drivers, finally convinced that the war was over."[19]

But in late 1952, Skinner's ambitious program was dismantled on the grounds that any attempt to promote industry or otherwise stimulate the civilian economy would interfere with the national defense. Conservative Governor Ford Q. Elvidge, who replaced Skinner after Eisenhower's election in 1952, had "no use for governmental planning, a communist concept, and no sense of aesthetics or even fair play," Alexander recalled. "Anyone hired by that idealistic dreamer, Skinner, must be all bad." Though work continued on a "comprehensive but rudimentary" general plan and on preparation of zoning and building ordinances for later use, most of the larger planning for commercial and domestic development was abandoned. Only the governor's house and several remarkable schools, begun before the end of Skinner's administration, were completed, buildings whose character would serve as reminders of the Guam that was never achieved.[20]

The sensibly composed tripartite governor's house, or House of Guam, included comfortable but unostentatious private family quarters, a large

central section for public entertaining and cere-
monial functions, and separate guest quarters, all
opening freely onto terraces and gardens, and functionally and esthetically interconnected by porches.
Neutra's planning rationale raised significant social as well as diplomatic issues. "Colonial areas
throughout the world," he observed, "are rapidly
emerging from the attitudes of former years. A
Governor is no longer an aloof ruler surrounded
by military splendor and palatial settings. Today
he is no more than the highest ranking servant of
the people and his dwelling is nothing sumptious,
but rather should have the privacy and serenity of
any decent middle class dwelling."[21]

The handsome Adelup School near Agana, the
Guam capital, intended as a prototype for future
development, combined elementary school facilities
with an adult educational center and a family
recreational area. Like its more modest counterparts
at Umatec and Incryan, it had long, low wings with
clerestory windows and walls opening to the out-
of-doors, recalling Neutra's earlier innovations in
Southern California and Puerto Rico.[22]

As a team, Neutra and Alexander were probably at their best on these planning projects of the
early 1950s. In formulating the plans, each made
basic conceptual contributions, with Neutra taking
chief responsibility for architectural design and
Alexander assuming control of planning organization and logistics. In a 1951 letter on the problems
of Elysian Park Heights, Neutra closed with the
warm assurance that he thought of Alexander "with
pride and happiness as . . . a friend and human
being with whom I have something in common,
after much lonely navigating through life." Initially,
Alexander reciprocated this affectionate respect.
Though he grew increasingly impatient with
Neutra's dramatic "Great Man act" and frequently
resorted to turning a "tin ear" to his partners'
grand monologues, he particularly enjoyed certain
aspects of their early travels together. He recalled
with amusement how, when stopping in Honolulu
on their first visit to Guam, Neutra "kept hearing
Tyrolean airs on the Muzak system, but they were
all Hawaiian to me." Pursuing this paradox with
his usual intensity, Neutra learned to his great
satisfaction that a nineteenth-century Hawaiian
queen had temporarily detained and put under

house arrest a visiting Austrian band master, who
had forthwith been ordered to compose songs for the
royal court. He had consequently rearranged in the
"Hawaiian" manner tunes and folk songs from
Neutra's native land.[23]

On another leg of the Guam expedition the
two partners visited the Philippines, where at one
of Manila's schools of architecture, Neutra "gave a
two-hour, impromptu address . . . which was remarkable in displaying his knowledge of history and
his ability to identify events in the Far East with
simultaneous events in Europe. He spoke in an open
court and kept the students sitting on the ground
and hanging over the balconies spellbound." At a
lecture in Japan, however, Alexander "for the first
time . . . had a chance to see a manifestation of
Neutra's hunger for the adulation of the masses. . . .
Hundreds of people were milling around outside the
building, blocking the street. Riot police were trying
to control them, a mob made angry by refusal to
admit them to an already-crowded auditorium.
Neutra became a man possessed, jumped up onto
a granite plinth next to the stairway, and tried to
shout down the mob. He would try to give a lecture
outside and then inside, but he couldn't be heard
and we finally persuaded him to go inside where an
impatient crowd was being harassed by firemen
trying to clear the aisles. Neutra was in his heaven,
more stimulated by this event than by any other I
ever witnessed."[24]

Back home in Los Angeles, the tension between the partners became increasingly apparent.
This was owing not only to the differences in
temperament and personality that had initially
seemed an asset but also to the related awkward-
ness of the two-office arrangement, and to basic
differences in architectural design philosophy. To
protect his freedom to do residential design, the
area in which he had made and would continue to
make his most important actual and theoretical
contributions, Neutra kept an office "at home," on
the first floor of his Silverlake residence. As opposed to "the Silverlake office of Richard J. Neutra
and Associates," the "Glendale Boulevard office of
Neutra & Alexander" handled the larger projects of
planning and of public and commercial architecture, including multiple-family housing. Particularly after heart attacks in 1949 and 1953 forced

him to spend more time in bed, Neutra used Silverlake as his base of operations. Although he paid periodic, almost daily, visits to the Glendale Boulevard office, it was naturally dominated by Alexander's more constant presence. Most of the staff worked in one or the other office, although in the early 1950s Neutra's son Dion, who had just completed architecture school, moved back and forth between the two in an unofficial and difficult "liaison" capacity. After 1955 Dion worked exclusively in the Glendale Boulevard office. Alexander had brought to the new partnership several valued associates from his earlier practice, chief among whom was fellow Cornell graduate Robert Pierce,[25] who, not surprisingly, remained loyal to Alexander. This was true of secretaries and other staff members as well. Because he did indeed spend most of his time at Silverlake, monitoring from his bedroom command post the work of both offices as well as his own vast personal projects, Neutra came to feel estranged from the Glendale Boulevard office. The work there, he perceived with frustration, had developed increasingly "beyond his control." Alexander saw it from a different perspective, feeling both relief at Neutra's distance from the scene and annoyance at the fact that, in Alexander's view, Neutra was carrying something less than his share of the work. Yet contrary to Neutra's own suspicions, there were achitects in the Glendale Boulevard office who admired and appreciated him. James Pulliam, for example, saw him as "a really egocentric gentleman," but admitted that he "had a certain love for him. . . . He did marvelous things for architecture in Southern California. It took a strong ego to accomplish those things." Frederick Lyman recalled that Neutra "was a rascal in some ways. . . . He was big on getting you to work extra time for nothing. But we got so much out of it. I didn't mind, we kind of loved him."[26]

In addition to the temperamental and organizational conflicts between Neutra and Alexander, there were basic differences in the two men's design philosophies. Alexander later admitted that he was "not enthusiastic" about Neutra's "stark design." The Lovell house was not his "cup of tea." He was, in fact, more sympathetic in the 1950s to the efforts of such architects as Edward Stone, Minoru Yamasaki, and Eero Saarinen to bring warmth to mod-

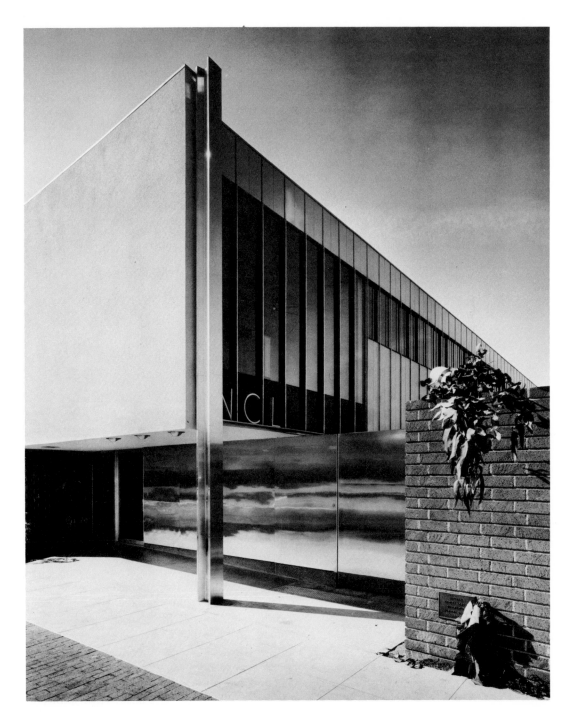

273. *Neutra and Alexander*, National Charity League, Los Angeles, 1953

274. *Neutra and Alexander*, National Charity League, 1953

ernism via various new "expressionistic" forms and decorative effects. Though after the end of the Alexander partnership Neutra's office would tend to move in that same direction, in the early 1950s Neutra rejected such "frills" and "arbitrary" effects. As a member in the late forties of the St. Louis Jefferson Memorial Competition jury, Neutra had voted enthusiastically for Saarinen's winning arch design, but in a critique of the architect's later work, he told Alexander that Saarinen was "a fox," meaning "that one didn't know which way he would jump next—every design was a surprise—inconsistent." Alexander, on the other hand, found Neutra's commitments to continuity and "consistency" esthetically and programmatically contrary to his own sentiments. While occasionally such tensions produced felicitous results, more often they led to watered-down compromises that failed to maximize the vision of either man.[27]

A series of commissions for school and university buildings illustrated this uneven achievement. A building for the National Charity League of Los Angeles (1953), housing office headquarters and the League's nursery school for emotionally disturbed children, was protected on its busy Hollywood Boulevard front by high walls enclosing outdoor play areas. On the handsome front facade overlooking the playground, a long, sleek band of second-story ribbon windows moved west from the glazed two-story stairway entrance corner. Aluminum panel sheathing, spiderleg outrigging, and immaculate detailing connected the building with Neutra's earlier work. Complementing the machine images of the main building were the intersecting one-story classroom wings of brick, stucco, wood, and glass. The building's combination of relaxed informality and restrained compositional elegance made it one of Neutra & Alexander's finest, though the partners' early disagreement over a design detail reflected their differing esthetic approaches. To help support the League financially, Neutra made a proposal that Alexander "found strange, that the surrounding wall on Hollywood Boulevard be designed to receive a series of identical advertis-

275. *Neutra and Alexander*, National Charity League, 1953

ing posters." Neutra argued that "any design whatever, if repeated enough, would be attractive." He had demonstrated this principle on a larger scale a few blocks west on the same street in the early 1930s with the repetitive billboards placed high on the Laemmle Building to advertise the films of Universal-International. For the Charity League building, however, both Alexander and the clients vetoed the idea.[28]

Similar programmatic requirements for child observation facilities at the UCLA Kindergarten and Elementary School (1957) and the USC Child Guidance Clinic (1963), employed stucco, brick, and a more explicit interaction with outdoor plantings to achieve more informal effects. Less focused and less compositionally compelling than the National Charity League, each satisfied the functional prerequisites but gave less to the neighboring architectural landscape. Neutra & Alexander's two Alamitos Schools, Garden Grove, Orange County (1957), were updated versions of Neutra's public schools of the thirties and of the large Kester Avenue School (1951), Van Nuys, California, commissioned before the formation of the Neutra & Alexander partnership. Though well above the quality of the average public school, they were less distinguished than the firm's large commission for Palos Verdes High School, completed in the early 1960s. Once again, responding creatively to Palos

Verdes code specifications for pitched, red-tile roofs, Neutra & Alexander produced 138,000 square feet of detached, parallel classroom wings connected by covered walkways for a student population of 2,000. Facing the ocean and surrounded by the hills of the spectacular Palos Verdes peninsula, the logically planned and beautifully detailed school had crisp white walls and red-tile roofs, and gave delight not only to its immediate users, but to the larger community as well.[29]

One of the ongoing commissions Alexander brought to the partnership was for the developing campus of Orange Coast College, south of Los Angeles. In the early fifties Neutra contributed design ideas for a business education building, a science building, and athletic facility, and a large theater with a stage opening to an outdoor amphitheater. Neutra, Alexander remembered, was particularly bewildered by the Orange Coast board members' concern with the details of the football stadium, an aspect of American culture for which Neutra lacked sufficient appreciation, and he "could hardly believe his ears at a Board meeting one night when the members started their cross-examinations. Where was the space for the pom-pom girls and the cheer leaders? Where was the space for the ambulance? It must be practically on the field—the ambulance attendant wants to see the game too! After the meeting, Neutra described the [en-

235

276. *Neutra and Alexander*, UCLA
Elementary School, Los Angeles, 1957

visioned] game which he had never seen, as a pagan ceremony full of primitive tribal rites and ritual." As Alexander was aware, the Orange Coast campus, planned in incremental stages over a period of years, lacked a central unifying orientation that would have strengthened the aggregate of competent, though unspectacular, architecture. Similarly respectable but unremarkable examples of late modern academic architecture were produced by Neutra & Alexander on other campuses: the large fine arts buildings at California State College, Northridge (1959), and the University of Nevada, Reno (1961), and the library complexes for Simpson College, Indianola, Iowa (1956–61), and Adelphi University, Garden City, New York, (1955–63).[30]

The best college building by Neutra & Alexander was done for the small, venerable St. John's College, founded in Annapolis, Maryland in the late seventeenth century. The curriculum focused on Socratic discussions of the great books of history. All involved were concerned that the new buildings relate to the predominately red-brick eighteenth- and nineteenth-century architecture of the college and the town. Neutra had earlier lectured at St. John's and had aroused enough enthusiasm there to make him seem to be the logical modernist contender. His and Alexander's designs for a connected cluster of structures housing the music department, a related auditorium, and the science department with laboratories and planetarium formed two-and-a-half sides of an open court that comfortably complemented the older neighboring structures. Variations in scale of the cluster's various elements, framed and accented by the familiar steel spider-legs, gave to the structures a "constructivist" complexity missing from the relatively blander composition of the firm's other college buildings.[31]

Though poor upkeep would subsequently compromise their effectiveness, the St. John's buildings aroused generally favorable comment at the time of completion (1958). Architect Alexander Cochran, whose Baltimore firm performed supervisory services, found it "one of the finest pieces of architecture that this, our region, has been fortunate enough to possess." St. John's discerning philanthropic benefactor, Paul Mellon, who helped finance the project, told Neutra that the buildings exemplified "the contributions which your great skills and

277. *Neutra and Alexander*, UCLA
Elementary School, 1957

278. *Neutra and Alexander*, Palos Verdes
High School, Palos Verdes, California, 1961

279. *Neutra and Alexander*, St. John's College, Annapolis, Maryland, 1958

280. *Neutra and Alexander*, chapel, Miramar Naval Station, La Jolla, California, 1957

taste have made to the American scene. From the outset I was particularly happy with your choice as the architect of Mellon Hall, and Frances Scott Key Hall, and the beautiful end result of your labors is a satisfaction to us all." Similar, more modest, programmatic requirements for a small auditorium, planetarium, and galleries led to competent but less satisfying structures for the Dayton, Ohio, Museum of Natural History (1956–58). Much of the spirit of the Annapolis buildings, however, was replicated in the dramatically sited museum and visitor's center for the Painted Desert and Petrified Forest of Arizona (1957–61).[32]

Of all Neutra & Alexander's public commissions, the least successful genre was church architecture. Of their ambitious plans for the Riviera Methodist Church, Redondo Beach, California (1958), only the Sunday school wing was completed as designed; the sanctuary was reconceptualized, at the congregation's request, by another local firm in a more traditional style of stripped neoclassicism. However, Neutra's designs for the chapel at the Miramar Naval Base, La Jolla, California (1957), and the Claremont Methodist Church, Claremont, California (1959), were completed essentially as planned. While Claremont, especially, testified to the adventurous spirit of a minister and congregation determined to "go modern," the resulting church was a rather bland hodge-podge of badly related constituent elements. Striving, no doubt, for the free-form, expressionist drama of Le Corbusier's Ronschamps Chapel (1955), Neutra and Alexander fell far short of such richness, while missing as well the crisp, cool, minimalist serenity of the International Style. The less pretentious box of the Miramar Chapel (1957) was equally unconvincing as a spiritual or an esthetic experience. As an intensely spiritual though religiously unorthodox and unaffiliated "seeker," Neutra was intrigued by the challenge of modern religious architecture. "What should a church look like?" he once asked a St. Louis audience. "Most of them," he answered, "look as if they had been designed by atheists." Though Neutra was interested in and well informed about both biblical scholarship and Christian history and theology, his Christian churches contained less "spiritual" and architectural energy and sophistication than his unbuilt Jewish designs of the middle 1920s. He was,

281. *Neutra and Alexander,* chapel
Miramar Naval Station, 1957

282. *Neutra and Alexander*, Hacienda
Motor Hotel, San Pedro, California, 1954

283. *Neutra and Alexander*, Hacienda
Motor Hotel, 1954

240

unfortunately, never commissioned to design temples or synagogues in his post-Chicago years.[33]

Neutra and Alexander's best commercial buildings were the Hacienda Motor Hotel, near the harbor in San Pedro (1954), and the offices and community center for the Amalgamated Clothing Workers of America, in downtown Los Angeles (1956). Both won *Progressive Architecture* Design Award Citations. Conceived as a resort spa, the San Pedro hotel consisted of detached rows of rooms gently descending the sloping site. Each looked over the roof of the other to the Los Angeles harbor and ocean beyond. The central entrance to the office and restaurant building bore a free-form "boomerang" canopy slab that would come to be a trademark of motel and restaurant architecture of the fifties.[34]

The sprawling, one-story office building, community center, and auditorium for the Amalgamated Clothing Workers bore certain resemblances to the handsome office building for the Northwestern Mutual Fire Association, commissioned before

Alexander's arrival and completed in 1950 on Westmoreland Avenue near Wilshire Boulevard. The front facades of both buildings used the then-novel aluminum louvers for light control and esthetic effect. Though less finely detailed than the Northwestern Mutual, the Amalgamated Building served its clients' needs admirably, while offering esthetic bonuses in the subtle proportions of its intersecting wall planes and a stunning abstract wall mural in the lobby by the Brazilian artist Roberto Burle Marx. In contrast to the Northwestern Mutual, whose high-level maintenance kept it crisp and alive as a fifties period piece, poor upkeep would affect the Amalgamated Building as intensely as it would most modernist structures, an unfortunate attribute of the genre that frequently seemed a less noticeable liability in "traditional" buildings. Moreover, the Burle Marx mural in the Amalgamated lobby was inexplicably painted over in the 1970s. Poor maintenance and, more damagingly, an unsympathetic addition by subsequent owners also compromised the subtle delicacy of the small office

241

285. *Neutra*, Northwestern Mutual
Building, 1950

286. *Neutra and Alexander*, Amalgamated
Clothing Workers of America Building,
Los Angeles, 1956

287. *Neutra and Alexander*, Amalgamated Clothing Workers of America Building, 1956, Roberto Burle Marx completing his mural

288. *Neutra*, Northwestern Mutual Building, 1950

building for the Ferro Chemical Corporation, near Cleveland (1957), commissioned by Stanley Elliott the owner of a nearby Neutra house.[35]

Neutra & Alexander's largest government commissions were housing developments of the mid to late 1950s for the Mountain Home Air Force Base, Boise, Idaho, and the Lemoore Naval Air Base, near Fresno, California. Of the two, the latter was more architecturally distinguished. Varying in size and esthetic complexity as they traversed the ranks of officers and enlistees, the houses at Lemoore featured familiar Neutra trademarks that visibly connected it with his private residences and his Avion and Channel Heights designs of the forties. An even more satisfying updating of old ideas was the realization, at last, of the Ring Plan School, first designed in the late twenties. Constructed of stucco, as opposed to the originally designated metal, the Lemoore school was otherwise a complete reification, and was appropriately named the Richard J. Neutra School. Its most remarkable aspect was that now, three decades after it was origi-

nally conceived, the once radical design seemed so thoroughly mainstream.[36]

In the 1950s Neutra and Alexander, like most architects of that or any time, sought commissions they did not win, and won commissions which were never realized. Of the former, the most significant were the Sydney, Australia, Opera House and the Air Force Academy, Boulder, Colorado, later won respectively by Jorn Utzon and Skidmore, Owings and Merrill. Commissions unexecuted—for financial or political reasons—included a vast civic center for Johannesburg, South Africa; a large city theater for Cologne, West Germany; an Air Force housing project for Spain; and the central redevelopment of Caracas, Venezuela.

The three most noted buildings designed by Neutra & Alexander, all completed in the late fifties and early sixties, after the end of the partnership were the Lincoln Memorial Museum and Visitors' Center, Gettysburg, the United States Embassy in Karachi, West Pakistan; and the Hall of Records for the County of Los Angeles. Located near the

289. *Neutra and Alexander*, Richard J. Neutra School, Lemoore Naval Air Base, Lemoore, California, 1961

edge of the famous Civil War battlefield and the spot where Lincoln delivered his address, the Gettysburg Visitors' Center, relabeled by Neutra the Lincoln Memorial Museum, was designed to house a 10,000-square-foot nineteenth-century cycloramic painting of the Battle of Gettysburg by Paul Philippoteaux, as well as other battle-related artifacts. The cylindrical painting demanded a round drum enclosure, attached to which was a long rectangular wing for park administration offices, a gift shop, and other visitors' facilities, topped by an observation deck for viewing the battlefield. Built of concrete and rough Pennsylvania fieldstone, the structure was supervised by Thaddeus Longstreth, Neutra's associate of the forties, who had set up a practice in neighboring New Jersey. Resolutely composed in Neutra's late modernist idiom, the building would become particularly vulnerable to the postmodern critique of the 1960s and '70s in its total lack of deference to its nineteenth-century *raison d'être*. Built to house a nineteenth-century painting, on the spot where Lincoln had uttered some of that century's most famous words, and overlooking a

nineteenth-century cemetery of solemn, Victorian, neoclassical votive monuments, the building itself contained no historical references. In the modernist canon of Neutra's generation, neoclassical fragments or other historic allusions were—at Gettysburg, as everywhere else—simply out of the question. But no building anywhere could have used them more convincingly.[37]

Such was not the case with the new American Embassy in Karachi, West Pakistan, where monumental modernism seemed the order of the day. Commissioned as one of a series of new embassies by distinguished American architects, the Karachi building was to take its place in the parade of monuments that would ultimately include Edward Stone's building for New Delhi, John Warneke's for Bangkok, Walter Gropius's for Athens, and Eero Saarinen's for London. Alexander recalled that Neutra's response was that "those other designs were just pretty buildings, whereas ours was 'stripped for action.' . . ." Alexander admitted that "the site was small and constricted on a city street in an ugly neighborhood." But he was equally cer-

244

tain that the solution "did little to overcome it."
Alexander learned while visiting Karachi of the
ready availability of cylindrical molds for casting
concrete vault forms, and was determined to utilize
such forms in an effort to counter what he believed
to be Neutra's overly stark design of the main
administration wing. The result was a meaningless
series of equally bland "vaults" used to decorate the
façade of the rear warehouse storage wing. Though
it was no better or worse than most of its sister
embassies of the fifties, the lack of resolution in the
Karachi building illustrated sadly the unresolved
tensions of fifties modernism in general and of the
Neutra & Alexander partnership in particular.[38]

Similar problems surfaced in the Los Angeles
Hall of Records, given to a team of local architectural firms who delegated design primacy to
Neutra and Alexander. It was planned for the anach-
ronistic storage of records in bulk, at the absolute
insistence of county officials, but as Neutra & Alexander had predicted, the county shortly turned to
an almost total reliance on microfilm, rendering
the new building's stack areas functionally obsolete.

Whatever the interior programmatic problems, however, the design of the façade had significant potential as a highly visible landmark of downtown Los
Angeles. Later Alexander claimed that he had
initially deferred to Neutra to produce the design,
but that despite the time pressure nothing appeared
but a few dreamy sketches of "abstract elevations."
"Finally, in desperation," Alexander averred, "I
spent a weekend analyzing the site, the depart-
mental space requirements, the staff and visitor
loads, paper processing, the work flow, etc., and
produced schematic sketches substantially identical
to the final design and the completed building."
Neutra, of course, made similar claims to authorship, particularly in regard to the base-to-cornice
light-controlling, energy-conserving louvers. Yet
credit for the design of the Los Angeles Hall of
Records was a dubious distinction for either of
the partners, since the result was one of rather
bland mediocrity. Alexander's penchant for warm-
ing Neutra's stark modernity with "colorful, organic," artwork led to cacophony on the building's
north façade and to mixtures of too many compet-

290. *Neutra and Alexander*, Lincoln
Museum and Visitors Center, Gettysburg,
Pennsylvania, 1961

245

291. *Neutra and Alexander*, United States Embassy, Karachi, West Pakistan, 1959

ing and incompatible materials elsewhere. Neutra left no record of his private opinion of the result or of whether, if working alone, he could somehow have achieved more.[39]

The personal and professional tensions between Neutra and Alexander mounted steadily over the years. Even in the relatively benign early days there were basic disagreements. On the first flight to Guam, Alexander remembered, Neutra "started to discuss the roles that he and I would play in approaching the Governor and his 'court.' I told him I was opposed to the whole concept, that he should be himself and I myself and that was enough. He persisted in outlining our 'roles.' I told him I hated the idea that so intrigued him, that it seemed false and dishonest in principle and that I especially disliked the role he described for me—that of a businessman versus his artist image. . . . In spite of my objections, he was to reintroduce the subject many times. From my standpoint it was one of his fundamental faults. . . ." Indeed, Alexander would keep insisting in his pragmatic, American way that Neutra "be himself," failing to realize how much of that self *was* truly a dramatic "actor," whose complex images of life and reality had been formed and nurtured in another time and place.[40]

Though originally Alexander appreciated certain of Neutra's qualities and genuinely attempted to accommodate the older man, his growing impatience soon outran his sympathy. Ultimately Alexander perceived Neutra as "a veritable tyrant in his own home office," where he had several secretaries, "including his long-suffering wife, Dione, working around the clock on worldwide correspondence, publications, and an always current book, calculated to make him immortal. Although I seldom visited [Silverlake], I could count on hearing his demands shouted intemperately on the intercom. Yet, he completely transformed his manner when he visited our joint office every afternoon, putting on the aloof Great Man act . . . covering insecurity with obscure, over-assured declarations or with the silence of a wise owl, blinking and nodding his head."[41]

Neutra would insist that his daily critiques of the work of the Glendale office greatly improved its quality. He also believed that Alexander failed to appreciate how important the "worldwide correspondence, publications, and . . . always current book" were for promoting the work of the firm. Neutra believed, perhaps correctly, that Alexander resented his greater fame and the extent to which

VIEW FROM SE-
L·A·CY· HALL OF RECORDS

many were drawn to Neutra the dramatic evangelist, a role with which Alexander—like Schindler—could never identify. Yet the fact that journalists and critics tended to *want* to give Neutra more credit than his partner or associates should have told Alexander something about their relative drawing power. In any case, Alexander grew increasingly resentful of what he saw as Neutra's ploys to steal the spotlight. John Entenza, he recalled, had once "told me that Neutra always sought a position

on the extreme right of a group having its picture taken so that the caption would read, 'from left to right, Richard Neutra,' etc. John had experienced some rude and forceful pushing by Neutra on occasion to carry out this plan. I soon observed the truth in the charge and found the means of supplanting him at the extreme right." Indeed, as such frustrations mounted, Alexander grew increasingly bitter and began to consider dissolving the relationship. "Even though Neutra was fifteen years my

292. *Neutra and Alexander*, County Hall of Records, Los Angeles, 1962

247

293. *Neutra and Alexander*, County Hall of Records, 1962

senior, we had entered our joint work as equals, at least in my eyes, and in equal sharing of income," Alexander recalled. "I introduced him to a class of work which he had not been able to get or carry out on his own, in spite of his claims to projects which turned out to have been unbuilt dreams. Most of the time "he was more a burden than a help. Some of our work did come through his blown-up 'fame,' but I always had to seek work that would pay more than its share to overcome the inefficiency of work with him to keep us solvent. He did not come close to carrying half the load in our joint practice. . . ." Alexander was also under-

standably upset over the way the Silverlake office would periodically engage in nonresidential work, in violation of their agreement.[42]

The immediate impetus for the break came in 1958, when Alexander received an invitation in the mail to the opening of a "Neutra exhibition" at the UCLA art galleries. He found it strange that Neutra had not mentioned the show in their almost daily meetings, but assumed that it covered Neutra's pre-1950 work. He was startled when he entered the gallery to find Neutra & Alexander projects featured as well. Though on the first page of the exhibit catalogue Neutra acknowledged his "many associates of past years, and in particular, my friend and partner, Robert Alexander," and though the catalogue featured only three Neutra & Alexander buildings, two of which were properly labeled, Alexander took umbrage at what he considered to be an act of personal and professional bad faith. Alexander told Neutra that "it was clear that [Neutra] would never learn to be a partner," and that he had "resolved never to sign another contract with him." They would work together to complete projects already under way, but each would seek new commissions under his own name. Though they had been partners in name and in fact, Neutra and Alexander had never been able to agree on the details of a legal partnership agreement. Hence the separation was less complicated legally than it might have been otherwise. Though by the late 1950s each partner had reservations about the other, the break seemed to come as a surprise to Neutra, and consequently he had greater misgivings and regrets. He also had more to lose from the strains and complications of severing the relationship. Nearing seventy years of age, he had less time to rebuild his practice than Alexander. He also realized that he had grown to depend on his younger partner and would miss his support, particularly on the larger projects that required complicated dealings with clients and contractors. Neutra could never believe that Alexander did not reciprocate this feeling of interdependency and felt, perhaps justly, that Alexander underrated his special kinds of contributions.[43]

During this period Neutra was completing his autobiography, *Life and Shape*, and when he became convinced that Alexander's decision was irrevocable he remarked to Dione that he would have to "rewrite the last chapter." His ultimate bitterness at what he regarded as his partner's betrayal caused him totally to omit Alexander's name from the book. Alexander operated from the Glendale building until 1960, when he moved to a downtown office. Neutra was particularly shocked when Dion went with him. In the 1960s, following the break, Alexander's practice flourished as he acquired and completed such commissions as Bunker Hill Towers in central Los Angeles and the campus of the new University of California, Irvine. Neutra, meanwhile, after nursing the wounds occasioned by the break, continued his practice from the Silverlake office, where, despite its own share of pain and vicissitude, he had through the years found sustaining satisfaction.[44]

294. *Neutra*, Logar House, Los Angeles,
1951

Survival

Throughout the 1950s Neutra focused much of his attention and energy in the Silverlake office on projects unconnected with the Alexander partnership. Until 1958–60, when the partnership ended, that office concentrated on residences and managed to achieve new breakthroughs in that genre. The Silverlake home-studio was also the place where Neutra conducted his vast correspondence, entertained friends and clients, and did most of his thinking and writing. This was partly an accommodation to his psychological estrangement from the Glendale Boulevard office, where Alexander held forth, and to the physical constraints of a serious heart condition. Following his first coronary in 1949, and particularly after the second one in 1953, Neutra reluctantly deferred to his doctor's warning that bed rest and a slower work pace were essential to his survival. He thereafter conducted much of his business in bed—from composing and checking drawings to receiving his staff and clients.

"I can do more than any coronary-inflicted person you may know," he wrote his sister-in-law Verena, "lying on my bed, using two public phones at the bedside and three intercommunication stations—one even over a distance of five hundred meters crossing public streets—plus three different call bells. . . . Drafting boards and easels fold down over my bed, electric lights and radiogramophone are easily operated in a dashboard over my head; a bedside table of handy design, rolling on casters, permits the use of a . . . tape recorder and contains drawer compartments for every grade of pencil, crayon, fountain pen, and desk supply. An electric clock gives me the time as it runs out. I use every minute from morning to late night. I have a view through the tree foliage over Silverlake; an elevator brings me and my drawings right from my room onto the ground floor where . . . special assistants at typewriter and drafting board carry on the work of an executive office." Fascinated as always with Machine Age gadgetry, Neutra turned even his sickbed into a technological adventure.[1]

In 1953, on the occasion of his second heart attack, a memorable coincidence helped to alleviate Neutra's physical and emotional pain. After several days in an intensive care unit he was moved to another room for continued recuperation, and when he insisted that he did not need or want to be in a private room, he was randomly assigned to a large double room. The other occupant was Rudolph Schindler, who was recovering from surgery for cancer. Unaware at the time that his illness was terminal, Schindler was as stunned as Neutra was at the fateful reunion. They had hardly met or spoken for over twenty years, but they warmed to the tragicomic possibilities of the situation and slowly reestablished their long-broken friendship. In talking with Schindler about the reunion and the earlier break, his friend Esther McCoy sensed a still-lingering bitterness, but members of both families who visited the room daily recalled a happier mood of spirited conversation—mostly of Vienna and of times and places past.[2]

In the Silverlake office throughout the fifties and sixties Neutra continued his atelier system of collaborators, assistants, and apprentices. The latter were usually students who worked part-time or for part of a year, in most cases without pay. The three collaborators who stayed the longest and made the greatest contributions were Benno Fischer, Sergei Koschin, and John Blanton. Fischer, a Polish Jew,

251

had been interned during the war in the Flossen-burg concentration camp and, after liberation, had immigrated to New York, where he had worked briefly for the General Panel Corporation of Walter Gropius and Konrad Wachsman. As an architecture student in Warsaw during the 1930s, Fischer had admired Neutra's work, and in 1947, at the age of thirty-two, had moved to Los Angeles and happily joined his office.[3]

Koschin, a White Russian aristocrat only six years younger than Neutra, had come of age during the Russian Revolution and had received his archi-tectural training in the 1920s at the famed Vutemas. There he had known Tatlin, Malevich, El Lizitssky, and the brothers Vesnin. In 1927 he had spent two months at the German Bauhaus, where he had par-ticularly admired Gropius, Mies, and Kandinsky. He had then worked for a year in Italy, during which time he met Le Corbusier. In the late 1920s and early 1930s he served as Le Corbusier's host and associate on the design and building of the Moscow Centrosoyos. Captured and interned by the Germans in World War II, he had worked after liberation for the American occupying forces. Like Fischer, he had followed and admired Neutra's work in the thirties, and in 1949 had migrated to Los Angeles specifically to attempt to get work in his office.[4]

The much younger John Blanton joined the staff in 1950, shortly after graduating from the Rice School of Architecture in Houston. Particularly impressed with Neutra's work of the forties, Blanton came to Silverlake as an unabashed devotee and remained through the years one of Neutra's most appreciative and empathetic followers. Compared to his own modest Texas upbringing, the Silverlake ambience and Neutra mystique seemed to Blanton unbelievably sophisticated. As a place to begin a career in architecture, it was, he admitted, all quite "euphoric."[5]

Other associates from the forties through the sixties whose stays were shorter but whose contribu-tions were significant included Edward Farrell, Paul Hoag, Grant King, Augusto Lodi, Perry Neuschatz, Dion Neutra, Donald Polsky, Frederick Reichl, Richard Rennacher, Robert Simpson, Toby and Gaselis Schmidbauer, Gunnar Serneblad, Maxwell Starkman, Volker Traub, Hans von Escher, Herbert

Weisskampf, and Egon Winkens. Like Fischer, Koschin, and Blanton, these various associates served as project "job captains," taking the original concept and layout—as devised or approved by Neutra—through working drawings and construc-tion supervision. Frequently several people collab-orated on a project. Other key staff members in the Silverlake operation were Neutra's executive secretaries. His sister-in-law Regula Thorston served from 1947 to 1956; her successor, Dorothy Serul-nic, continued until 1967. Both combined efficiency with great personal zest and dedication to the de-manding Neutra mission.

Neutra keenly appreciated the contributions of his staff, believing that "at the present time, 'lone wolf' careers are much less possible than when I myself started on a foreign continent which would have no part of 'modern architecture.' Such a career now is less possible, less necessary, less desirable." Yet Neutra never found anyone with quite the perfectionist devotion to detail that he and others recognized in himself. "Perfectionism is really the reason for his success," Dione wrote in her diary in June 1950. "The unending toil and patience he expends on each detail have brought him his success. This is also the reason that nobody can pinch hit for him because no one has the pa-tience and the fine feeling [*Fingerspitzengefühl*] . . . out of which a composition is arrived at."[6]

The contractor Neutra favored for building his later houses was Fordyce "Red" Marsh, a self-taught craftsman who in the fifties worked on several dozen Neutra jobs. Marsh saw most people as being either pro or con on Neutra, with rela-tively few taking an in-between position. Both personally and professionally he counted himself among the stauncher admirers. Marsh found it significant that as buildings got underway, Neutra frequently asked his clients for a family photo-graph to mount on the site to remind the workmen that they were building for real and particular people. Though Marsh's high bids frequently led clients to other contractors, Neutra enjoyed point-ing to Marsh's work as a model.[7]

Marsh also participated in a memorable en-counter with Ayn Rand, who in *The Fountainhead* had created Howard Roark, a mid-century symbol of the architect as superman. It happened, Regula

Thorston recalled, one hot summer day in 1952 when she, Marsh, and Neutra were inspecting a site in the San Fernando Valley and Marsh expressed a desire to visit the nearby von Sternberg house, which he had never seen. Neutra was certain that Ayn Rand, the current owner, would be happy to receive them and forthwith proceeded to drop in unannounced. As an admirer of Neutra and a proud Neutra house owner, Rand received him cordially, Regula remembered—until she fixed upon the tall, handsome, blue-eyed, red-headed Marsh. Then moving past Neutra, who was unaccustomed to such brush-offs, she put her hands on Marsh's broad shoulders and solemnly told him that he *was* Howard Roark, that he epitomized the image upon which she had based her book. Poor Marsh, Regula noted, was totally bewildered, never having heard of either Rand or Roark. Rand's mesmerized fascination with her reified superman was broken only when she realized that it was time for a radio speech of another of her heroes, Senator Robert Taft of Ohio, currently seeking the Republican presidential nomination. Neutra, offended by the double upstaging, decided that as a loyal Democrat he did not want to listen to Taft, and left with his entourage before "Roark" got to tour the house.[8]

Neutra's residential designs of the fifties and sixties continued the trend, begun in the forties, of breaking with the cool, hard, crisp machine images of his earlier work. Sensitive to the criticism that his and others' modernist buildings were too "cold" and "tense," he took steps in the post-war period to make them project a softer, warmer, more relaxed atmosphere. He decided by the late forties that he had for the most part mastered the means of producing architecture. Now he must focus more explicitly on the ends—the subtle, elusive effects of building for the senses. The synthetic aluminum, concrete, and stucco packaging of the thirties gave way more frequently to natural stone and wood, now used in tandem with the harder industrial materials. An increased use of subtly placed mirrors, outdoor water roofs and shallow lily pools stressed the power of reflected images. The spiderleg outrigging projection of the roof beams, developed in the late forties, became one of the most distinctive trademarks of Neutra's later work—suggesting the extension of the building to infinity while simul-taneously anchoring it to the earth. A nonstructural, modernist equivalent of the Gothic flying buttress, the wood or metal spiderleg now became Neutra's most ubiquitous "ornament."

Yet there were negative as well as positive accoutrements of the more casual and informal style. Always receptive to new, off-the-shelf materials, Neutra, like most architects of the 1950s, fell prey to the lure of glass-louvered windows. Heralded as safer, more flexible, and less expensive than the handsome and dramatic steel casements, glass louvers had a cheap and insubstantial air that was totally inconsistent with the laconically elegant mien of most of Neutra's houses. Easy to break and penetrate, they also increased a building's vulnerability to burglary. Along with the increase of glass louvers, moreover, was the greater use of larger spans of plate glass, with the consequent decrease in metal or wood mullions and spandrels. As a result, Neutra abandoned much of the lively geometry of the fenestration patterns so convincingly carried out in such earlier buildings as the Lovell house (1929) and the Anna Sten house (1934).

Another problem of the later houses, both functionally and esthetically, was the frequent placement of garages to the front rather than to the less conspicuous side or rear, as had been the case in most buildings of the thirties. Here as always, Neutra blithely assumed that his clients would be as neat and orderly as his architecture and would refrain from leaving the doors open and using the garages as cluttered storage areas. This was a problem for "naturally messy" clients, who often must have wanted a modernist building in the hope that somehow, by osmosis, it would "straighten out" their lives. Instead, such houses usually spotlighted messiness, with damage to the architect's intentions and to the owners' self-image. When a gaping garage functioned as the real entryway, the formal "main" entrance was usually ignored. Entering the house via cluttered garage and kitchen made residents and visitors miss the architect's intention to create a particular series of processional experiences. Connected with Neutra's long-time preference for multiuse spaces was the the elimination of discrete dining areas. All of these factors contributed to the decline of the drama, elegance, and cool sophistication of the earlier period. To UCLA linguist Edward Tuttle, Neutra's later houses seemed, in fact, to be "so aggressively informal" that to maintain civility a person living there would "feel constrained to sleep in a necktie." Ironically, Neutra must unconsciously have felt the same vibrations as several later clients recalled his eccentric habit of receiving them in his bedroom wearing ordinary pajamas and an incongruous necktie.

As his houses moved, moreover, from the cool, crisp industrial materials and the white-gray ambience of the thirties to softer, warmer, more textured woodsiness, complemented by a greater range of colors, the buildings gave up the earlier "neutrality" that had frequently deferred to an eclectic variety in furnishing and decorating. The spare use of antiques from all periods, for example, was more possible and successful in houses of the thirties than in the more deliberately programmed informality of the fifties, where Danish Modern or the Eames lounge chair frequently seemed the only alternative to the standard Neutra built-ins. This coincided significantly, not only for Neutra but for his modernist peers generally, with the change in the cultural identity of clients from the avant-garde pioneers of the twenties and thirties to the middle-class majority that made up the public of most mid-century modernists.

Whatever the differences between the gestalt of the fifties and that of the thirties, however, there were significant similarities and continuities as well. In both periods, for example, Neutra continued to link windows in long, repetitive bands and to prefer flat roofs as more "honest" and economical. Though he could build imaginatively with shed and gabled roofs, he argued for flat, shallow "water roofs" reflecting the contiguous elements of nature whenever codes and clients permitted. Neutra's deference to nature and his long-acknowledged skill in siting and landscaping continued, as before, to win him well-deserved praise. Though embodying less dramatic contrast than those of the twenties and thirties, Neutra's houses of the post-war period continued to exemplify "the machine in the garden." As such, they encouraged the tactile and olfactory senses that photographs could never capture. Indeed, dependent as they were on the scent, size, and arrangement of plantings and the wind-swept ripples of the pools and water roofs, many of the better effects of Neutra's architecture

were more fragile and elusive and poetically subjective than critics of his work have ever understood. It was, in fact, these subtle appeals to the senses that best exemplified the theories of *Survival Through Design,* for which Neutra coined the formidable label "bio-realism."

All of Neutra's architecture emphasized repetition and regularity, but it also contained, in the more inspired examples, a built-in readiness for unexpected delight. Generally, he insisted, he was not as interested in producing individual *tours de force*—like Schindler or Le Corbusier—as in developing an overall *oeuvre* of consistent and distinguished, if unspectacular, elements. Neutra's penchant for repetition suggested, at its best, a sturdy sort of drama and pervasive serenity, while producing, at its worst, an ordinary blandness devoid of surprise. The latter problem, however, occurred less often in the early period than in the later.

One salient characteristic that, early and late, pervaded Neutra's achitecture was its dependence for success on excellent workmanship and careful, painstaking maintenance. If, indeed, as Neutra claimed, his smooth, sleek surfaces were easier to clean than the "Victorian curlicues" of his youth, they were also less able to conceal the dirt they collected. Neutra seldom displayed a conscious interest in texture and patina, though his older, better-maintained buildings indeed developed such qualities, particularly in the juxtaposition of vines and plantings. It was, in any case, generally important for all Neutra buildings to be neat, freshly painted, and carefully maintained.

Another characteristic common to both periods was an inconsistent record of energy conservation. Generally concerned with proper orientation, not only to the contours of the particular site but to the rays of the sun, Neutra protected vulnerable exposures with cantilevered overhangs. Yet his love of glass rendered him insufficiently cognizant of the heat gain and heat loss occasioned by such expanses. He also failed to realize that a smaller window segment might better frame a landscape than would a whole wide expanse of undivided glass. Building in the pre-War period before the advent of air conditioning, Neutra was particularly sensitive to air circulation patterns. Both functionally and poetically he placed great reliance on the tactile and olfactory properties of "the breeze from the garden." Indeed, whatever the pros and cons and the obvious differences between the two periods, the most important element of all his best architecture was its nature-related quality of profound serenity.

Many of these qualities continued to point up the debts Neutra owed to Japanese esthetics and the continuing impact upon his development of the simple, timeless, abstract elegance of Japanese design. Whenever Neutra's work moved closest to perfection, it was the kind of perfection implicit in the haiku rather than in the classical English sonnet. In the 1920s, and particularly following his visit to Japan in 1930, he was most impressed by the white and gray palette of such classic structures as the main pavilion of Katsura Palace, Kyoto (late sixteenth century) and its modernist legacies in such works as Yamada's recently completed Electrical Testing Factory in Tokyo. In the 1950s and '60s, however, the changing character and rationale of his work turned him increasingly to the darker, more textured, and informal vernacular. How was it, he once asked his son Raymond, that with all its apparent similarity of elements, a city like Kyoto was never, never boring? By the imaginative manipulation of a few simple modules, he surmised, by ever deferring to the richness of nature, by caring for the landscape with love and attention and repairing it when necessary with skill and finesse, much of the subtlety and beauty of Kyoto could be achieved in a "modern" city designed by Neutra.[9]

Beyond the low-cost housing developments of Channel Heights of the early 1940s, the Lemoore Naval Air Force Base of the 1950s, and the Bewobau developments in Germany of the 1960s, the closest Neutra came to realizing such a townscape was an interrelated group of nine houses that he began in the late forties and completed in the early sixties. Acquiring a tract of land near his own VDL House, he sold lots only to contractually committed clients and reared a Neutra village that was indeed "never boring." Though the Reunion, Flavin, Ohara, and Akai houses on Argent Place were the most individually distinguished, the neighboring houses facing Silverlake Boulevard comprised a more coherent group.

Neutra's growing fame and his pattern-book vocabulary of deliberately replicable formulas led in the fifties and sixties to a vast quantity of work. Lacking in their individual elements the complex geometry of the earlier buildings, the best of Neutra's later houses became spatially more complex, with a cubistic building up of volumetric spaces and intersecting axes. The largely esthetic devices of sliding planes and overreaching parapets, and particularly the accents of the extended-beam, spiderleg outrigging, imparted a more "constructivist" ambience than had usually been apparent in his earlier, more planar buildings.

In the fifties and sixties, as in the earlier period, it was important for Neutra to become deeply involved with his clients. He had once told Dione that it was "necessary for him to fall in love with them, to weave a kind of legend around their lives which had little to do with reality, but made it possible for him to spend so many hours on their project. Occasionally the legend would endure, at other times it would break apart and then the disappointment would occur; however that was the only way he could work."[10]

There were among the commissioners of these later Neutra houses numerous exceptions to the middle-class orientation of most mid-century modernist clients. Had they, in fact, been building in the 1930s, when modern architecture was more avant-garde, some of them undoubtedly would have turned to Neutra then as well. James Logar, a businessman, and his wife Olive, for example, had "eccentric" notions for the times about education, diet, and architecture. They were fervent vegetarians and preferred to teach their children at home rather than expose them to the corrupting world of public education and the "junk food" they would encounter there. They also wanted a "nature-near" house in the mountains of what was then considered a remote area of the San Fernando Valley, appropriate as a home and a school for their three sons. They decided on Neutra after reading the *Time* cover story of 1949, and over the course of the next two years, as the house was being built, they became devoted followers. Built by Marsh, the house formed an irregular *L* or open triangle, with the large central living, study, and dining areas flanked to the southeast by kitchen and garages and to the northwest by the bedroom wing. All rooms opened to patios and to spectacular views of the mountains and valley.[11]

While their house was being designed and built in 1951, Neutra arranged for the Logars to visit the house he had just completed in Highland Park, Los Angeles, for Jay Hinds, an engineer, and his wife Katharine, a social worker. Olive Logar wrote Neutra that it was "like a robin's nest high up in a tree, overlooking the city. They are the happiest people and entirely satisfied with every detail." The Hindses had encountered Neutra when they lived in New Mexico through photographs of his work in the Museum of Modern Art publication *If You Want to Build a House*. When they later moved to Los Angeles, they contacted him and commissioned a small *L*-shaped two-bedroom dwelling. Constructed by Marsh, it was close to the street on the entrance side, while the master bedroom and the living, dining, and kitchen areas to the rear looked out over a sloping ravine. In addition to his usual "ornamental" trademarks, Neutra exemplified his talent for making small elements have a large effect by attaching a long, narrow storage room perpendicular to the west side at its southwest corner. When viewed below from the west, the simple storage bin took on the character of an asymetrically placed abstract sculpture, while losing none of its functional utility.[12]

For two musicians, Frederick and Mary Jane Auerbacher, and their children Neutra had the chance in 1952 to build a rustic lodge high in the San Bernardino Mountains, which were covered in the winter months by heavy amounts of snow. Convincing his clients of the fallacy of the argument that houses in snow areas demanded steeply pitched roofs, Neutra insisted that snow on flat roofs provided good insulation and avoided the problem of precipitous snow slides that could suddenly block entrances or "dump a load of slush on an unwary bystander." With its redwood board and batten, its elegant proportions, its simple, built-in furniture and interior details, the Auerbacher lodge was an almost perfect product of Neutra's design skills and Marsh's craftmanship. John Blanton remembered the ineluctable feeling in the office from the beginning that "this was going to be one of the good ones." Fred Auerbacher especially appreciated Neutra's "seeing to it that every little detail was 'just right.' . . ."[13]

One of Neutra's most admired houses of the fifties was built in Ojai, California, for James and Orline Moore, disciples of the Indian mystic Krishnamurti, who lived nearby. The main house (1952) crowned a beautiful knoll and looked down upon the roofs of the connected two-room guest house below. Conceived as an oasis in the middle of a forty-acre ranch in the high, arid Ojai Valley, the house was surrounded by moat-like lily pools, which also served as reservoirs for irrigating the gardens and humidifying the air. The sublime proportions and the relationship of nature and architecture particularly pleased Orline Moore, who found the house exhilarating not only on the typically sunny days but on the occasionally "misty, gloomy" ones as well, when she felt herself a part of "the mystery over the mountains." In 1954 the Moore house won the national American Institute of Architects' First Honor award.[14]

A tiny 1,000-square-foot house for an Occidental College art professor, Constance Perkins, became one of Neutra's acknowledged gems. "It's not with the wealthy that the future of contemporary architecture lies," Neutra once told an art conference that Perkins had hosted. "It is with the people in the middle. They are the onces who can afford to be uninhibited and imaginative and to whom living with beauty is more important than ostentation." That convinced Perkins that she might be able to afford a house by an architect she had long admired, and between 1953 and 1955 the two worked together on design details and color selection in the close, intense way that Neutra enjoyed. Raised over a carport at street level, the house's flat roof slab rested on the beams that extended beyond the enclosed volume to form the familiar spiderlegs. A fish pool, designed by one of Perkins's students, entered the living room beneath the mitred glass. An opaque glass screen perpendicular to the entrance wall tied the main house to the garage below and shielded the private porch off the living room from the front entrance stairs. A studio-bedroom and guest room lay in back of the kitchen and living-dining areas.[15]

The same reflecting pools and extended beam spiderlegs framed and ornamented the much larger house for the noted painter Robert Chuey and his wife, the poet Josephine Ain (1956). Josephine's first marriage had been to Gregory Ain, whom she had met following the breakup of his first marriage while she was living briefly with Galka Scheyer in the Neutra house on Blue Heights Drive. Josephine had known the Neutras and Schindlers in the 1930s, and it was her delight with the Scheyer house that made her choose Neutra when she and Chuey decided to build in the mid–1950s. Perched on the

298. *Neutra*, Hinds House, 1951

299. *Neutra*, Hinds House, 1951

300. *Neutra*, Auerbacher Lodge, Luring Pines, California, 1952

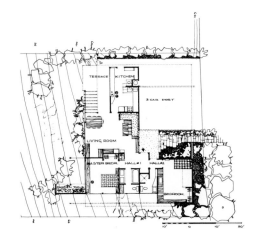

301. *Neutra*, Hinds House, Los Angeles, 1951

302. *Neutra*, Auerbacher Lodge, 1952

303. *Neutra*, Moore House, Ojai, California, 1952

304. *Neutra*, Moore House, 1952

259

305. *Neutra,* Moore House, 1952

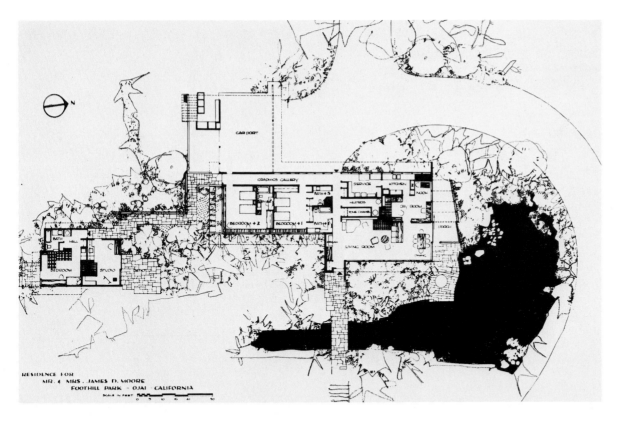

RESIDENCE FOR
MR. & MRS. JAMES D. MOORE
FOOTHILL PARK - OJAI - CALIFORNIA

ridge of the Santa Monica Mountains at the top of Sunset Plaza Drive, the Chuey site, which was not far from Scheyer's, had the same spectacular views of mountains, city, and ocean. A large living room with floor-to-ceiling glass opened west to terraces, southeast to gardens and reflecting pools, and northeast to the glazed studio filled with Chuey's vast canvases. Bedrooms and kitchen lay to the north. The house encouraged a lively social life of parties, poetry readings, and the showing of Chuey's paintings. As an early follower of the psychologist Timothy Leary, Josephine also participated in LSD experiments.[16] "This house has the quality of an absolute presence," she wrote Neutra in a typically intense letter. "You are an alchemist who has transmuted earth, house, and sky into a single enchantment. . . . This house seems to have a spiritual existence. . . . It remembers that being is a miracle. I can only hope that I can in some measure grow up to the wholeness and balance embodied here. . . . If I had the means I would build your homes everywhere for all people. We wish to thank you and everyone involved in the building of what to us is the immaterial materialized. One can be silent here."[17] In the 1950s and '60s Neutra built dozens of similarly outstanding houses in Southern

California, including, particularly, the Heryford house, Los Angeles (1951); the Nash house, Camarillo (1957); the Clark house, Pasadena (1957); the Oxley house, La Jolla (1958); the Singleton house, Los Angeles (1959); and the Ohara house, Los Angeles (1961).

In contrast to the intersecting planes and volumetric spaces of such relatively "constructivist" designs, Neutra also developed in the fifties and sixties a smaller and less successful genre, of what Neutra collaborator John Blanton labeled "post and beam boxcar" houses. These generally took the form of a long central space, usually built on a scenic hillside slope, with a balcony deck running the length of the house overlooking a pool or garden and the grand view beyond. Underneath the raised main floor lay basement spaces usually developed as garages or utility or recreational rooms. Included in this genre were the expensive Bel Air houses for the Staller and Brown families (1955), the Radoz house, San Pedro (1958), and such smaller structures as the Linn house (1961) on the ridge of Mulholland Drive. The best of this genre was the Slavin house, Santa Barbara (1956), where, at Blanton's suggestion, a "jog" was inserted in the line of the facade by pulling the deck forward from

307. *Neutra*, Perkins House, Pasadena,
California, 1955

308. *Neutra*, Perkins House, 1955

309. *Neutra*, Perkins House, 1955

310. *Neutra*, Chuey House, Los Angeles, 1956

311. *Neutra*, Chuey House, 1956

312. *Neutra*, Cheuey House, 1956

313. *Neutra*, Chuey House, 1956

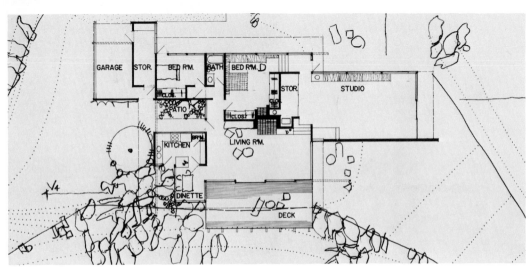

314. *Neutra*, Heryford House, Los Angeles, 1951

315. *Neutra*, Heryford House, 1951

316. *Neutra*, Singleton House, Los Angeles, 1959

317. *Neutra*, Singleton House, 1959

318. *Neutra*, Singleton House, 1959

same neighborhood signaled an even more interesting achievement: the Hafley-Moore "twin houses" of 1953.

Olan Hafley had first heard of Neutra in the 1930s from a high school civics teacher in Du Quoin, Illinois, who had enthusiastically presented Neutra as "the architect of the future." Twenty years later Hafley, now a General Motors executive in Southern California, and his wife Aida found it natural to turn to Neutra when they decided to build a house. When the owner of the adjacent lot expressed similar interests, Neutra was able, at roughly the same time, to design neighboring houses, which though differing in numerous ways, showed definite affinities. The larger, two-story Hafley house was more open to the street than its lower, more protected companion, though a fetchingly designed pergola connected the two structures over a common driveway entrance. An amusing legacy of the designing and building period was a favorite phrase of the Hafley's parakeet, who had learned the often-repeated solution to the varied vexations of building a house. "Ask Mr. Neutra!" the parakeet would squawk, long after the Hafleys had settled into their home. "Ask Mr. Neutra! Ask Mr. Neutra."[19]

Because he built the great majority of his houses in Southern California, the formulas he perfected there were naturally conditioned by its climate and geography and by his nearness to the actual building operations. He was proud of his houses in other parts of the world to which he transported the famous modernist Southern California ambience—with notably mixed success. Even when building in northern California he experienced certain problems with the less predictable climate there. Though the Nelson house in Orinda (1951) and the Schwind house in Hillsborough (1956) were thoroughly competent inland exercises of relaxed fifties modernism, the Connell house at Pebble Beach, near Carmel, California (1958), had serious problems of climate control. Arthur Connell recalled that "the original concept seemed so absolutely right that it was never altered in any important aspect, although Richard himself had not as yet seen the site." Yet "the house turned out to be not ideally suited for the environment, although it certainly capitalized on the outstanding view. The main problem . . . was that Cypress Point is exposed to northwest and southerly winds which

the southern half of the house and articulating the break appropriately with a spiderleg. This avoided the blander, "boxcar" effect of the Staller house, where a solid slab, inserted in the middle of the façade, formed a less convincing articulating device. The Slavin house was marred only by a tunnel-like first floor entrance hall and stairway that led to the main floor and by the oppressively cramped and virtually windowless kitchen, located claustrophobically in the middle of the house. Neutra had little interest in cooking, and unless clients had firmly held ideas of their own, good kitchens were not one of his strengths.[18]

Throughout the 1950s and '60s, code restrictions continued to coax from Neutra pitched roof houses of a generally high calibre, from the Coe house (1950) to the Oberholtzer house (1961) on the Palos Verdes peninsula. The Matlock house, Long Beach (1952), was a particularly strong example of Neutra's ability to adapt his style to the pitched roof format, though another project in the

exceed 30 knots with gusts to 50 and 60 on occasion, and these can persist for long periods. I feel certain that the air flow through the house could be as much as 1 or 2 knots, despite all windows and doors being closed, and the heat just never went off." In addition to the high fuel costs, "the house leaked somewhere in every rain storm . . . but then there were many beautiful calm days when the sea breezes moved gently through the house and the clear sun beat down."[20]

Connell, indeed, had pleasant memories not only of the house but of his engagingly eccentric architect as well. "In one of the early planning visits to Silverlake," he recalled, "my wife and I arrived to find him . . . propped in bed, sheets, blankets, and comforters in disarray, wearing pajamas, but also, incongruously, a necktie. Intermixed with this melange were his pastel crayons, many of which were broken, and the dust from them had invaded everything, including his hair and moustache. He made no reference to any of this and proceeded as though the meeting were in any of the many rooms at Silverlake he used for clients' conference."[21]

Most other clients in even colder climates, however, found that Neutra's houses, if properly built and insulated, fared well in all seasons. Frederick and Cecel Fischer, in Spokane, Washington, for example, built in 1951 and wrote in the winter of 1952 that "our blizzards, with snow whirling in zig-zag flurries on the patio, were sights to behold through our 36 feet of glass trimmed in 'silver,' especially in the evening when the apple wood blazed away in the fireplace. With shrubs, rocks and trees almost completely obliterated with a blanket of snow and 24" or more of snow on the roof, your house, Mr. Neutra, reacted as though it had nested all winter in the Mediterranean sunshine . . . we have the feeling of living outdoors the year around. . . . The sun warms the whole house so completely. . . ." Fischer and his whole family were deeply involved with music and the arts. When asked once where they had first heard of Neutra, Fischer replied that "it was like asking where we first heard of Bach." They had known and admired Neutra's work for some time, he added, but it was the *Time* cover story that gave them the impetus to contact him.[22]

Indeed, there were few clients after 1950, par-

319. *Neutra*, Slavin House, Santa Barbara, California, 1956

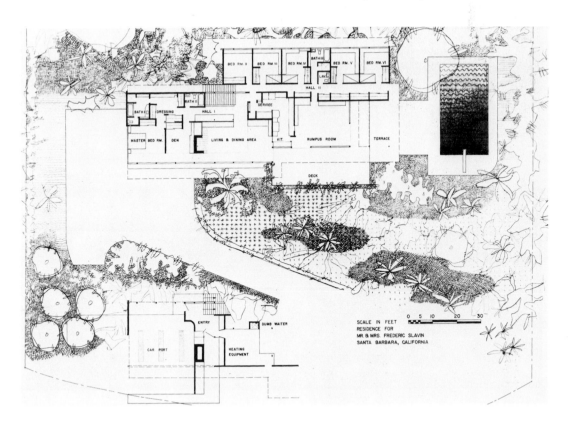

320. *Neutra*, Slavin House, 1956

321. *Neutra*, Hafley-Moore Houses, Long
Beach, California, 1953

322. *Neutra*, Nelson House, Orinda,
California, 1951

270

ticularly those in distant parts of the country, who were not influenced by the *Time* article. These more distant clients were usually affluent business or professional people, able to appreciate and afford fine things. Most considered other leading architects as well, including, in several cases, Frank Lloyd Wright, but decided that Neutra better fitted their needs. Several were convinced after hearing him lecture or after reading his books. Many shared the experience of Mildred Warner and her husband, the eminent University of Chicago anthropologist Lloyd Warner, who decided in the mid-1950s to give up their large old Georgian home near the university and build a smaller, modern house on the dunes of Lake Michigan, southeast of Chicago. For ideas, Mildred Warner pored through the architecture periodicals at the Chicago Art Institute and discovered that "every house I liked was a Neutra house." With only a moderate budget, they contacted Neutra, who conceived a design that intrigued and delighted them. Later they regretted their decision not to use the more expensive thermopane glass and thus effect better temperature control, but in general the house offered great comfort and "composure." Personally, they found Neutra both fascinating and difficult, but they were equally certain that he was "an under-recognized genius."[23]

When Nora O'Brien had a heart attack in 1946, she and her husband, a Shreveport, Louisiana, businessman, decided to give up their large, traditional two-story house and build a smaller modern one-story house. They were first drawn to Wright and even went to Wisconsin to visit him at Taliesin, but decided that his demanding ideas offered them too little flexibility. When the *Time* cover story presented Neutra both as a disciple of Wright and a designer of simpler, more relaxed buildings, they called him and commissioned him. For the warm, humid Louisiana climate, Neutra complemented the indoor living space with ample use of breeze-catching screened porches. Like most of Neutra's houses in smaller American cities, the O'Brien house (1950) occasioned considerable comment among the local cognoscenti. "They speak of it as the 'Neutra House,'" O'Brien wrote, "and seem delighted that a house designed by Mr. Neutra is being erected here in Shreveport." Another Southerner, physician Philip J. Livingston, also considered Wright but ultimately chose Neutra to design a handsome house (1956) in a lush hillside dogwood grove in Chattanooga, Tennessee.[24]

H. H. Everist, owner of a large heavy-construction firm in Sioux City, Iowa, had, like O'Brien and Livingston, the means and the taste to commission practically anyone he chose. "Building the first Neutra designed residence in this area," Everist wrote later, "we often think of the manner in which this commission was made." First, they had sent out two form letters. "The earliest was mailed to more than fifty architectural firms or individuals, all of whom had wide reputations and many published examples of their work. This initial letter elicited varying responses, of course, but after careful consideration, we winnowed twelve firms from the lot and mailed our second letter. These twelve represented the peak of architectural eminence. At least five were of international stature." Everist remembered that the most interesting and positive replies came from Wright, Neutra, and Mies van der Rohe. Though similar in both plan and detail to Neutra's other houses of the fifties, the Everist house (1951) was one of his most successful mid-continental designs. The clients enjoyed his periodic visits and appreciated his enthusiasm for other examples of Sioux City architecture, particularly the work of William Steele, a Prairie School follower of Sullivan and Wright, who had designed the local courthouse and Everist's childhood home as well.[25]

After the John Nicholas Brown house of the late 1930s, the second Neutra house on the American East Coast was for a New York businessman, Lorin Price, at Bayport, Long Island (1951). Built of beautiful fieldstone, with a flagstone covering for both terrace and interior floors, the house was trimmed in natural brown wood and metal and featured the usual Neutra ornamental trademarks. Facing south to the Atlantic Ocean, the Price house sat sternly on the Long Island landscape like a lonely, sturdy, low-lying rock. For Henry and Betty Corwin in Weston, Connecticut (1955), and Alan and Janet Glenn in Stamford, Connecticut (1960), Neutra built fetching wooden houses, deftly sited on wooded New England knolls. For his old Brownsville, Texas, client George Kraigher, now retired on a Connecticut farm, Neutra designed a simple wooden house, (1958) less dramatic and compelling than the first house for Kraigher but melding

323. *Neutra*, Nelson House, 1951

324. *Neutra*, Connell House, Carmel, California, 1958

271

325. *Neutra*, Fischer House, Spokane,
Washington, 1951

326. *Neutra*, Everist House, Sioux City,
Iowa, 1951

and wooden Miller house (1956) were mid-century modernist California houses transplanted to the east, but the concrete block Hasserick house (1958) and fieldstone Coveney house (1960) took more convincing note of the climate and materials of eastern Pennsylvania. While the Hasserick house was later damaged by an awkward enlargement, the Coveney house was allowed to grow gracefully with sympathetic additions designed by Longstreth. The large, rectangular Friedland house (1958) was less impressive in its overall gestalt than in various details of ornament and fenestration, which recalled Neutra's larger houses of earlier decades.

A large country house for the Pitcairn family, set deep in the woods at Bryn Athyn, Pennsylvania, again revealed Neutra's genius for siting and for inflecting the building to the natural landscape. Yet the house's outlying bedroom wings were insufficiently integrated with the main element of the front living areas. The mirrored image of the curving front stairway proved gimmicky and disorienting in so grand a setting. A familiar perpendicular Neutra slab wall divided the front facade into two incongruously different images. To the right of the slab and the main front entrance ran a grand and rather formal two-story expanse of windows. To the left, by contrast, off the living room area, lay a woodsy, informal deck supported by incongruously diagonal wooden braces and suggesting the ambience of a rustic ski lodge. Either unaware of this palpable dichotomy, or unwilling or unable to address or ameliorate it, Neutra and Longstreth used the slab to hide it, though with less than convincing or felicitous effect.

An even more disappointing misuse of a grand setting occurred in a 1964 house in Richmond, Virginia, that Neutra and Longstreth designed for Walter Rice, a high official of Reynolds Aluminum who later became the Nixon-appointed United States ambassador to Australia. The house was set high on an island in the James River rapids, but the familiar trademarks of Neutra's late modernist style were sadly compromised by an unnecessary extravagance of overly rich materials. Instead of the concrete or stucco so comfortably identified with modernist architecture, for example, the main facades were covered with thinly cut wedges of south Georgia marble. A vast mirrored wall "doubled" the main stairway as awkwardly as at the Pitcairn

admirably with the rural New England setting. Contesting Neutra's belief that snow on flat roofs provided insulation, and unable to believe that Neutra ever used pitched roofs, Kraigher made the unfortunate decision to engage a local builder to add a hipped roof, compromising the building's formerly crisp serenity.

With his old associate Thaddeus Longstreth, Neutra built six houses in the Philadelphia area. The charmingly modest stucco Cohen house (1955)

house and the Adelphi College Library. In smaller spaces and in quieter, subtler ways Neutra frequently used mirrors as effective space extenders, but here the effect was pretentious and disconcerting. In these occasional lapses from architectural excellence, however, in the waning years of the late modern movement, Neutra and Longstreth were hardly alone.

Neutra's late houses outside the United States ranged from merely competent to excellent. Of the first category, the DeSchulthess house, Havana, Cuba (1956), exemplified Neutra's problems in the too-large, too-rich category, while the Gonzales-Garrondona house, Caracas, Venezuela (1962), recalled, in its stepped hillside layering, happier memories of his larger thirties houses. In their slightly heavier, blockier proportions, the Kemper house, Wuppertal, Germany (1967), and the Delcourt house, Croix, France (1968), emphasized resoundingly Neutra's preferences for the horizontal. And like his Everist house in Iowa and its various contemporaries built across America, they bore a striking resemblance to the similarly blocky late houses of Gerrit Rietveld. Among Neutra's better German designs were the Pescher house, Wuppertal (1968), and the Rang house, Königstein (1961), near Frankfurt. Both were one-story structures with intersecting wings and varying levels sprawling laconically amid pools and rockwalled gardens.

Two excellent houses in the spectacular Swiss Alps—Casa Tuia, for the Grelling family, Ascona (1961), and the Bucerius house, Nevegna (1966) —employed flat roofs, glass walls, and the standard Neutra elements with a lightness and deftness that complemented their sitings. Client preferences and local code restrictions called for broken shed roofs on the sprightly Rentsch house, near Wenger and Bern (1964). Its resulting resemblance to the ski lodge vernacular lessened its late-Neutra modernist impact, but not its deference to its rugged surroundings.

Characteristically, and appropriately, some of the best late residential work of Neutra and his associates was the multiple-unit housing built in the early sixties for the Bewobau Corporation near Hamburg and Frankfurt am Main, Germany. With compact but spacious apartments, typically interacting with private garden courtyards, the Bewobau

327. *Neutra*, Everist House, 1951

propects were practical and felicitous in the crisp, simple Neutra manner of yore. He had been considered by developer William Levitt for the American equivalent—Levittown—and he and Longstreth had drawn beautiful proposals. The fear, however, that Levittowners would still not accept the flat roofs and other Neutra modernist trademarks as images of "home" led Levitt to turn instead to variations on the Cape Cod and other American styles.[26]

273

328. *Neutra*, Hasserick House, Philadelphia, 1958

329. *Neutra*, Pitcairn House, Bryn Athyn, Pennsylvania, 1962

330. *Neutra*, Hasserick House, 1958

331. *Neutra*, Kemper House, Wuppertal,
Germany, 1967

332. *Neutra*, Bucerius House, Navegna,
Switzerland, 1966

276

333. *Neutra*, Bewobau Housing, Walldorf, Germany, 1960

334. *Neutra*, Bucerius House, 1966

335. *Neutra*, Bewobau Housing, 1960

336. *Neutra*, Bewobau Housing, 1960

337. *Neutra*, unbuilt designs for Levittown, late 1950s

338. *Neutra*, unbuilt designs for Levittown, late 1950s

339. *Neutra*, Medical Clinic, San
Bernardino, California, 1953

340. *Neutra*, Medical Clinic, 1953

One of the several sources of friction between Neutra and Alexander had been the violation of the agreement that the Silverlake office would design only residences and would not engage in public and commercial work. In fact, throughout the 1950s Neutra acquired certain commercial commissions, independent of Alexander, and directed them to his Silverlake staff as a respite from their otherwise total absorption in house design. The best of these "bootleg" commissions included the San Bernardino Medical Clinic (1953) and the Mariners' Medical Center, Newport Beach, commissioned in the late 1950s and completed in the early sixties. Dr. Max Goodman, owner of a nearby Neutra residence, was instrumental in commissioning the San Bernardino clinic, whose simple geometry and linear fenestration recalled Neutra's earlier work of the thirties. The more complexly "decorated" Mariners' Medical Center, Newport Beach, alternated one- and two-story spaces with pools and small, exquisitely planted gardens. As Neutra intended, the doctors and dentists there reported that the beautiful and interesting surroundings helped distract patients' attention from their less pleasant medical problems. "It has increasingly . . . become clear to us," one wrote, "that this is by no means just a building to you, and [that] we, as well as you, are engaged in a problem of 'applied physiology.'" *L'Archittetura* editor Bruno Zevi, a longtime Neutra supporter, found particularly pleasing proof in the Newport Beach building of Neutra's continuing vitality. "By now," he wrote Dione, "the beautiful buildings by Richard are so many that one could not classify them anymore. But I must say this has a 'human' and 'humanistic' quality . . . which seems quite rare. It will be a pleasure and privilege to publish it in the magazine" and "to devote to it an article in my weekly column." Though technically in violation of his agreement with Alexander, Neutra's "bootleg" structures of the fifties and early sixties were among the best public buildings he built in those years.[27]

Zevi's tribute typified the countless and continuing encomiums Neutra received throughout the fifties and sixties from architects, editors, critics, and historians—as his achievement became more and more uneven. In the middle 1950s, the early modernist Henry van de Velde, addressed Neutra, then in his sixties, as his "admirable young comrade in arms . . . a real master pioneer, to whom the 20th century style owes its inception." In the early 1960s, after Neutra had passed seventy, Columbia historian James Marston Fitch continued this line of praise by recounting an informal conversation among fellow critics and architects in San Francisco. "Your name came up," Fitch wrote. "We all agreed that your contribution to world architecture was very great, that you had not gotten the credit it seemed to us you deserved, and that we should all write you a note telling you so."[28]

Such praise continued throughout the 1960s, despite the generally declining quality of Neutra's larger work, the complex problems of the organization of his practice, and his deteriorating physical and mental health. Despite such exceptions as the residentially scaled Mariners' Medical Building, a general sense of fatigue characterized Neutra's later, larger buildings—as indeed it did the work of so many of his modernist peers. Political and budgetary constraints could not alone account for the bland lifelessness of such late modernist monuments as the Roberson Arts Center, Binghamton, New York (1965); the University of Pennsylvania dormitories, Philadelphia (1969); the Laveta Medical Tower, Orange, California (1966); and the university laboratories for Mymensingh, East Pakistan (1963). As he had with numerous buildings in the Alexander years, Neutra reflected the anxious vulnerability of his modernist generation by attempting to "warm" such structures with superfluous and disingenuous gimmicks. The curvilinear "sunscreens" at LaVeta, for example, an idea of Koschin's that was approved by Neutra, were sad reverberations of the more lyrically convincing late "brutalist" conceptions of Koschin's first master, Le Corbusier.

The most celebrated large building of Neutra's last decade was the Community Drive-In Church, Garden Grove, California, designed for the dynamic evangelist Robert A. Schuller. Beginning his ministry in suburban Orange County in the early 1950s on less than a shoestring, Schuller, unable to afford a church, had held his first service in a rented drive-in movie theater, vacant on Sunday mornings. He preached from the concession stand, conveying his sermons via the standard sound boxes attached to each car. This appealed to casual, mobile Angelenos, always most comfortable inside their own cars, and particularly to the handicapped,

341. *Neutra*, Mariners Medical Building, Newport Beach, California, 1963

invalids, and others unable to attend regular services conveniently. Later, as his ministry prospered, Schuller built a small church building, but he continued to hold the popular outdoor services several miles away in the drive-in movie lot. In the early 1960s, when he commissioned Neutra to design a larger, grander building, he asked him to combine the drive-in element with a standard sanctuary for able-bodied, well-groomed, traditional churchgoers.[29]

Neutra did this by placing the pulpit at the northeast corner of the sanctuary, with large opening glass walls connecting it to the parking lot and to those seated there in the "pews from Detroit." With the exception of that functional element and of certain on-rushing streamlined motifs in the adjoining bell tower, however, the buildings made little reference to its automotive audience and to the design possibilities inherent in that condition. The result was a mixture of late modernist forms with the sadly familiar efforts to warm it all up with craggy blond fieldstone laid in vertical patterns. Neutra had once remarked to Lloyd and Mildred Warner that he tried to "imagine out" the verticals

281

342. *Neutra*, Mariners Medical Building, 1963

282

343. *Neutra*, La Veta Medical Building, Orange, California, 1966

344. *Neutra*, Mymensingh University, Bangladesh, 1963

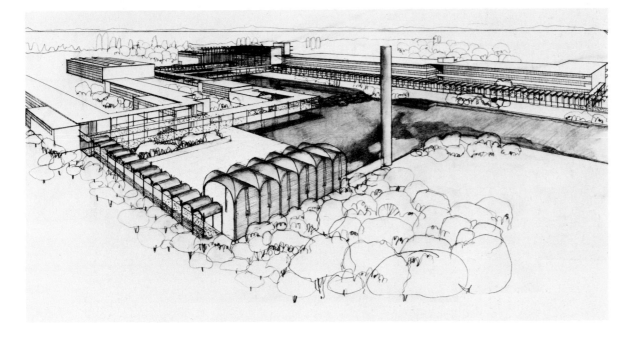

345. *Neutra*, Community Church, Garden Grove, California, 1962; Tower of Hope, 1966

346. *Neutra*, Community Church, 1962

347. *Neutra*, Community Church, 1962

348. *Neutra*, Community Church, 1962

349. *Neutra*, drawing of family attending services in car, Community Church, 1962

in his buildings. Here and in other of his designs of the sixties, standing the stones unnaturally on end reflected his and the modern movement's confused sense of direction. In the mid-1960s the Tower of Hope, largely designed by Koschin and Dion Neutra, rose above the sanctuary, more prominent than anything else in Orange County except the nearby "Matterhorn" at Disneyland. Neutra's fusion of commitments to humanist and scientific thinking impressed Schuller greatly. He was, the famous minister later asserted, one of the five most important human influences on his development. The others were John Calvin, Fulton Sheen, Norman Vincent Peale, and Billy Graham.[30]

As an extension of his social and architectural thought, particularly his ideas on the "biorealistic" intersection of urban planning, design esthetics, and physiological psychology, Neutra established the Richard J. Neutra Institute in the early 1960s, a nonprofit organization with branches in Los Angeles and Zurich. Strongly supported by such former clients as Betty Ford, Maurice Heller, and Sidney Troxell and by such community leaders as Judge Shirley Hufstedler, the Institute's purpose was "to ameliorate, by the fast advancing insights of all sciences, the human setting in which to live, to work, to rest." Its motto was the same as the title of Neutra's book, "Survival Through Design," and its first aim was "to broaden and deepen the channels of communication" among the planning, design and scientific professions via seminars, lecture series, exhibitions, publications, and broadcasts of symposia. It compiled bibliographies and served as "a clearing house for material published and unpublished . . . to render wider accessibility to the broadest public concerned with the human setting as the essential basis of welfare everywhere."[31]

The Institute's other stated aims were the "stimulation of mutually linked research in both the environmental sciences and the planning professions," the application of scientific advances to actual planning projects, and the education of ordinary "consumers" of the environment, "from kindergarten to college," as well as publishers of textbooks, organizations of teachers, and students' groups. "A better-informed public," Neutra believed, "will realize the decisive meaning of a biologically bearable environment. Not least, this must encompass sensory satisfaction and harmonious shape, which are necessary prerequisites for an unimpaired wholeness of living." As a raiser of public consciousness, the Institute's best moments were the lectures and seminars held at Silverlake. Like many other aspects of Richard Neutra's life, its ambitious reach exceeded its grasp, and by 1967 its active program had fallen far behind its ever-compelling aims. Like other aspects of the work and ideas of Neutra and his generation, the Institute suffered from too great an insistence on equating "survival" so exclusively with the modern movement. The eclipse of modernism in the 1960s and '70s was already suggesting the necessity of a more inclusive net.[32]

350. Richard and Dione Neutra, early
1960s

Eclipse

At its late modernist best and its mediocre worst, Neutra's work of the 1950s and '60s reflected the same anxieties, both consciously and unconsciously, that vexed Walter Gropius and other modernists of that generation. This was not the case with Le Corbusier's confident, continuing brilliance or with Ludwig Mies van der Rohe's unabashed elegance and persistence in continuing to do "the wrong thing" well. The developing work of Neutra and Gropius shared many characteristics, early and late, just as the two men shared various convictions about the modern movement and their respective roles in it.

As early as 1951, for example, American Institute of Architects president Ralph Walker issued a manifesto in the *AIA Journal* obliquely attacking Gropius and Neutra and the European emigré architects of the 1920s and '30s. "The real problem facing the architectural profession," Walker wrote, "is how best to release the potentialities of the civilization developing here in this country. We cannot look to Europe, as it means looking to a civilization which for the last 75 years has been bent upon destroying itself, and the prophets it has sent to the United States are wholly negative in philosophy—stripping down culture to unattractive minima or in twisting neurosis into Nihilism. We must ourselves and in our own way, find the architectural answer to our needs, and in the very beginning cease imitating despair and negation to find a positive way toward an architectural form. Imitation of a universal form is fatal and indicates laziness, for if truly creative men are developed by our schools, there will be little unanimity. We, as Americans, must beware of the *Schleiermachers*, i.e., veilmakers. . . ."[1]

Gropius sent copies of his response to Walker, to Mies, Neutra, Chermayeff, and Breuer: "I did not quite believe my eyes first, so I read it again to be sure. For as you write about architecture in this article, I cannot come to any other conclusion but that you meant to challenge the contributions made to our profession by men like Mies van der Rohe, Neutra, Chermayeff, Breuer and myself, who certainly represent among others that group of former Europeans you speak of."[2]

Written challenges such as Walker's were easier to dismiss, however, than the actual challenge of new architectural sensibilities and the suggestion that new movements and new heroes were assuming the stage. Neutra was baffled, for example, by the rise of Louis Kahn in the late fifties and sixties and by what his own generation saw as Kahn's overly wrought "formalism," too dependent, Neutra thought, on historic allusion and grand brooding geometry. He pointed, with justification, to the functional and particularly the climate control problems of Kahn's Richards Medical Laboratories at the University of Pennsylvania, where in lieu of overhangs or other types of sunscreens, the occupants had been forced to cover glazed areas with aluminum foil, and where filing cabinets and laboratory equipment had to be placed against outside windows owing to lack of floor and wall space. He failed to acknowledge that occasionally his own clients, in less dramatic situations, had been forced to some of the same expedients and that the Richards Towers, whatever their operational failures, contained a rich and resonant poetry that was almost totally lacking in his own nearby student dormitory buildings. He had similar "formalist" criticism of Kahn's government building for Bangladesh, though again his own nearby university buildings at Mymensingh offered little comparison in cultural or textural richness. Closer to home was Kahn's design for the Salk Laboratories, La Jolla. Neutra despaired of what he saw as Kahn's "blindness to nature" in covering the plaza between the main wings with concrete rather than natural plantings. Here Neutra failed to see how "trivial" Kahn would have found such plantings and how essential the relatively empty plaza was to integrating the wings and directing the eye to the even grander natural scene of the Pacific Ocean coast beyond. Neutra was considered for the Bryn Mawr dormitory commission which Kahn ultimately got. Kahn's rise to international acclaim late in life confirmed, ironically, Neutra's suggestion to Dione early in his own career that great architects really matured in their seventies. His own ascendancy had come and gone earlier—a fact he was understandably reluctant to acknowledge.[3]

Many of the stirrings implicit in Kahn's architecture were further rationalized and lifted into consciousness by Robert Venturi's epochal critique of modernism, *Complexity and Contradiction in Architecture* (1966), a book that perplexed but interested Neutra. Attacking "the puritanically moral language of orthodox modern architectures," Venturi called for an architecture and for a new appreciation of architecture that was "hybrid rather than 'pure,' compromising rather than 'clean,' distorted rather than straightforward, ambiguous rather than 'articulated' . . . inconsistent and equivocal rather than direct and clear." Indeed, in his call for "messy vitality over obvious unity," Venturi went beyond Kahn's formal complexity to attack the modern movement in its most vulnerable areas.[4]

The architectural eclipse of Neutra and his generation both reflected and precipitated his own physical and psychological malaise. For his heart condition and his recurring depression, he took vast quantities of variously prescribed drugs. Neutra was a moderate drinker, but the combination of drugs and alcohol frequently made him even more unstable and aggravated the darker side of his nature. When under particular stress, he often exploded with an impatient hostility that made those around him forget or lose interest in his brighter, more brilliant sides.

A 1965 encounter with David Travers, John Entenza's successor at *Arts and Architecture*, typified this condition. Before a speaking engagement of Neutra's that Travers attended, Neutra had so offended the editor that he wrote Neutra the following morning "to advise you that an association of your name with the magazine *Arts and Architecture* is no longer possible in any manner so long as I am in a position to prevent it. Your calculated and insulting discourteousness toward Mrs. Travers and myself last evening leaves me no honorable alternative. I cannot pretend not to have perceived it. Unfortunately, it is too late to strike your name from our masthead of the April issue; it will not appear in May."[5]

Neutra responded immediately with typically contrite and obviously sincere apologies. "In my heart," he wrote, "I know beyond doubt that there was . . . no intent of doing such a thing as insulting you or, for heaven's sake, Mrs. Travers—while I was nervously trying to put together . . . slides I suddenly needed [and] did not have along. . . . But the main thing is that you did feel hurt by something I did, or perhaps said . . . and I request you, from the bottom of my soul, that you forgive me, whatever it was. . . . When you, as I recall, said smilingly your name, stepping into that corridor with the chairpile on which I fingered those slides, holding them up and looking at them against a bulb in the ceiling, I was, as a matter of fact, for a second very happy to forget the whole lecturing business, and curse it. But here it was pressing on me. And when Mrs. Travers seemed to say with a warm expression, yes, she was interested in philosophy, I would have loved to pour out that I really was too, and, that in spite of all I flippantly might have said, I too believed: The human individual does count more than anything and no 'averages' will ever do our world real justice. . . . At the end of my life and work, I know that your task too is a very difficult and lonely one, and I have often in public and abroad spoken of your *Arts and Architecture* and that I am happy it connects, from Los Angeles, America with the wide world."[6]

"Dear Mr. Travers," Neutra concluded, "I should tell you that you naturally could not see into my heart that evening. It pained me very badly before I had to come. I took a lot of nitroglycerine against my angina pectoris and drank half a tumbler of vodka. I only remember that I wildly improvised. . . . But one thing I know, I would love to see Mrs. Travers and yourself, whom it seems I have offended without anywhere being clear about it in my mind. In all sincerity, I again beg both your forgiveness. . . . Let me telephone and don't lose your time being angry about something which really is not, and was not there." Travers replied that he was "sorry if I misinterpreted your actions and demeanor toward Mrs. Travers and myself and shall be happy to treat the affair as closed."[7]

Neutra's uneven public behavior, moreover, devolved into even more complex intensity in his dealings with members of his family circle. Regula Thorston, for example, his admiring sister-in-law and devoted office manager, found Neutra so difficult and demanding that in 1956 she resigned her position, to Neutra's surprise and regret. Even Dione, his most loyal defender, found him at times almost unbearable, and admitted that the marriage could probably not have lasted had it not been for the frequent respites of travel and escape from the harsh professional and personal realities. In her diaries, she chronicled their brightest and darkest moments. John Blanton called her a "pathological truth-teller."

"The charming, witty Richard Neutra his audiences know," she wrote in a typical entry in 1954, "is a very different person from the one his intimates know. He can be so disagreeable that I can hardly stand him. He talks in either a very overbearing voice, or he whines. I don't know what I dislike more. All the time, however, I tell myself that the RJN his audiences know is the real one. The one we know all too often is the harrowed man, overburdened, cornered, who cannot see a way out of his dilemma, always groping and hoping to find someone to share his burden and help him. He does acknowledge that both Regula and I do this, also Dion in a more restricted way. That his draftsmen want to go home at 5:00 P.M. is utterly incomprehensible to him." She admitted that the "thing I miss most is the lack of joy, the ability to celebrate, to be glad about a new job, a new honor, a new invitation. He immediately forsees all the difficulties . . . and so all these events pass without pause. . . ." He seemed unable to stop for the smaller pleasures of life. Once, for example, after visiting a client in Palos Verdes, Neutra would only

take the time for "a snack at a drugstore, although of course I would have enjoyed it much more to eat a leisurely dinner . . . but RJN dislikes it very much to sit and sit and so we ate at this ugly lunch counter in the drugstore." When she chided him for this, he remarked that she could relax with her next husband.[8]

In the mid-1950s, as in the late '30s, Neutra was again persuaded to seek psychological counseling. This time he saw Dr. Friederick Karpf, who confessed to Dione "how exhausted he always was after a session with RJN, who was so clever and intelligent that it was strenuous to keep a jump ahead of him." As in the 1930s, however, Neutra continued to pride himself on his powers of "self-analysis," and the consultations ended with only temporary improvement in his psychological condition. In various journal entries throughout his life —from his Viennese adolescence to his post-war despondency to his recurring periods of depression in America—Neutra's self-analysis was frequently quite astute, assessing, in fact, more perceptively than his critics the complex causes and catastrophic consequences of his strident, insecure, self-defeating aggressiveness. Yet there were also times when Dione found him naively unaware. Once when she reminded him of the psychosomatic component of most physical pain and the effect upon health of human unhappiness, he replied that that did not apply to him. "I looked at him in blank amazement. 'I consider myself a happy person,' he said. 'How do you think I could fascinate people, audiences, clients, if I did not radiate happiness?' "[9]

Shortly after the break with Alexander, Dione wrote that Neutra had "become so dependent that he does not want to look through his [mail] pouch, but wants me or the secretaries to take the responsibility. . . . There may be great commissions coming his way, but in the present state of mind, he is afraid to tackle them. . . . The question is: should he? Or should he decline? If he declines, he will be unhappy, if he accepts, he will be unhappy. He is very much afraid that now that Dion, Regula, Alexander have left him, I shall leave him too because if he becomes more and more frantic and difficult to live with, I shall not want to stay. I, of course, reassure him that I would never desert him, however impossible he becomes." On April 8, 1959, she noted, "Today is RJN's birthday. I am worried

351. Richard and Raymond Neutra, late 1960s

greater delight, Dione recalled, in cultivating friendships with the journalist Chet Huntley, the philosopher Maynard Hutchins, the editor Norman Cousins, and the physician Elmer Belt. Dione also recorded the lighter side of their personal relationship. Late one evening in 1961 when Neutra came to bed, she admitted, she was initially in an unreceptive and "belligerent mood, tired of the whole setup. This constant tension, these constant complaints. However, as soon as RJN lies down with me, he relaxes," she observed. "He tried hard to amuse me and finally said something so funny that I had to laugh and the ice was broken."[11]

After Dione, the least clouded intimate relationship Neutra had was with his youngest son Raymond. Born in 1939, by which time there was money for both necessities and amenities, Raymond attended the best private boarding schools in Southern California. After graduating from Pomona College, he attended the Medical School of McGill University in Montreal and went on to become a successful physician and epidemiologist. Long fascinated with the medical sciences, Neutra approved of his youngest son's career choice and was proud of his personal and intellectual development. Handsome, affable, intelligent, and highly motivated, Raymond inherited the better qualities of each of his parents. Yet though he felt admiration and affection for both of them, he was also able, with penetrating perception, critically to interpret their complex personalities.

At a young age Raymond realized that his father played few of the conventional paternal roles, but expected instead that young Raymond act like a mature little adult whom the senior Neutra could use as a sounding board to test out *his* theories or unload *his* problems. For a young man with his own developing needs this was both flattering and frustrating. Raymond saw his father as having personal identity problems that continued all his life, though he found less uncertainty in his convictions and achievements as an architect. He admired the intensity with which "RJN" pursued his goals—even though his failure to achieve them caused him, inevitably, great personal anguish. Pushing, pushing all his life to achieve his frequently unrealistic ambitions, Neutra set himself up, Raymond believed, for the "Faustian tragedy" of his declining years.[12]

As a physician, Raymond could readily attest

about him and his future, although I try not to think about it because his life should not end in disaster." In an earlier entry written when Neutra was out of town she had written that it was "amazing what tenseness this man can create. Everything seems so simple when he is gone. We all work quickly and happily at our different self-imposed tasks, without rush or hurry, without being chided for things forgotten! However, ten days of this and I long to have him back. He is so vital, so interesting. . . ."[10]

Dione was, in fact, always able and willing to see the other side. "I still congratulate myself," she wrote, "to be the wife of Richard Neutra, and accept that the highlights, the trips, the acclaim balances itself with the daily pinpricks of complaining and wailing." In her diaries she cited the continuing high points. On February 5, 1960, at a dinner party, for example, "RJN was in very good spirits and had an animated discussion with Aldous Huxley, which he seemed to enjoy." He took even

to the seriousness of his father's physical and psychological illnesses, but he was equally certain that Neutra used them cunningly, both as a rationale for his failures and as a handy excuse for doing and not doing as he wished. Raymond, and others, more than once saw Neutra stage a heart seizure when he needed to win sympathy. Still, Raymond noted, his father's arteriosclerosis was so serious that after 1949 he could have gone at any time. Psychologically, he observed, Neutra was a milder, more "controlled" version of the manic-depressive. The depressions seemed to "come down" on him, competing with the alternately creative and destructive "highs" of the cycle. Frequently, though Neutra may never have acknowledged this, the depressions furnished a safety valve for the demanding and sometimes terrifying highs, and represented for him a "safer" place to be. Raymond believed that though he welcomed criticism from peers he respected, Neutra held certain distorted images of reality that, if challenged or violated, would make him frantic. It was important for him to believe, for example, that everyone who worked for him loved him devotedly, and he refused to countenance any thoughts to the contrary. Conversations with his father were, on the one hand, exciting and stimulating, Raymond recalled, but there was also frequently a certain "craziness" involved. Neutra, Raymond sensed, had a way not unlike that of a good courtroom lawyer of pushing people to more extreme positions than they wished to espouse and then taking delight in revealing their vulnerability.[13]

Raymond also saw his mother as complexly involved in Neutra's behavior, not merely a smiling, innocent bystander who protected and defended him. She had made deliberate and not totally unselfish decisions about the kind of life she wanted to live even while giving up a promising musical career to devote herself to him. In Neutra she early saw potential—unshaped genius—and decided to devote her life to helping him realize it. They formed indeed a symbiotic unit; they acted as one person. She strongly encouraged the Faustian contract. Her ego needed his success and the constant sense of urgency in their lives that frustrated but also thrilled her. She found much of her excitement vicariously through him. She goaded him to be "interesting" and controversial. He did not have the option of not being famous. Other-

wise, he feared, she might lose interest. Still, Raymond appreciated his parents immensely. In myriad, though sometimes conflicting ways, they had opened his eyes to life's richest possibilities.[14]

Richard Neutra's relationship with his second son, Dion, was personally and professionally more complex and tragic. It was classically tragic in the age-old sense that each found himself—like other sons and fathers—caught in the other's fatal flaws. Each seemed unable, particularly in the fifties and sixties, to work successfully with or without the other. Growing up in the 1930s, Dion missed the attention that his parents, particularly his mother, felt compelled to give to Frank, their mentally retarded oldest child, before Frank was finally committed to an institution. He also missed the attention and advantages they were later able to give to Raymond. Neutra pressed Dion to become an architect, while wisely allowing Raymond more of a choice of career. From the age of twelve Dion was expected to spend his afternoons at the drafting board, and though he remembered enjoying aspects of this, he later regretted having missed many of the more innocent pursuits of childhood. Neutra was determined that Dion should follow in his footsteps, but in his ambition to make Dion a great architect Neutra prescribed and monitored the process too literally. Though he could write thoughtful paternal letters of advice, he generally neglected to encourage his son's personal development. After graduating in the late 1940s from the Architecture School of the University of Southern California, Dion studied for a year in Switzerland. He then intended to work independently of his father, but the elder Neutra, citing his own declining health, urged Dion to commit himself to the family enterprises. Between 1950 and 1955 Dion moved back and forth between the Silverlake and Glendale Boulevard offices. Thrust into the ambiguous and potentially threatening role of "the boss's son," he was eyed suspiciously by the older associates. After 1955 this was partially ameliorated by his decision to work exclusively in the Glendale Boulevard office of Neutra & Alexander.[15]

Throughout the 1950s, as a member of both offices, he—like the other associates—played vital roles in the designing and execution of the two firms' buildings. Most close observers, including his father, appreciated his technical and engineer-

352. Dion and Richard Neutra, mid-1960s

after the breakup of the Neutra & Alexander partnership. After several years in the Alexander office, Dion then worked briefly for Richard Dorman before finally attempting to practice on his own.[16]

In a Father's Day greeting of 1961, Dion spoke to the senior Neutra of their frustrated relationship. "I really am sympathetic to your situation," he wrote, "but somehow one of my gifts has not been to convey this very successfully. It is complicated by the fact that I am somehow implicated by the situation, as well [as] our inability to communicate, which produces frustration, resentment, and distortion. . . . I am sorry that you tend to look at things from the dark side at least when I've observed you. I have learned this from you. And it causes people to be a bit uncomfortable. People want to associate with one who is happy, optimistic and a 'good fellow,' good loser, one who doesn't burden you with his problems. . . . I'm sorry this doesn't work out better for both of us. '. . ."[17]

Dion's plans to develop his own practice, however, were again curtailed by another emergency, which pulled him back closer to the Neutra architectural orbit. The crisis this time was a bad stroke of fate that seemed to epitomize his father's declining fortunes. For in the early morning of March 27, 1963, the Silverlake studio—the Van der Leeuw Research House—was almost completely destroyed by fire. Apparently caused by an electrical short circuit, the fire occurred while Richard and Dione were away in the Middle West. Their housekeeper, Evelyn Francis, barely escaped. The Neutras returned and tried to live in the undamaged guest house, but they could not bear to stare at the charred ruins and moved to a nearby vacant Neutra house on Earl Street. Except for the materials Neutra had given to UCLA in the mid-1950s—drawings, letters, and personal memorabilia—most of his recent work and the family's most treasured personal possessions were destroyed. "Everything is gone," Dione wrote despondently. "The past is finished. All the clipping books, all the client and appreciation letters, all the books containing his contributions, not to speak of his own [books], all his medals and degrees and competitions won. All the publicity material. All the reprints of magazines. In short, all our working tools, all negatives, all photographs, all lecture tapes, hundreds of hand sketches, drawings of him by others, autographed books, etc.,

ing talents and his steady contributions toward "making things work." The senior Neutra was most critical of Dion's reserved, "unanimated," diffident personality and his failure to approximate his own "largeness of vision," and delight in ideas and intellectual wordplay. Neutra found Dion, like Alexander, too concerned with money and the "business" of architecture, as opposed to its spiritual and psychological essence—though, as Alexander pointed out, someone had to attend to such things to allow Neutra freedom in the more ethereal realms. Alexander and Dion had, in fact, good rapport, because they frequently thought in similar ways not only on day-to-day pragmatics but on esthetic issues as well. They also shared a common ambivalence toward the man with whom they found themselves so complexly allied. It was no surprise then—to anyone but his parents—when Dion elected to go with Alexander

etc." Dorothy Serulnic, however, remembered Neutra's own rather different reaction when they arrived from the airport to confront the scene. He looked at it silently for about five seconds, she recalled, and then started discussing the details of rebuilding.[18]

When it came to designing and planning "VDL II" on the site of the home they had all shared so long, it seemed somehow natural to both father and son that they should share in conceptualizing its new form. Perhaps both hoped that this joint enterprise might heal old wounds and prepare the way for a steadier future relationship. They agreed that the new house would rise on the old slab, and would employ the old modules, but decided to take appropriate cognizance of the changes in Neutra's style and ideas since he built the first house thirty years before. Larger panes of glass, more mirrors and reflecting pools, and softer, more varied textures and materials would give new meaning to VDL II. In the day-to-day role of supervising architect, however, Dion found himself making many design decisions, while his father increasingly spent more time on the lecture circuit. Absent for months during the crucial finishing stages, the senior Neutra returned to view many of his son's decisions with critical dismay. At Dione's insistence he tried to keep these feelings to himself, but he felt impelled to apologize to Blanton about what he regarded as cacophonous colors and a disconcerting mixture of too many materials. He told Dorothy Serulnic that he believed the new house had less "soul" than the old one. Rather than bridging the gaps in the relationship, the rebuilding of the house tended to confirm them.[19]

Finally realizing, however, that many of Dion's problems were partially caused by his overprotectiveness, Neutra resolved—since all signs pointed to a partnership—to attempt to take a back seat and let Dion run the office. To Dione's relief, they traveled more than ever, as Neutra assuaged his personal unhappiness with the still abundant acclaim of his public. Between 1966 and 1969 they even decided to live in Vienna, using the guest house of the city's Arbeiterkammer as headquarters for their almost incessant traveling. Neutra enjoyed living again in Vienna, though he continued to feel hurt that he received no commissions in his native city. All major office work was still air-mailed for his approval, but the thrust of the late work bore Dion's signature. This caused further friction with the firm's older associates who, accustomed to answering only to RJN, resented Dion's newly solidified power. By 1967 they had, for various reasons, all gone elsewhere. Koschin retired. Blanton and Fischer set up their own offices. Dorothy Serulnic resigned because, with RJN gone, it was "no longer any fun." The amount of work dwindled.

One late building, however, in which Neutra took particular interest, was a Washington, D.C., house for Ann and Donald Brown. As a Smith College undergraduate in the late 1940s, Ann Brown had studied architectural history with Oliver Larkin and Henry-Russell Hitchcock and, under their tutelage, had been introduced to the work of Neutra. When she and her husband found themselves able to build a house in the late 1960s, she eschewed the more fashionable post-modern avant-garde and opted instead for Neutra's "good old modern" style. In the completed house she skillfully mixed furniture by Le Corbusier with Chippendale antiques and abstract paintings and sculpture—an effect to which Neutra gave smiling approval. The general success of the "old-fashioned" Brown house suggested what Neutra—if possessed of greater patience—could have done in his late years with such small commissions. Like Louis Sullivan in the late part of his life, Neutra might have been able to weather changing tastes by doing—in the old way —a few jobs well. But that, alas, he was unable to do.[20]

In June 1969 Neutra returned to Los Angeles to accept an honorary doctorate from UCLA—one of countless such honors he received in those years. He and Dione naturally stayed at Silverlake, which had lain virtually empty since its mid-sixties rebuilding, and finding it once again pleasant and stimulating, decided to return to California permanently. Neutra enjoyed teaching in the fall of 1969 at the California Polytechnic Institute in Pomona and continued to work, as he had in Vienna, on the manuscript of another book called "The Man in the Middle Is the Measure." Yet his unhappy restlessness demanded further travel, and in the spring of 1970 he and Dione left again for an extended European lecture tour.

In Wuppertal, Germany, they visited his clients, the Peschers and Kempers, and on April

353. Neutra amidst ruins of burned-out VDL House I, Los Angeles, 1963

354. Neutra viewing ruins of VDL House I, 1963

355. *Richard and Dion Neutra*, VDL House II, Los Angeles, 1966

356. *Richard and Dion Neutra*, VDL House II, 1966

297

357. *Richard and Dion Neutra*, VDL
House II, 1966

interest in realizing unattained goals. However bleak the present might seem, there were always new projects or ideas to sustain him.[22]

Though ever the immigrant, he shared certain qualities with a famous native-born character of American fiction. Like the Great Gatsby of F. Scott Fitzgerald, Neutra's "dream must have seemed so close that he could hardly fail to grasp it. He did not know that it was already behind him somewhere back in that vast obscurity. . . ." Like Neutra, Gatsby believed in "the orgiastic future that year by year recedes before us. It eluded us then, but that's no matter—tomorrow we will run faster, stretch out our arms further . . . and one fine morning . . ." And so, Fitzgerald concluded, "we beat on, boats against the current, borne back ceaselessly into the past."[23]

At the memorial service at Garden Grove Church, Dione sang the two Bach songs Neutra had liked most: "O Jesulein Süss," and "Komm Süsser Tod." Raymond, Dion, and Schuller spoke to an audience that Neutra would have considered unacceptably small. *Saturday Review* editor Norman Cousins placed Neutra, for the third time, on the magazine's cover, though in the article inside critic Wolf von Eckardt admitted that he "sometimes found [Neutra's] vanity, which rivaled that of Frank Lloyd Wright, a trifle irritating. He used to call, it seemed to me, a bit too insistently to offer me an interview. The last time he called, I said just as insistently that I was on a deadline. 'Aren't you ever on a lifeline?' he retorted."[24]

Eulogies poured in from all over the world, but most were shorter and less effulgent than might have been expected. Most offered only simple biographical sketches and mentioned chiefly the earlier work. Bruno Zevi's was particularly harsh. "A strange, puzzling figure," he wrote in *L'Architettura*. Though Neutra had been "in touch with three key characters of the modern movement," he had failed, Zevi believed, "to grasp their secret. On the artistic grounds: he does not inherit Loos' 'Raumplan,' he misses Mendelsohn's vital component, he rejects Wright's articulated plan and that consciousness in the 'nature of materials' which even his compatriot R. M. Schindler had intimately caught." Zevi made no mention of what Neutra *had* learned from those and other masters, and of how his own synthesis had transcended their categories. "On a

16, 1970, while photographing the Kemper house, Neutra collapsed and died of a massive heart attack. When Dione was called from the nearby Pescher house she asked to be left alone with him for a moment, as she recalled kaleidoscopically their shared experiences of fifty years—a half century of mixed, but ultimately satisfying, memories.[21]

Neutra himself had long been obsessed with the absolute certainty of his imminent demise. All letters had to be signed before he went to bed, since he might not live to sign them the next morning. He was constantly rewriting his last will and testament. "Death is a pretty quick event," he wrote to a friend, following the death of László Moholy-Nagy. "Flesh is like the grass—unprotected." In 1969, he wrote moving obituaries in the *Los Angeles Times* on the occasion of the deaths of Gropius and Mies. The old modernist fraternity was rapidly thinning out. At seventy-eight, he insisted, he was ready to die. Yet his sheer longevity and recurring vitality countered his professed readiness for death. He was kept from its reach by his actual will to live, by his

psychological level," Zevi insisted, "he possessed several impossible temperaments: one dogmatically puritan, the other arrogant and unpleasant, the third megalomaniac to an insufferable degree. . . ."[25]

The seventies were not Neutra's—or modernism's—decade. Indeed, most of the praise and the balanced assessments had come earlier. In the 1950s Zevi himself had eloquently expressed the prevailing mood: "Poet in the houses of Lovell, von Sternberg, and Tremaine, he emerges in the history of modern architecture as a major literate: synthesis of a thorough European education and a favorable American environment, his architecture shows the missionary ambition to sacrifice the exceptions on the altar of a higher and civilized construction norm. . . . Some exceptional works notwithstanding, the characterization of Neutra and his cultural significance remain therefore in the literary sphere. His architecture has an essayistic valor, searches a rule, an education, a logic, shuns eccentricities, caprices, extravagances, reflects the conscience of a moralistic task in the professional practice. It is afraid of confusion, of disorder, of lack of system. . . . it follows a constant directional principle . . . detests the strokes of genius, the brilliant ideas, the stimuli of curiosity and oratory, bends every excess to a discipline, to an organized thought which develops in graduated and always superintended variations which do not wish to astonish. . . . Altogether he attacks the masters greater than he for their incapacity to equalize. They invented the modern architecture, but he alone gave it respectability and prestige."[26]

In 1967 the anthropologist Robert Ardrey pursued the same line from another perspective. "There is probably no city in the world," he wrote Neutra, "where the influence of your work and your ideas cannot be read in stone and stucco, realized by men you never met. This is the genuine immortality, when what a man has done so thoroughly imbues his time that it takes on a kind of anonymity. Like a sperm in a gene-pool, nobody quite remembers who was the donor, but there it is, a portion of a population's resource forever. Your concepts of living have in many ways been that. I can remember times in Los Angeles in the '30s when there was only one man, Richard Neutra, and you said, 'That's a Neutra house.' Nobody else could have built it. And then later you looked at a house

and you said: 'Look at the Neutra influence.' But then later on, unless you were a Neutra fan and connoisseur, you wouldn't say it because your concepts had spread so widely and deeply into domestic architecture that they had become part of the modern way of life."[27]

Indeed, Neutra's greatest period of personal creativity had been the years between 1927 and 1949, during which time he was without doubt the leading modernist residential designer. As with most practitioners of any art, the quality of his work following that peak period had fallen off and became less consistent, though throughout his life Neutra continued to produce examples of respectable and, at times, inspired architecture. As significant as his own work, however, was the role he played as modernist missionary, propagating the gospel of modern architecture and its relation to human psychological and physiological needs.

In 1968 the Southern California chapter of the American Institute of Architects nominated

358. *Neutra*, Brown House, Washington, D.C., 1968

359. Neutra, at signing of Humanities Bill with President and Mrs. Johnson, 1965

visiting Neutra in 1928 in Los Angeles, where he "worked as a lonely pioneer designing modern buildings, the like of which were then unknown on the West Coast. Against very great odds, he stuck to his new artistic approach and by skill and stamina, he slowly achieved a true breakthrough." Mies van der Rohe wrote that "the mainstream of today's architecture is the result of the threads of thought and activity of a handful of men who persevered in their efforts and maintained their ideals." Neutra's work, Mies asserted, "over the long span of years has become one of those threads. By his example, he has influenced and taught a generation of architects, for which the profession and the world is in his debt."[28]

Sybil Moholy-Nagy argued that "in honoring Richard Neutra, the Institute would honor architecture in its three major and historical functions: as the art of designed environment, as expressed life orientation and conviction, and as prophecy of a better future." Neutra's work, she believed, "has been expressive of these three commitments for half a century. The sum total of his buildings is much more important than judgment passed on the success or failure of individual solutions. While the 'big names' among architectural firms—those who started together with Richard Neutra as pioneers and environmental teachers of America—have sold out flatly to package deal and bland commercialism . . . he has retained the quality of the prototypical building, no matter how unrewarding financially this may be. It is safe to say . . . that without Richard Neutra the vital beginnings of a California Architecture made by such men as Gill and Schindler would have been lost in the ill-smelling swamp of speculation developments. By keeping his personality inviolate, he kept the idea of a west coast style alive." She urged the AIA "to decide for this award, if only to restore faith in its professional integrity."[29]

Neutra for the national institute's highest award—the AIA Gold Medal. In support of its case, it solicited letters from leading international architects and critics. Kenzo Tange wrote that Neutra was "one of the architects whom I most admire and respect." The Japanese, he noted, were particularly drawn to the "exquisite sensitivity in his space and his delicate treatment for structures and materials." Gropius called Neutra one of the "leading modern architects since the beginning of the new movement in the early 20s of this century." He recalled

Yet though most of its respondents expressed surprise that Neutra had not already received the Gold Medal, the AIA declined to honor him in 1968. In his late years, he had evidently offended too many of his peers—as his work had come to seem increasingly *déjà vu.* It would in fact be another nine years before he would win the Gold Medal—posthumously. The fact that he did receive it in 1977 suggested that even at the height of post-modern eclecticism, the world of architecture might be ready at least for new historical appraisals. In 1979 the Museum of Modern Art celebrated its fiftieth anniversary with a show on the modern art of the twenties, which featured handsome models of Gropius's Bauhaus, Neutra's Lovell house and other classics of modern design. Perhaps because it was less well known on the East Coast, there seemed to be particularly intense interest in Neutra's building. And in 1980, as if to confirm this growing interest and awareness, the Museum announced a Neutra retrospective to open in 1982 —the fiftieth anniversary of the epochal show that had given Neutra his greatest early acclaim.

Eclipse—if defined as "a reduction or loss of splendor, status, reputation" came to Neutra and his generation in the sixties and seventies. They had once bravely "beat on, boats against the current." How would they fare, when, contrary to their credos and their fondest self-images, they were borne, like all mortals, "back ceaselessly into the past?" Would their stars reappear when the oscillations of history readjusted the light? The evidence strongly suggested they would.

360. Neutra, beneath portrait of Emperor Franz Josef, Vienna, late 1960s

Appendix A
Neutra, Schindler, and the Lovell Health House

Since the issue of how and why Neutra got the commission to design the Health House for Philip and Leah Lovell has become a controversial one, the following letters between the Neutras and the Lovells from the late 1960s and early '70s are reproduced in an effort to clarify the matter.

There is even controversy, however, as to how and why these particular letters originated.

In Vienna to Los Angeles *(p. 71), Esther McCoy wrote:* "In February 1969 Neutra showed me a letter written to him by the Lovells, the gist of which was that they had always intended Neutra to design the town house, liked it, and considered Neutra a genius.

"Lovell told me several weeks later, 'He is a sick man, he had a heart attack and might die any day. They started driving out to see us—bringing an autographed book and articles about Neutra. Then they brought this letter they wanted us to sign.'

"Leah said, 'When we read that letter it had too many things in it that weren't true so Philip said we would write our own letter. If that letter means that much to him, well, it's all so far in the past. . . .'"

As in several other instances, however, the Lovells' memory was in error—particularly in regard to Neutra's "driving out" and asking them to sign a prepared letter. Neutra had apparently not been in contact with the Lovells for some time when Philip initiated the new round of communications with a letter of December 10, 1968, suggesting that he might like to sell the beach house and build another one. Since Richard and Dione were in Vienna for an extended stay at this time, their son Dion, in charge of the office, received and acknowledged Lovell's letter and forwarded it to his father. Since Neutra had long been disturbed by the reverberations of Schindler's insinuation that Neutra had "taken" the Lovell commission from him, Neutra took this opportunity to attempt to clarify the matter and to ask Lovell to write to him and try to reconstruct the chain of events. The letters begin with Lovell's initial query of 1968. (Neutra and Lovell's erratic spelling has not been corrected.)

Dec. 10, 1968

To Richard Neutra Sr. & Dion Neutra:

Greetings:—Nixon won out on the slogan "Its time for a change." And that's the way with the Lovells, who, in spite of many, many years are still around, and in excellent health—and incidentally give my best wishes to your mother, Dion.

Purpose of this communicado???—Since the firm of Schindler & Neutra have been my guiding lights for nearly half a century, I'm going to the surviving members of the team as the passage of time has changed my purposes. In short, I am seeking a purchaser for the beach house. Both of you are undoubtedly familiar with it in every aspect—but I don't know whether you know that it has been made a "National Monument" by the Parks Division of the Dept. of the Interior. What that means, I don't know—maybe I can now sell kosher hot dogs in it!!!

Soooooo—just in case—since you both know all the people worth while who have both dinero and the appreciation for good architecture, if you know of such a person or persons who would be willing to part with $125,000 net to us, with an allowance of $5,000 off the purchase price for re-habilitation of this menage, this beach house is now for sale. We'd like to move to Malibu—and maybe build a house there. Age 73 does not deter me—how about you Richard? If any commissions are involved it would have to be added to the above price.

Good luck and best wishes
Philip M. Lovell

December 16, 1968

Dear Dr. Lovell:

How nice to hear from you—such a charming letter indeed!

I suppose you may have heard from the owners of the Health House, Dr. and Mrs. Topper, that I have been keeping in touch in trying to preserve the architectural merits of your first efforts with my dad. It is amazing to notice that whereas the architecture seems to bear the test of time, some of the mechanical installations are becoming obsolete, such as the heating and plumbing, etc. Even some of the steel needs painting occasionally!

Thank you very much for thinking of us in connection with the necessary sale of the Schindler beach house. I am sending a copy of your letter together with this one to Esther McCoy, architectural historian, who may well have some thoughts as to how it should best be disposed of. Also to my aunt, Regula Thorston, who has been in the real estate business and may have interested buyers. Also to another aunt, Elizabeth von Wetter who is also in the real estate business in the Naples-Long Beach area.

I assume that your "bottom" price is $125,000 plus commissions. We would certainly enjoy serving you once again and age 73 certainly does not deter me. I will have to let my dad speak for himself, but I know that he has always been very fond of you both and would find it most stimulating to see how the passage of time have changed everyone's idea and program!

May I enclose our family Christmas card along with our best wishes for the holiday season? This year it was designed by our 16 year old daughter.

Cordially,
Dion Neutra
for Richard and Dion Neutra,
Architects and Associates.

jetzt: Plösslg. 2, 1040 Vienna, Austria
January 28, 1969

Dear Dr. Lovell,

I can hardly express to you, how I felt after so long a time to receive your letter. It was very delayed till our office in Los Angeles and my son Dion, who is my partner, could reach me after a little new Years-holiday.

Both, Dione and I thought very intensely of you both, and we found your way of writing, your humor quite as in the olden days! We enjoyed your letter so very much and are happy, you are both well.

It is an honour to me, that after forty years, you seem to keep me still in good memory.—

It may interest you, that a couple of weeks ago, I spoke here in public at an exhibition of R. M. Schindler, who had been my best friend, and who never had a better friend than me.

I talked about both your houses, of which only the beach-house, of course, could be seen by the audience in enlarged photographs. I mentioned your third house in Wrightwood, but I forgot to talk about your clinic downtown, which was the first thing, you trusted me with. I spoke of it, what a great stimulating clients you and Lea had been to architects—.

You must remember very well, when you spoke to me about the house at Griffith Park first, I at once wanted to do it with R. M. S. and was happy at this thought, speaking to you about it. It is terrible to me, that in America and even here in Vienna it is whispered—it was me, who stole your sympathy and confidence away from my best friend. How can anyone believe such a thing of me! I suffer from this suspicion my whole life!

Before we can do anymore happily for you, which we would love, I beg you to write me at least a short letter,—or as long as you wish,—that I have not done anything so mean against a friend, whom infact I wanted to see and have you look at then as my partner. When you told me to go ahead alone, I did it with anxiety, and only, when he himself did not wish to join me.

I know I have served you and Lea, first with a bleeding heart but always with loving devotion. And what I accomplished with very hard work at Griffith Park, is now like your house at the beach as you know highly considered by the profession and many, many other people, around the world as something like a historical monument.

To have you to remember the whole history, you showed me, when your house at Griffith Park was about a third finished, complete plans of Fred Monhoff! You remember him? It was in Spanish style and the project for your lot at Griffith Park.

When I was given the Hall of Records to design and build, much later, downtown, Fred Monhoff was the county architect, and first very bitter against me! God, I could swear, that I had not stolen anything from him either!—I had not known anything else, but loved to invest my deepest devotion in this house for you both, and in yourselves. Please write me, that you remember all this is true, and as you once have written me many, many years ago, that I had acted as a fair and faithful architect, indeed, to you both and to your children.—I had a fire, and it destroyed my house, library, past correspondence and all.—Do you remember Mr. Topper, who was a little friend of poor David. He owes your health-house now and loves to remember it, when he was a boy.—He has 3 little boys himself, but they are growing up.

Please give me the great comfort, that I have been most honest as a friend and in this service of designing a house which like your beach house has become a national monument. I need this comfort from you and you are the only one, who can give it to me.—

My sincere warmest wishes are with you both.

I am cordially and devotedly yours,
Richard J. Neutra.

There are numerous errors of historical fact in Lovell's answer, especially on the issue of how he met and commissioned Neutra and Schindler. Lovell was guilty of "Freudian forgetfulness" or of a misguided desire, especially in the fifth paragraph, to reconstruct events as he wished in retrospect, they might *have happened.*

Feb. 9, 1969

My dear Richard:

You ask me to give you a resume of what transpired over 40 years ago vis-a-vis the buildings I had built by you and R. M. Schindler. To the best of my ability here is a true account of the circumstances that existed in those days. First I must explain my own personal circumstances in order to understand some decisions which I made at that time.

I was at the height of my relationship with the L. A. Times. I had taken up a column which at that time was over 30 years old and which was overwhelmingly the most popular part of that newspaper. In very short order I had an office consisting of over 30 rooms and had up to 37 people helping me in my clinic. I was making good money, and decided that what I wanted most for this money was to have a house in the mountains, land near Fallbrook, a house at the seashore, and a city home. I looked around for an architect who would reflect my views—views which in my field were at that time, and even today far from orthodox—in fact I was and still am far to the left in most of my medical and social views. I encountered several men who are probably not familiar to you—orthodox men who built the standard "little boxes" made famous by Pete Seegurs [sic] songs. This was before I contacted either you or RMS.

It was at this time quite by accident I became acquainted with 3 of you—Wright, RMS and you Richard. My views were the same as yours. I repeated to both of you (in one interview I discarded Wright) my views both negative and positive. I was vehement that creating a building, which became an integral part of a city, should be outlawed by the plans of every dam fool woman who wants a home. The American or European housewife does not create her own automobile, her shoes, her food, or virtually anything else she and her family uses. In short the cities of the world are and were a bastardly hodge podge of chop suey created by millions of morons—the average family. Here in this new and pioneering country, the family arriving from Georgia wanted a house just like she had there, the one from Michigan a house just like she had there, and so on ad infinitum, ad nauseum. Where these might have had some value in their original locale, i.e. to fight cold and snow, etc.—here she was in a semi Paradise, and carried her old hodge-podge to this new country.

In addition to having no social concept, no experience in this wonderful new country of Calif., no technical experience, 98% of our native Californians thoroly disagreed with me in my health views. Believing firmly then and now that only in Natural forces lies men's happiness—i.e. we needed and wanted sun, air, harmony of lines, and the ability to do many health things which I advocated, such as outdoors sleep, nude sunbathing, a pool that was never to be chlorinated, light, air, sunshine, clean lines, no hodge podge jungle of ideas—I looked around for an architect. I encountered several before I accidentally ran across both you and RMS—but when I encountered both of you, it was like a breath of fresh air. Instead of opposition I met approval (Richard you and RMS were the "Hippies", the protesters of those years in the field of architecture—and I was the master "Hippy" of my forte, not believing in the "Establishment" of orthodox medicine, and most other things pertinent to the "Establishment of those days) and a few days after I met both of you—I believe it was the same week—I then made my decision that I would engage both of you to formulate architectural plans for the buildings I wanted.

At first I intended to have both of you work jointly—I made an appointment and called at Kings Road, expecting to meet with both of you. Instead you were not there and I proceeded to talk with RMS on the presumption that you were both partners. It was not until several weeks later that I found out I was mistaken—that you were not partners—perhaps you had been, but not at that time. But by this time RMS had submitted drawings, sketches, etc. and I kept my mouth shut as to the partnership. It was then I decided that I would distribute the 4 buildings on a financial basis—I knew that the country, beach, and mountain homes were to be secondary to my city home, where my clinic was located. Adding my outlay for the 4 projects, I figured that my city home on Dundee would equal in outlay the other 3 projects—i.e. beach, mountain and ranch. In point of fact the city house cost much more than the other 3 houses. By this time Frank L. Wright was out—in fact somewhere about that time I even spoke to his son—but there was no contact. Long before I started the city house I had determined that you, and only you, were to be the architect for my city home—even though I had a conference over the phone with Wright, etc.

Further, I had had an argument with RMS—I was thoroly dissatisfied with the material he put in the Mt. Cabin—celotex on the exterior—came the first winter storm, and the walls which were half an inch thick became 2 inches thick—and nearly 6 ft of snow at that winter—result, a portion of the living room collapsed —and then I was sure Schindler would not do any further work for me. But by this time I had made my arrangement with you, and you were in the process of building. As the building progressed, more and more I was enamored—not only did you conform to my "radicalism" that I wanted air, light, outdoors sleeping, the ability of the sun to penetrate, etc. but by this time I also had a shock with the beach house—the sleeping porches which RMS created became rain pools—impossible to maintain when it rained, and, you undoubtedly noticed that after 1 year we "windowed" up the front from the intermediate door. This did not make me too happy with RMS—but with Dundee Dr., your creation, I did not have a single complaint. Everything I represented you produced for me—and it seemed that it was your philosophy as well as mine.

Not only did you create a masterpiece, but you did it so economically that I was surprised and pleased. The supervision you gave it was unparalleled. RMS came to Newport but once or twice a week at the utmost—you were on the job daily. and after more than that. Nothing escaped your attention. Not a single thing displeased me. Not a single mistake of any consequence was made. The city house for nearly 2 decades became a house of comfort, happiness, and above all, radical drugless health.

Most men get accreditation after they die. Of the 3 people who entered my architectural life at that time only you are still alive—and I am shortly going to celebrate my 74th birthday. If I had to live those years over and over again, again and again I would choose both of you—in my book only 3 architects that came under my observation are and were GREAT—you, RMS, and Wright. On Wright—I couldn't get along with him in a thousand years—but both of you were patient with my lack of professionalism but markedly sympathetic with my ideas—and you both carried them out superbly.

I want to emphasize and reiterate (why it should come up I do not know) but in the field of architecture that has come under my control, I would do it again and again with both of you—I am sorry that my division that I would ask both of you to create buildings for me on a finance basis of division rather that on a numerical basis of so many buildings for you and so may for him.

And finally Richard, let me say this—altho I shall shortly be 74, when as and if I create a new home—and there's a possibility as I'm getting this home ready for sale—there is one man now living whom I would choose overwhelmingly—and his name happens to be Richard Neutra. And if RMS were living now I would say the same for him.

Cordially yours,
Philip M. Lovell.

February 13, 1969

Dear dear Mr. Neutra,

Philip showed me a copy of a letter he sent you and how sorry I was that he had already mailed it for I would so much have liked to sign it, too, and add to it that I, also think you the great architect of our day. I cannot say enuf as so how highly I look up to you as the foremost designer of our day, of how deeply sorry I am if I have ever said or done anything that would hurt you in any way.

That you have been dedicated to your art as few people are, is so so evident to anyone that has given any thought at all to the field of architecture—in fact, all who have known of your devotion have felt as we do, that you are undoubtedly the great artist of your day. The future will be the richer for having had the genius of your work as background. Please know that we honor and respect you for the much you have given to enrich our world. We feel rich in having known not only your work, but you personally.

Very Sincerely yours
Leah Lovell.

By this time, the Neutras had returned to Los Angeles, and Neutra answered the Lovells' letters by hand.

22 Febr. 1969

Dear Philip, Dearest Leah—from Richard!

This is nothing which I will dictate into a typewriter to a third person!—*I embrace you both from all my heart*—you never had ever called me by my first name—and I have always thought of you—like the thousands and thousands who have looked at your Griffith Park house, as: *Dr. and Mrs. Lovell!*—I had to look *deep into your hearts*—and into mine too—to build your house—and watch your children—it was one of my life's awful days when I learned about David.—He was such, *such* a wonderful boy!—(Right now the tears come into my eyes, when I think of him—and of you that day—!) You *must* write me of your grandchildren and children—how often you can see them.—How is Dundee Drive in *their* memory?

My dear ones, both your letters are written me by mistake! Never, never have I said that *you would have to explain your good feelings toward me*! You surely have not to apologize for *anything* to me!—I am three years older than you, Philip, and I never had in all my life better, more trusting, more wonderful clients than you and Leah—each in his and her way! (Even Mrs. Westerman was a dear one, God bless her soul.) —How can you so misunderstand my feelings to you both, and about that experience I had with you?

In many ways, you might be surprised how

deeply and lovingly I know you, *and how fate has related you to each other*—before I was made to step into your life and while I worked with a devotion for you *two human beings*.—You would be happy and astounded how lovingly I looked into your souls to have the fascination to do the best by you. Every human being is entitled to his privacy and I respected it, but wanted to give *you two a common good to cherish together*, and still each in his own way—Leah with her fine, even dainty, taste and soul, and you, Philip, with your roughnecky outside in shirtsleeves throwing a half-crushed wood box across the room into the fireplace!—But I knew, inside, you have a tender soul too—a little like sweet David.—You have been the turning point in my life (not only to architecture, as they say, from the technical-constructivistic to the humane-biological as its main interest and goal!)—You are right. I wanted to be RMS' best friend—he never has had a better one in his awful loneliness, which before me he never covered up with his smile he had to carry as tragically as his gifts.—He *knew* he never had a better, a more worthy friend than he had in me and that I had done *nothing whatever* to push him out of your friendship, as they here to my deep grief have said!—I love you Leah and love you Philip—I am the last human being on earth you have to make up with —I don't remember one harsh word! No architect ever found more loving and beloved FRIENDS!

My son Dion, my partner, and Dione share my feelings for you!

February 1969!

Dear Richard and Dione!

Warm greetings from Philip and me. I have read and reread your dear letter. It is needless to say how glad we both were to get it and to know that you are both well and that you remember us kindly.

We treasure deeply all the memories of yesterday that bring back our building era! And our friendships for one another that grew out of that enriching life.

It was indeed wonderful for Philip and me to have met you and to have had the privilege of giving to you the opportunity to have expressed yourself as you did—so richly and so well! As I look back on it all, my heart fills with joy at the enrichment it meant to us all. It opened a new and creative world to us all! How we grew and how our world widened with the growth!

If we made little mistakes in our growing, we are deeply sorry and the joy that fills our hearts rightnow at having the rich experience we did have together will more than make up for the misunderstandings.

We love our memories of yesterday of which you are a very very rich part. You gave us much—you opened our eyes to a world so new to us then and so rich in its development of us—We have much, much to be grateful for and we are.

Now that we are truly matured, we can look back on that rich rich past and be glad for it—we love the memory of each one of our friends of those early glowing days!

You have enriched our lives in knowing you— and we look back now with deep gratitude and love for each of those dear ones who grew up into a world that was wondrous and new—so new to us in those long-time-ago days!

We love the memories and we love you who are a rich rich part of those memories. I am so happy to be here to write and tell you how very much you have given to us and how grateful we are for the richness that came to us thru you.

To you both and to your loved ones, we send love and glowing memories of days long since past but never forgotten.

Our love again!
Leah and Philip Lovell.

After Neutra's death, Dione read through the foregoing correspondence, and—disturbed by the inaccuracies (particularly Lovell's earlier contention that he had met and commissioned Neutra and Schindler at the same time), wrote Lovell again and asked for clarification. He replied as follows:

Aug. 6, 1971

My dear Dion & Dione:

Before me I have several letters between us— actually I do not know the purpose of them. Much of it goes back forty or more years, and of course memory does not apply accurately to those days. Perhaps I may be confused as to dates and episodes—it is only the main events that are prominent. As I told you before, when I first met RMS & Richard, I thought they were partners—or at least they consorted together professionally. It wasn't until a few days later I found out I was mistaken. Yes, I did not ask Richard to do the main house until some time later—perhaps you are right, 4 years later. I know I did discuss it with him. At that time, so alike did I appraise these 2 men that my sense of fairness allotted to each of them a parallel amount of expenditure, even tho RMS portion was executed first, together with the cabin he built in

Wrightwood, and the beach house RMS built—also the ranch house RMS built.

My appreciation of these 2 men was such that I recognized both of them as not only unusual but very potential geniuses. But my intention was economic in the allotment of work for each—I intended to spend the same amount for both. When all accounts were settled, Richard spent more than twice as much for his one house than RMS for the 3. Of course you know what happened to 2 of RMS buildings—one was set on fire accidentally by a German refugee kid I had there who decided to go swimming while he filled a gasoline can. The other, in Wrightwood, built of a new material at that time, Celotex—came the winter storms, a good snowfall, and on the next visit to Wrightwood, the Celotex walls were swollen to twice their normal size, the flat roof had collapsed and the underpinning had also collapsed—and there was no choice. Its cost wasn't very much—less than $8,000—the ranch house was somewhat higher—but it too went down the drain via the fire route—and that left only 2 buildings by these 2 geniuses—the beach and Dundee.

That was as far as I can recall—both men were of the highest character, both geniuses and innovators for instance your father was an innovator—he told me that Dundee was the first building in which steel framework was used for a resistance, and thus he made a special and excellent deal with Truscon Steel associated with Bethlehem steel—and was thus an innovator insofar as this was also the first building having a steel framework west of the Mississippi. He was either the first or nearly so with a number of other ideas such as the first to use 8 to 10 ft. vitrolite glass panels for entire bathrooms, the first to use ultra violet glass as glazing, the first to design a swimming pool which did not require chlorine, which to me is deadly poison, so that each poolful of water was used for irrigation, and no one bathing therein ever emerged with pink eye, etc.

Both men were geniuses—and so was Wright—except that I could not and would not get along with Wright in those days—he met Leah several times and tried to get my work—but I told him I was quite satisfied with Neutra and Schindler—it was she who introduced him to Aline Barnsdall [sic]—at that time she was conducting a school.

Anyhow, if you are going to write his biography, know this—Richard Neutra was unquestionably a genius, at that time very little recognized—both of them men of the highest technical and character quality—for instance I never paid the subcontractors myself—I would give Richard a check for 8 to 10 thousand dollars to pay each current contractor, and he thus handled all the finances. With both I told them my views —I wanted something than the customary house, usually a relic of the house they had in Peoria—I wanted something distinctly Californian—I wanted open spaces, maximum light, maximum sun, as near earthquake[-proof] as possible, outdoor sleeping, facilities for nude sunbathing, etc. etc. And both of these men were the only ones I trusted to fulfill these ideas. In short these men were geniuses of their time who had to wait for recognition long after they had created their works—both of the highest integrity and creative imagination, and with both of them, I hope I have earned their respect and friendship thruout the years. And now as I approach my 77th birthday, my memory of these men is warm and responsive.

Good luck Dion, and Dione—one of these days do drop in Dione—with your cello—

Best wishes,
Philip.

These letters are in the possession of Dione Neutra. Philip Lovell gave me his permission to publish them when I talked with him in Newport Beach, February 16, 1973.

Appendix B
The Buildings of Richard Neutra

This list is compiled from a number of sources, though it is based primarily on the records of the Neutra office. Particularly in regard to dates, the office records have sometimes been in error as have numerous published sources over the years that were based upon those records. Corrections of such errors have come chiefly from correspondence or conversations with Neutra clients. As a last resort, or when in doubt, however, I used the Neutra office data. Still, compilations such as this are highly vulnerable undertakings, and persons able to make additional corrections are urged to contact the author, care of the Department of History or School of Architecture, University of California, Los Angeles.

Addresses have been taken from the list published and circulated by the Neutra office. Their publication should *not* be taken by the reader as an invitation to trespass beyond the public street in attempts to view the buildings. While commercial and public buildings may be visited during office hours, no attempt should be made to visit private dwellings without first obtaining permission from the owners.

An overwhelming majority of occupants of Neutra buildings responded warmly to my inquiries and to my request to visit them. Only a few failed to answer my letter.

Following is a chronological list based upon the date that work on each building was substantially completed. It differs frequently, sometimes by several years, from the date of the design conception as often given by the Neutra office. Through the years, Neutra's various offices collaborated with other firms, particularly for supervision of projects outside Los Angeles. Those firms are not listed here unless there is evidence that they had a significant part in the design process. This list, furthermore, does not attempt to include the frequently elusive contributions of associates within the Neutra office who worked on particular jobs, though an attempt to assess their general input is made throughout the text. The letters "N & A" appear by commissions from the Neutra and Alexander office in the 1950s and early 1960s. The name of Neutra's other (Silverlake) office changed in the early 1950s from Richard Neutra, Architect, to Richard Neutra and Associates and in the late 1960s to Richard and Dion Neutra. These changes are discussed in the text, but except for the separate N & A designation, no distinctions are made here among those several variations.

Finally, only built commissions are listed here. Such important unbuilt projects as Rush City Reformed (late 1920s), the League of Nations building (1926), and Elysian Park Heights/Chavez Ravine (early 1950s) are discussed in the text.

1915

Officers' Tea House
Trebinje, Serbia
(demolished)

1922

Public Housing Project
Luckenwalde, Germany (DDR)
(address and condition unknown)

Berliner Tageblatt Building addition (with Eric Mendelsohn)
Jerusalemerstrasse, Berlin, Germany (DDR)

Forest Cemetery Gatehouse and Related Buildings
Luckenwalde, Germany (DDR)
(greatly altered)

1923

Zehlendorf Houses (with Eric Mendelsohn)
Onkel-Tom-Strass 91
Zehlendorf, Berlin, Germany

1925

Pergola and Wading Pool, Hollyhock House (with Rudolph Schindler)

Hollywood Boulevard and Vermont Avenue
Los Angeles, California

1927

Jardinette Apartments
5128 West Marathon Street
Los Angeles, California

Lovell Physical Culture Center
154 West 12th Street
Los Angeles, California

1929

Lovell (Health) House
4616 Dundee Lane
Los Angeles, California

1932

Van der Leeuw Research House
2300 Silver Lake Boulevard
Los Angeles, California

Exhibition House
Austrian Werkbund
between Veitengengasse and
Jagdschlosegasse, Lainz,
Vienna, Austria

1933

Koblick House
98 Fairview Avenue
at Camino al Lago
Atherton, California
(greatly altered)

Mosk House
2742 Hollyridge Drive
Los Angeles, California
(altered)

Laemmle/Universal-International
Building
Hollywood Boulevard and
Vine Street
Los Angeles, California
(altered beyond recognition)

1934

Beard House
1981 Meadowbrook Lane
Altadena, California

Rajagopals House—addition and
remodeling
2126 North Gower

Los Angeles, California

Scheyer House
1880 Blue Heights Drive
Los Angeles, California
(altered)

Sten/Frenke House
126 Mabery Road
Santa Monica, California

Comet Orange Shop
709 South Broadway
Los Angeles, California
(altered beyond recognition)

1935

Largent House
Burnett and Hopkins Streets
San Francisco, California

Von Sternberg House
10000 Tampa Avenue
Northridge, California
(demolished)

California Military Academy
5300 Angeles Vista Drive
Los Angeles, California
(altered)

Corona Avenue School
3825 Bell Avenue at Bear Street
Los Angeles, California

1936

Kun House #1
7960 Fareholm Drive
Los Angeles, California

Plywood Model House
427 Beloit Avenue
Los Angeles, California

Richter House
1820 Kenneth Way
Pasadena, California
(demolished)

Ruben House—addition and
remodeling
50 Haldeman Road
Los Angeles, California

1937

Barsha House
4859 Westpark Drive
Los Angeles, California

moved to:
Channel Road and Mesa Road
Santa Monica Canyon,
Los Angeles, California

Darling House
90 Woodland Avenue
San Francisco, California

Davis House
2914 West 21st Street
Bakersfield, California

Ford House—addition and
remodeling
2430 Leavenworth Street
San Francisco, California

Hofmann House
1408 La Cuesta Road
Hillsborough, California

Kaufman House
234 Hilgard Avenue
Los Angeles, California

Koblick House
1818 Silverwood Terrace
Los Angeles, California

Kraigher House #1
Brownsville, Texas

Malcolmson House
491 Mesa Road
Los Angeles, California

Miller House
2311 North Indian Avenue
Palm Springs, California

Landfair Apartments
Ophir Drive and Landfair Avenue
Los Angeles, California

Strathmore Apartments
11005 Strathmore Drive
Los Angeles, California

Catalina Ticket Office
542 West 6th Street
Los Angeles, California

Emerson Junior High School
1650 Selby Avenue
Los Angeles, California

Leighton Cocktail Bar
449 South Hill Street
Los Angeles, California

Scholts Advertising Building
1201 West 4th Street
Los Angeles, California

1938

Brown House
Fishers Island
New York
(destroyed by fire)

Lewin House
512 Ocean Front
Santa Monica, California

Schiff Apartment Duplex
2056-2058 Jefferson Street
San Francisco, California

1939

Davey House
Los Ranchitos de Aguajitos
Monterey, California

Eurich House
13081 West Sunset Drive
Los Altos Heights, California

Gill House
542 Suncourt Terrace
Glendale, California

Johnson/Stafford Houses
180-184 Marvin Avenue
Los Altos, California

McIntosh House
1317 Maltman Avenue
Los Angeles, California

Sciobereti House
35 Alamo Avenue
Berkeley, California

Ward-Berger House
3156 Lake Hollywood Drive
Los Angeles, California

National Youth Centers
Sacramento and San Luis
Obispo, California
(demolished)

1940

Beckstrand House
1400 Via Monte Mar
Palos Verdes, California

De Graaf House

1900 Palatine Road
Portland, Oregon

Hauswirth House
11 El Portal Court
Berkeley, California

Kahn House
66 Calhoun Terrace
San Francisco, California

Sweet House
541 Suncourt Terrace
Glendale, California

Evans Plywood Building
Lebanon, Oregon

N.Y.A. Rose Parade Float
Pasadena, California
(demolished)

1941

Bald House
McAndrew Road
Ojai, California

Maxwell House
475 Bowling Green Way
Los Angeles, California

Avion Village Housing Project
(with David Williams and
Roscoe DeWitt)
Grand Prairie, Texas

1942

Bonnet House
2256 El Contento Drive
Los Angeles, California

Branch House
7716 Firenze Avenue
Los Angeles, California
(altered beyond recognition)

Nesbitt House
414 Avondale Avenue
Los Angeles, California

Rethy House
2101 Santa Anita Road
Sierra Madre, California

Van Cleef House
651 Warner Avenue
Los Angeles, California

Channel Heights Housing

Western Avenue and 25th Street
San Pedro, California

Hacienda Village Housing
(with Paul Williams, Wurdeman
and Becket, et al.)
East 1036 Street and
Compton Avenue
Los Angeles, California

Kelton Apartments
646-648 Kelton Avenue
Los Angeles, California

Progressive Builders Homes
6306-6339 Denny Avenue
Burbank, California

Pueblo Del Rio Housing
(with Gordon Kaufman, Paul
Williams, Wurdeman and Becket,
and Ralph Cornell)
53rd Street and Holmes Avenue
Los Angeles, California

1944

Prototype Schools and Health
Centers
Puerto Rico

1945

Margolis Stores
Palm Canyon Drive
Palm Springs, California
(demolished)

Norman Clinic
6th Street and Grand Avenue
San Pedro, California
(altered beyond recognition)

1946

Kaufmann Desert House
470 West Vista de Chino
Palm Springs, California
(altered)

Ayeroff Brothers Appliance Store
1066 South La Cienga Boulevard
Los Angeles, California
(altered)

Bekey Factory
752 Gladys Avenue
Los Angeles, California
(altered)

Hughes Auto Showroom
Vineland and Kling
Los Angeles, California

Bailey Case Study House
219 Chautaugua Boulevard
Los Angeles, California
(with later Neutra additions)

1947

Brown House
1861 Heather Court
Los Angeles, California

Schmidt House
1460 Chamberlain Road
Pasadena. California
(altered)

Norwalk Garage
2926 West 21st Street
Bakersfield, California
(altered)

1948

Atwell House
7500 Fairmount
El Cerrito, California

Goodson House
8310 Grandview
Los Angeles, California
(destroyed by fire)

Sokol House
2242 Silver Lake Boulevard
Los Angeles, California

Tremaine House
1636 Moore Road
Montecito, California

Treweek House
2250 Silver Lake Boulevard
Los Angeles, California

Tuta House
1800 Via Vidalia
Palos Verdes, California

Elkay Apartments
638 Kelton Avenue
Los Angeles, California

Aloe Health Equipment and
Supply Building
11th and Flower Streets
Los Angeles, California
(altered)

Holiday House
27400 Pacific Coast Highway
Malibu, California
(greatly altered)

1949

Chase House
4254 Cresta Avenue
Hope Ranch, Santa Barbara
California

Freedman House
315 Via De La Paz
Los Angeles, California

Hines House
760 Via Somonte
Palos Verdes, California

Greenberg House
10525 Garwood Place
Los Angeles, California

Reunion House
2440 Earl Street
Los Angeles, California
(altered)

Rourke House
9228 Hazen Drive
Beverly Hills, California

Sanders House
Via Somonte and Via Del Monte
Palos Verdes, California
(altered)

Wilkins House
528 Hermosa
South Pasadena, California
(altered)

Mill Creek Summit Maintenance
Yard
Mill Creek, California

1950

Beckstrand Lodge
Drycreek Ranch
Meadow, Utah

Hees House
250 Trino Way
Los Angeles, California
(altered beyond recognition)

Kun House #2
7947 Fareholm Drive
Los Angeles, California

Miller House
6400 Drexel Avenue
Los Angeles, California

O'Brien House
4740 Richmond Avenue
Shreveport, Louisiana

Wirin House
2622 Glendower Avenue
Los Angeles, California

Coe House
Via Lomita
Rolling Hills, Palos Verdes,
California

Glendale Office Building
2379 Glendale Boulevard
Los Angeles, California

Northwestern Mutual Fire
Association Building
621 South Westmoreland Avenue
Los Angeles, California

Swim Stadium, Orange Coast
College (N&A)
2701 Fairview Road
Costa Mesa, California

1951

Brod House
Oakwood and Sycamore
Arcadia, California

Everist House
200 West 45th Street
Sioux City, Iowa

Fischer House
1618 Pinecrest Road
Spokane, Washington

Goldman House
3970 Archdale Road
Encino, California

Heryford House
3444 Bonnie Hill Drive
Los Angeles, California

Hinds House
3940 San Raphael Avenue
Los Angeles, California

Hunter House
2311 Bancroft Avenue
Los Angeles, California

Logar House
17728 Ridgeway Road
Granada Hills, California

Meltzer House
1508 Murray Drive
Los Angeles, California

Mosby House
3 Artamos Drive
Missoula, Montana

Nelson House
511 Miner Road
Orinda, California

Price House
255 South Gillette Avenue
Bayport, Long Island, New York

Kester Avenue Elementary School
5353 Kester Avenue
Los Angeles, California

1952

Auerbacher House #1
Pleasant Drive and Frontier Drive
Luring Pines, California

Goodman House
4227 Golden Avenue
San Bernardino, California

Heller House
811 Camden Drive
Beverly Hills, California
(demolished)

McElwain House
6323 Lindley Avenue
Reseda, California
(greatly altered)

Marshall House
Rancho Santa Fe, California

Matlock House
1560 Ramillo Avenue
Long Beach, California

Miller House
941 Arlington Avenue
El Cerito, California

Moore House
512 North Foothill Road
Ojai, California

Van Sicklin House
Rancho Santa Fe, California

Adelup School (N&A)
Adelup Point, Guam

Football Stadium addition,
Orange Coast College (N&A)
2701 Fairview Road
Costa Mesa, California

Umatac School (N&A)
Umatac, Guam

1953

Auerbacher House #2
121 Sierra Vista Drive
Redlands, California

Elliott House
7125 Conelly Boulevard
Bedford, Ohio

Governor's House (N&A)
Agana, Guam

Hafley-Moore Twin Houses
5551, 5561 La Posada
Long Beach, California

Hall House
900 Bay Avenue at 9th Street
Newport Beach, California

Kesler House
1367 Monument Street
Los Angeles, California

Kramer House
108 West 8th Street
Norco, California

Moore House
2507 Valley Drive
Manhattan Beach, California

Schaarman House
7850 Torreyson Drive
Los Angeles, California

Beckstrand Medical Building
1090 Atlantic Avenue
Long Beach, California

Business Education Building,
Orange Coast College (N&A)
2701 Fairview Road
Costa Mesa, California

National Charity League
Administration Building
(N&A)
5000 Hollywood Boulevard

Los Angeles, California

San Bernardino Medical Center
1700 Waterman Avenue
San Bernardino, California

Speech Arts Building,
Orange Coast College (N&A)
2701 Fairview Road
Costa Mesa, California

1954

Hammerman House
(address withheld at request of
owner)
Los Angeles, California

Weston House
3220 Durand Drive
Los Angeles, California

Eagle Rock Park Clubhouse
1100 Eagle Vista Drive
Los Angeles, California

San Pedro Hacienda (N&A)
First Street and Miraleste Avenue
San Pedro, California
(demolished)

1955

Brown House
10801 Chalon Road
Los Angeles, California

Cohen House
8805 Cheltenham Avenue
Springfield Township,
Pennsylvania

Corwin House
Huckleberry Lane
Weston, Connecticut

Hansch House
4070 Olive Knoll
Claremont, California

Kronish House
9439 Sunset Boulevard
Beverly Hills, California

Perkins House
1540 Poppy Peak Drive
Pasadena, California

Roberts House
539 South Grand Avenue
Covina, California

Serulnic House
3947 Markridge Road
Tujunga, California

Staller House
901 Bel Air Road
Los Angeles, California

Weihe House
25 Sweet Bay Road,
Portuguese Bend
Palos Verdes, California

Gemological Institute of America
11940 San Vincente Boulevard
Los Angeles, California

Logar Store (N&A)
Chatsworth and White Oaks
Streets
Granada Hills, California

Mountain Home Air Force Base
Housing (N&A)
Mountain Home, Idaho

National Charity League (N&A)
Observation Nursery School
5000 Hollywood Boulevard
Los Angeles, California

Science Building, Orange
Coast College (N&A)
2701 Fairview Road
Costa Mesa, California

1956

Adler House
1438 North Kenter Avenue
Los Angeles, California
(greatly altered)

Artega House
12960 Gladstone
San Fernando, California

Chuey House
2460 Sunset Plaza Drive
Los Angeles, California

Cohen House
27360 Pacific Coast Highway
Malibu, California

DeShulthess House
15012 Avenida Quijano
Havana, Cuba

Kilbury House

920 Via Nogales
Palos Verdes, California

Livingston House
1718 Minnekada Road
Chattanooga, Tennessee

Miller House
109 South Whitehall Road
Norristown, Pennsylvania

Schwind House
1430 Carlton Road
Hillsborough, California

Slavin House
1322 Dover Road
Santa Barbara, California

Troxwell House
766 Paseo Miramar
Los Angeles, California

Amalgamated Clothing Workers
of America Office Building
(N&A)
2501 South Hill Street
Los Angeles, California

1957

Clark House
1780 Devon Road
Pasadena, California

Flavin House
2218 Argent Place
Los Angeles, California

Gillen House
7 Quail Canyon Road
San Bernardino, California

Nash House
35 Marine View Drive
Camarillo, California

Sorrells House
Shoshone, California

Wise House
1371 Paseo Del Mar
San Pedro, California

Yew House
2226 Silver Lake Boulevard
Los Angeles, California

Alamitos Intermediate School
(N&A)

Dale and Lampson Streets
Garden Grove, California

Alamitos Lawrence School
12521 Monroe
Garden Grove, California

Dayton Planetarium and
Museum of Natural History
(N&A)
2629 Ridge Avenue
Dayton, Ohio

Ferro Chemical Company (N&A)
450 Krick Road
Bedford, Ohio

Library addition, Orange
Coast College (N&A)
2701 Fairview Road
Costa Mesa, California

Miramar Chapel (N&A)
U.S. Naval Air Station
Miramar, California

UCLA Kindergarten and
Elementary School
(N&A)
10636 Sunset Boulevard
Los Angeles, California

1958

Cole House
1362 Kashlan Road
La Habra, California
(greatly altered)

Connell House
Pebble Beach, Carmel, California

Friedland House
1020 North Lane
Gladwyn, Pennsylvania

Hailey House
3319 Tareco Drive
Los Angeles, California

Hasserick House
3033 School House Lane
Philadelphia, Pennsylvania
(altered)

Huebsch House
320 de la Fuente
Monterey Park, California

Hughes House

1560 Oriole Lane
Los Angeles, California

Kaufman House addition
3574 Multiview Drive
Los Angeles, California

Kraigher House, #2
Bethlehem Road
Litchfield, Connecticut

Leddy House
2501 Dracena Street
Bakersfield, California

Oxley House
9302 Farris Road
La Jolla, California

Rados House
2209 West Daladier Drive
San Pedro, California

Art and Science Building,
St. John's College (N&A)
Annapolis, Maryland

Claremont Methodist Church
(N&A)
1616 North Hills Avenue
Claremont, California

Riviera Methodist Church
(N&A)
375 Palos Verdes Drive
Torrance, California
(greatly altered)

1959

Dailey House
953 Granvia Alta Mira
Palos Verdes, California

Larsen House
5435 Jed Smith Road
Calabasas, California

Lew House
1460 Sunset Plaza Drive
Los Angeles, California

Loring House
2456 Astral Drive
Los Angeles, California

McSorley House
1248 La Peresa Drive
Thousand Oaks, California

Ninneman House
4218 Via Padova
Claremont, California

Oyler House
771 Thundercloud Lane
Lone Pine, California

Pariser House
Union and Judith Streets
Uniontown, Pennsylvania

Singleton House
15000 Mulholland Drive
Los Angeles, California

Warner House
22 Summit Drive
Chesterton, Indiana

Crescent Professional Building
8105 Third Street
Los Angeles, California

Fine Arts Building (N&A)
California State University
18111 Nordhoff Boulevard
Northridge, California

United States Embassy
(N&A)
Brunton Road and Victoria Road
Karachi, West Pakistan

1960

Bell House
222 East Constance
Santa Barbara, California

Bizzari House
6070 Kenridge Drive
Cincinnati, Ohio

Bond House
4499 Yerba Santa Drive
San Diego, California

Coveney House
301 Hughes Road
King of Prussia, Pennsylvania
(altered)

Glen House
130 Brookhollow Lane
Stamford, Connecticut

Inadomi House
2238 Silverlake Boulevard
Los Angeles, California

Kambara House
2232 Silverlake Boulevard
Los Angeles, California

Pickering House
225 Via Genova, Lido Isle
Newport Beach, California

Quant House
13 Castle Rock Road
Apple Valley, California

Sale House
1531 Tigertail Road
Los Angeles, California

Bewobau Housing
Quickborn and Waldorf, Germany

1961

Cytron House
2249 Benedict Canyon Drive
Beverly Hills, California

Field House
4341 Lanai
Encino, California
(altered beyond recognition)

Levit House
1705 Summitridge Drive
Beverly Hills, California

Linn House
7820 Mulholland Drive
Los Angeles, California

List House
679 Manhattan Road, S.E.
Grand Rapids, Michigan

Oberholtzer House
27274 Eastvale Road
Rolling Hills
Palos Verdes, California

Ohara House
2210 Argent Place
Los Angeles, California

Rang House
Hardtbergweg 15
Koenigstein/Taunus, Germany

Tuia House
Strada del Roccolo 11
Ascona, Switzerland

Arts Center, University of Nevada

(N&A)
Reno, Nevada

Buena Park Swim Stadium and
Recreation Center
7225 El Dorado Drive
Buena Park, California

Lemoore Naval Air Base Housing
(N&A)
Lemoore, California

Lincoln Memorial Museum
(N&A)
Gettysburg National Park
Gettysburg, Pennsylvania

Painted Desert and Petrified
Forest Visitors Center
(N&A)
Painted Desert, Arizona

Palos Verdes High School
(N&A)
600 Cloyden Drive
Palos Verdes, California

Richard J. Neutra School
(N&A)
Lemoore Naval Air Base
Lemoore, California

Santa Ana Police Facilities
(N&A)
Civic Center Plaza
Santa Ana, California

Simpson College Library
(N&A)
Indianola, Iowa

United Auto Workers Building
(N&A)
8503 Rosemead Avenue
Pico-Rivera, California

1962

Akai House
2200 Argent Place
Los Angeles, California

Erman House
16535 Oldham Street
Encino, California

Goldman House
3417 Southern Hills Drive
Des Moines, Iowa

Gonzales-Gorrondona House
Avenida de la Linea 65
Caracas, Venezuela

Hendershot House
2866 Westbrook Avenue
Los Angeles, California

Hrabe House
5851 Clear Valley
Calabasas, California

Maslon House
70-900 Fairway Drive
Cathedral City, California

Pitcairn House
2860 Papermill Road
Bryn Athyn, Pennsylvania

Stone-Fischer Houses
3631, 3831 Oakfield Drive
Los Angeles, California

Garden Grove Community Church
12141 Lewis Street
Garden Grove, California
(altered)

Los Angeles County Hall of
Records (N&A)
320 West Temple Street
Los Angeles, California

1963

Child Guidance Clinic, University
of Southern California (N&A)
746 West Adams Boulevard
Los Angeles, California

Mariners Medical Arts Center
1901 Westcliff Drive
Newport Beach, California

Mymensingh Agricultural
University
Bangladesh (East Pakistan)

Swirbul Library,
Adelphi University
Garden City, Long Island
New York

1964

Kuhns House
4359 Camello Road
Woodland Hills, California

Rentsch House
Wenger, Switzerland

Taylor House
3816 Lackerbie Court
Glendale, California

Poster Apartments
6847 Radford Avenue
Los Angeles, California

1965

Rice House
1000 Old Cork Lane
Loch Island
Richmond, Virginia

Van der Leeuw Research House
#2
2300 Silverlake Boulevard
Los Angeles, California

Congregational Church
Los Altos and Hacienda Boulevard
Hacienda Heights, California
(altered)

Reno Convention Hall
Reno, Nevada

Roberson Memorial Center
30 Front Street
Binghampton, New York

St. Andrew Methodist Church
3945 Bradley Road
Santa Maria, California
(altered)

1966

Bucerius House
Navegna, Switzerland

Virzintas House—remodeling
4338½ Laurel Canyon Road
Studio City, California

Von Huene Cabin
Joaquins Road
Mammoth, California

La Veta Medical Square
100 West La Veta Avenue
Orange, California

Tower of Hope
Garden Grove Community Church
12141 Lewis Street
Garden Grove, California

1967

Kemper House
Dornerweg 100
Wuppertal, Germany

Muffer Cabin
Mono Street
Mammoth, California

Shinoda House
1124 Camino del Rio
Santa Barbara, California

1968

Brown House
3005 Audubon Terrace, N.W.
Washington, D.C.

Orange County Courthouse,
Civic Center Plaza
6th and Main Streets
Santa Ana, California

Pescher House
Am Freudenberg 75
Wuppertal/Hahnenberg, Germany

Stern House
621 North Camden Drive
Beverly Hills, California

1969

Delcourt House
Avenue General de Gaulle
Croix, France

Graduate Student Housing,
University of Pennsylvania
(with Bellante and Clauss)
Philadelphia, Pennsylvania

Notes

Introduction: Neutra and Modernism

1. Jose Ortega y Gasset, *The Dehumanization of Art* (Princeton: Princeton University Press, 1968), pp. 12–13, 54; André Malraux, "Museum Without Walls," in *The Voices of Silence* (Princeton: Princeton University Press, 1978), pp. 100, 119.
2. Quoted in Robert Adams, "What Was Modernism?, 1977 Faculty Research Lecture at the University of California, Los Angeles. I am grateful to Professor Adams, first for the brilliant lecture and second for providing me with a copy of it.
3. Ibid.
4. Ibid.
5. For the etymology of the term "modern" see the *Oxford English Dictionary*.
6. Robert Venturi, *Complexity and Contradiction in Architecture* (New York: Museum of Modern Art, 1966), p. 22.
7. Robert Venturi, Denise Scott-Brown, Steven Izenour, et al., *Learning From Las Vegas* (Cambridge: M.I.T. Press, 1972), pp. x, xi.

Genesis 1892–1914

1. Graf quoted in William Johnston, *The Austrian Mind: An Intellectual and Social History, 1848–1938* (Berkeley and Los Angeles: University of California Press, 1972), p. 31; Schnitzler quoted in Adolf Opel, "Introduction: The Legacies of Dissolution," in Nicolas Powell, *The Second Spring: The Arts in Vienna, 1898–1918* (Greenwich, Conn: New York Graphic Society, 1974), p. 19; Kraus quoted in Erwin Mitsch, *The Art of Egon Schiele* (London: Phaidon, 1975), p. 18.
2. Zuckerkandl quoted in Opel, "Legacies of Dissolution," p. 29.
3. Walter Jaksch to author, February 17, 1979; Josephine Neutra Weixlgärtner to author, November 17, 1978; Weixlgärtner to Dione Neutra, September 29, 1975, Dione Neutra Papers, copy in possession of author; Richard Neutra, *Life and Shape* (New York: Appleton-Century-Crofts, 1962), pp. 42–43.
4. Weixlgärtner to author, November 17, 1978; Richard Neutra, Diary, n.d. (1917?), book 5, p. 7, Neutra Archive, Special Collections, University Research Library, University of California, Los Angeles.
5. Neutra to Dione Neutra, n.d.; Neutra to Lily Niedermann, n.d., Dione Neutra Papers, copies in possession of author.
6. Weixlgärtner to Dione Neutra, May 29, 1975; Weixlgärtner to author, November 17, 1978; Richard Neutra, Diary, n.d. (1917?), book 5, pp. 7–11.
7. Weixlgärtner to author, November 17, 1978; Neutra, *Life and Shape*, p. 49.
8. Neutra, *Life and Shape*, p. 34.
9. Neutra, "Data on RJN's Early Life," unpublished early draft for "Early Influences" chapter in *Life and Shape*, typescript in possession of the author; Neutra, *Life and Shape*, pp. 36–41.
10. Ibid.
11. Ibid.
12. Ibid.; Weixlgärtner to author, November 17, 1978.
13. Weixlgärtner to author, November 17, 1978; Jaksch to author, February 17, 1979; Neutra, *Life and Shape*, pp. 54–55, 82–87.
14. Official transcript, Richard Neutra, Sophiengymnasium, Vienna.
15. Neutra, *Life and Shape*, pp. 43–44, 54; Conversation with Dione Neutra, March 8, 1979.
16. Neutra, Diary, 1910–13, passim. Mentions and lists of titles of books Neutra read are scattered throughout his diary, chiefly between the years 1910–13, books 1–3. Extended commentaries on reading and related matters are specifically cited below.
17. Ibid.

18. Neutra, Diary, December 27, 1910, book 1, p. 20; January 2, 1913, book 2, p. 29.

19. Ibid., March 18, 1913, book 2, p. 46.

20. Ibid., passim, 1910–13, books 1–3.

21. Ibid., April 1, 1912, book 1, p. 98; December 5, 1910, book 1, pp. 6–7; February 5, 1912, book 1, p. 88.

22. Ibid., September 22–23, 1910, book 1, pp. 4–5; Stefan Zweig, *The World of Yesterday: An Autobiography* (Lincoln: University of Nebraska Press, 1964), p. 42; Johnston, *Austrian Mind*, pp. 125–26.

23. Johnston, *Austrian Mind*, p. 116.

24. Neutra, *Life and Shape*, pp. 46–58.

25. Ibid.; Weixlgärtner to author, November 17, 1978.

26. Neutra, Diary, passim, but especially November 10, 1912, book 2, p. 27; January 27, 1913, book 2, pp. 29–31; February 4, 1913, book 2, p. 4.

27. Neutra, Diary, June 3, 1917, book 5, pp. 13–14; The visit with Klimt occurred while Neutra was on leave from the army completing his degree at the Technische Hochschule.

28. Ibid., February 16, 1918, book 5, p. 126; Weixlgärtner to author, November 17, 1978.

29. Neutra, "Data on RJN's Early Life."

30. Neutra, Diary, March 31, 1913, book 2, pp. 48–51.

31. Neutra, *Life and Shape*, p. 76; Neutra, Diary, September 22, 1910, book 1, p. 3.

32. Neutra, "Biographical Notes," early unpublished draft for "Early Influences" chapter in *Life and Shape*, typescript in possession of author; Neutra, Diary, September 17, 1912, book 1, p. 134.

33. Neutra, Diary, October 3, 1912, book 4, pp. 7, 13, 17–18, 21.

34. Ibid., October 3, 1910, book 1, pp. 10–11.

35. Ibid., September 11, 1911, book 1, pp. 67–68; April 15, 1912, book 1, pp. 114–17; April 23, 1914, book 2, pp. 135–36.

36. Ibid., August 24, 1913, book 2, pp. 75–81.

37. Neutra, *Life and Shape*, p. 80; Dione Neutra, conversation with author, February 20, 1972, Los Angeles.

38. Neutra, Diary, October 4, 1911, book 1, pp. 72–76.

39. Neutra to Dione Neutra, n.d. (1921?), Dione Neutra Papers, copy in possession of author.

40. Neutra, Diary, March 2–3, 1911, book 1, pp. 34–39.

41. Ibid., April 8, 1911, book 1, pp. 44–45.

42. Ibid., February 4, 1911, book 1, pp. 25–31.

43. Ibid.

44. Ibid.

45. Ibid., September 26, 1910, book 1, pp. 6–7.

46. Neutra. *Life and Shape*, p. 66.

47. Heinz Geretsegger and Max Peintner, *Otto Wagner, 1848–1918* (New York: Praeger, 1970), pp. 9–18; Leonardo Benevolo, *History of Modern Architecture*, 2 vols. (Cambridge: MIT Press, 1971), 1:284–89; Robert L. Delevoy, "Otto Wagner," *Encyclopedia of Modern Architecture* (New York: Abrams, 1964), pp. 319–20. I am also indebted to Barbara Geilla, who allowed me to read a draft of the first chapter of her doctoral dissertation on Rudolph Schindler, which dealt in part with Wagner.

48. Ibid.

49. Geretsegger and Peinter, *Otto Wagner*, pp. 147–72.

50. Ibid.; Neutra, Diary, September 13, 1913, book 3, pp. 21–23.

51. Neutra to Robert Judson Clark, December 30, 1964, copy in possession of author.

52. Richard Neutra, official transcript, Technical Institute of Vienna (Technische Hochschule); the record of Neutra's attendance, professors, and examinations was summarized in a letter of February 2, 1979, to Walter Jaksch from Alfred Lechner, a staff member at the Technical University, as the Technische Hochschule was renamed. Copy in possession of author.

53. Ibid.

54. Ibid.; Neutra, *Life and Shape*, pp. 79–80; Neutra, Diary, June 8, 1912, book 1, p. 125; November 5, 1913, book 2, p. 93.

55. Ludwig Münz and Gustav Künstler, *Adolf Loos: Pioneer of Modern Architecture* (New York: Praeger, 1966), pp. 25–27; Benevolo, *History of Modern Architecture* 1:298–306; Robert L. Delevoy, "Adolf Loos," *Encyclopedia of Modern Architecture*, pp. 177–78.

56. Nikolaus Pevsner, "Introduction," in Münz and Künstler, *Adolf Loos*, p. 18.

57. Ibid.; Neutra, "What Attracted Me to the U.S. and How Did I Get There?", unpublished early draft for Loos section of *Life and Shape*, typescript in possession of author.

58. Neutra, Diary, October (n.d.), 1912, book 2, p. 162; November 10, 1912, book 2, pp. 23–25; (n.d.) 1914, book 3, pp. 60–84.

59. Ibid.; Neutra, review of *Adolf Loos* by Münz and Künstler, *Architectural Forum*, July–August 1966, pp. 88–89, 116.

60. Ibid.

61. Neutra, Diary, June 23, 1914, book 2, p. 143; Neutra to Schindler, June 14, 1914, in Esther McCoy, *Vienna to Los Angeles: Two Journeys* (Santa Monica, Calif.: Arts and Architecture

Press, 1979), p. 109. Neutra's sketches of Wright buildings occur on undated Diary pages, 1914, book 3, pp. 93–100.

62. Neutra, *Life and Shape*, pp. 171–73.

63. Neutra, Diary, January 5, 1914, book 2, p. 132.

Trial, 1914–1923

1. Neutra, *Life and Shape*, pp. 97–126.

2. Neutra, Diary, February 7, 1916, book 4, pp. 49–50; Neutra, *Life and Shape*, pp. 126–27.

3. Neutra, Diary, November 30, 1916, book 2, pp. 143–49. For unexplained reasons, this record of the emperor's funeral appears in Neutra's diary out of chronological context; it follows a notation for June 23, 1914.

4. Ibid., January 17, 1917, book 2, pp. 155–59.

5. Neutra, *Life and Shape*, pp. 128–31; Neutra to Lilly Niedermann, January 1, 1920, Dione Neutra Papers; Neutra, Diary, April 6, 1919, book 7, pp. 2–5.

6. Neutra, *Life and Shape*, pp. 132–42; Lawrence Weschler, interview with Dione Neutra, Los Angeles, April 10, 1978, Oral History Program, UCLA; Thomas S. Hines, interview with Regula Niedermann Fybel, May 16, 1974, Los Angeles.

7. Ibid.

8. Ibid.

9. Neutra, Diary, October 6, 26, 1919, book 8, pp. 26–27; 44–45.

10. Neutra, Diary, September 20, 1919, book 8, p. 15; Neutra to Rudolph Schindler, November 10 and 17, 1919, in McCoy, *Vienna to Los Angeles*, pp. 113–15; Neutra to Dione Neutra, n.d. (1923), Dione Neutra Papers.

    Neutra seemed undeterred by Schindler's criticism of the United States and continued to defend the Americans, whom he saw, from a distance, as being essentially idealistic. During the war, for example, Neutra had received a letter from Schindler dated February 9, 1915, stating:

    I am getting along as well in America as I could have expected. The work in the office [Ottenheimer, Stern and Reichert] is tiresome and hopeless, although I acquire a lot of knowledge and use my free time as well as possible.

    My trip to San Francisco, but especially my stay in New Mexico among Indians and cowboys are unforgettable experiences. That part of America is a country one can be fond of, but the civilized part is horrible, starting with the President down to the street-

    sweeper. They all are dilettantes and the greed for money has taken on such dimensions that everybody is already born a cheat. Everything here is to be had for a price. . . .

    Why should such people, who are lazy in their innermost being, possess good architecture? Everything is speculation and imitation. One erects houses and by and by they deteriorate and nobody cares a hoot. They are inhuman from start to finish.

    The stay here has been very beneficial to me personally. My view regarding life has become much clearer and simpler and allows less and less for compromises. Lately I ask myself more and more whether it is not a worthier goal in life to be a vagabond. Earning a living will aways produce pettiness. . . ."

    This letter was discovered by Dione Neutra in her late husband's papers sometime after she gave the bulk of Schindler's letters to Neutra to the Schindler Collection at the University of California, Santa Barbara. It was not included in Mc-Coy's edition of the letters cited above.

11. Neutra to Dione Neutra, n.d. (1923?), Dione Neutra Papers.

12. Neutra wrote to Mütterli that he was happy he "did not come too late. The poor old man was so emaciated when we lowered him into the coffin. . . . He is buried in the same grave with my mother as he wished it. He outlived her for twelve years, without being really able to live without her. When I arrived my father was overjoyed as if he knew the end was near. . . . He was comforted to know what path I hoped to travel. . . . I hope not to be a disgrace to him, who was from beginning to end such a good and diligent man. . . ." Neutra to Lilly Niedermann, March 17, 1920, Dione Neutra Papers.

13. Weschler, interview with Dione Neutra, April 10, 1978; Neutra, *Life and Shape*, pp. 142–46. In a letter to her mother, Dione wrote that it was "a great thrill to hear Eric Korngold. I understand perfectly well all the objections one could voice against him. . . . His exuberance, his wit, which he richly mixes with his pathos, originate from the same source. But he *is* a human being. I am happy to have had a chance not only to hear him but to see him and there was for me a lot to observe. . . . His roaring agitation produces a thin thread of spittle dropping from his wide-open mouth. This is not beautiful, but strangely does not seem abhorrent to the beholder. . . ." She

added that she "fell in love with his voice, which he mistreats so outrageously. Once harsh, puffed up, then strident and overturning into a pitiful falsetto. . . ." Dione Niedermann to Lilly Niedermann, March 20, 1920, Dione Neutra Papers.

14. Weschler, interview with Dione Neutra, April 10, 1978; Neutra to Lilly Niedermann, March, n.d.; April, n.d.; May, n.d.; June, n.d. 1920, Dione Neutra Papers.

15. Neutra to Lilly Niedermann, June. n.d., 1920, Dione Neutra Papers.

16. Weschler, interview with Dione Neutra, April 10, 1978; Dione Niedermann to Neutra, n.d., 1920, Dione Neutra Papers; Neutra, *Life and Shape*, pp. 146–49.

17. Neutra, *Life and Shape*, pp. 149–52; Weschler, interview with Dione Neutra, April 10, 1978; Neutra to Dione Niedermann, two letters, May, n.d., 1920, Dione Neutra Papers.

18. Dione Niedermann to Lilly Niedermann, n.d., 1921; Neutra to Dione Niedermann, October 23, 1921, Dione Neutra Papers; Neutra, *Life and Shape*, pp. 149–52.

19. Arnold Whittick, "Erich Mendelsohn," *Encyclopedia of Modern Architecture*, pp. 183–86; Benevolo, *History of Modern Architecture*, pp. 453–56; Wolf Von Eckardt, *Eric Mendelsohn* (New York: Braziller, 1960), p. 11; Wolfgang Pehnt, *Expressionist Architecture* (New York: Praeger, 1973), pp. 117–26, Arnold Whittick, *Eric Mendelsohn* (London: Leonard Hill, 1956).

20. Neutra to Lilly Niedermann, Fall, n.d., 1921, Dione Neutra Papers.

21. Hermann George Scheffauer, "Dynamic Architecture, New Forms for the Future," *The Dial* 60 (March 1921):323–28; Neutra to Lilly Niedermann, October 16, 1921, Dione Neutra Papers.

22. Von Eckardt, *Eric Mendelsohn*, p. 11; Neutra to Lilly Niedermann, October 16, 1921; November 9, 1921; November, n.d., 1921; Neutra to Dione Niedermann, Fall, n.d., 1921; August 3, 1922; Fall(?), n.d., 1922, Dione Neutra Papers.

23. Neutra to Dione Niedermann, April, n.d., 1922; Dione Neutra Papers. Mendelsohn to Louise Mendelsohn, June 22, 1922, in *Eric Mendelsohn: Letters of an Architect*, ed. Oskar Beyer (London: Abelard-Schuman, 1967), p. 56.

24. Neutra to Frances Toplitz, Fall, n.d., 1922, Dione Neutra Papers.

Over fifty years later, Louise Mendelsohn, widow of the architect, expressed to the author in an interview (Los Angeles, April 30, 1977) and a letter (November 26. 1978) her recollection that *"in no way has* Neutra designed anything for the Mosse building . . . he was 'employed' at E. M.'s office and followed Eric's design, All the details too! He supervised the final building but E. M. is entirely responsible for *any* design details." Certainly attribution of design input from junior employees of an established office is usually difficult, if not impossible, to determine. In Whittick's *Eric Mendelsohn*, Pehnt's *Expressionist Architecture*, and Bruno Zevi's *Eric Mendelsohn: Opera Completta* (Milano: ETAS Kompass, 1970), Neutra is listed as "collaborator." In UCLA's Neutra Archive there exist approximately one hundred sketches, drawings, and design studies for furniture and larger design details of the Mosse project, most of which are almost certainly in Neutra's hand. Neutra apparently took these drawings when he left Mendelsohn's office (along with those of other projects on which he worked) as an important part of his early professional portfolio. They apparently traveled with him to New York, Chicago, and Los Angeles as he sought work in various architectural offices, and were part of the collection of his papers he gave to UCLA. The Mosse drawings at UCLA seem, for the most part, to be skillful and convincing attempts on Neutra's part to draw in the Mendelsohn style, though certain details, especially in the designs for the furniture and cabinetry of Lachmann Mosse's office, suggest influences from Frank Lloyd Wright and an intricacy of detail and layering not usually found in Mendelsohn's bolder, plainer, and more schematic drawings. While the basic and original design(s) therefore must be credited to Mendelsohn, it is reasonable to believe that Neutra, in the course of his long involvement with various aspects of the project, must have made some creative contributions of his own.

25. Neutra, *Life and Shape*, pp. 156–57.

26. Neutra to Lilly Niedermann, n.d., 1922; Neutra to Dione Neutra, January, n.d., 1924; Dione Neutra to Lilly Niedermann, July, n.d., 1923; Neutra to Lilly Niedermann and Dione Neutra, January, n.d., 1923, Dione Neutra Papers.

27. Neutra to Dione Niedermann, September 15, 1921, Dione Neutra Papers. The Demian reference is to Hermann Hesse's novel.

28. Neutra to Dione Niedermann, September, n.d., 1921; July, n.d., 1922, Dione Neutra Papers; Neutra, *Life and Shape*, pp. 155–56.

29. Neutra to Dione Niedermann, October, n.d., 1923; August 3, 1922; Neutra to Lilly Niedermann, n.d.,

1922, Dione Neutra Papers.

30. Weschler, interview with Dione Neutra, April 10, 1978.

31. Neutra to Frances Toplitz, Fall, n.d., 1922; Neutra to Dione Niedermann, November, n.d., 1921, Dione Neutra Papers.

32. Neutra to Lilly Niedermann, n.d., 1922, Dione Neutra Papers.

33. Dione Niedermann to Neutra, December, n.d., 1921, Dione Neutra Papers.

34. Neutra to Dione Niedermann, December, n.d., 1921, Dione Neutra Papers.

35. This matter was discussed in a series of eight undated letters between Richard and Dione, August–September 1922, Dione Neutra Papers.

36. Neutra to Lilly Niedermann, December, n.d., 1922, Dione Neutra Papers. Weschler, interview with Dione Neutra, June 10, 1978.

37. Neutra to Alfred Niedermann, October 5, 1920, Dione Neutra Papers.

38. Neutra to Lilly Niedermann, n.d., 1920, Dione Neutra Papers.

39. Neutra to Lilly Niedermann, n.d., (1921?), Dione Neutra Papers.

40. Neutra to Lilly Niedermann, March, n.d., 1923, Dione Neutra Papers.

41. Harwell Hamilton Harris, "AIA Gold Medal Award to Neutra," *North Carolina Architect*, May–June 1977.

42. Neutra to Frances Toplitz, n.d., 1921; Neutra to Lilly Niedermann, November 5, 1922, Dione Neutra Papers. "Selbskritik," Letter to editor, *The Nation*, CXV (November 15, 1922) :526.

43. This is documented in Neutra and Schindler's exchange of letters between 1919 and 1924, published in McCoy, *Vienna to Los Angeles*, pp. 104–40.

44. Neutra to Pauline Gibling Schindler, October 13, 1920, Dione Neutra Papers. Rudolph Schindler to Neutra, March 12, June 12, August 10, November 19, 1921; Neutra to Schindler, April 25, July 9, 1921, McCoy, *Vienna to Los Angeles*, pp. 131–39.

45. James J. Forrestal to Neutra, December 11, 1920; Neutra to Dione Niedermann, February, n.d., 1921, Dione Neutra Papers.

46. Henry Menkes to Neutra, July 15, 1923, Dione Neutra Papers.

47. Weschler, interview with Dione Neutra, June 10, 1978.

48. Ibid.; Neutra to Lilly Niedermann, August, n.d., September 1, 1923, Dione Neutra Papers.

49. Neutra to Lilly Niedermann, November 9, 1921, Dione Neutra Papers.

50. Neutra to Dione Niedermann, December 12, 1922, Dione Neutra Papers.

Exploration, 1923–1926

1. Neutra to Dione Neutra, October 24, 1923, Dione Neutra Papers.

2. Neutra to Dione Neutra, January, n.d., 1924; February, n.d., 1924; Neutra to Lilly Niedermann, November, n.d., 1923, Dione Neutra Papers.

3. Neutra to Dione Neutra, February, n.d., 1924; November (?), n.d., 1923, Dione Neutra Papers; Neutra, *Life and Shape*, p. 205.

4. Neutra to Lilly Niedermann, January, n.d., 1924; Neutra to Dione Neutra, December, n.d., 1923, Dione Neutra Papers.

5. Neutra to Dione Neutra, December, n.d., 1923, Dione Neutra Papers.

6. Neutra to Dione Neutra, November 5, 1923; January, n.d., 1924; February 13, 1924, Dione Neutra Papers. Promotional brochure of the library committee, "An Appeal to the Friends of Jewish Culture," copy in possession of author.

7. "An Appeal to the Friends of Jewish Culture"; "Architecture and Architects," *Encyclopedia Judaica* 3: 350; Neutra to Dione Neutra, January, n.d., 1924, Dione Neutra Papers.

8. Neutra to Dione Neutra, February (?), n.d., 1924; Rudolph Schindler to Neutra, January, n.d., 1924, Dione Neutra Papers.

9. Neutra to Dione Neutra, January 3, 1924; May 23, 1924, Dione Neutra Papers. Later the Neutras made the painful discovery that Frank had suffered brain damage during the difficult delivery and was mentally retarded as a result.

10. Neutra to Dione Neutra, February, n.d., 1923, Dione Neutra Papers.

11. Neutra to Dione Neutra, February 23, 1924, Dione Neutra Papers.

12. Neutra, *Life and Shape*, pp. 174–79; Neutra to Dione Neutra, February, n.d., 1924, Dione Neutra Papers.

13. Neutra, *Life and Shape*, pp. 190–202; Neutra to Frances Toplitz, March 3, 1924, Dione Neutra Papers.

14. Neutra, *Life and Shape*, p. 190.

15. I. A. Reinhardt, "To the Architectural Profession," December 19, 1924, Dione Neutra Papers.

16. Neutra to Frances Toplitz, April 10, 1924, Dione Neutra Papers. At about this same time Neutra also designed a "congressional building for Vienna" and "a library for a Southern university," neither of which was ever built. No docu-

mentation has thus far come to light to explain these projects.

17. Neutra, *Life and Shape*, pp. 179–81; Neutra to Dione Neutra, April (?), n.d., 1924, Dione Neutra Papers.

18. Neutra to Dione Neutra, March 3, 1924; March or April, n.d., 1924, Dione Neutra Papers.

19. Schindler to Neutra, April 14, 1924, Dione Neutra Papers.

20. Neutra, *Life and Shape*, pp. 181–82; Neutra to Dione Neutra, March or April, n.d., 1924, Dione Neutra Papers.

21. Ibid., Neutra to Dione Neutra, April 20, 1924, Dione Neutra Papers.

22. Neutra, *Life and Shape*, pp. 183–84; Weschler, interview with Dione Neutra, June 19, 1978; Neutra to Dione Neutra, April, n.d., 1924, Dione Neutra Papers.

23. Dione Neutra to Lilly Niedermann, June, n.d., 1924; Neutra to Frances Toplitz, May 31, June 20, 1924, Dione Neutra Papers.

24. Neutra to Frances Toplitz, May 31, 1924, Dione Neutra Papers; Neutra, *Life and Shape*, pp. 186–87; Dione Neutra to Lilly Niedermann, July 12, 1924, Dione Neutra Papers.

25. Dione Neutra to Lilly Niedermann, July 12, 1924; Neutra to Lilly Niedermann, October (?), n.d., 1924, Dione Neutra Papers.

26. Frank Lloyd Wright to Neutra, November 3, 1924; Schindler to Neutra, November 22, 1924; Dione Neutra to Lilly Niedermann, November, n.d., 1924; Neutra to Frances Toplitz, November, n.d., 1924, Dione Neutra Papers.

27. Weschler, interview with Dione Neutra, June 10, 1978.

28. Ibid.; Frank Lloyd Wright, *An Autobiography* (New York: Horizon, 1977) pp. 530–31; Neutra to Lilly Niedermann, January 17, 1925, Dione Neutra Papers.

29. Neutra, *Life and Shape*, pp. 185–86; Neutra to Ralph Fletcher Seymour, July 21, 1951, Dione Neutra Papers.

30. Neutra to Frances Toplitz, November 26, 1924, December, n.d., 1924, Dione Neutra Papers; Weschler, interview with Dione Neutra, June 10, 1978.

31. Neutra to Frances Toplitz, January 26, 1925, Dione Neutra Papers.

32. Schindler to Neutra, November 22, 1924; Dione Neutra to Alfred and Lilly Niedermann, January 14, 1925, Dione Neutra Papers; Weschler, interview with Dione Neutra, July 14, 1978.

33. A slightly different version of this material was published by the author as "Preserving the Visi-

ble Past: The Schindler House and the Los Angeles Preservation Movement," *L.A. Architect*, September 1978, pp. 2–3.

34. Weschler, interview with Dione Neutra, July 14, 1978; Dione Neutra to Lilly Niedermann, February 16, 1925, Dione Neutra Papers.

35. Thomas S. Hines, interviews with Pauline Schindler, February 9, 1972, July 1, 1976, Los Angeles.

36. Weschler, interview with Dione Neutra, July 14, 1978; Dione Neutra to Verena Saslavsky, n.d., 1925, and to Lilly Niedermann, n.d., 1925, and August 4, 1926, Dione Neutra Papers.

37. Harwell Harris to Pauline Schindler, 1974, quoted in McCoy, *Vienna to Los Angeles*, p. 54.

38. Weschler, interview with Dione Neutra, July 14, 1978; Neutra to Frances Toplitz, April 21, 1925; Dione Neutra to Lilly Niedermann, n.d., 1925, and November 5, 1926; Neutra to Verena and Ruben Saslavsky, n.d., 1926, Dione Neutra Papers.

39. Weschler, interview with Dione Neutra, July 14, 1978.

40. c.f. David Gebhard, *Schindler* (New York: Viking, 1972), pp. 92–93.

41. Neutra to Alfred and Lilly Niedermann, February 21, 1925; Neutra to Lilly Niedermann, August 19, 1925, and n.d., 1926; California Lamb's Club brochure, n.d., Dione Neutra Papers; *Los Angeles Times*, August 9, 1925.

42. Neutra to Lilly Niedermann, May, n.d., 1925, Dione Neutra Papers.

43. Willy Boesiger, ed., *Richard Neutra 1923–50: Buildings and Projects* (New York: Praeger, 1964), p. 195.

44. Richard J. Neutra, *Wie Baut Amerika?* (Stuttgart: Julius Hoffmann, 1927); Alfred Niedermann to Neutra, n.d., 1926; Julius Hoffmann to Neutra, December 8, 1926, Dione Neutra Papers; Dione Neutra to author, July 27, 1979. I am greatly indebted to Regula Niedermann Fybel's translation of *Wie Baut Amerika?* deposited in the UCLA Research Library's Department of Special Collections.

45. A. Lunarcharsky to Neutra, September 22, 1927; The *Architect's Journal* of London quoted in promotion brochure of Julius Hoffmann; *Berliner Tageblatt*, September 11, 1927; *Magazine for Politics and Culture*, n.d., all in Dione Neutra Papers.

46. Henry-Russell Hitchcock, Jr., review of *Wie Baut Amerika?* in *Architectural Record*, 63 (June 1928), 594–95.

47. Anonymous [Pauline Schindler], review of *Wie Baut Amerika?* in *City Club Bulletin*, July 30 and August 6, 1927. Pauline Schindler authorship was

confirmed in a conversation between Dione Neutra and author, July 27, 1979.

48. Ibid.

Breakthrough, 1926–1930

1. Schindler to Neutra, February 9, 1915, Dione Neutra Papers.

2. Thomas S. Hines and Rochelle Kappe, interview with Harwell H. Harris, September 16, 1976, Los Angeles. Examples of Schindler's efforts at self-promotion will be given in later chapters.

3. John Ritter, "World Parliament, The League of Nations Competition, 1926," *Architectural Review*, 136 (July 1964):17–23; Weschler, interview with Dione Neutra, July 14. 1978; Dione Niedermann to Alfred and Lilly Niedermann, n.d., 1926, Dione Neutra Papers.

4. Dione Neutra to Lilly Niedermann, September 29, December 7, 1926, Dione Neutra Papers.

5. Weschler, interview with Dione Neutra, July 14, 1978; Ritter, "World Parliament," p. 22.

6. In his article "World Parliament," Ritter summarized the matter succinctly:

All that the jury eventually produced was a list of nine first, nine second, and nine third prize winners, reflecting their diverse opinions; a poor result for the League, and galling for the 377 entrant firms of architects, especially since it had been only a single stage competition, with long and complex requirements.

The League then appointed a committee of five diplomats to make the decision: they proceeded (after the event) to raise the originally very strict price limit for the buildings by 50 percent, and they added the provision of a World Library to the programme, to be paid for . . . by John D. Rockefeller. Then, in December, they reported that they found the entry by Messrs. Nénot and Flegenheimer the most suitable, but in view of certain objections they asked three other prize winners, Messrs. Broggi, Lefèvre and Vago, to collaborate.

The League did its best in the hopeless situation that had been presented to them by the jury but, understandably M. Le Corbusier objected at this stage. His own scheme had been the only one to have been estimated (by a Swiss building journal) as within the original cost limit, so there seemed to be some discrimination against him. He also asked why the new library had been added to the pro-

gram instead of forming a separate job. His objections were not admitted but controversy continued to flare in the press; the publicity was historically important, since a modern project was for the first time seen as a very serious contender for a building complex of international importance.

The problem did not end there because, with the Library added, the original site appeared inadequate and the League had to find somewhere else to build. They eventually chose the Ariana park, on the hillside above the old lake-side site; but as this had been left to the city by a private citizen, specifically as a public park, permission had to be sought from his heirs, one of whom required Le Corbusier's collaboration. Eventually a compromise was reached: that, together with any other prize winners who so wished, he could submit another project. Le Corbusier's revised project is familiar through his public works, and he explained it to the committee in April, 1929. However, it was not accepted; and here the matter closed, except for some further argument, in which Le Corbusier accused the official architects of plagiarizing his first scheme. This seems extremely unlikely on examination: the building as finally completed clearly owes almost everything to the collaborator Joseph Vago. . . .

7. Lilly Niedermann to Dione Neutra, May 8, 1927, Dione Neutra Papers.

8. Lilly Niedermann to Dione Neutra, July 8, 1927, Dione Neutra Papers.

9. Dione Niedermann to Lilly Niedermann, August 17, 1927; Alfred Niedermann to Richard Neutra, n.d., 1927, Dione Neutra Papers. In her essay in *Vienna to Los Angeles*, Esther McCoy presented only Schindler's version of the incident: "Schindler's and Neutra's entry had won a prize of sorts. Le Corbusier claimed that his plan had originally won first prize, then the plan was rescinded and no winner was named. So in 1930 [*sic*] three copies were chosen to be exhibited in Europe—Le Corbusier's, [Hans Wittmer and] Hannes Meyer's, and Schindler's and Neutra's. The benefits to Neutra, then in Europe, were somewhat greater than to Schindler, for Schindler's name had been removed from their plan when it was exhibited. . . . Schindler had heard in 1930 from architects in Vienna and from his sister that his name was missing from the exhibition material and that Neutra accepted complete credit." Schindler later told McCoy "that the Lovell House commission

was to Neutra an act of self-survival, but the removal of his name from the League of Nations entry was an act of malice" (*Vienna to Los Angeles*, pp. 62–63). In his autobiography, *Life and Shape*, pp. 221–22, and in *Richard Neutra, 1923–50*, Neutra was careful to cite Schindler's participation. In Ritter's "World Parliament" article, however, only Neutra's name is listed.

10. Harwell H. Harris, foreword to McCoy, *Vienna to Los Angeles*, p. 9.

11. AGIC promotional blurb, copy in possession of author; Weschler, interview with Dione Neutra, July 14, 1978.

12. Weschler, interview with Dione Neutra, July 14, 1978.

13. Schindler's financial records indicate that Neutra was paid part of the fee on such jobs as the Leah-Ruth Shop—Schindler Papers, University of California, Santa Barbara; see also Gebhard, *Schindler*, pp. 93–98; and on AGIC, McCoy, *Vienna to Los Angeles*, p. 53.

14. "Architectural Group Prepares Drawings for Limit-Height Apartment Building," *Los Angeles Journal of Commerce*, September 24, 1927, p. 1.

15. Neutra to John Beardsley, September 7, 1929; Neutra to Alfred Niedermann, May 5, 1927; Dione Neutra to Lilly Niedermann, n.d., 1927, Dione Neutra Papers; Weschler, interview with Dione Neutra, July 14, 1978.

16. "The Garden Apartment House," *Christian Science Monitor*, July 12, 1928.

17. Ibid.

18. Henry-Russell Hitchcock, Jr., "Foreign Periodicals," *Architectural Record*, 64 (December 1928), p. 537; Willard D. Morgan, "C.M.D. Architecture Receives Editorial Acclaim," *Central Manufacturing District Magazine* (Los Angeles) April 1930, pp. 32–35; Weschler, interview with Dione Neutra, July 14, 1978.

19. Thomas S. Hines, interview with Pauline Schindler, February 9, 1972, Los Angeles; interview with Philip Lovell, February 16, 1973, Newport Beach.

20. Ibid.

21. Ibid.

22. c.f. Gebhard, *Schindler*, pp. 80–89.

23. Philip Lovell to Neutra, February 9, 1969, in the Appendix to this chapter. Hines, interview with Philip Lovell. February 16, 1973. For contrasting views, see the Appendix and McCoy, *Vienna to Los Angeles*, pp. 65–71.

24. Dione Neutra to Lilly Niedermann, September 29, 1926. Dione Neutra Papers; Thomas S. Hines, interview with Dione Neutra, February 20, 1972,

Los Angeles; Weschler, interview with Dione Neutra, July 14, 1978; Hines and Kappe, interview with Harwell Harris, September 16, 1976.

25. Neutra, "Halle für Körperkultur des Dr. Ph. M. Lovell, Los Angeles," *Das Neue Frankfurt*, May 1928, pp. 90–91; Hines, interview with Philip Lovell, February 16, 1973; Hines, interview with Dione Neutra, February 20, 1972; Weschler, interview with Dione Neutra, July 14, 1978. Neutra to Dione Neutra, August 24, 1927; Dione Neutra to Lilly Niedermann, April 2, 1928, Dione Neutra Papers. The fact that Neutra began work on the project in May 1927 is noted in his final statement to Lovell, May 15, 1930, Dione Neutra Papers.

26. Dione Neutra to Lilly Niedermann, April 2, 1928, Dione Neutra Papers. In November 1928 Pauline invited the Neutras to Carmel for a much-needed vacation. Richard gave a lecture and Dione a concert, both of which were warmly promoted and reviewed in *The Carmelite*. Neutra, Pauline wrote, "is one of these two or three true descendants of the lineage of Sullivan and Wright, to whom architecture is not merely an expression of a civilization, but a conditioning agent of future cultures." She found the work of Neutra and those few contemporaries to have "the quality, the feeling, of great architecture. It is organic. It is as recognizably great . . . as life is recognizable against the contrast of death." *The Carmelite*, November 28, 1928, p. 11.

27. Hines, interview with Dione Neutra, February 20, 1927; Weschler, interview with Dione Neutra, July 14, 1978.

28. Neutra, *Life and Shape*, p. 207; Hines, interview with Philip Lovell, February 16, 1973.

29. Neutra, *Life and Shape*, p. 221.

30. Ibid., pp. 220–24.

31. Frank Lloyd Wright to Neutra, n.d. (1929?), Dione Neutra Papers.

32. Neutra to Philip Lovell, May 15, 1930, Dione Neutra Papers.

33. Philip Lovell, "Care of the Body," *Los Angeles Times Sunday Magazine*, December 15, 1929, p. 26.

34. Ibid.

35. Weschler, interview with Dione Neutra, July 14, 1978; Neutra, *Life and Shape*, p. 225; Philip Lovell, "Mr. Neutra, Architect," posted statement, copy in possession of author.

36. Neutra's volume was a companion to *Russland* by El Lissitsky, and *Frankreich* by Roger Ginsburger, the husband of Dione's sister Doris. All were published by Schroll of Vienna in a series

called *Neues Bauen in der Welt* ("New Building in the World").

37. Neutra to Philip Lovell, May 15, 1930, Dione Neutra Papers.

Confirmation, 1930–1932

1. Neutra to Dione Neutra, June 2, 1930, Dione Neutra Papers.
2. Neutra, *Life and Shape*, pp. 226–54; Weschler, interview with Dione Neutra, July 18, 1978; Kunio Maekawa to Richard Neutra, June 12, 1930, Dione Neutra Papers.
3. Neutra, "Japanische Wohnung, Ableitung, Schwierigkeiten," *Die Form*, March 15, 1931, pp. 92–97; "Umbildung chinesischer Städte," *Die Form*, May 15, 1932, pp. 142–49; Neutra, *Life and Shape*, pp. 226–52.
4. Weschler, interview with Dione Neutra, July 18, 1978; Neutra, *Life and Shape*, pp. 252–57. Neutra's chronology of the European trip had become somewhat confused by the time he wrote his autobiography in the early 1960s.
5. Neutra, *Life and Shape*, pp. 252–57.
6. Ibid.
7. Hines, conversation with Dione Neutra, November 24, 1979; Weschler, interview with Dione Neutra, July 18, 1978; Christopher Byal and James Young, "A Dialogue with Richard Neutra," *Opus* 10 (Spring 1970) :10 *Opus* was a student publication at the California Polytechnic Institute, Pomona.
8. Byal and Young, "A Dialogue With Richard Neutra," pp. 15–16.
9. Hines, conversation with Dione Neutra, November 24, 1979; Weschler, interview with Dione Neutra, July 18, 1978.
10. Ibid.
11. Virginia Weisshaus to Neutra, August 10, 1931, Dione Neutra Papers.
12. Ludwig Mies van der Rohe, signed but untitled printed statement, Dione Neutra Papers.
13. Reyner Banham, "CIAM," *Encyclopedia of Modern Architecture*, pp. 70–73.
14. Ibid.; Karl Moser and Sigfried Giedion, "invitation on 3e Congrès internationaux d'Architecture moderne," in possession of author; Le Corbusier, "Rapport de Le Corbusier sur le parcellement du sol des villes et les immeubles destinés a l'habitation" and Neutra, "Maison haute, moyenne, ou basse en circonstances americaines," typescripts in possession of author.
15. Neutra, *Life and Shape*, pp. 254–55; Byal and Young, "A Dialogue with Richard Neutra," p. 20.

16. Weschler, interview with Dione Neutra, July 18, 1978.
17. Neutra to Schindler, December 9, 1930, Schindler Collection, University of California, Santa Barbara.
18. Neutra to Dione Neutra, December 2, 1930, Dione Neutra Papers.
19. Neutra to Dione Neutra, December 24, 1930, Dione Neutra Papers.
20. Ibid.
21. Ibid.
22. Neutra to Dione Neutra, December 20, 1930, January, n.d., 1931, Dione Neutra Papers; Louis Sherwin, "Neutra Finds Our Skyscrapers Deny City Place in the Sunshine," New York *Evening Post*, January 12, 1931, p. 3.
23. Neutra, *Life and Shape*, p. 259; "Architecture Is Advancing in West; California House Chosen for Museum Display," *Pasadena Star News*, August 31, 1931.
24. Neutra to Schindler, January 14, 1931; January 28, 1931; Schindler Collection; Philip Johnson to Neutra, May 26, 1931, Dione Neutra Papers.
25. Neutra, *Life and Shape*, pp. 259–61; Hines, conversation with Dione Neutra, January 25, 1979; Philip Johnson to Neutra, December 11, 1930, Dione Neutra Papers.
26. Neutra to Lilly Niedermann, January, n.d., 1931, Dione Neutra Papers; Neutra to Schindler, January 14, 1931, Schindler Collection.
27. Neutra to Lilly Niedermann, January, n.d., 1931; Neutra to Dione Neutra, January, n.d., 1931, Dione Neutra Papers.
28. Hines and Kappe, interview with Harwell H. Harris, September 16, 1976.
29. Ibid.; Harris, "AIA Gold Medal Awarded to Richard Neutra," *North Carolina Architect*, May–June 1977.
30. Ibid.
31. Ibid.; M. T. Cantell to Neutra, April 7, 1931; Dione Neutra to Verena Saslavski, July 15, 1931; course announcement flyers from the University of Southern California and the Chouinard School of Art, Dione Neutra Papers.
32. Dione Neutra to Frances Toplitz, Dione Neutra to Verena Saslavsky, July 15, 1931, Dione Neutra Papers.
33. "Architect Back From Long Tour," *Los Angeles Times*, April 9, 1931.
34. Alfred Barr, foreword to *Modern Architecture* (New York: Museum of Modern Art, 1932), pp. 12–17.
35. Ibid.
36. Ibid.

37. Ibid.; Van der Leeuw to Neutra, June 2, 1931, Dione Neutra Papers.

38. Henry-Russell Hitchcock, "Richard J. Neutra," in *Modern Architecture*, pp. 157–60.

39. Neutra to Hitchcock, March 12, 1932, copy in possession of author.

40. H. I. Brock, "Architecture Styled International," *New York Times Magazine*, February 7, 1932, p. 11.

41. See, for example, "International Stylists' Designs Thrill Crowds; Los Angeles Architect Included With World's Twelve Leading Exponents of New Motif," and "Art 'Boom' in Prospect During Olympic Games," *Los Angeles Times*, July 24, 1932; Dione Neutra to Frances Toplitz, July 30, 1932, Dione Neutra Papers.

42. "New Architecture Revealed in Exhibit of International Scope," *Southwest Builder and Contractor*, July 22, 1932, clipping in Dione Neutra Papers.

43. Henry-Russell Hitchcock, *Modern Architecture: Romanticism and Reintegration* (New York: Harcourt, Brace, 1929), pp. 117, 204–5.

44. Schindler to Hitchcock, January, n.d., 1930; Hitchcock to Schindler, February, n.d., 1930, Schindler Collection.

45. Philip Johnson to Schindler, January 9, 1932; January 24, 1932; March 17, 1932; Schindler to Johnson, March 9, 1932, Schindler Collection.

46. Philip Johnson and Henry-Russell Hitchcock, "The Extent of Modern Architecture," in *Modern Architecture*, p. 22.

47. See Gebhard, *Schindler*, pp. 121–60.

48. Schindler to Josef von Sternberg, July 10, 1929, Schindler Collection.

49. Neutra to Schindler, December 9, 1930; January 14, 1931; January 28, 1931; Schindler to Neutra, June 15, 1931, Schindler Collection.

Modernity, 1932–1940

1. "Garden Homes for Workers," *Christian Science Monitor*, July 26, 1932; Max Eisler, "Die Werkbundsiedlung in Wien," *Moderne Bauformen* 31 (September 1932): 435–59, Unless otherwise noted, building analyses are based on the author's study of plans, drawings, specifications, and photographs in the Neutra Archive, UCLA Special Collections, and visits to buildings.

2. Ibid.

3. Richard Neutra, *Life and Shape*, pp. 263–68; Hines, interview with Dione Neutra, Los Angeles, March 19, 1980.

4. Ibid.

5. Ibid.

6. See "Research House in Los Angeles Backed by Dutch Philanthropist," *Southwest Builder and Contractor*, 82 (October 13, 1933): 15–17; "Versuchshaus am Silbersee," *Das Werk* 21 (July 1934), 202–5; Thomas Whittemore to Neutra, March 24, 1940, in possession of author.

7. Hines, interview with Dione Neutra, March 20, 1980; Bertha Mosk to Neutra, October 26, 1933; January 26, 1938, Neutra Archive.

8. Hines, interview with Dione Neutra, March 20, 1980; Hines, interview with Lette Valeska, March 12, 1980, Los Angeles; Hines, interview with Greta and J. R. Davidson, June 27, 1974, Ojai.

9. Ibid.; Hines, interview with Gregory Ain, April 25, 1977, Los Angeles. Ain insisted that his chief contribution to all of the projects on which he worked was doing the working drawings and attending to construction details while Neutra took responsibility for the conception of the designs.

10. Hines, interview with Dione Neutra, March 20, 1980. Ain later admitted that he did not care for the layout of the Beard house, and one night after hours did a design of his own. As a play on William Beard's name he labeled his project "the Billy Whiskers house." Neutra, he recalled, was not amused.

11. Neutra quoted in "Los Angeles Architect Wins Awards on Three Homes in Competition," *Southwest Builder and Contractor* 84 (June 7, 1935): 11.

12. Joseph Hudnut and Jury, "Better Homes in America," *Architectural Forum*, April 1935, p. 399; William Beard to Neutra, March 1, 1935, Neutra Archive. Like other Neutra clients of the period, the Beards wrote an impassioned testimonial about their house, which included the following passages:

> There have been numerous attacks in recent years on functional modern homes, their designers, and their occupants, on the theory that such structures are little more than barns to be occupied only by persons of inferior mentality. As an antidote to some of this criticism the undersigned present their reactions to their life in the modern home of which they have been the owners.
>
> In the first place, a modern home requires a minimum of furniture and equipment. There is no place for mere "things" —for bric-a-brac, chandeliers with imitation candles, sea shells, and colored stones. To the newcomer, this often seems like an insuperable obstacle for the "collectors' instinct" is strong in the human animal and is not easily drowned. But if one remains in a mod-

ern structure one ultimately passes successfully through this transition stage and from
mere necessity learns to stop gathering in the
odds and ends of the earth. When this has
become second nature, one at last enjoys the
simplicity of the modern home and gets a
new sense of material release. As bondage to
mere objects dies out, the budget shrivels,
and the mind is no longer distracted by cu-
pids carved in nearby chairs or curly-cues in
ballustrades. In both thought and action one
is now rid of useless baggage and has a peace
and contentment that comes from true simplicity. It takes time, but the reward is well
worth the effort, as we can testify. Not only
has our modern home destroyed the magpie
spirit, but it has taught us that a home can
be as easy to operate as a car. The simple
interior and metal furniture, the absence of
needless halls and stairs, the effective kitchen
layout conspire to make household operations
rapid and effective, leaving time for other
things. Under modern high-pressure living,
this evidence of needless drudgery, this elimination of any need for servants, has proved
a second welcome relief to us. The home
thereby comes to be a house of good cheer
rather than a chore.

   Our home also represents an honest
adaptation of structure to immediate needs
and hence a minimum of waste and expense.
Here are no small windows blindly patterned
after English homes where they were originally installed generations ago to avoid a
heavy luxury tax on large windows. Here is
no money idly frittered away on an imitation
thatch roof, or a mansard roof copied from
Paris where it was designed to get around the
local height limitations on buildings. Here
are no bogus sagging beams, no artificial
chimneys, no thin veneer panels made to resemble great oak doors. Here are no signs of
needless depreciation, paid for at heavy expense in order to make the house look old.
The very act of living in such a home is a
challenge to all hypocrisy, and a stimulus to
clear thinking and efficient living which undoubtedly have a positive influence on our
thoughts and deeds.

13. Hines, interview with Dione Neutra, March 20,
1980.

14. Ibid.; Lillian Richter to Neutra, January 19, 1938,
Neutra Archive.

15. Hines, interview with Dione Neutra, March 20,
1980; Augusta Owen Patterson, "Desert at the

Doorstep," *Town and Country*, November 1945,
pp. 120–23.

16. Grace Lewis Miller to Museum of Modern Art,
quoted in her letter to Neutra, May 27, 1938, Neutra Archive.

17. Ibid.

18. Kathryn Davis to Neutra, February 11, 1938;
Harry Koblick to Neutra, January 20, 1938, Neutra Archive.

19. The Wards lived in their house a relatively short
time and sold it to the Bergers, under whose name
it was published. Hines, interview with Dione
Neutra, March 20, 1980; Hines, interview with
Helen Barsha, March 20, 1980, Los Angeles. Like
other Neutra clients of the period, the Barshas
wrote a letter of appreciation to Neutra in the
form of a modernist manifesto, entitled "So We
Built a Modern House" (Neutra Archive).

   About two years ago we decided to build a
house. We had no definite style in mind and
as we were in that all too common position
of knowing practically nothing about building, we started reading all the magazines and
books we could lay our hands on and discussing the problem with anyone who would talk
to us. As we got into the subject we became
aware of something lacking in most homes.
There seemed to be too much attention paid
to correctness of period and ornamentation;
not enough to living.

   Then, one day, we happened on a European book which had some photographs and
plans of what we thought were queer looking
structures. With their flat roofs and lack of
ornamentation, they looked boxy and square.
The window area seemed far out of proportion to the area of the rest of the house;
nevertheless, there was something intriguing
about them. As we studied the plans, we saw
that they were not just a collection of rooms
held together by walls, but that the plan had
been designed as a whole, that each room had
a definite relations with the others, and that
the exteriors were determined by the interiors
(completely in reverse of the conventional
design).

   The next problem was to find an architect in this part of the country to give us such
a fine home. We heard of a man who had
achieved recognition because of his modern
work in this country and who lived in Los
Angeles. We lost no time in arranging a
meeting with Richard Neutra.

   From the first, we were favorably impressed with his attitude toward designing a

home. He did not ask us how much we wanted to spend or how many rooms we wanted—then tell us that he would show us a plan in a week. Instead, he met with us several times and we discussed all of our living problems in the minutest detail. In fact, by his questions, he opened our eyes to a new conception of house planning.

After he had firmly implanted in his his mind our needs and desires, we went looking at lots. We had a particular tract in mind which fronted on a park—affording a delightful view. Here again, we saw a different method, the lot was not chosen for its pretentious possibilities or because it looked good as a lot. Mr. Neutra took into consideration the view, the surroundings and the possibility of designing a house that would get the most out of the lot.

At about this time we became beset with new worries. Our friends and others who should have known what they were talking about, tried to dissuade us from continuing. They use all the arguments that we had given ourselves at first—modern houses were too radical, they were cold, sterile, unlivable, and ugly. But their arguments were to no avail because we had visited quite a few Neutra homes by this time and had talked with the people living in them. Without exception, these people were more than enthusiastic in describing the pleasure they derived from their homes. Their arguments were far stronger to us than those of people who hadn't actually experienced a Neutra home. So we continued.

By now, we had plans to look at. We saw now the result of all our discussions with Mr. Neutra. We also saw, that because of the functional design, we were able to take advantage of many new construction methods and materials without being restricted by period or style. We were getting a home fitted to present day living and not a relic of the past.

We built the house. Mr. Neutra had planned in such detail and supervised the construction so wisely that extras, which are usually a big item in residential construction, were kept down to less than $\frac{1}{2}$ of 1% of the cost of the building.

In his logical and thorough way, Mr. Neutra had seen the project in its entirety. In order to make it a more perfect whole, he had gone as far as to design the landscaping and all the interiors.

So far everything had worked out even better than we had planned. But we still had to put the house to the real test—LIVING.

We have now enjoyed our home for a year, long enough to give us a hint of the pleasure we shall get out of it in the years to come. Our lives have been far richer because we gritted our teeth and, despite opposition, went ahead with a modern house. Home has become to us not just a place to sleep and eat, but a living something from which we get a spiritual and physical benefit.

The large areas of glass which so many people deride, give us constantly changing views of the landscape. They make each room seem to project itself into the landscape and we get a feeling of living in the open without having to suffer any of the discomforts. They make every room cheerful despite the weather.

Because of the simplicity of design, the correct proportioning and the open layout of the plan, all the rooms, as well as the exterior, seem to be much larger than they really are. We actually have the effect of a home costing twice as much as it really does. We also get a feeling of spaciousness impossible in any other design.

We find that our house is easy to live in. It is easier to clean and stays clean and orderly better than conventional houses cluttered with roccoco furniture and knickknacks. The use of simple light-colored wall and ceiling surfaces, combined with well-designed lighting, is less costly and prevents eyestrain. Our furniture is designed for use as well as beauty. It not only looks inviting, it is comfortable. We find that people visiting us never feel ill at ease, everything in the house makes them relax and enjoy themselves.

We find our house easy to live with. Each room serves at least two purposes. Our living-dining room serves as library, music room and card room. Our bedroom serves also as a study. The kitchen serves as a breakfast room. We actually use each room a large portion of the day.

We find out house easy to entertain in. We have had small and large groups, formal and informal parties, musicals, games, discussions; and in each instance, the house seemed designed for that particular occasion.

We find that all the old arguments against modern architecture are false. That if one studies it and gets close to it, he will learn to appreciate it. What to the uninitiated looks like angular, sterile, boxiness is actually good, clean, simple line and plane, unencumbered by useless ornamentation. As good art must be simple of line and thought, so must good architecture.

We find that we have a house that expresses our personalities in a way that no conventional house could. Our house was designed for us and calls on no tradition to give it beauty, but takes everything from the present to give us pleasure.

We find (and this pleases us most of all), that our friends are becoming converted to our ideas now that they have had an opportunity to see good modern design actually doing the things it is supposed to do.

In short, we find that modern architecture has one distinct disadvantage. It has become practically a religion with us. We are now intolerant of everything in life that is not thoroughly modern.

20. Harry McIntosh to Neutra, February 28, 1952, Neutra Archive; Hines, interview with Harrison McIntosh, March 9, 1980, Claremont, Calif.; Hines, interview with Gerard Gill, September 19, 1977, Glendale, Calif.

21. Hines, interview with Dione Neutra, March 20, 1980; "Diatalum Dwellings," *Architectural Forum*, September 1942; John Cushman Fistere, "House Looking Westward," *Ladies' Home Journal*, June 1938; "Modern Rides Out of the West," *Better Homes and Gardens*, September 1938.

22. Hines, interview with Dione Neutra, March 20, 1980; "Exhibition House Group," *Architectural Forum*, July 1936, pp. 38–39.

23. Hines, interview with Dione Neutra, March 20, 1980.

24. "First Prize in the Special Class," *House Beautiful*, September 1934.

25. von Sternberg to Neutra, February 18, 1932; Neutra to von Sternberg February 20, 1932; Neutra to von Sternberg, April 21, 1934, Neutra Archive.

26. Josef von Sternberg, *Fun in a Chinese Laundry* (New York: Macmillan, 1965), pp. 270–72.

27. Ibid.; von Sternberg to Neutra, n.d., 1935, Neutra Archive; Neutra to von Sternberg, n.d., quoted in von Sternberg, *Fun in a Chinese Laundry*, pp. 271–72.

28. Neutra, *Life and Shape*, pp. 283–89.

29. Ibid.

30. Ibid.

31. Aline Barnsdall to Neutra, February 15, 1939, Neutra Archive.

32. Hines, interview with Dione Neutra, March 20, 1980.

33. Anita Loos to author, October 6, 1978.

34. Hines, interview with Dione Neutra, March 20, 1980; Maurice Zolotow, "Newly Discovered Hollywood Novel by Charles Reznikoff," *Los Angeles Times Book Review* (January 8, 1978), p. 3; Albert Lewin to Neutra, September 10, 1940, Neutra Archive.

35. Ibid.; Hines, interview with Mary [Stotherd] Wescher, October 17, 1978, Los Angeles.

36. Hines, interview with Julius Shulman, October 11, 1976, Los Angeles.

37. Ruth Ruben to Neutra, June 6, 1936; January 19, 1938, Neutra Archive; Hines, interview with Ruth Ruben Morris, Los Angeles, March 18, 1980, Los Angeles.

38. Dixie [Darling] Bayer to author, January 15, 1979; Hines, interview with Dione Neutra, March 20, 1980.

39. Hines, interview with Dione Neutra, March 20, 1980.

40. Two letters from Mona Hofmann to Dione Neutra, and to Richard and Dione Neutra, n.d., 1938, Neutra Archive.

41. Hines, interview with Elizabeth Ford, June 25, 1978, San Francisco.

42. Ilse Schiff to author, January 8, 1979.

43. Ibid.

44. Sidney Kahn to "Ricardo" and Dione Neutra, n.d., 1949, Neutra Archive.

45. Hines, interview with Simone Sciobereti, June 23, 1977, Berkeley; Raymond H. Sciobereti to Neutra, n.d., Neutra Archive; Hines, interview with Alvin Eurich, March 1, 1980, New York.

46. Hines, interview with George Kraigher, October 24, 1977, Litchfield, Conn.; Kraigher to Neutra, October 26, 1938; February 9, 1938, Neutra Archive.

47. Ibid.

48. "Arts Patron John N. Brown Dies at 79," *Los Angeles Times*, October 15, 1979, p. 18; John Nicholas Brown, "Memorandum For Mr. Richard J. Neutra in Answer to Questionnaire," n.d., 1936, Neutra Archive.

49. Ibid.; Anne (Mrs. John N.) Brown to author, April 11, 1979.

50. Hines, interview with Dione Neutra, March 19, 1980; Brown to Neutra, October 22, 1936, Neutra

Archive. Neutra, "Residence John Nicholas Brown, Fishers Island, New York," in *Richard Neutra, 1923–50*, pp. 42–47.

51. Brown, "Memorandum for Mr. Richard J. Neutra."

52. Ibid.

53. Ibid.

54. Brown to Neutra, December 1, 1936; April 20, 1937; Neutra to Buckminster Fuller. March 21, 1937, Neutra Archive.

55. Harry Polhemus to Neutra, September 8, 1938, Neutra Archive; Anne Brown to author, April 11, 1979.

56. Brown to Neutra, August 18, 1938; Neutra Archive.

57. Anne Brown to author, April 11, 1979.

58. Ibid.; Brown to Neutra, July 6, 1939, Neutra Archive; Hines, interview with J. Carter Brown, Washington, D.C., April 13, 1979.

59. Hines, interview with J. Carter Brown, April 13, 1979.

Community, 1932–1942

1. Hines, interview with Gregory Ain, April 25, 1977, Los Angeles; Hines, interview with Dione Neutra, May 1, 1980, Los Angeles; Carl Laemmle to Neutra, March 26, 1934, Neutra Archive. C.f. "A Restaurant in Los Angeles," *Architectural Review*, November 1934, pp. 159–61.

2. Lewis Mumford, *The Brown Decades: The Arts of America, 1865–1895* (New York: Dover, 1955), p. 241; Philip K. Wrigley to Neutra, September 1, 1937, Neutra Archive.

3. C.f. "A One-Story Special Purpose Office Building, Sholtz Advertising Building," *Architectural Record*, December 1937, pp. 102–3; "Office Building," *Architectural Forum*, March 1942, pp. 166–67.

4. "An Architect Tries For Informality in the Schoolroom," *St. Louis Post-Dispatch*, September 13. 1936, p. 3; "Test Tube School Open," *Los Angeles Times*, October 14, 1935; "Southland to Give Unique School Plan," *Los Angeles Times*, November 18, 1935; Richard J. Neutra, "New Elementary Schools For America," *Architectural Forum*, January 1935, pp. 25–32.

5. Ibid.; Dione Neutra, mimeographed Christmas letter, 1935, Dione Neutra Papers (copies also in possession of author); Doyt Early to Neutra, October 18, 1935, Neutra Archive.

6. Georgina Ritchie to Los Angeles Board of Education, March, n.d., 1936; Ritchie to Neutra, January 24, 1950, Neutra Archive.

7. "Boys' School, California Military Academy," *Architectural Record*, September 1936, pp. 192–93.

8. Hines, interview with Dione Neutra, May 1, 1980; Weschler, interview with Dione Neutra, July 21, 1978; Paul E. Gustafson, "Modern School," *California Arts and Architecture*, November 1941, pp. 28–29; Richard J. Neutra, "Architect and Educator Joined Hands to Make New Los Angeles School Esthetic and Functional," *School Management*, March 1941, pp. 196–98; "New Building Dedicated," *The Emersonian*, November 23, 1937, p. 1; Oliver Larkin, *Art and Life in America* (New York: Holt, Rinehart & Winston, 1960), p. 446.

9. The competition entries were published in *Richard Neutra, 1923–50*. The unbuilt museum project was published in *Arts and Architecture*, May 1944, p. 35.

10. Dione Neutra, Mimeographed Christmas letters, 1936, 1937; Hines, interview with Dione Neutra, May 1, 1980; Weschler, interview with Dione Neutra, July 21, 1978; c.f. "Apartment Houses, Landfair Dwellings," *Architectural Forum*, May 1937, pp. 399–402. Neutra's files and memoranda on the Rabinovitch lawsuit are in the Neutra Archive.

11. C.f. Esther McCoy, *Richard Neutra* (New York: Braziller, 1960), p. 13.

12. Hines, interviews with Regula (Thorston) Fybel, May 16, May 30, June 27, July 24, 1974, Los Angeles.

13. Luise Rainer to Neutra, February 16, 1938, Dione Neutra Papers.

14. McCoy, *Richard Neutra*, p. 13. For a joint treatment of the Kelton, Strathmore, and Landfair apartments see "Three Privately Developed Apartment Houses," *Pencil Points*, January 1944, pp. 51–58. "Richard J. Neutra," *L'Architecture D'aujourd'hui*, May–June 1946.

15. Weschler, interview with Dione Neutra, July 21, 1978; Dione Neutra, Mimeographed Christmas letter, 1934.

16. Hines, interview with Dione Neutra, May 1, 1980; "Laurence Westbrook, 74, Dies; Roosevelt Administrative Aide," *New York Times*, January 26, 1964.

17. The progress of the Jacksonville Park Living Project is covered in detail in the correspondence file of the Neutra Archive.

18. Richard J. Neutra, "Building For Youth," *California Arts and Architecture*, April 1941, pp. 28–29. A drawing of the Rose Parade float is in the NYA file, Neutra Archive.

19. Richard J. Neutra, "Report to the National Youth Administration," May 26, 1939, typescript in Neutra Archive.

20. L. Deeming Tilton, California State Planning Board, to Neutra, October 10, 1939, Neutra Archive.

21. For example, while Neutra was developing the Avion designs Williams sent him a beautiful old photograph of a house near San Antonio, with unadorned surfaces, breeze-catching porches, and a low-pitched roof. "Please copy!" Williams wrote on the back. "This is Spanish architecture by Spaniards to suit their own needs and the exactions of an insistent climate." Williams' undated note on the back of the photograph is in the Avion Village file, Neutra Archive.

22. David Williams to Richard and Dione Neutra, May 21, 1941, Neutra Archive.

23. "Modernity Keynote for Village" and "NAA Housing Plans to be Streamlined," *Dallas Morning News*, March 20, 1941.

24. Tom Treanor, "The Home Front," *Los Angeles Times*, April 2, 1941.

25. Laurence Westbrook to Neutra, March 17, 1949, Neutra Archive.

26. Weschler, interview with Dione Neutra, August 3, 1978; Hines, interview with Dione Neutra, May 1, 1980.

27. "Six Hundred Unit Permanent Housing Development in Harbor Area," *Southwest Builder and Contractor*, June 18, 1943; "Channel Heights Homes to be Dedicated Sunday," *Los Angeles Daily News*, November 13, 1942.

28. Hines, interviews with Myrtle Dessery, August 9, 1980, and with Evelyn Dessery Sichi, August 11, 1980, Los Angeles.

29. David Williams, Federal Works Agency interoffice communication, December 20, 1941; and Laurence Westbrook to Neutra, February 6, 1942, excerpts in Channel Heights file, Neutra Archive. One such respondent was my student Mark Smith, whose senior thesis "Richard Neutra and Le Corbusier" (1978) gave me new insights into Channel Heights as well as Neutra's other works.

30. "Neutra's Neophytes," *Architectural Forum*, August 1935, pp. 7–8; Ben G. Silver to Neutra, February 17. 1939, and Neutra to Silver, February 25, 1939, in possession of author.

31. Hines, interview with Ain, April 25, 1977; Dione Neutra, Christmas letter, 1937, Dione Neutra Papers.

32. Hines, interview with Ain, April 25, 1977; Hines and Kappe, interview with Harwell H. Harris, September 16, 1976.

33. Neutra to Gregory Ain, March 24, 1935; Copy in possession of author.

34. Hines, interview with Ain, April 25, 1977.

35. Hines, interview with Raphael Soriano, June 21, 1977, Tiburon, Calif.

36. Ibid.

37. Hines and Kappe, interview with Harris, September 16, 1976. Harris, "AIA Gold Medal Awarded to Neutra."

38. Hines and Kappe, interview with Harris, September 16, 1976.

39. Hines, interview with Greta and J. R. Davidson, June 27, 1974, Ojai, Calif.; Weschler, interview with Dione Neutra, August 3, 1978.

40. Weschler, interview with Dione Neutra, July 21, 1978; Dione Neutra, Christmas letters, 1935–40.

41. Weschler, interview with Dione Neutra, July 21, 1978; Dione Neutra, Christmas letters, 1938.

42. Mary Beard to Dione Neutra, September 1, 1938; March 13, 1939; June 29, 1939, Dione Neutra Papers.

43. Dione Neutra, Christmas letters, 1934–40. Walter Gropius to Neutra, May 18, 1938; László Moholy-Nagy to Neutra, April 19, 1939; Le Corbusier to Neutra, October 8, 1935; Amédée Ozenfant to Neutra, October 8, 1939; J. J. P. Oud to Neutra, February 2, 1939; Ernst May to Dione Neutra, nd.; José Luis Sert to Neutra, February 5, 1940; March 6, 1942; Frank Lloyd Wright to Dione Neutra, September 1, 1937, in possession of author. Neutra, *Life and Shape*, pp. 261–63. The Aalto visit is discussed in Hines and Kappe, interview with Harris, September 16, 1976.

44. Nancy Newhall, ed., *The Daybooks of Edward Weston* (Millerton, N.Y.: Aperture, n.d.), II, California, p. 102. The Neutra entry is dated January 3, 1929.

45. Erik Erikson, *Childhood and Society* (New York: W. W. Norton, 1963), pp. 24, 279.

46. Quoted in Dione Neutra, Christmas letter, 1938.

47. Mary Beard to Dione Neutra, January 18, 1939; November 7, 1939, Dione Neutra Papers; Dione Neutra, Christmas letter, 1939.

48. Neutra to Dione Neutra, Mexico City, n.d., 1937, Dione Neutra Papers.

49. Dione Neutra, Christmas letter, 1938.

50. Dione Neutra, Christmas letter, 1940.

51. Ibid.

52. Ibid.

53. Ibid.

54. Pauline Schindler to Neutra, n.d., 1936, in possession of author.

55. Philip Johnson, quoted in Robert Hughes, "Doing Their Own Thing," *Time*, January 8, 1979, pp. 54–55.

56. Dione Neutra, Christmas letters, 1938–40.

57. Henry Robert Harrison, "Richard J. Neutra, A Center of Architectural Stimulation," *Pencil Points*, July 1937, pp. 410–11.

58. Ibid.

Transition, 1941–1949

1. Maxwell Fry to Neutra, September 9, 1940, in possession of author.

2. Ibid.

3. "Puerto Rico," *Architectural Forum* 82, March 1945, pp. 119–20.

4. Neutra, "The Caribbean Part of America," unpublished typescript, in possession of author.

5. Neutra, "Puerto Rico—Island of Promise," *Survey Graphic* 33, June 1944, pp. 193–95.

6. "Puerto Rico," *Architectural Forum* 82, March 1945, p. 121.

7. Olegaria R. de Rivera to Governor Rexford Tugwell, October 2, 1944; Luiz Munoz Marin to Neutra, February 21, 1945, Neutra Archive.

8. Herbert Johnson to Neutra, February 5, 1946, Neutra Archive.

9. William Gray Purcell to Neutra, n.d., in possession of author.

10. Neutra, "Comments on Planetary Reconstruction," *Arts and Architecture* 61, December 1944, pp. 21–22.

11. Ibid.

12. "California's Neutra Urges Modern Planning To Repair War Damage," *Michigan Society of Architects Weekly Bulletin* 18, December 5, 1944, p. 6.

13. Neutra, Address to the Vancouver Institute, quoted in "Architectural Lag Dangers Outlined," undated unidentified clipping in Neutra Archive; Neutra, "Los Angeles Inventory," *Arts and Architecture* 60, November 1943, p. 16.

14. Hines, interview with Sybil Maxwell, October 19, 1978, Los Angeles; Charles and Sybil Maxwell to Neutra, February 19, 1952, Neutra Archive; "A Home for Genius," *Home Magazine, Los Angeles Times*, November 11, 1945, pp. 3–4.

15. "Report of the Jury, Honor Awards Program, 1938–1946, Southern California Chapter, American Institute of Architects," *Southwest Builder and Contractor*, September 27, 1946, pp. 14–15.

16. See "Community Projects." *Arts and Architecture* 59, August 1942, pp. 30–31.

17. For the cover story, see *Saturday Review* 39, June 1956, pp. 9–10.

18. Hines, interview with Dione Neutra, May 1, 1980; Hines, conversation with Edgar Kaufmann, Jr.,

June 13, 1981, Los Angeles.

19. Hines, interview with Thaddeus Longstreth, October 21, 1977, Princeton, N.J.

20. "Neutra Home Design Wins Architect Award," *Los Angeles Examiner*, June 26, 1949, p. 25; "Neutra, Wurdeman & Beckett Win Awards," *Building News*, June 9, 1949, p. 1.

21. Neutra to Julius Shulman, March 3, 1947, Neutra Archive; Julius Shulman, "A Photographer's Perspective on Neutra," *AIA Journal* (March 1977), 54.

22. Neutra to Edgar Kaufmann, Sr., March 3, 1947, Neutra Archive.

23. "A Modern House Uses Its Setting to Help Provide Luxurious Living," *Architectural Forum* 91, September 1949, p. 52; "Urbanity in the Wooded Foothills," *Interiors* 111, October 1951, p. 81.

24. Neutra to Entenza, July 16, 1947, Neutra Archive; Esther McCoy, "Introduction," *Case Study Houses 1945–1962* (Los Angeles: Hennessey & Ingalls, 1977), p. 8.

25. Hines, interview with Mrs. Stuart Bailey, October 6, 1980, Los Angeles.

26. Stuart G. Bailey to Neutra, June 13, 1958, Neutra Archive. In addition to the unbuilt Huggins Case Study House and the greatly modified Scott house, Neutra also designed two unbuilt houses for Long Beach, the Alpha and Omega Case Study houses of 1946 and 1947.

27. Betty Branch to Neutra, January 15, 1942; Russell Branch to Neutra, April 20, 1942, Neutra Archive.

28. Russell Branch to Editor, *Architectural Forum* 89, July 1948, p. 30.

29. Stanley Frankel to Editor, *Architectural Forum* 89, October 1948, p. 28.

30. Russell Branch to Neutra, August 14, 1948, Neutra Archive, printed in *Architectural Forum* 89, October 1948, p. 28.

31. See Thomas S. Hines, "Designing For the Motor Age: Richard Neutra and the Automobile," *Oppositions*, Fall 1979.

32. "On Planning Man's Physical Environment At Princeton University's Bi-Centennial Conference," *Architectural Forum*, April 1947, pp. 12–13, 97–100; Dione Neutra, "Highlights of My Life with Richard Neutra," typescript in possession of author, pp. 13–14.

33. Gropius to Neutra, July 31, 1944; Neutra to Gropius, August 5, 1944; Neutra to Kameki Tsuchiura, November 18, 1947; Sybil Moholy-Nagy to Richard and Dione Neutra, May 30, 1947, Neutra Archive.

34. "Homes Inside Out," *Time* 49 (February 3,

1947); "New Shells," *Time* 54 (August 15, 1949), pp. 58–66.

35. Neutra, *Survival Through Design* (New York: Oxford University Press, 1954), p. 229.

36. Maxwell Fry, "The Interpretation of Environment," *Arts and Architecture* 71, April 1954, p. 21; Robert H. Hutchins, "Design For Living," *The Nation*, February 20, 1954, p. 152; Lewis Mumford, "The Sky Line: Terminals and Monuments," *New Yorker* 30, March 20, 1954, pp. 106–7.

37. Douglas Haskell, "Planning Our Plans," *Saturday Review* 37, February 20, 1954, pp. 15–16.

Crisis, 1950–1960

1. Weschler, interview with Dione Neutra, August 9, 14, 1978; Robert E. Alexander, unpublished memoirs, passim, Alexander Papers, Cornell University. Copy in possession of author.

2. This 1972 citation was quoted in the "Baldwin Hills Village" section of Alexander's unpublished memoirs.

3. Hines, interview with Robert Alexander, December 11, 1978, Los Angeles.

4. Ibid.; Hines, interview with Simon Eisner, November 4, 1976, Los Angeles.

5. Neutra, "History and the Setting for a Project of Rehabilitation," unpublished memorandum, in possession of author, pp. 4–5.

6. Ibid.

7. Neutra, "Elysian Park Heights, a Project of Urban Reconstruction," pp. 1–2; and "Elysian Park Heights, Urban Reconstruction and Housing," p. 1, unpublished memoranda, in possession of author.

8. Neutra and Alexander, "Submission to the City Planning Commission of the City of Los Angeles: Site Statistics," unpublished memorandum, in possession of author.

9. Hines, interview with Eisner, November 4, 1976; *Los Angeles Times*, June 2, 1952; Neutra to William Wurster, November 12, 1951, Neutra to William Wurster and Catharine Bauer, March 4, 1953, Neutra Archive.

10. Hines, interview with Eisner; Neutra, "Elysian Park Heights," pp. 2–4.

11. Hines, interview with Eisner.

12. Ibid.; *Los Angeles Times*, May 22, 23, 1952.

13. *Los Angeles Times*, August 30, September 3, October 28, 29, 1952.

14. "Chronological Facts Regarding Low-Rent Program of Los Angeles Housing Authority, Remarks of Hon. Chet Holifield of California, in the House of Representatives, Wednesday, April 22, 1953," *Congressional Record*, 83d Cong., 1st sess.

15. *Los Angeles Times*, June 4, 1978.

16. Hines, interview with Alexander; "Sacramento Redevolpment," in Willy Boesiger, ed., *Richard Neutra, 1950–60, Buildings and Projects* (New York: Praeger, 1959), pp. 206–15.

17. "Special Design Award: City Planning," *Progressive Architecture*, January 1955, pp. 104–7; Joseph T. Bill to Neutra, February 25, 1959, Neutra Archive; Allan Temko, "Sacramento's Second Gold Rush, *Architectural Forum*, October 1960, pp. 124–29.

18. "Comprehensive Planning and Design on Guam," *Richard Neutra, 1950–60*, pp. 228–31; *New York Times*, August 3, 1952.

19. Robert Alexander, "Neutra and Alexander," in unpublished memoirs, pp. 7–11, 17–19.

20. Ibid.

21. "House of Guam and Governor's Residence," *Richard Neutra, 1950–60*, p. 232.

22. Ibid., pp. 234–37; Maria Wong to Neutra, June 16, 1962, Neutra Archive.

23. Neutra to Alexander, January 13, 1951, Neutra Archive, Alexander, "Neutra and Alexander," unpublished memoirs, pp. 6–7. Alexander's efforts to show affection and concern for Neutra as late as 1956 are documented in the following letter (Alexander to Neutra, March 15, 1956, Neutra Archive):

> When you told me the doctors recommend three operations, my outward reaction, I'm sure, did not express my concern. We talked about many other things through necessity. Believe me, I wish there were some way to give you perfect health so that we could concentrate on the really exciting and fulfilling things in life.
>
> Thanks so much for letting me see the new book. It is beautiful, and it gave me a real lift just to skim through it, which is all I could do at noon hour. I did manage to read the introduction and the first essay.
>
> Every human being extends something of himself into the world he lives in. A seemingly small, even insignificant kindness may have an impact on another who may pass it on to others in an ever widening, rippling circle in the pool of humanity. This circle may continue forever, achieving a real immortality. This not only may, but *does* happen constantly, and your excursions in the realm of the body, the mind, and the heart are overwhelming—it seems to me. It is our

professional obligation to help man find happiness, and you have brought him a full measure now and for time to come.

No one should know better than you that life cannot be measured properly by the clock or the revolutions of our planet. Intensity and quality surely count more than hours, and by these measures, who has lived or is living more than you? I think this is especially true when there is no immediate concrete objective in view, no walls to scale, no dragon to slay, but when you are simply *being*, being yourself, fascinated and fascinating, living life with great zest and gusto! These rare occasions I treasure even more than those equally exciting times when we are searching for some solution to an architectural problem or more often trying to map a campaign of human strategy or tactics.

You have been disappointed, I know, by my constant busyness in the office. I have, too, for I enjoy *nothing* as much for instance, as working out a clean and satisfying solution to a plan for St. Johns or the Hall of Records or the Dayton Museum. I also know full well the infinite pains it should take to develop basic concepts into good architecture and should love to follow every job through all stages, especially if we could do it in detail together, when I learn so much.

But if you have to be even somewhat free, from concern over the equally infinite "business" inherent in substantial architectural practice, I must spend a *lot* of time on things which would only frustrate you, I believe. This is the way in which you are enabled to be involved in projects of greater scope. . . .

24. Alexander, "Neutra and Alexander," unpublished memoirs, pp. 6–7, 11–13.

25. In addition to Pierce, the Neutra and Alexander roster included Andrew Balfour, Al Boeke, Robert Clark, Robert Kennard, Jean Killion, Frederick Lyman, Howard Miller, Adolfo Miralles, Disuke Nagano, Dion Neutra, James Pulliam, John Rollo, Toby Schmidlbauer, Hans von Escher, H. Thomas Wilson, Zelma Wilson, and Bernard Zimmerman. Executive secretaries, who also functioned as project coordinators, included Jan Kerwin, Irma Zakon, and Yvonne Kennedy. The structural engineering firm of Parker and Zehnder had its offices in the Glendale Boulevard Building and worked on most of Neutra and Alexander's projects.

26. Weschler, interview with Dione Neutra, August 9, 14, 1978; Hines, interview with Alexander, December 11, 1978. Lyman and Pulliam, quoted in John Dreyfuss, "Neutra: Greatness Rewarded," *Los Angeles Times*, March 13, 1977.

27. Hines, interview with Alexander, December 11, 1978; unpublished memoirs, pp. 1, 49, 56.

28. Ibid., p. 29. See figures 106–109 in Esther McCoy, *Richard Neutra*.

29. For plans, photographs, and further descriptions of these buildings, see the second and third volumes of *Richard Neutra, Buildings and Projects*, (New York: Praeger, 1959–66).

30. Ibid.; Alexander, "Neutra and Alexander," unpublished memoirs, pp. 20, 26–27; Hines, interview with Alexander, December 11, 1978.

31. *Richard Neutra, 1950–60*, pp. 178–79; Alexander, "Neutra and Alexander," unpublished memoirs, pp. 34, 36–40.

32. Alexander Cochran to Neutra, November 18, 1958; Paul Mellon to Neutra, July 21, 1959, Neutra Archive.

33. "What Should a Church Look Like?", *St. Louis Globe-Democrat*, February 8, 1959; see also the second and third volumes of *Richard Neutra, Buildings and Projects*, passim.

34. *Richard Neutra, 1950–60*, pp. 130–37.

35. Ibid., pp. 100–5, 138–41.

36. *Richard Neutra, 1960–66, Buildings and Projects*, pp. 74–83.

37. Ibid., pp. 156–65.

38. Ibid., pp. 224–33; Hines, interview with Alexander, December 11, 1978; Alexander, "Neutra and Alexander," unpublished memoirs, pp. 49–51.

39. *Richard Neutra, 1960–66*, pp. 200–11; Alexander, "Neutra and Alexander," unpublished memoirs, pp. 43–47.

40. Alexander, "Neutra and Alexander," unpublished memoirs, pp. 7–8.

41. Ibid., pp. 13–14.

42. Ibid., pp. 48, 69–72; Weschler, interview with Dione Neutra, August 9, 14, 1978.

43. Ibid.

44. Ibid.

Survival, 1950–1970

1. Neutra to Verena Saslavsky, December 4, 1953, Dione Neutra Papers.

2. Hines, interview with Mark and Pauline Schindler, July 1, 1976, Los Angeles; Hines, conversation with Mary Schindler, Los Angeles, May 4, 1977; Hines, interview with Regula [Thorston]

Fybel, June 27, 1974; Esther McCoy, *Vienna to Los Angeles*. p. 63.

3. Hines, interview with Benno Fischer, December 5, 1978, Los Angeles.

4. Hines, interview with Agnes Koschin, December 5, 1978, Los Angeles.

5. Hines, interview with John Blanton, December 1, 1978, Los Angeles.

6. Neutra, "The Creative Team," *Architecture and Buildings*, June 1956; Dione Neutra, Diary, June, n.d., 1950, Dione Neutra Papers.

7. Hines, interview with Fordyce Marsh, December 12, 1978, Los Angeles.

8. Ibid.; Hines, interview with Regula [Thorston] Fybel, June 27, 1974.

9. Hines, interview with Raymond Neutra, February 16, 1978.

10. Dione Neutra, Diary, May, n.d., 1942, Dione Neutra Papers.

11. Hines, interview with Regula [Thorston] Fybel, June 27, 1974. Illustrations of most of the buildings discussed in this chapter can be found, among other places, in three late books by Neutra: *Life and Human Habitat* (Stuttgart: Alexander Koch, 1956); *World and Dwelling* (Stuttgart: Alexander Koch, 1962); and *Building With Nature* (New York: Universe Books, 1971).

12. Olive Logar to Neutra, March 14, 1951; Jay and Catherine Hinds to Neutra, March 12, 1952, Neutra Archive.

13. Frederick Auerbacher to Neutra, April 8, 1952, Neutra Archive.

14. Orline Moore to Neutra, February 11, 1952, Neutra Archive.

15. Neutra, quoted in Margaret Stovall, "Home of the Week," *Pasadena Independent Star News*, December 5, 1960.

16. Hines, interview with Josephine Ain Chuey, August 5, 1978, Los Angeles.

17. Josephine Chuey to Neutra, October 1, 1956, Neutra Archive.

18. Hines, interview with John Blanton, December 1, 1978.

19. Hines, interview with Aida Hafley, Long Beach, August 30, 1977.

20. Arthur Connell to author, September 10, 1977.

21. Ibid.

22. Frederick and Cecel Fischer to Neutra, February 27, 1952, Neutra Archive.

23. Mildred Warner, taped message to author, n.d., 1979.

24. Nora O'Brien to author, January 18, 1979; Philip Livingston to author, January 4, 1979.

25. H. H. Everist, Jr. to author, February 16, 1979;

Everist to Neutra, March 27, 1952, Neutra Archive.

26. Hines, interview with Thaddeus Longstreth, October 21, 1977. Actually, after their first submissions to Levitt were rejected, Neutra and Longstreth offered pitched-roof designs, but these still seemed too modern to Levitt and were likewise turned down.

27. Thomas W. Doan to Neutra, August 17, 1962; Bruno Zevi to Dione Neutra, August 28, 1964, Neutra Archive.

28. Henry van de Velde to Neutra, July 7, 1953; James Marston Fitch to Neutra, 1963, Neutra Archive.

29. Hines, interview with Robert A. Schuller, Los Angeles, February 12, 1981.

30. Ibid.

31. "Aims and Purposes: Richard J. Neutra Institute," n.d., copy in possession of author; Hines, interview with Dorothy Serulnic, December 7, 1978, Los Angeles.

32. Ibid.

Eclipse, 1970–1980

1. Ralph Walker, "The Education Necessary to the Professional Practice of Architecture," *Journal of the American Institute of Architects*, March 1951, p. 125.

2. Walter Gropius to Ralph Walker, March 19, 1951, copy in possession of author.

3. Hines, interview with Dione Neutra, February 9, 1981.

4. Venturi, *Complexity and Contradiction in Architecture*, passim; Richard Longstreth to author, March 16, 1981.

5. David Travers to Neutra, April 2, 1965, Neutra Archive.

6. Neutra to Travers, April 4, 1965, Neutra Archive.

7. Ibid.

8. Dione Neutra, Diary, August, n.d., 1954; April 6, 1959, Dione Neutra Papers.

9. Ibid., October, n.d., 1954; November, n.d., 1955.

10. Dione Neutra to Dr. Frederick Karpf, February 10, 1959; Diary, April 8, 1959; December, n.d., 1959, Dione Neutra Papers.

11. Dione Neutra, Diary, August, n.d., 1954; February 5, 1960; July 27, 1961.

12. Hines, interview with Raymond Neutra, February 16, 1978.

13. Ibid.

14. Ibid.

15. Ibid.; Hines, interview with Regula [Thorston]

Fybel, June 27, 1974; with Benno Fischer, December 5, 1978; with John Blanton, December 1, 1978; with Robert Alexander, December 11, 1978.

16. Ibid.

17. Dion Neutra to Richard Neutra, June 18, 1961, Dione Neutra Papers (copy in possession of author).

18. Dione Neutra, Christmas letter, 1963, copy in possession of author; Hines, interview with Dorothy Serulnic, December 8, 1978.

19. Weschler, interview with Dione Neutra, August 18, 1978; Hines, interview with John Blanton, December 1, 1978, and Dorothy Serulnic, December 8, 1978.

20. Hines, interview with Ann Brown, April 12, 1978, Washington, D.C.

21. Hines, interview with Dione Neutra, February 9, 1981.

22. Ibid.; Neutra to Garrett Eckbo, n.d., Neutra Archive.

23. F. Scott Fitzgerald, *The Great Gatsby* (New York: Charles Scribner's Sons, 1953), p. 182.

24. Hines, interview with Dione Neutra, February 9, 1981; Wolf Von Eckardt, "Richard Neutra, Survival Through Design," *Saturday Review*, June 6, 1970, pp. 62–63.

25. Bruno Zevi, "From the Loos-Mendelsohn-Wright Triangle," *L'Architectura* 16 (November 1970), 425.

26. Bruno Zevi, "Richard Neutra," English translation, in typescript, of Zevi's article from the special Neutra issue of *Il Balcone* (1954), Dione Neutra Papers, copy in possession of author.

27. Robert Ardrey to Neutra, January 22, 1967, Dione Neutra Papers.

28. Letters to Board of Dirctors, AIA, from Kenzo Tange, October 17, 1968; Walter Gropius, October 2, 1968; Ludwig Mies van der Rohe, October 29, 1968; Neutra Archive.

29. Sybil Moholy-Nagy to Board of Directors, AIA, October 3, 1968, Neutra Archive.

On Sources

A formal, alphabetized, tabular bibliography would be an unnecessary duplication of the notes to the text. What follows here is an introduction to the major categories of source material relating to Neutra's life and work. Readers desiring specific citations should refer to the notes for the appropriate chapter and paragraph. Neither a complete bibliography of writings by or about Neutra nor a bibliography of the history of modern architecture, this is instead an acknowledgment of the sources, published and unpublished, that most influenced the writing of this book.

Manuscripts

As the notes will indicate, the majority of references for this study are primary sources from two major collections: the Richard J. Neutra Archive, Special Collections, University Research Library, University of California, Los Angeles, and the Dione Neutra Papers, still in her possession at 2300 Silver Lake Boulevard, Los Angeles, and lent to me during my research.

The Neutra Archive, UCLA, contains material that Neutra gave to the university in 1955–56, with additional, miscellaneous donations from the Neutra family since that time. The archive includes drawings and blueprints of most of Neutra's buildings and projects through the mid-1950s. Client correspondence, arranged alphabetically, and office correspondence, arranged chronologically, exist for the same period. Similar materials for the post-1955 years remain, at the time of this book's production, in the Neutra office, 2379 Glendale Boulevard, Los Angeles, though the architect's son and associate Dion Neutra is now in the process of donating and transferring these materials to UCLA. Though the UCLA Archive contains numerous photographs, the basic photographic file resides with the Neutra office materials that are in the process of being transferred. In addition to the above categories, the UCLA Archive contains the eight volumes of Neutra's loosely chronological early unpublished diaries, 1910–1920, variant manuscripts of his books and articles, and tapes of his lectures.

The Dione Neutra papers contain primarily her and her husband's personal letters and memorabilia and her unpublished diaries, which run from 1932 to the present period. The largest number of letters are ones the two Neutras wrote to each other when apart and to Dione's parents, Alfred and Lilly Niedermann, from ca. 1920 to 1938, when the Niedermanns moved to Los Angeles. This Neutra-Niedermann correspondence, which Lilly Niedermann saved and returned to her daughter, is a major source of information for the two most crucial decades of Neutra's life and career. Dione Neutra's annual Christmas letters to family and friends provide important summaries of key events and achievements in their lives. Like the remaining papers in the Neutra office, Dione Neutra's personal papers will ultimately join those of her husband in the UCLA Archive. In quoting from the German language material in this collection, I have used Dione Neutra's English translations almost exclusively, with only occasional variant translations of my own.

The Art Museum collections at the University of California, Santa Barbara, contain the drawings and papers of Neutra's colleague Rudolph Schindler and shed light on their relationship, particularly between 1912 and 1930. This museum also holds the drawings and papers of Gregory Ain, who worked for Neutra in the early 1930s.

The papers of Neutra's partner Robert Alexander (1950–1960) are located at Cornell University. They contain correspondence, drawings, and other materials relating to Neutra-Alexander buildings and projects and, most importantly, Alexander's unpublished memoirs, a copy of which he gave to me for use in writing this book.

In addition to these public and private manuscript collections, I collected during the course of this research numerous primary documents in my personal file, which I intend ultimately to donate to the UCLA Neutra Archive. Particularly significant are documents, and memorabilia given to me by Dione Neutra and solicited letters and taped interviews from Neutra clients and associates. Especially noteworthy here are letters to me from Josephine Neutra Weixilgärtner and Walter Jaksch regarding hitherto obscure details of Neutra's early life in Vienna, and from Louise Mendelsohn regarding Neutra's years with her husband in Berlin. All are specifically cited in the notes to Chapters 1 and 2.

Interviews

Almost equal to manuscripts as primary source materials are my taped interviews with Neutra's family, associates, and clients, in my possession, and Lawrence Weschler's extensive interviews in 1978 with Dione Neutra for the UCLA Oral History Archive, Powell Library, UCLA. As the notes will indicate, I began interviewing certain crucial clients and associates of Neutra in the early 1970s as a matter of general cultural and architectural interest even before it was clear that such interviews would ultimately contribute to this book. Casual conversations, as cited, frequently provided useful data. In addition to the numerous Neutra clients, cited in the notes, the following relatives, friends, and associates were interviewed by me in the 1970s and early 1980s: Gregory Ain, April 25, 1977, Los Angeles; Robert Alexander, December 11, 1978, Los Angeles; John Blanton, December 1, 1978, Los Angeles; Norman Cousins, March 17, 1980, Los Angeles; Greta and J.R. Davidson, June 24, 1974, Ojai, California; Simon Eisner, November 4, 1976, Los Angeles; Benno Fischer, December 5, 1978, Los Angeles; Regula Niedermann (Thorston) Fybel, May 16, May 30, June 27, July 24, 1974, Los Angeles; Harwell Harris (w/Rochelle Kappe), September 16, 1976, Los Angeles; Agnes Koschin, December 5, 1978, Los Angeles; Thaddeus Longstreth, October 21, 1977, Princeton, New Jersey; Philip Lovell, February 16, 1973, Newport Beach, California; Fordyce Marsh, December 12, 1978, Los Angeles; Louise Mendelsohn, April 30, 1977, Los Angeles; Carey McWilliams, February 5, 1979, Los Angeles; Dion Neutra, December 12, 20, 1978, Los Angeles; Raymond Neutra, February 16, 1978, Los Angeles; Mark Schindler, July 1, 1976, Los Angeles; Pauline Schindler, February 9, 1972, July 1, 1976, Los Angeles; Dorothy Serulnic, December 7, 1978, Los Angeles; Julius Shulman, October 11, 1976, Los Angeles; Raphael Soriano, June 21, 1977, Tiburon, California; Lette Valeska, March 12, 1980, Los Angeles; Frank Wilkinson, October 5,

1981, Los Angeles. Numerous conversations with Dione Neutra, recorded and unrecorded, yielded information and clarified issues as did the more formal, taped interviews of February 20, 1972, March 19, 20, 1980, and May 1, 1980. Crucial information and confirmation of data came from Lawrence Weschler's official UCLA Oral History interviews with Dione Neutra, conducted on April 10, June 10, July 14, July 18, July 21, August 3, August 9, August 14, 1978.

Published Books

The content of Richard Neutra's major books are discussed in the text. Those treating themes and ideas in the development of modern architecture include his autobiography, *Life and Shape* (New York: Appleton Century-Crofts, 1962); his two early books on American architecture, *Wie Baut Amerika?* (Stuttgart: Julius Hoffman, 1927); and *Amerika: Die Stilbildung Des Neuen Bauens in Den Vereinigten Staaten* (Vinena: Schroll, 1930); *The Architecture of Social Concern in Regions of Mild Climate* (São Paulo, Brazil: Gerth Todtmann, 1948); *Survival Through Design* (New York: Oxford University Press, 1954); and *Mystery and Realities of the Site* (Scarsdale, N.Y.: Morgan and Morgan, 1951). Four other monographs, composed largely by Neutra, are catalogues of his buildings and include the three-volume set, edited by Willy Boesinger, introduction by Sigfried Giedion, of Neutra's work from 1923 to 1966: *Richard Neutra, Buildings and Projects* (New York: Praeger, 1966); *Life and Human Habitat* (Stuttgart: Alexander Koch, 1956); *World and Dwelling* (New York: Universe Books, 1962); and *Building with Nature* (New York: Universe Books, 1971). Neutra's and Schindler's letters to each other are published in Esther McCoy, *Two Journeys: Vienna to Los Angeles* (Santa Monica, California: Arts and Architecture Press, 1979). McCoy's introductory essay falls somewhere between a personal memoir and a secondary reconstruction, since she knew and was associated with most of her subjects. The differences in viewpoint between her work and this one reflect, among other things, the sources each relied on. Other books in the primary documents catagory include Frank Lloyd Wright, *An Autobiography* (New York: Horizon Press, 1977), and the autobiography of Josef von Sternberg, *Fun in a Chinese Laundry* (New York: Macmillan, 1965). The Museum of Modern Art's 1932 catalogue, *Modern Architecture*, introduction by Alfred Barr, was revised by its other authors, Philip Johnson and Henry-Russell Hitchcock, as *The International Style* (New York: Norton, 1932).

Difficult to classify in its wide-ranging sweep

through history and psychology is the work of Erik Erikson, particularly *Childhood and Society* (New York: Norton, 1963), which furnished ever-fresh insights into Neutra's psychological development.

The best recent histories of modern architecture include Kenneth Frampton, *Modern Architecture: A Critical History* (New York: Oxford University Press, 1980); Leonardo Benevolo, *History of Modern Architecture*, 2 vols. (Cambridge, Mass.: MIT Press, 1971); and the two volumes by William Jordy in the *American Buildings and Their Architects* series: *Progressive and Academic Ideals at the Turn of the Twentieth Century* and *The Impact of European Modernism in the Mid-Twentieth Century* (Garden City, N.Y.: Doubleday, 1972). I do not forget, however, older treatments of the modern movement that shaped my thinking at an earlier stage, particularly Henry-Russell Hitchcock, *Modern Architecture: Romanticism and Reintegration* (New York: Payson and Clarke, 1929); and Hitchcock, *Modern Architecture: Nineteenth and Twentieth Centuries* (Hammondsworth, England: Penguin, 1963); Sigfried Giedion, *Space, Time, and Architecture: The Growth of a New Tradition* (Cambridge, Mass.: Harvard University Press, 1965); Reyner Banham, *Theory and Design in the First Machine Age* (New York: Praeger, 1960); and Banham, *Age of the Masters: A Personal View of Modern Architecture* (New York: Harper and Row [1962], 1975); Vincent Scully, *Modern Architecture* (New York: Braziller, [1961], 1974); and John Burchard and Albert Bush-Brown, *The Architecture of America: A Social and Cultural History* (Boston: Little-Brown, 1961). The book I recall as first introducing me to Neutra was Wayne Andrews, *Architecture, Ambition and Americans* (New York: Free Press, 1964).

Monographs on the cultural and architectural environments that specifically nurtured and reflected Neutra's development in Vienna, Berlin, and Los Angeles include: William Johnston, *The Austrian Mind: An Intellectual and Social History, 1848–1939* (Berkeley: University of California Press, 1972); Allan Janik and Stephen Toulmin, *Wittgenstein's Vienna* (New York: Simon and Schuster, 1973); Nicholas Powell, *The Sacred Spring: The Arts of Vienna, 1898–1918* (Greenwich, Conn.: New York Graphic Society, 1974); Carl E. Schorske, *Culture and Politics in Fin-de-Siècle Vienna* (New York: Knopf, 1980); Heinz Geretsegger and Max Peintner, *Otto Wagner, 1848–1914* (New York: Praeger, 1970); Ludwig Münz and Gustav Künstler, with an introduction by Nikolaus Pevsner, *Adolf Loos: Pioneer of Modern Architecture* (New York: Praeger, 1966); Peter Gay, *Weimar Culture: The Outsider as Insider* (New York: Harper and Row, 1968); Arnold Whittick, *Erich Mendelsohn*

(London: Leonard Hill Books, 1956); Wolf von Eckardt, *Eric Mendelsohn* (New York: Braziller, 1960); Wolfgang Pehnt, *Expressionist Architecture* (New York: Praeger, 1973); Hans M. Wingler, *The Bauhaus: Weimar, Dessau, Berlin, Chicago* (Cambridge, Mass.: MIT Press, 1969); Carey McWilliams, *Southern California Country: An Island on the Land* (New York: Duell, Sloan, and Pierce, 1946); Reyner Banham, *Los Angeles: The Architecture of Four Ecologies* (New York: Harper & Row, 1971); Esther McCoy, *Five California Architects* (New York: Reinhold, 1960); McCoy, *Richard Neutra* (New York: Braziller, 1960); McCoy, *Case Study Houses, 1945–1962* (Los Angeles: Hennessey and Ingalls, 1977); David Gebhard, *Schindler* (New York: Viking, 1972); Gebhard and Harriette von Breton, *LA in the Thirties* (Salt Lake City: Peregrine Smith, 1975); and Rupert Spade, *Richard Neutra* (New York: Simon and Schuster, 1971). Frederick Wight's essay, "Is Planning Possible; Can Destiny be Designed?," introduced the catalogue of Neutra's first one-man show at the UCLA Art Galleries (Los Angeles, 1958).

Newspapers and Periodicals

Contemporary newspapers and periodicals provided useful material for the most productive period of Neutra's life (1920–1970). Newspapers that I consulted included the *Christian Science Monitor, Dallas Morning Herald, Los Angeles Daily News, Los Angeles Examiner, Los Angeles Times, New York Evening Post, New York Times, Pasadena Independent Star News, St. Louis Globe-Democrat*, and the *St. Louis Post-Dispatch*.

Popular periodicals that I consulted included: *American Home, Better Homes and Gardens, Dial, Fortune, House Beautiful, House and Garden, Ladies' Home Journal, Nation, New Yorker, Saturday Review, Survey Graphic, Time*, and *Town and Country*.

Trade and professional journals that I consulted included: *American Architect, American Artist, American City, American Historical Review, American Institute of Architects, Journal, Arbitare, Architect and Builder, Architect and Buildings News, Architect and Engineer, Architect's Journal, Architect's Year Book, Architecture, Architecture and Building, Architectural Association Journal, Architectural Design, Architectural Forum, Architectural Record, Architectural Review, Architekten, Architectoniki, L'Architecture, L'Architecture d'Aujourd'hui, Architecture: Formes et Fonctions, L'Architecture Française, Arkitektur, Architektur und Wohnforen, L'Architettura, Arquitectura, Art Digest, Art News, Art and Industry, Arts and Decoration, Der Aufbau, Bauen-wohnen, Bau-*

kunst und Werkform, Bauwelt, Beaux-Arts Institute of Design, New York, Bulletin, The Builder, Building News, Cahiers d'Art, (California) Arts and Architecture, Casabella, Connaissance des Arts, Design, Design and Environment, Deutsche Architektur, Deutsche Bauzeitung, Domus, Federal Architect, Die Form, Habitat, L'Homme et l'architecture, Housing, Industrial Design, Inland Architect, Interiors, Journal of Modern History, Kenchiku Bunka, Kokusai Kentiku, Kunstwerk, Landscape Architecture, Library Journal, Los Angeles Journal of Commerce, Magazine of Art, Michigan Society of Architects, Weekly Bulletin, Modern Hospital, *Moderne Bauformen, National Parent-Teacher, National Sculpture Review, Das Neue Frankfurt, Die Neue Stadt, North Carolina Architect, Nuestra Arquitectura, Oppositions, Pencil Points, Progressive Architecture, Revista de Arquitecture, Royal Architectural Institute of Canada. Journal, Royal Institute of British Architects, Journal, School Management, Society of Architectural Historians. Journal, South African Architectural Record, Southwest Builder and Contractor, Techniques et Architecture, Town Planning Review, Werk, Western Architect and Engineer, Western Building,* and *Zodiac.*

Illustration Credits

With a few exceptions, the illustrations for this book came from the Neutra Archive, UCLA Special Collections; from Dione Neutra's personal collection; and from the Neutra office's photography file. Photographers and sources of photographs are cited in alphabetical order. Numbers refer to the number of each photograph, not to page numbers. Unidentified photographs are cited under Photographer Unidentified.

J. H. Brenenstul, 167

Mrs. John N. Brown, 180, 182

Harold Holliday Costain, 181, 184

Simon Eisner, 266

Amir Farr, 293, 346, 347

Foto-Sessner, 350

Regula Fybel, 20

Hesse Photograph, 332, 334

Donald J. Higgins, 246

Thomas S. Hines, 86, 130, 163, 168, 169, 175, 209, 210

Jordan Lagman, 345

Charles A. Libby and Son, 325

Gary Lovell, 68

Luckhaus, 85, 88, 89, 92, 93, 111, 118, 119, 122, 124, 132, 139, 147, 152, 154, 157, 158, 159, 160, 161, 166, 188, 190, 191, 193, 194, 198, 200, 201, 203, 204, 206, 236

Willard Morgan, 71, 72, 73, 80, 82, 83, 84, 91

Mott Studios, 174, 176

Nadel/Los Angeles Housing Authority, 268

Neutra Archive, 6, 7, 8, 14, 17, 18, 19, 23, 25, 27, 28, 29, 30, 35, 36, 38, 39, 47, 48, 50, 51, 52, 53, 54, 55, 56, 57, 58, 59, 60, 61, 62, 63, 64, 65, 74, 75, 76, 78, 79, 81, 103, 104, 107, 121, 123, 134, 135, 145, 148, 149, 173, 179, 187, 205, 208, 215, 219, 226, 228, 229, 230, 235, 244, 251, 263, 349

Neutra Office, 77, 258, 259, 269, 270, 271, 292, 295, 301, 306, 313, 320, 333, 337, 338, 344,

Dione Neutra, 2, 3, 4, 15, 16, 21, 22, 32, 33, 34, 37, 40, 41, 42, 43, 46, 70, 97, 101, 102, 351

Rondal Partridge, 291

Rogers Studio, 178

Schindler Collection, UCSB, 44, 69

Mark Schindler, 45

Julius Shulman, 96, 114, 126, 127, 128, 129, 131, 133, 136, 137, 143, 151, 155, 156, 162, 164, 170, 171, 172, 199, 202, 211, 212, 213, 214, 216, 221, 222, 223, 225, 232, 233, 234, 237, 238, 239, 240, 241, 242, 243, 245, 247, 248, 249, 250, 252, 253, 254, 255, 256, 257, 260, 261, 262, 273, 274, 275, 276, 277, 278, 280, 281, 282, 283, 284, 285, 286, 287, 288, 294, 296, 297, 298, 299, 300, 302, 303, 304, 305, 307, 308, 309, 310, 311, 312, 314, 315, 316, 317, 318, 319, 321, 322, 323, 326, 327, 329, 339, 340, 341, 342, 354, 356, 357

Eberhard Troeger, 335, 336

United States Navy, 289

UCLA Special Collections, 49

Lawrence S. Williams, 290, 328, 330

W. F. Woodcock, 112

Index